Advance Praise for *American Ingrate*

"Benjamin Weingarten professionally and thoroughly dissects the strange case of Rep. Ilhan Omar (D-MN), and demonstrates that much about the congresswoman is an enigma at best and a fraud at worst. We do not know, and authorities are apparently not interested in, her strange marriage…her tax avoidance, her violations of campaign financing laws, and her apparent disgust with a country that she…sought out and presently finds profitable. Weingarten's case study of Omar serves as a larger indictment of the therapeutic mindset, which Omar manipulated so well on her way to notoriety and power. Weingarten suggests that if Omar had not existed, she would have had to be invented, given that she is a metaphor for a larger American pathology of progressive virtue-signaling, and, ultimately, self-loathing."

—**Victor Davis Hanson**,
The Hoover Institution,
Stanford University

"*American Ingrate* is a serious, deeply researched work that makes the compelling case Rep. Ilhan Omar is the new face of the Democratic Party, and delves deeply into her background and beliefs. It compellingly sets forth the argument that she not only personifies, but leads a Progressive-Islamist alliance held together by the glue of hatred of America, of Judeo-Christian values, of Western civilization, and of Israel. Read it and weep. Or better, read it and fight back. This is a manual in that fight."

—**Dennis Prager**, national radio talk show
host and columnist, co-founder of PragerU,
and *New York Times* bestselling author of
ten books, including, most recently, the
first two volumes of *The Rational Bible*,
a five-volume commentary on the Torah

"It has become clear that left-wing ideology and extreme identity politics have cultivated a dangerous strain of anti-Semitism in the Democratic Party that is part and parcel of its increasingly anti-Judeo Christian and anti-Western orientation. Benjamin Weingarten has done a brilliant job of illustrating this phenomenon through the story of Rep. Ilhan Omar's rise to power despite her holding views about Israel, the Jewish people, and America's role in the world, which would have been unacceptable just a few years ago. *American Ingrate* is required reading for anyone seeking to understand the modern Democratic Party's posture towards Israel and its reflexive anti-Americanism."

—**Newt Gingrich**,
former Speaker of the House

"Since she first emerged as a public figure in Minneapolis, Ilhan Omar has been accorded coverage fit for an old-fashioned fan magazine like *Tiger Beat*. The mainstream media have turned away from any serious examination of Omar's shocking personal background or her foggy Islamist Marxism as though she were just any other prominent Democrat. Benjamin Weingarten pierces the fog in his penetrating study of Omar. In my own writing, I have followed Omar closely from the moment she appeared on the scene as a conquering hero of the left in August 2016, yet I learned new things about her on virtually every page of *American Ingrate*. Omar is a leading indicator of the direction of the Democratic Party. This is therefore both an impressive and important book."

—**Scott Johnson**,
Power Line

"*American Ingrate* is a sharply critical reckoning—cultural, political, and intellectual—with Ilhan Omar, one of the most divisive and destructive figures in American public life. The Democratic party's inability, or unwillingness, to censure or even criticize the Minnesota congresswoman for her hateful remarks about other

Americans, American Jews, is evidence that one of the country's two major political parties is trending in a dangerous direction—not progressivism but Middle East-style sectarianism. Benjamin Weingarten has the full story. His comprehensive research, unearthing Ms. Omar's hidden past and unpacking her third-worldist ideological convictions, is an invaluable and timely contribution to the key debates shaping our American moment."

—**Lee Smith,** investigative journalist and
author of *The Plot Against the President*

"Ilhan Omar, the subject of Benjamin Weingarten's timely and copiously researched book shares Jeremy Corbyn's Communism, and his hatred of Jews and Israel and support for Islamic terrorists in the United States and terrorists worldwide. And as Weingarten demonstrates, she also hates the United States of America. While she doesn't hold a formal leadership role in the Democratic party… [s]he is playing a central role in Corbynizing the Democratic Party. Weingarten's book sounds a critical warning bell. Ilhan Omar is no mere 'symbol' of diversity. She is a hardcore, radical ideologue who went into politics to advance her goal of weakening America while making the United States an unhospitable place for Jews and for everyone who doesn't share her bigoted, hatred for Americans, America, and everything it stands for."

—**Caroline Glick,** award-winning
columnist and author of *The Israeli
Solution: A One State Plan for
Peace in the Middle East*

AMERICAN INGRATE

ILHAN OMAR AND THE PROGRESSIVE-ISLAMIST TAKEOVER OF THE DEMOCRATIC PARTY

BENJAMIN WEINGARTEN

Post Hill
PRESS

A BOMBARDIER BOOKS BOOK
An Imprint of Post Hill Press
ISBN: 978-1-64293-426-7
ISBN (eBook): 978-1-64293-427-4

American Ingrate:
Ilhan Omar and the Progressive-Islamist Takeover of the Democratic Party
© 2020 by Benjamin Weingarten
All Rights Reserved

Cover Design by Cody Corcoran

Post Hill Press
New York • Nashville
posthillpress.com

Published in the United States of America

In loving memory of Hadassah Linfield.

Table of Contents

Foreword by Andrew C. McCarthy

It was a point so straightforward, so obvious, that it should not have needed making. Sometimes, though, these are the points that most need making because they are the ones most apt to be missed. Sharia supremacists, and in particular, the jihadists at the point of the spear, agitate (and, in the case of the jihadists, slaughter) *for a reason*.

This simple truth is still obscure today because it was consciously avoided when jihadists declared war on the United States by bombing the World Trade Center on February 26, 1993. Our determination to combat the atrocities while turning our eyes from what animates them remains strong—even after 9/11, even after nearly two decades of fitful war made seemingly unwinnable and "endless" (to borrow President Donald Trump's description) by the price tag our government placed on success: its mulish insistence that fundamentalist Islamic cultures would quickly transform into Western democracies.

Willful Blindness. That's what I called it at the time, and in a memoir about the oddity of being on the front lines of a national security struggle… as a *prosecutor* of all things. The phenomenon that our enemies were at war with us—projecting force against our homeland, on an attack scale never accomplished by our mortal Nazi and Soviet enemies—yet we judged indictments and subpoenas as an adequate response.

The determination to treat a security challenge as a law enforcement problem signaled a failure of will. Even with the post-9/11 course correction, which finally placed military, intelligence, and diplomatic assets in the forefront, with law enforcement in a support role, this failure seemed to become more, not less, apparent. It instructed our adversaries that, at its core, the American superpower was mired in self-doubt. Its ruling elite, in particular, were more curious about what we must have done to provoke the ire of Muslim militants than convinced about the need to prevail over an ancient yet newly energized totalitarianism.

The self-doubt about our culture and history, about whether we are more villains than a beacon, is a dire condition. Over the long haul, it may be an existential one. The reasons are richly documented by my friend Ben Weingarten in *American Ingrate*, his startling account of the life and times of Ilhan Omar, a Somali immigrant who is now a United States congresswoman, elected in 2018 by a Minnesota district dominated by Islamists and Leftists.

Ms. Omar is no jihadist. We go back to the beginning, though: Jihadists attack for a reason. That reason is the implementation and spreading of Sharia governance. The objective is nothing less than the supplanting of the existing system—in our case, America's liberty culture and Constitution—with an authoritarian system that coerces people to live a particular way. The way the avant-garde construe Islamic law. Sharia: a corpus largely set in stone a millennium ago, which, as interpreted by dominant fundamentalists, is systematically statist, discriminatory, and intolerant to the point of cruelty.

Islamists—adherents to "political Islam," a confusing term since classical Islam does not separate mosque and state—are best understood as *Sharia supremacists*. This term underscores their objective. The most effective Islamists are not the jihadists, although they are adept at exploiting the atmosphere of intimidation the jihadists create. The Muslim Brotherhood, the world's most influential and successful global Sharia supremacist movement, has always regarded violence as just one item on an ideologically aggressive menu. The Brotherhood has always thrived on the campus, has always been educated, disciplined, and savvy. It prefers to infiltrate the institutions of influence: government, law, media, and academia.

These sophisticated Islamists have always grasped that to succeed in the West, a long-term, incrementalist strategy would be necessary. The strategy would convert the West's liberties—free speech, association, political participation, religious observance, access to the courts—into its own arsenal.

To succeed, moreover, requires alliances. None has been more valuable than the anti-Western Left.

The alliance between Islamists and Leftists is not intuitive. The Left's signature is radical egalitarianism—ostensibly, a striving for equality of results rather than of opportunity. On the surface, that would seem to be a non-starter for Sharia supremacists—as would be abortion, women's rights, LGBTQ rights, and so on. Yet, in reality, radical egalitarianism is more radical than egalitarian—as with Islamists, the thumb is inexorably placed on the scale for favored over disfavored groups.

As a group's favorability is directly proportional to its transgressiveness toward bourgeois culture, Islamists do quite well in the Left's order of things. This is borne out by history: in Nasser's Egypt and Khomeini's Iran, to take two modern examples. While Islamists and Leftists have different visions of the good society, they find it natural to align against the existing Western (or at least, Western-influenced) order. Once that order is overthrown, the competing authoritarians turn on each other. But while a Western order exists, their mutual interest in undoing it makes for an effective collaboration.

As Weingarten illustrates, Ilhan Omar is the instantiation of this Islamist-Leftist collusion. Born into the privileged segment of war-torn Somalia's Islamist elite, she makes her way to the comparative paradise of America. But she does not see a shining city on a hill. The United States gives Omar peace, security, education, and opportunity. She, however, sees only racism, religious bigotry, persecution, and global aggression—which, naturally, is her reckoning of American sacrifices of blood and treasure to improve the lives of Muslim-majority nations, notwithstanding jihadist attacks on our nation.

Omar's is the story of how a committed ideologue at the crossroads of statism—both the Islamist and Leftist varieties—thrives in the society whose upheaval she seeks. It is the story of modern America, too paralyzed by political correctness to examine closely the neon signs of fraud and deceit in the rise of a radical who has become the darling of progressive Western media.

It is the story that presses the question of whether the West is sufficiently confident in its worthiness to fight against the threat that Ilhan Omar and her cohort represent.

PART I

Who is Ilhan Omar and What Does She Stand For?

CHAPTER 1

ROOTS OF ILHAN OMAR'S RAGE AND RISE

A Strange Way to Say "Thank You"

Freshman Congresswoman Ilhan Omar (D-MN) has lived the American dream. Yet to hear her tell it, America has always been a nightmare. For most people, the chance to come to the United States and leave behind life in a refugee camp with days filled performing menial labor in the sub-Saharan sun, under the constant threat of violence and disease—having escaped a war-torn, corrupt, and repressive homeland—would be an unfathomable dream come true.

Yet Rep. Omar gives a distinctly different impression. Central to her autobiographical narrative is just how disappointed she was when she first arrived on our shores. The girl who had purportedly escaped a violent assault on her family home in civil-war-stricken Somalia, and departed the dangerous, ramshackle, jungle-like conditions of a Kenyan camp for America, was amazingly ungrateful.[1] In fact, she was disgusted. In interview after interview, the progressive provocateur describes her initial impressions upon arriving in the U.S. according to some variation of the following:

> The America we were going to was [portrayed as] very glossy and picturesque—the only things that existed were white

picket fences and beautifully mowed lawns and everybody seemed to have everything that they need. When we arrived, our first experience was driving through Manhattan. There was graffiti everywhere. Trash everywhere. Panhandlers and people who were homeless sleeping on the streets. I remember looking to my dad for answers. I said, "This doesn't look like the America you promised." He said, "Well we haven't gotten to our America yet, you just need to be patient."[2]

It got worse from there. According to Omar:

Upon arriving here in the United States, I quickly realize (sic) that the opportunities I saw were not fully accessible to the people already living here. My first impressions of America were visible homelessness with…the struggles of classmates that weren't able to afford lunch, the lack of updated textbooks or no textbooks at all, families working two jobs to pay the rent and to put food on the table. I remember confronting my grandfather and my family members about the tangible disconnection between our dreams and the reality. They encouraged me not to complain but to do something about it. I learned that if you want a certain world, you have to organize for it.[3]

Clearly, America failed to live up to Omar's ideals. The most aspirational spin she could put on her experience upon arriving in the U.S. is that she could "organize" to achieve them. As we will soon explore, however, what Omar sought to organize to achieve was inconsistent if not incompatible with traditional American ideals. Omar's philosophy is not the stuff of Madison, Hamilton, and Jay.[4]

As will become clear, to this day America has failed to meet Omar's expectations. She bites the hand that provided her family a roof over its head, an education, and a land of such bounty that she could spend her days as an activist charting her course to political prominence. She sits insolent even now, from her rarefied perch as a prominent member of the

United States House of Representatives. Through it all, Omar has been consumed with what she perceives as America's vices, with nary a word for its virtues. Why such seeming disdain? In her telling, the U.S. was conceived in sin, built on oppression and bigotry, its people hypocritical in word and deed, and marked by ignorance and ugliness. Try though she might to reframe her contempt as constructive criticism for a nation she believes has not fulfilled its lofty principles, this position rings hollow.

After leveling a litany of calumnies against the United States during her first term in the U.S. House, the backlash proved so great that she was compelled to address her apparent seething anti-Americanism. She mustered the defense that, "I probably love this country more than anyone that (sic) is naturally born."[5] Needless to say, such a statement strains credulity. Clearly, Ms. Omar doth protest too much.

Privileged Beginnings in a Marxist-Islamist Paradise *Culture Shock*

It is understandable that an immigrant might at first feel alienated in a distant land with a foreign culture. But in the case of Rep. Omar, the challenge may have been particularly acute for a reason that has gone largely overlooked. Setting aside her disappointment in America given her expectations, and the identity-based lens through which she came to view her experiences so negatively, Omar may have been miffed because, by her own account, she had come from an affluent and evidently politically connected Somali family.[6] In the parlance of her progressive faithful, she was *privileged*. *spoiled brat*

Ilhan Omar was born on October 4, 1982, to a family of "civil servants and educators." Her mother, Fadhuma Abukar Haji Hussein, reportedly worked as an assistant to the minister of petroleum, and later served as a department director.[i,7] Her father, Nur Omar Mohamed, was a teacher trainer.[ii] Following her mother's death when Omar was two years old, her

---

i   Omar's mother's name has been reported as Fadhuma Abukar Haji Hussein, but as with much else in her family background, as we will explore, there is little corroborating documentation.

ii   Evidence suggests that Omar's father also goes by the name "Nur Said Elmi Mohamed," as well as "Nur Said," which will become relevant in a later chapter. See: https://alphanewsmn.com/investigation-suggests-omar-married-brother/. Issues surrounding Omar's family, including its members' names, will be discussed at length, as their significance is explored in a later chapter.

father, and grandfather, Abukar, director of Somalia's National Marine Transport, raised her.[8] According to one profile, Omar and numerous relatives originally resided in something of a "compound, complete with domestic help," in the coastal capital of Mogadishu.[9] Their home was "filled with history books and African art."[10] Omar received schooling in Islamic studies from a young age.[11] Her family had sufficient food such that it could afford to share with the poor beggars who congregated outside its grounds.[12] Given this comfortable upbringing in an undeveloped country reliant on foreign aid, it is evident that Omar's family was part of Somalia's ruling class prior to its descent into chaos and war in 1991. Left undiscussed when Omar has broached her background is the nature of the regime her family served.

The Somalia into which Omar was born, and under which her family thrived, was a Marxist-Islamist dictatorship.[iii] Its president, Major General Mohamed Siad Barre, rose to power in a military coup in 1969. In 1974, Somalia became the first black African state to ink a friendship treaty with the Soviet Union, with President Barre seeking to solidify his stranglehold on power with Kremlin support.[13] Here is what *The New York Times* wrote of

---

iii   The terms "Islamist" and "Islamic supremacist" are herein used interchangeably to describe the belief in and desire to impose Sharia law universally, by means violent and/ or peaceful. Former federal prosecutor Andrew C. McCarthy's description of "Sharia supremacism" during June 2016 testimony for the Senate Judiciary Committee reflects the "Islamist" or "Islamic supremacist" ideology: "[T]here is a sharia-supremacist construction of Islam to which millions of Muslims have adhered for centuries. It is virulently anti-Western, misogynist, anti-Semitic, and homophobic. It rejects basic tenets of Western liberalism, including the power of people to chart their own destiny and make their own laws in contravention of sharia. It rejects individual liberty and equality. It brooks no separation between spiritual life and civil society. It is a comprehensive framework for human life, dictating high public matters of government, economy and combat, as well as such intimate personal matters as hygiene and relations between the sexes. It endorses violent jihad to implement and spread sharia. And it regards the United States, closely trailed by Israel and Europe, as the principal enemies of Islam that must be defeated." See full testimony here: https://www.judiciary.senate.gov/imo/media/doc/06-28-16%20 McCarthy%20Testimony.pdf. It is also worth noting what Supreme Court Justice Robert Jackson—of the Nuremberg Trials—stated in penning the foreword to a 1955 book titled *Law in the Middle East.* Justice Jackson described Sharia thusly: "In any broad sense, Islamic law offers the American lawyer a study in dramatic contrasts. Even casual acquaintance and superficial knowledge...reveal that its striking features relative to our law are not likenesses but inconsistencies, not similarities but contrarieties. **In its source, its scope and its sanctions, the law of the Middle East is the antithesis of Western law.**" [Emphasis added]

his ruling ideology in an October 1977 piece titled, "Somalia Trys (sic) to Live by Both the Koran and 'Das Kapital:'"

> President Siad Barre has often insisted that Marx and Mohammed are not only compatible but also complimentary, that the religious asceticism of Islam can combine with the concept of mass discipline inherent in "scientific socialism" to forge a strong national will and lift the country from the ranks of the 25 poorest nations.

> "Islam and socialism supplement each other because both advocate the advancement of the interest of the people, of mankind—justice, dignity, prosperity and equality," be (sic) has written.[14]

Somalia's United Nations (UN) profile describes Barre's state ideology as combining "aspects of the Qur'an with the influences of Marx, Lenin, Mao, and Mussolini…"[15] Like the notorious figures on whom he modeled his rule, Barre fostered a cult of personality, maintaining order over rivalrous clan-based factions who might threaten his power by harshly repressing, arresting, torturing, and persecuting them.[16,17]

Though neither Rep. Omar nor her family members are known to have ever addressed it publicly, those in positions like Omar's father and grandfather were important Communist apparatchiks. As the *Washington Post* detailed in an April 1980 article:

> Teachers and civil servants were required to attend weekly indoctrination classes run by the Soviet-created Political Office of the Presidency, and any Somalian official "judged to have a 'non-socialist attitude' [was] retired or dismissed from government service," the CIA reported.

> The Russians virtually took over the Somalian armed forces with a contingent of civilian advisers and some 1,300 military officers. Somalian officers were required to attend indoctrination classes on Marxist-Leninist ideology and

soon found that their careers were influenced more by the Soviets' evaluations than by their superiors.[18]

Somalia's UN profile adds that "civil servants attended reorientation courses that combined professional training with political indoctrination, and those found to be incompetent or politically unreliable were fired."[19]

The Barre regime apparently deemed Omar's relatives neither incompetent nor politically unreliable, given how they prospered under the regime's rule. That Omar's father was a "teacher trainer," presumably indoctrinating other teachers in the potentate's philosophy, and that her grandfather served in a senior governmental capacity, suggests that at a minimum they feigned loyalty to the authoritarian Barre regime and its radical political philosophy. The reason this is significant—and making it all the more glaring that journalists have refused to explore the views of Omar's father and grandfather in any detail—is that Omar has crafted a story of her background that relies heavily on the influence of both men, as well as the other "teachers" in her family.[20]

Indeed, Omar has said that she was "raised by educators."[21] She has been less specific about what she was taught. Is it not reasonable to think her tutelage was in accord with, or at least bore the residue of, the Barre regime's radical Left-Islamist ethos? Omar and her grandfather are said to have "bonded over their desire to be part of the political process," with Omar's romantic narrative dating her entrance into the political arena to her time as a teenager serving as her grandfather's translator at local Democratic-Farm-Labor (DFL) Party conventions in Minnesota.[22]

As for the views her elders imparted to her, says Omar: "Being able to dream about the prosperity for your children, having access to *economic sustainability* and *equitable housing* were some of the conversations I had with my grandfather."[23] [Emphasis added] Congresswoman Omar describes learning about apartheid South Africa from her grandfather, which colored her perspective on the boycott, divestment, and sanctions (BDS) movement that targets Israel.[24] She speaks of being "informed about the Cold War and the kind of struggles that some of the African nations that remained under colonial power were going through. And the idea of Pan Africanism, the work that needed to get done there, a lot of the struggles

20

that were happening in the Middle East for peace, all of that, the United States' role in that was…very much a part of our informed lives," from the time she was four to eight years old.[25]

Consistent with the Marxian regime under which her family lived, Omar said that she "was always made aware of inequality in society, that there was a class system."[26] Through what prism did Omar view these issues then? Through what prism does Omar view these issues now? Her rhetoric speaks for itself. It is sadly true that Omar's radically Leftist worldview, which we will explore in great detail throughout this book, could have been absorbed as she was politically assimilated into the Leftist enclave in Minnesota that she now represents. But her family's ideological milieu would still seem germane. That it has gone unquestioned and even unspoken seems curious. We asked Rep. Omar about her family's politics and activities during the Barre years, but neither she nor her office provided a response.

It is notable too that Rep. Omar counts as a critical political "mentor and confidante" Habon Abdulle, a fellow Somali Minnesotan. Abdulle was pictured with the freshman congresswoman and her family during her swearing-in ceremony for the U.S. House of Representatives.[27] She is another child of the regime, described as "royalty," as the daughter of Somalia's first minister of defense.[28] As we will explore later, Omar's ties to Somalia's political class—a political class leading one of the most corrupted, violent, and repressive Sharia-based regimes in the world—remain quite deep. Omar has purportedly even leveraged her ties back home to threaten those who might expose damaging information that would derail her political career in America.[29]

Heretofore we have remained silent on the role of Islam in Omar's family and its potential influence on her political philosophy. This factor would be worthy of exploration even setting aside Omar's public embrace of her Islamic identity, given the predominance of Islam in Somalia, and its role in the Barre regime. It is therefore odd that Omar has said that the Somalia of her birth was "very secular"—for Islam was the state religion, and Barre's system mixed Islam with Leftism. Omar has also submitted, unprompted, that while Wahhabism, the Sunni Islamist movement, was beginning to take hold in Somalia when her family departed, "my grandfather and others had a complete distaste for it."[30]

Nevertheless, Omar has said that in college she sought to harmonize the Leftist views to which she adhered with her Muslim faith, stating: "A lot of the social justice issues that I care about stem from this idea of wanting equality and fighting for equality. That is something that is very much part of the principle of the teachings of Islam. That we are all created equal and that we should all be treated equally in our society…I wanted to live that out."[31] She further stated that "Advocacy, fighting for justice… is very inherently Islamic."[32] Omar was not the first to note these parallels. Leading Muslim Brotherhood scholar Sayyid Qutb literally wrote the book on this topic in his 1948 treatise *Social Justice in Islam*—the relevance of which will become clear later in this book. The preamble to the Somali Constitution under the Barre Somali Revolutionary Socialist Party regime called for "creat[ing] a society founded on social justice…" through implementing his Marxist-Islamist program.[33] The first article of the current Somali Constitution, which is subordinate to Sharia law, too says Somalia is founded on "social justice."[34] It is telling given Omar's embrace of her Islamic identity and how forthcoming she is on so many other issues that details on the relationship between her background, faith, and politics are so scant. What we will be able to surmise after examining Omar's desired policies, her methods for achieving them, and the company she keeps, is that it is unclear where her Leftism ends and her Islamist sympathies begin.

An Ingrate's Obama-esque Rise

Rep. Omar's unlikely journey to the pinnacle of power on Capitol Hill began when she, her father, and one of her sisters obtained asylum and arrived in America in 1995. Ilhan, father Nur, and sister Sahra originally settled in Arlington, Virginia, before heading to the home of the Somali diaspora in the U.S., Minneapolis, Minnesota, in 1997. There, they lived in Minneapolis's Cedar-Riverside neighborhood, which has come to be known as "Little Mogadishu."

As noted, Omar was politically active from a young age, including attending Minnesota DFL caucuses with her grandfather. In high school, Omar was a "student organizer." There, she claims to have formed a "unity and diversity group—a United Nations of students." Adds Omar: "I've been organizing ever since."[35] Indeed, Rep. Omar, like President Barack Obama, has been described as a longtime community organizer. We will discuss the parallels between these two figures, and how the latter helped pave the way for the former, in a later chapter.

In 2002, at the age of nineteen, Omar married Ahmed Hirsi (formerly "Ahmed Abdisalan Aden") in her "faith tradition," though they did not obtain a marriage license under Minnesota State law. Between 2002 and 2008, they had two children. During this time, Omar says she attended a small private college while working.[36] Though there is limited information concerning this period of her life, we do know that in 2005 she served as a "community educator" at the University of Minnesota, reportedly teaching new Americans about "nutrition, education, and financial management."[37] According to an archived biography on her website, at some point, she also worked at retailer Best Buy.[38] These did not appear to be the makings of a state legislator, let alone a national political figure and international celebrity. Omar eventually enrolled full-time at North Dakota State University (NDSU) in 2009, graduating with a degree in Political Science and International Studies in 2011. She has been described as a "low-profile" student. The only group with which she seemed to associate at school was the Muslim Student Association (MSA), with which she helped organize an "Islam Awareness Week."[iv,39] At NDSU, Omar befriended the future executive director of the Minnesota branch of the Hamas/Muslim Brotherhood-linked Council on American-Islamic Relations (CAIR), Jaylani Hussein.[40,41,42] We will discuss the significance of these ties in a later chapter.

It was also just before her time at NDSU that Omar supposedly divorced Ahmed Hirsi, again in her "faith tradition," while entering into a relationship with a British citizen and future classmate named Ahmed Nur Said Elmi, whom she legally married in 2009. A student with that name was enrolled at NDSU while Omar attended the school, and address records indicate that Omar, Elmi, and Hirsi all lived at the same address in Fargo, North Dakota as of August 2009, and concurrently at a different Fargo address as of November 2010. According to Omar, she

---

iv   It bears noting that MSA, the preeminent Islamic student group in North America, spawned from and is central to the aims of the Islamic supremacist Muslim Brotherhood. See: https://www.investigativeproject.org/documents/misc/31.pdf.

and Elmi ended their relationship in 2011, that is, the same year Omar graduated. Omar claims she reconciled with Hirsi shortly thereafter. By June 2012, the couple welcomed its third child. While Omar and Hirsi remarried in their faith tradition, Omar and Elmi did not legally divorce until six years after they supposedly split, in 2017. Omar and Hirsi only legally married in 2018. By 2019, Omar and Hirsi legally divorced, with Rep. Omar embroiled in potential ethics violations involving an alleged affair with a political consultant of hers.[43,44,45] We will discuss why these twisted family matters go far beyond merely representing tabloid fodder in a later chapter.

Omar's Obama-esque, meteoric political rise accelerated following her graduation from college. From 2012-2013, while working for the Minnesota Department of Education as a child nutrition outreach coordinator, Omar served as campaign manager in the successful run of a Minnesota State Senate candidate, and then, as campaign manager in the successful run of a Minneapolis City Council candidate. She left her post at the Minnesota Department of Education to serve this councilman as a senior policy aide from 2013 to 2015.[46,47] During this period she also obtained a Humphrey Policy Fellowship at the University of Minnesota, gaining a political credential. Perhaps most importantly, she won an election for DFL vice chair in the 60th State Senate district. As DFL vice chair, the self-identified progressive Somali woman in her early thirties cemented her role as a conduit for the party to Somali immigrants and stood well-positioned to appeal to the disproportionately young constituents in her district, given the large college student population it encompasses.[48] Both the Somali and college student constituencies would soon prove central to her future electoral triumphs.

Prior to her own electoral victories, Omar was involved in a heated 2014 Democratic primary race for Minnesota House District 60B between long-time Representative Phyllis Kahn and Minneapolis school board member Mohamud Noor. During the race, Omar was involved in election controversies. In one case, while overseeing the early voting process, she is alleged to have to coordinated efforts with a Somali-American election judge, who seemingly sought to coax one or several voters into supporting "our Muslim Brother" (Noor), rather than the "old Jewish lady" (Rep. Kahn).[49]

Omar also reportedly ended up concussed during a brawl that broke out at a DFL caucus, in a precinct in which she did not live, and for which she had reportedly been told in advance not to attend under threat.[50] Suffice it to say, she was clearly comfortable operating in the hurly-burly of politics.

In the next campaign cycle in 2016, Omar threw her own hat in the ring for Kahn's Minnesota State House seat. This was a bold move. Kahn was a 44-year incumbent, regarded as a Minnesota icon, who is evocative in philosophy and background of Senator Bernie Sanders—albeit of higher intellect and a more pleasant demeanor. Also in the race for the party nomination was the aforementioned Mohamud Noor. In some ways, this state race presaged the party-wide phenomenon currently underway in the Democratic Party, in which a generational, identity-based, and to a lesser extent ideological divide revealed itself in a struggle between the "Woke" newcomer and the perceived insufficiently Woke establishmentarian.[v]

Deploying a campaign strategy that relied on juicing turnout among college students at the University of Minnesota and Augsburg University, and carrying a large percentage of the Somali constituency unique to her district, Omar triumphed over not only Noor but also the incumbent State Rep. Kahn. This was no small feat. Rep. Omar knocked off the tied-for-longest-serving legislator in Minnesota's history. Omar then cruised to victory in the general election.[51]

As State Rep. Kahn described the race when we met in September of 2019, it was "out with the old, in with the new." From her vantage point, and on the basis of the public record, substance lost to style. But Omar's victory showed a political shrewdness that has marked her career. Not just national but international media celebrated Omar as the first Somali-American, Muslim woman elected to state legislative office in the nation—the

v   To this end, in a sign of the times Rep. Kahn, a longtime member of the DFL Feminist Caucus—who Rep. Omar herself praised for having "pav[ed] the way for women to partake politically and in activism"—was accused by some on the Left of sexism during the 2016 race. The charge stemmed from Kahn's quip that that Omar was, "younger than me...prettier than me. She appears nicer than me. She agrees with anything that anyone says to her. So, it was tough competition." See: https://www.minnpost.com/mnopedia/2019/03/founded-in-1973-the-dfl-feminist-caucus-gave-women-a-stronger-voice-in-the-party/, http://www.startribune.com/rep-phyllis-kahn-shamefully-disenfranchises-young-voters/376636071/, and https://www.minnpost.com/community-voices/2016/04/rep-kahn-threatens-her-legacy-sexist-rhetoric/.

fashionable hijab-wearing arch-Leftist refugee feted by the press as a foil to the hated newly elected President Donald Trump. In September 2017, Omar made the cover of *Time Magazine*.[52] In May 2018, she had a cameo in a Maroon 5 music video.[53] Later that year, a documentary filmmaker released *Time for Ilhan*, a documentary capturing Rep. Omar's successful run for state representative in 2016, only adding to her lore.[54]

Consequently, when Democratic Congressman Keith Ellison announced his intent to run for Minnesota State Attorney General, Omar jumped at the opportunity and ran for his congressional seat. Just as Ellison was undeterred in his run by allegations of spousal abuse, Omar was undeterred by allegations of campaign finance violations—which would resurface after the election.[55,56] Omar clinched the House primary—again besting members of the DFL establishment in good standing—which in the ardently left-wing district encompassing Minneapolis and its suburbs effectively sealed her victory for the seat itself. Omar was thus swept into office, joining forces with what would become known as the progressive freshman "Squad" headlined by Rep. Alexandria Ocasio-Cortez (D-NY). Along the way, Rep. Omar appears to have returned to a life of privilege, transitioning from "Little Mogadishu" and the Cedar-Riverside neighborhood over which public housing towers loom, to a luxury condo in an upscale Minneapolis neighborhood, where she presently resides when she is not in Washington, D.C.[57]

Beyond Rep. Omar's brash and bigoted rhetoric, she is largely portrayed as a national sensation on the basis of her symbolic significance, given the predominately left-wing media's obsession with identity politics, and Omar's place atop its hierarchy. To support the likes of Rep. Omar on these bases is to virtue-signal, something her own Squad mates have acknowledged.[58] Whether tokenized or not, Omar is happy to embrace such identity politics as a self-described "intersectional feminist."

Regardless, the superficial focus on her vitriol and politically useful traits and background should not diminish from the fact that she adroitly navigated crowded fields of skilled Democrats, and clearly mounted intelligently crafted campaigns to achieve high office well before she was forty years old. Respect for her political acumen however—and belief that Omar's rise foretells a takeover of the Democratic Party by her ideological compatriots—should not be confused with belief in the merit of her political positions. On the contrary, the Unwoke will find her positions not only incompatible with but subversive of the country and the values it has historically upheld. In the next chapter, we will explore Omar's positions.

CHAPTER 2

OMAR BLAMES AMERICA FIRST

Knowing One by Their Idols

Whether as a function of her having marinated in the Leftism of Minneapolis, her upbringing, or some combination of the two, it speaks volumes that Rep. Ilhan Omar counts among her idols notorious former Black Panther and Communist Party USA (CPUSA) leader Angela Davis. At an April 2019 "Black Women in Defense of Ilhan Omar" rally, flanked by Davis and others, a sentimental Omar strode to the lectern and stated:

> I'm a little emotional. Everyone knows that I refuse to cry. I talk about this all the time. I always say that nobody really deserves my tears or any of my sisters' tears. Um, but you all have moved me to tears with your love, and um, and I am just grateful to all of you. To one of my idols, Angela Davis, I just… [Omar cries, crowd cheers] yeah, I just, I, I can't tell you how enormously inspiring you have been to me throughout my life. And the work that you have done in making us realize that we have to be internally liberated to fight for external liberation has been lifesaving for people

like me who had to navigate what it feels like to grow up black in this country. So, thank you.[1]

Jane Kamensky, the Harvard professor and director of the academic library that recently acquired Davis's life papers, says that "Angela Davis is at the intersection of feminism, American political radicalism and global political radicalism."[2] This is perhaps the best that can be said of her. It may also be what historians are saying about Rep. Omar someday.

The episode for which Omar's hero Davis gained worldwide infamy—at least it should have been infamy—is worth recounting. As conservative author and publisher Roger Kimball described it in a *Wall Street Journal* editorial:[i]

> In 1970 she [Davis] became romantically involved with George Jackson, a career criminal and Black Panther serving time in Soledad Prison for armed robbery.
>
> In 1970 Jackson was one of several prisoners implicated in the murder of a prison guard. That August Jackson's 17-year-old brother Jonathan burst into a Marin County courthouse during a trial. He distributed arms to the defendants, took the judge, the prosecutor and at least one juror hostage. **Some of the weapons, as later testimony at her trial revealed, had been bought by Ms. Davis two days before.** Jonathan intended to trade the hostages for the release of his brother and then flee to Cuba.
>
> In what became a shootout, Jonathan and two of the defendants were killed. **The judge's head was blown off by a shotgun taped under his chin. Another hostage was paralyzed for life. In 1971…George Jackson and several other inmates murdered three prison guards and two white inmates, before being shot himself.**

---

i   The author has consulted with Roger Kimball's publishing company in the past.

**After the bloody courthouse melee, Ms. Davis fled and
went underground.** The FBI apprehended her in New
York some months later.[3] [Emphasis added]

Davis was ultimately acquitted of murder. As famed lawyer and author
Alan Dershowitz, who worked as an unpaid consultant on an aspect of
the Davis case, described it: "She claimed that as a black, a woman, and a
Communist, she could not receive a fair trial in any American court. She
was acquitted, so maybe she was right!"[4]

But her complicity in evil causes only grew. A supporter of the Soviet
invasions of Czechoslovakia and Afghanistan, and a two-time vice presidential candidate on the CPUSA ticket, in 1979 the Red regime awarded
Davis the Lenin Peace Prize for her efforts. She received the award in a ceremony held on Soviet soil best-described as a revolting, treacherous lovefest.
Davis was likewise celebrated by the East German leadership responsible
for building the Berlin Wall.[5]

Last but not least, undermining her future criminal justice bona
fides—but further linking her to Rep. Omar—Dershowitz relates an anecdote regarding Davis and Soviet Jews. When Dershowitz heard that Davis
was heading to Moscow in the 1970s to receive some kind of human rights
award, he claims to have called her office to ask her to lobby the Communist regime on behalf of Jewish prisoners of conscience who sought to
immigrate to Israel. Dershowitz writes that: "Several days later, I received
a call back from Ms. Davis's secretary informing me that Davis had looked
into the people on my list and none of them were political prisoners. 'They
are all Zionist fascists and opponents of Socialism.' Davis would urge that
they be kept in prison where they belonged."[6] Some kind of idol for Rep.
Omar indeed.

Following in the footsteps of Ms. Davis, Congresswoman Omar
combines a "Blame America First"-infused radical progressive ideology,
with intersectionalism and the poisonous politics of identity. Consequently, Rep. Omar undermines our country rhetorically and threatens it
substantively.

This is to say nothing of Rep. Omar's anti-Jewish bigotry—sometimes, though not always hidden under the thinly veiled guise of

anti-Zionism—that we will argue represents a corrosive underlying animus towards Western civilization. Nor is it to mention Omar's myriad ties to Islamists and Islamist-tied and/or corrupt foreign regimes that literally threaten American life and limb, and similarly abhor the West. We will limit the focus of this chapter to Omar's radical rhetoric and give these related points their proper due in subsequent chapters.

Blame America First Redux

At the 1984 Republican National Convention, a first-time attendee and self-described "born Democrat" walked up to the podium and engaged in the kind of political heresy that today might lead to bodily harm.[7] Describing critics of President Ronald Reagan's administration, she said this:

> They said that saving Grenada from terror and totalitarianism was the wrong thing to do - they didn't blame Cuba or the communists for threatening American students and murdering Grenadians - they blamed the United States instead.
>
> But then, somehow, they always blame America first.
>
> When our Marines, sent to Lebanon on a multinational peacekeeping mission with the consent of the United States Congress, were murdered in their sleep, the "blame America first crowd" didn't blame the terrorists who murdered the Marines, they blamed the United States.
>
> But then, they always blame America first.
>
> When the Soviet Union walked out of arms control negotiations, and refused even to discuss the issues, the San Francisco Democrats didn't blame Soviet intransigence. They blamed the United States.

But then, they always blame America first.

When Marxist dictators shoot their way to power in Central America, the San Francisco Democrats don't blame the guerrillas and their Soviet allies, they blame United States policies of 100 years ago.

But then, they always blame America first.

The American people know better.[8]

Let us hope that the late U.S. Ambassador to the UN Jeanne Kirkpatrick is still right about our fellow Americans. As for Rep. Omar, she is in the running for leader of the modern-day "Blame America Firsters." Her views in both the domestic and foreign policy realms reflect, as we will detail in the next chapter, that an anti-American ethos lies at the core of her political philosophy.

Congresswoman Omar disputes this. She claims that she loves the country more than native-born Americans. By all rights she should, given what America has provided her. But when it comes to patriotism, you do not "hurt the ones you love." Try though she might to claim that her scathing criticism of the country is constructive, forcing us to live up to our principles, Omar's incessant excoriation of the U.S., and its people, does not prove her affection. It shows once again her ungratefulness and contempt. Rep. Omar's commensurate policy views only bolster this contention, as do her retrograde political partners at home and abroad.

Rep. Omar's rhetoric reflects Howard Zinn's version of U.S. history.[9,10] Her politics are clearly derivative of such a vision. Omar considers America an evil, oppressive, colonialist occupier. And if America is as, shall we say, "deplorable" and "irredeemable," as Omar portrays it, then by her logic—and that of her idols such as Angela Davis, and others across the Left-Islamist axis who we will come to meet—then "justice" requires overthrowing the established order. Consider what Rep. Omar has said about this nation of which she claims to be so enamored.

Castigating America for its Actions at Home

On Thanksgiving of 2017, then-Minnesota State Rep. Omar tweeted: "As we celebrate with loved ones today, take a moment to recognize our indigenous neighbors whose land we occupy as we continue to fight for a more equitable and just Minnesota."[11] Earlier that year, Rep. Omar had retweeted a tweet that read, "The original fake news: Columbus discovering the United States Happy #IndigenousPeoplesDay," adding her own message: "No glory for invaders #IndigenousPeoplesDay."[12] In Omar's reading of history, America has only grown more wicked since. The congresswoman beseeches us to "confront that our nation was founded by genocide and we maintain global power through neocolonialism…We must confront that our nation was founded by the genocide of indigenous people and on the backs of slaves, that we maintain global power with the tenor of neocolonialism."[13]

Not to be outdone, on Independence Day 2018, Rep. Omar found it fitting to remind us that "We shouldn't revise history. We're a country built on stolen land and the backs of slaves. Independence Day allows us to reflect on how far we've come and how much farther we have to go. Leveraging our voice to fight for justice is as American as it gets. Happy 4th of July."[14] Should she not have concluded this tweet with: "Unhappy 4th of July?" Incidentally, Omar has provided no such qualifications in tweets celebrating Somalia's Independence Day in recent years.[15,16] If her love for any country is unconditional, certainly it is not for America. And considering its past as Rep. Omar understands it—a past in which the U.S. was a genocidal, occupying, neocolonialist oppressor—on what grounds would she or anyone love it? You will not find a single other country for which Rep. Omar expresses even a fraction of such scorn, save for Israel or Saudi Arabia.

Central to Rep. Omar's critique of America is the idea that we are a hypocritical nation.[ii] According to the congresswoman, "We have values and ideals of prosperity and equality and protecting human dignity…All of

---

ii   It bears noting that as a longtime progressive community organizer, Rep. Omar, in focusing on hypocrisy, is following the fourth rule of the founder of modern community organizing, Saul Alinsky. In his *Rules for Radicals* Alinsky calls for followers to "Make the enemy live up to its own book of rules." See: https://en.wikiquote.org/wiki/Saul_Alinsky.

these things are part of the American value system. But in actuality we have mass incarceration. We have people who literally are sleeping outside in sub-zero weather. We have all kinds of atrocities. We are caging children at our borders. We have police officers who are shooting unarmed black men. So we have practices that really do not live up to the values and the ideas that are very much part of our DNA."[17] Leaving aside Rep. Omar's hyperbolic and dubious claims, and one's inability to see them as coming from a place of love, you will never once hear her exalt America with comparable feeling. That this is a nation uniquely dedicated to liberty, and as a consequence, the most prosperous nation in the history of mankind, responsible for raising the living standards not just of millions of Americans of every color and creed, but of billions of people across a globe in which tyranny and misery still largely reign, is the kind of statement Rep. Omar will never bring herself to utter. Instead, righteous indignation rests on her lips. Rep. Omar likewise believes U.S. foreign policy is hypocritical, as we will discuss in the next section.

Congresswoman Omar is not just miffed about America's conception in sin, and its purported hypocrisy in the decades since. She takes issue with her fellow citizens in the here and now. Chiding critics of refugee resettlement, in May of 2019, Rep. Omar said that "ignorance really is pervasive in many parts of…this country. And as someone who was raised by educators, I really like to inform people about things that they might be ignorant to (sic), willingly or unwillingly."[18] Leaving aside the irony of Rep. Omar's improper grammar, this statement comes from someone whose refugee-heavy district has produced dozens of terrorists, and who has had to have multiple interventions regarding her own anti-Semitic bigotry. Yet Rep. Omar knows better than the dimwitted, deplorable "bitter clingers."

At an Iftar dinner that same month, recounting a conversation with Speaker Nancy Pelosi (D-CA), Rep. Omar similarly lamented, "I know in this country we have religious liberty. Not everyone understands that. Ignorance is very pervasive in this country. I am worried that when I show up in November [2018], as the victor of that election, that they will do everything to make sure that I will not be able to wear my headscarf to represent my constituents."[19]

It is worth emphasizing that Rep. Omar believes it vital to wear a hijab to "represent my constituents." Beyond what this says about Omar's district, and her view as to what representation entails, it appears the irony is lost on her that it is her party that rejects even the smallest expressions of religiosity in the public square, and whose progressive cohort often attacks traditional believers. Omar herself enjoys the right in this haven of religious liberty to criticize non-Muslims for their deeply held beliefs. What she cannot abide is any criticism of her own religion, which she casts as "Islamophobic" hate speech.

As an aside, Omar reportedly only began to wear the hijab after the September 11, 2001 attacks, by one account, "not so much out of religious conviction, she has said, as from a determination to show her cultural identity at a time when many Americans viewed Muslims with suspicion."[20] If a group of Jews or Christians today were to slaughter thousands of their fellow countrymen in the name of their faith, it is hard to imagine previously non-demonstrable coreligionists waking up tomorrow and deciding to don religious garb to make such a point. It is also notable that while to Rep. Omar, "the hijab means power, liberation, beauty, and resistance," the reality is that Islam commands Muslim women to wear it.[21,22] It is for this reason that Iranian women's rights activists have been *removing* their hijabs as a form of resistance against the theocratic Khomeinist regime.[23] One would have thought Rep. Omar as an ardent feminist and opponent of theocracy—at least as she defines it—would follow suit.

Rep. Omar seems to harbor particular hostility for our military—the institution responsible for protecting us from foreign enemies, and among the only ones Americans overwhelmingly still hold in high regard.[24] Her most wanton attack concerns the U.S. engagement in 1993 in the Battle of Mogadishu. That clash, in Omar's native Somalia, resulted in the "Black Hawk Down" tragedy. Rather than recognize that America's armed forces, as described by one veteran of the mission, sacrificed their lives "to support peacekeepers who were desperate to rescue the country from starvation and the ravages of civil war"—including defeating the warlords who were oppressing Rep. Omar's own *Majerteen* clan—Rep. Omar has savaged them.[25] She claimed that "...thousands of Somalis [were] killed by the American forces that day!" concluding the offending tweet with "#NotTodaySatan."[26] This is in addition to the fact that she vastly overstated the Somali death toll and neglected to mention that the deaths were largely the result of outnumbered Americans troops fighting for their very lives against a vicious Somali onslaught.[27] These being the facts, who is Rep. Omar calling "Satan?" And what does she have to say about Americans who paid the ultimate sacrifice as part of a humanitarian mission a world away, only for refugees like herself to figuratively spit on their graves?

Rep. Omar has also talked of meeting American veterans, "who say the most horrendous things, who have complete disregard for life."[28] Are these the words of someone who "probably loves this country more than" you?

Rep. Omar's hostility towards America pervades her views on any number of policy issues. In June of 2019, she sought to portray national sovereignty as antithetical to Americanism, writing, "It's un-American to criminalize immigrants for wanting to come to this country for a better life."[29] This leads one to wonder whether she believes we, or any nation, should have borders at all. That same month, Rep. Omar also said, "[W]e live in a society and govern in a body [Congress] that might value the life of a dog more than they value the life of a child who might not look like theirs."[30]

Relatedly, Rep. Omar demonizes both Immigrations and Customs Enforcement (ICE) and Customs and Border Patrol (CBP) as, "radicalized, criminal agencies…destroying families and killing innocent children."[31] Omar calls her desire to abolish ICE a "personal thing," as in her view ICE is "a tool to dehumanize and treat Muslims as second-class citizens within this country," notwithstanding the fact that Muslims in America enjoy rights they could never dream of being afforded in, say, any of the world's numerous Sharia-based states.[32,33] Regarding CBP officers, she has advocated for "eliminating their existence," and implied they are bigoted towards "black or brown people," in spite of the fact that more than half of all CBP agents are Latino.[34,35] It is unclear how Rep. Omar squares her condemnation of "dehumanization" with her desire to "eliminat[e]" the "existence" of fellow human beings.[36,37]

Rep. Omar has gone so far as to say our border security officers are engaged in torture. In July of 2019, she again slandered our homeland security officials, asserting, "Instead of addressing the unrest we have fueled, we are making it worse and then torturing the people who come to our border."[38] Of course, if Rep. Omar wants to see torture, she should visit with the law-abiding citizens trapped in gang-dominated areas of the Northern Triangle. Notably, Omar also defended fellow Squad mate Rep. Alexandria Ocasio-Cortez's preposterous and offensive characterization of migrant holding centers as "concentration camps."[39]

Meanwhile, as will become a recurring theme, Rep. Omar justifies her positions on immigration dishonestly. Omar's claims that U.S. authorities are committing "atrocities" on the southern border appear to be slanderous based on the cases she has cited. When Omar, for example, tweeted a story claiming U.S. culpability in the death of a migrant child who had entered the country through Mexico, she apparently failed to read it.[40] The child was given medical care in the U.S., in a bid to save her life, that she was unable to receive while traversing Central America.[41] Meanwhile, of course, it is the "Open Border" and "sanctuary" policies championed by Rep. Omar that serve as magnets for migrants to put their children in harm's way in the first place. And the aforementioned Northern Triangle countries to America's south that have devolved into dysfunction and chaos, incidentally, are not Jeffersonian democracies but rather far more closely approximate Rep. Omar's ideal political models.

Perhaps most prominently, Omar has howled against what she inaccurately describes as President Trump's "Muslim ban."[42] On top of such substantive positions, Rep. Omar's pro-alien sentiment is too reflected in her belief that the term "alien" itself is, to use one of her favorite words, "dehumanizing." As we will soon see, however, she shares no such compunction with decrying millions of fellow Americans who happen to hold different political views as ignorant bigots, nor, well, *dehumanizing* the president of the United States.[43,44,45] Her compassion seems singularly reserved for non-citizens, not law-abiding Americans. If you blame America first, you put Americans second.

Omar has also attacked our justice system on multiple occasions, including telling a made-up story to a group of high school students designed to illustrate its deficiencies. As *The Federalist*'s John Daniel Davidson reported:[iii] "A recent profile of Rep. Ilhan Omar by the *Washington Post* made waves because of its revelation that the congresswoman lied to a group of high school students about witnessing racism and injustice in a Minneapolis courtroom. In an anecdote lifted almost verbatim from the plot of 'Les Miserables,' Omar claimed she saw a 'sweet, old…African American lady,' who had spent the weekend in jail for stealing a two-dollar loaf of bread to feed her 'starving 5-year-old granddaughter,' handed an eighty-dollar fine. Omar, unable to control her emotions, blurted out, 'Bullsh—t!' in the courtroom." If Rep. Omar has to lie and use profanity to prove America's cruelty, it is probably not as cruel as she would have us think.

Rep. Omar's critique of our criminal justice system is based on the idea that "tough-on-crime…is synonymous with further criminalization of black and brown youth."[46] The soft bigotry of her low expectations aside, the implication is that our justice system disproportionately targets people of color, rather than that people of color disproportionately commit crimes. Omar's view is not borne out by the facts.[47,48] Those facts have to be reckoned with, however uncomfortable it may make politicians and the public, in the immediate term to protect law-abiding Americans of all colors, and ultimately for families, civil society institutions, and policymakers to forthrightly grapple with and combat the underlying problems.

More fundamentally, in Rep. Omar's view, the injustice begins well before people are subjected to the systemically racist criminal justice system. Crime is society's fault, an outgrowth of "a lack of access to mental health care, unemployment, food insecurity, etc."[49] In the same address in which Omar lied to high schoolers, rather than share any wisdom or seek to inspire them, she complained that "…the only thing that made my family excited about coming to the United States was that the United States was supposed to be the country that guaranteed justice to all…I feel it necessary for me to speak about that promise that's not kept."[50] We in the United States just never seem to live up to her expectations.

Her rhetoric on the home front—and as we will soon see on the international front—stands firmly in the tradition of the likes of her idol Angela

Davis. Consider what Davis said just days after being released from prison in June 1972—an address whose primary theme is that America is a hypocritical prison:

> It has been said many times that one can learn a great deal about a society by looking towards its prisons. Look towards its dungeons and there you will see in concentrated and microcosmic form the sickness of the entire system. And today in the United States of America…there is something that is particularly revealing about the analogy between the prison and the larger society of which it is a reflection. For in a painfully real sense we are all prisoners of a society whose bombastic proclamations of freedom and justice for all are nothing but meaningless rhetoric.
>
> For this society's accumulated wealth, its scientific achievements are swallowed up by the avarice of a few capitalists and by insane projects of war and other irrational ventures. We are imprisoned in a society where there is so much wealth and so many sophisticated scientific and technological skills that anyone with just a little bit of common sense can see the insanity of a continued existence of ghettos and barrios and the poverty which is there. *[applause]*
>
> …We know that all we have to do is to redirect that wealth and that energy and channel it into food for the hungry, and to clothes for the needy; into schools, hospitals, housing, and all the material things that are necessary *[applause]*, all the material things that are necessary in order for human beings to lead decent, comfortable lives – in order to lead lives which are devoid of all the pressures of racism, and yes, male supremacist attitudes and institutions and all the other means with which the rulers manipulate the people….

Our condition here and now – the condition of all of us who
are brown and black and working women and men – bears
a very striking similarity to the condition of the prisoner…
Like the prisoner we are locked up with the ugliness of
racism and poverty and war and all the attendant mental
frustrations and manipulations.

…As black people, as brown people, as people of color,
as working men and women in general, we know and we
experience the agony of the struggle for existence each day.
We are locked into that struggle. The parallels between our
lives and the lives of our sisters and brothers behind bars
are very clear.[51]

As we will see in a later chapter, Rep. Omar's platform conforms well
to Davis's rhetoric.

Castigating America for its Actions Abroad

On top of America's rotten founding, rampant hypocrisy, monstrous
military, border practices, insufferable injustice, and ignorant citizens in the
main, Rep. Omar blames America for problems the world over. Maybe the
most far-reaching problem she attributes to America is the global refugee
crisis. In May of 2019, the congresswoman stood on the floor of the U.S.
House and declared:

The United States is responsible for nearly a third of the
excess carbon dioxide in the atmosphere today and, thus,
bears more responsibility for the climate crisis than any
other country. But the climate crisis is a major contributing
factor of yet another devastating crisis we are facing today:
the global refugee crisis…At a time when climate change
is making droughts and famines worse, making conflicts
fiercer and repression more brutal, our country is resettling
historically low numbers of refugees…Countries that are

responsible for perpetuating the climate crisis, like the United States, should rise as leaders in offering protection and refuge for displaced communities. It is our duty, as one of the richest countries in the world, to support the Paris Agreement…[52]

Yet the hundreds of thousands of people fleeing parts of Central America and the Middle East are doing so not because of the atmospheric byproducts of American industry—as Rep. Omar and her fellow Green New Dealers would have us believe—but largely because of the pathologies of the countries they are escaping. If Rep. Omar wants to make the case that the Obama administration caused the massive refugee flows by way of its foreign, and/or climate policies, she has not done so. And still, one wonders, if America is the root cause of the world's problems on climate and immigration, on top of the many other flaws Rep. Omar points out about it, why would people all across the world risk their lives to come to such a wretched place? And if Rep. Omar genuinely believes, as mentioned previously, that we are "torturing" those often illegitimately seeking asylum in America—individuals who disproportionately refuse to abide by our laws by skipping court appearances once here—how would she describe life under the governments from which said individuals are fleeing?[53,54] Does Rep. Omar believe they are beyond reproach?

Rep. Omar is adamant that America is the proximate cause of a whole host of problems worldwide. It is not surprising then that during a November 2019 campaign rally for socialist presidential candidate Senator Bernie Sanders (D-VT)—whom Rep. Omar endorsed along with Squad leader Rep. Alexandria Ocasio-Cortez—Omar expressed her "honor" and "excitement" to stand with a man who as president would "fight against Western imperialism."[55,56] She has taken this case on the road, going on international trips sponsored by pro-Communist groups like "Witness for Peace" (WFP) to press her case. Created in opposition to the Reagan Presidency, WFP seeks to "chang[e] U.S. policies and corporate practices that contribute to poverty and oppression in Latin America and the Caribbean," working "intentionally to undermine these oppressive systems."[57,58]

One way to meet WFP's goal is to delegitimize America. We know Rep. Omar agrees from the poorly choreographed display she put on in lambasting President Trump's Venezuela Envoy, former Reagan administration veteran Elliott Abrams. Seeking to settle a score on behalf of the Third World, when Abrams appeared before her at the House Foreign Affairs Committee (HFAC), she attacked him as a stand-in for America's "imperialist" sins dating back to the 1980s. Rep. Omar appeared to be reading from a script cribbing from an article on Abrams published in Qatar-backed *Al-Jazeera*, savaging Abrams himself, and his beliefs.[59]

It began when Rep. Omar incorrectly, and perhaps intentionally, referred to Abrams as "Mr. Adams," and, before asking him a question, asserted, "You pleaded guilty to two counts of withholding information from Congress regarding your involvement in the Iran-Cortra (sic) affair, for which you were later pardoned by President George H. W. Bush. I fail to understand, ah, why members of this committee or the American people should find any testimony that you give, ah, today, to be truthful." When Abrams sought to respond, stunned at the personal attack, Omar shot him down.

That set the stage for a round of questioning in which Omar sought to portray Abrams—and by extension the Republican administrations he has served, and America itself—as a monster. Rep. Omar laid the groundwork by placing the blame for the 1981 El Mozote massacre at the feet of the U.S. government, which Abrams had dismissed in prior testimony as Communist propaganda, as laid out in the *Al-Jazeera* article. When Rep. Omar asked if, given the massacre, Abrams stood by his statement that America's El Salvador policy in the Reagan years was a "fabulous achievement," he replied, "From the day that President [José Napoleón] Duarte was elected [in 1984] in a free election to this day, El Salvador has been a democracy. That's a fabulous achievement." The conversation went downhill from there:

> **Rep. Omar:** Yes or no, do you think that massacre was a fabulous achievement that happened under our watch?
>
> **Abrams:** That is a ridiculous question.
>
> **Rep. Omar (interrupting):** Yes or no?

Abrams: No.

Rep. Omar: I will take that as a yes.[60]

Omar used this line of questioning to portray Abrams—and again by extension the Trump administration and America itself—as someone who would "support an armed faction within Venezuela that engages in war crimes, crimes against humanity, or genocide," were it in the U.S. national interest. The irony was lost on Rep. Omar that Abrams is a staunch proponent of human rights, and she was in effect standing against a Venezuelan opposition to a socialist regime engaged in war crimes, crimes against humanity, and mass persecution.[61] Rep. Omar's questioning was simultaneously unoriginal, unintelligible, and unhinged—gratuitous in every respect. But she scored one for the oppressed of the Earth against the United States.

Speaking of Venezuela, Omar blamed not Chavismo-Maduro socialism for its collapse but, as one might expect by now, America. According to Rep. Omar, "a lot of the policies that we've put in place has (sic) kind of helped lead [to] the devastation in Venezuela and we've sort of set the stage for where we are arriving today [with] this particular bullying and the use of sanctions to eventually intervene and make regime change."[62] Keep in mind that the "regime change" Rep. Omar derisively references was Juan Guaidó succeeding President Maduro on an interim basis as he was constitutionally mandated to as president of Venezuela's National Assembly.[63]

Beyond ignoring such facts, by proffering the claim that America is engaging in a coup, she is creating a propaganda victory for the Left's greatest enemy—at least of recent vintage—Vladimir Putin's Russia, granted, along with others closer to Rep. Omar's heart, such as Iran, as we will touch on momentarily.[64,65] Further, again, it is telling that you will seek in vain to find a comment from Rep. Omar condemning Maduro's deployment of death squads against his political opponents.[66] None of this matters if your objective is to delegitimize the country you represent while bolstering your nation's opponents.

Regarding Iran, Omar blames America for the Khomeinist regime's aggression. By her logic, pulling out of the Joint Comprehensive Plan of

Action, referred to herein as the Iran nuclear deal or "Iran Deal"—through which the Obama administration underwrote the regime's jihadist and expansionist efforts to the tune of over 100 billion dollars—pushed Iran to engage in still more jihadist and expansionist efforts. In an October 2019 op-ed, Omar called the Trump administration's "maximum pressure" campaign against Iran—involving the imposition of crippling sanctions designed to squeeze the mullocracy—a "failed U.S. strategy."[67] That by late 2019 the totalitarian, anti-Western regime appeared to be straining to survive under the pressure of these efforts, reacting in desperation with widespread violence against citizens emboldened to protest its rule, would seem to contradict Omar's view.[68] Apparently, Omar believes the superior policy is to reward Iranian bellicosity against the West and our allies—that success would be defined by a stronger and more stable mullocracy.[69] She fails to address the fact that Iran's regime initiated and has been at war with the United States since 1979. It is therefore not surprising that Rep. Omar too opposes America's ongoing partnerships with several of Iran's foes. Nor is it surprising that she recoiled in the aftermath of the Trump administration's successful January 2020 strike on Major General Qassem Soleimani, head of the terrorist organization, the Islamic Revolutionary Guard Corps-Quds Force, and architect of Iran's global jihadist and imperialist efforts.[70]

And at root, as with domestic policy, in Rep. Omar's view, hypocrisy underlies U.S. foreign policy. In a March 2019 piece in *The New Yorker*, Benjamin Wallace-Wells describes an interview he conducted with Rep. Omar in which he recounts:

> I asked whether she [Omar] wanted to highlight the gap between how Americans valued the lives of citizens and those of non-citizens. That wasn't the core issue, she said. The core issue was America's hypocrisy, a term she used often. She believes that her upbringing has made her especially alert to it. "Now, abroad, we have ideals about providing support and guidance, and doing that in the most diplomatic way," she said. "But the way that in actuality gets carried out is not diplomatic and not caring

and not rooted in humanity. We are engaging in constant conflict that causes more human suffering than the one we went to go help. (sic) And we further and support (sic) policies that dehumanize and violate human rights. And this hypocritical way that we engage…is one that is duly noted by many people around the world." She paused. "What we seek to do is good. That is inherently in us. We think we're helping. But what we end up doing is causing hurt and furthering human suffering."[71]

Were it only that Rep. Omar took such a non-interventionist view in domestic matters.

No one would deny that there have been unintended consequences to a number of America's overseas engagements—some of which were ill-considered—thus harming our national interest. But Rep. Omar goes much further when she claims America seeks to "dehumanize and violate human rights." This is a particularly ironic assertion given several of the regimes America has challenged militarily in Omar's lifetime have collectively massacred thousands of innocents, imperiled millions more, and were among the worst human rights abusers on the planet.

We may with good reason view democracy-promotion and nation-building efforts in general with great skepticism, and as a fool's errand in places inhospitable to Western liberalism such as the Islamic world. We may argue that it would be far better to pursue a range of policies that would be entirely unacceptable to Rep. Omar, such as taking all possible measures to secure the homeland and its borders, while bolstering our military to such a degree and providing it such latitude in terms of rules of engagement that the costs to others of threatening the U.S. would be prohibitive. But would Rep. Omar really suggest there was malice behind helping to organize popularly elected governments in Iraq and Afghanistan? These efforts may have been naïve and thus misguided, but they were certainly not nefarious.

Rep. Omar's critiques of such measures cannot be taken in good faith because she consistently portrays America as the world's great antagonist. Yet the world's true despots, who threaten the liberties of others, are rarely if ever the objects of Omar's ire. In brief, the most charitable thing one can say about Rep. Omar, in the context of her harping on the United States' "hypocrisy," is that she lacks any sense of proportion and awareness.

But arguably the most sinister element of Rep. Omar's Blame America First worldview concerns her sentiments on the Iran-related matter of Islamic terrorism. Rep. Omar blames America for creating jihadis, through both our words and actions. In her telling: "Our president [Trump] is their [jihadis'] best PR person…It's a perfect selling and promotional tool. The president says, 'We are at war with Islam. We are at war with people who come from countries that are majority-Muslim countries. And we favor the people in those countries who are not Muslim.' What more do you need?"[72]

Who knew that imposing temporary travel restrictions on people seeking to enter the United States from countries with sizable jihadist populations, who were unable to be properly vetted, constituted a call to strap a bomb to oneself or take up arms against the infidel? Or is Rep. Omar claiming that America creates terrorists by forthrightly recognizing the ideology that animates them?

A consistent theme Rep. Omar sounds—undoubtedly to the delight of jihadists worldwide—is that of "blowback." The general idea of blowback is that by killing enemies in foreign lands, one creates collateral damage that "radicalizes" the impacted populations, thereby inspiring more combatants. In a May 2019 congressional hearing, Rep. Omar said, "we know that in Somalia, particularly in dealing with Al-Shabaab, since President Trump has gotten elected the number of drones have increased, but the number of attacks that Al-Shabaab has been able to carry out has also tripled. We also know the same to be true for Boko Haram."[73]

Subsequently, she made the argument more pointedly, arguing "it seems like…there is a direct sort of correlation between our droning and the increase of their [Somali jihadis'] assaults and…their recruitment."[74]

In the wake of a brutal Al-Shabaab attack on a Kenyan shopping mall in September 2013, Rep. Omar described such acts of terrorism as a response to, "our involvement in other people's affairs."[75] Notably in that same interview with Ahmed Tharwat—a man who characterized Israel as "Jewish ISIS," and has compared members of Hamas to victims of the

Holocaust—Rep. Omar seemed to draw moral equivalence between the U.S. government and Al-Qaeda.[76] Below is the relevant portion of the exchange:

> **Ilhan Omar:** …the thing that was interesting in the class [that Omar took on terrorism at NDSU] was every time the professor said "Al-Qaeda," he sort of, his shoulders went up, and you know…
>
> **Ahmed Tharwat:** He's in command, yeah.
>
> **Ilhan Omar:** Al-Qaeda, you know? Hezbollah. [Omar shrugs shoulders and says words in an affected voice]
>
> **Ahmed Tharwat:** He's an expert.
>
> [laughter]
>
> …
>
> **Ilhan Omar:** …You don't say, "America," with an intensity, you don't say, "England," with an intensity. You don't say, "the army" with an intensity.[77]

This back-and-forth speaks for itself.

Omar has gone beyond rationalizing jihad and treating jihadists as on par with Americans to defending jihadists themselves. In November of 2016, Omar interceded on behalf of a Somali-American man alleged to have attempted to join and fight for the Islamic State.[78] He was one of nine Somali Minnesotans hailing from Rep. Omar's Twin Cities home—an area that is a hotbed of U.S. jihadi activity—sentenced in one of the largest terrorist prosecutions in U.S. history.[79,80] A tenth charged co-conspirator had successfully joined the Islamic State in Syria.[81] As Minnesota State Representative-elect, Omar saw fit to write a letter to the judge presiding over the case asking for leniency in the sentencing of this aforementioned individual, though her general language seemed to indicate a plea for leniency on behalf of the entire terrorist cell. While others filed their letters with the court, Omar both delivered her appeal to the judge and released its text to the media, just days after her election.[82] In her letter, Rep. Omar wrote to Judge Michael Davis that lengthy sentences, "create an environment in which extremism can flourish, aligning with the presupposition of terrorist recruitment: 'Americans do not accept you and continue to trivialize your value. Instead of being a nobody, be a martyr.'" Rep. Omar added that, "The desire to commit violence is not inherent to people—it is the consequences (sic) of systematic alienation."[83] Again, jihad, like the rest of the world's ills, is seen as America's fault. Further, punishing jihadists only creates more of them. That Omar released this statement publicly reflects the overt nature of her radicalism. It amounted to a wink to jihadists in her district, and beyond, indicating they had a sympathetic ear in Ilhan Omar.

It is beyond instructive to juxtapose Rep. Omar's statements with the most infamous jihadist of our era, Osama bin Laden. In a 1998 interview with *ABC News*, playing on the self-loathing of the then-fringiest of fringe progressives, bin Laden told former correspondent John Miller:

> The call to wage war against America was made because America has spear-headed the crusade against the Islamic nation, sending tens of thousands of its troops to the land of the two Holy Mosques over and above its meddling in its affairs and its politics, and its support of the oppressive, corrupt and tyrannical regime that is in control. These are the reasons behind the singling out of America as a target.
>
> …The wrongs and the crimes committed against the Muslim nation are far greater than can be covered by this interview. America heads the list of aggressors against Muslims.
>
> …They rip us of our wealth and of our resources and of our oil. Our religion is under attack. They kill and murder our brothers. They compromise our honor and our dignity and

dare we utter a single word of protest against the injustice, we are called terrorists. This is compounded injustice.

… The leaders in America and in other countries as well have fallen victim to Jewish Zionist blackmail. They have mobilized their people against Islam and against Muslims. These are portrayed in such a manner as to drive people to rally against them. **The truth is that the whole Muslim world is the victim of international terrorism, engineered by America** at the United Nations. We are a nation whose sacred symbols have been looted and whose wealth and resources have been plundered. It is normal for us to react against the forces that invade our land and occupy it.[84] [**Emphasis added**]

It is important for Americans to understand the nature of their enemies if they are to be countered. Characteristic of jihadist ideology and tactics is an emphasis on deception. Under certain circumstances, Islamic law not only permits but commands lying and dissimulation in service of its goals.[85,86] Relatedly, Islamic supremacists are adept at devising propaganda that plays on Western guilt and self-doubt. Rhetoric that triggers the reflexive, "Why do they hate us?" response is particularly effective. Bin Laden sought to stir these emotions in his listeners and was adept at promoting the notion of blowback. Unfortunately, as Rep. Omar seems well aware, the blowback explanation for jihadism may have more receptive ears in the West today than it did in the bin Laden era.

Of course, claims of blowback being a root cause for jihadi actions may be disproven by observing that scores of those targeted by jihadis have never engaged in violence against them or their homelands. In recent years, jihadis have slaughtered not only thousands of non-Muslim civilians worldwide but thousands of noncombatant Muslim civilians in Muslim lands.

A more compelling causal explanation than blowback can be found in Islamic texts themselves. There is substantial justification for the theological and legal imperative to commit *offensive* jihad in the Islamic canon.[iv] The classical, authoritative manual of Islamic law, *Reliance of the Traveller*, which is sanctioned by Egypt's Al-Azhar University, the seat of Sunni Islamic scholarship, states unequivocally that:[87]

> Jihad means to war against non-Muslims, and is etymologically derived from the word *mujahada*, signifying warfare to establish the religion [Islam]...The caliph makes war upon Jews, Christians, and Zoroastrians (provided he has first invited them to enter Islam in faith and practice, and if they will not, then invited them to enter the social *order* of Islam by paying the non-Muslim poll tax (jizya...)...in accordance with the word of Allah Most High, "Fight those who do not believe in Allah and the Last Day and who forbid not what Allah and His messenger have forbidden--who do not practice the religion of truth [Islam], being of those who have been given the Book [namely Jews and Christians]--until they pay the poll tax [*jizya*] out of hand and are humbled" (Koran 9:29)...[88]

The Muslim Brotherhood is the tip of the Sunni Islamic supremacist spear from which jihadist groups like Al-Qaeda sprang. The Brotherhood is not shy about its mission. Its slogan reads: "Allah is our objective; the Prophet is our leader; the Quran is our law; Jihad is our way; dying in the way of Allah is our highest hope."[89] Without delving into an extensive Islamic exegesis, note too that Quran verse 3:151 calls for Muslims to "cast terror into the hearts of the Unbelievers [Christians in context]." There is no addendum reading "solely in a defensive capacity."[90] In short, the goal of inflicting terror is to force non-Muslims into submitting to Islam—it is

---

iv   Some will counter that there are multiple interpretations of Islam, and/or that the concept of offensive jihad is itself a misinterpretation. But the real questions are: (i) whether there is in fact a basis for offensive jihad according to Islamic law, and (ii) whether there are people who accept it as such. The answer to both of these questions is "yes." The well over 35,000 attacks carried out by Islamic terrorists since September 11, 2001, as documented at thereligionofpeace.com, attest to the latter. For a comprehensive treatment of the former, see Stephen Coughlin's *Catastrophic Failure*, and Dr. Andrew Bostom's *Sharia Versus Freedom*.

not merely to repel invaders, real or imagined. Bin Laden revealed the true nature of the jihadist cause as follows:

> ...[O]ur call is the call of Islam that was revealed to **Mohammed. It is a call to all mankind. We have been entrusted with good cause to follow in the footsteps of the Messenger and to communicate his message to all nations.**

> ...In our religion, we believe that Allah has created us for the purpose of worshipping him. He is the one who has created us and who has favored us with this religion. **Allah has ordered us to make holy wars and to fight to see to it that His word is the highest and the uppermost and that of the unbelievers the lowermost.** We believe that this is the call we have to answer regardless of our financial capabilities.

> **This too answers the claims of the West and of the secular people in the Arab world. They claim that this blessed awakening and the people reverting to Islam are due to economic factors. This is not so. It is rather a grace from Allah, a desire to embrace the religion of Allah.**

> ...I am one of the servants of Allah. We do our duty of fighting for the sake of the religion of Allah. **It is also our duty to send a call to all the people of the world to enjoy this great light and to embrace Islam and experience the happiness in Islam. Our primary mission is nothing but the furthering of this religion.**[91] [Emphasis added]

It should deeply concern every American that Rep. Omar's rhetoric parallels bin Laden's—and all the more so given that she sits on the HFAC. Unlike her fellow Democrats, who really may not know better, ignorance is likely no defense for Rep. Omar's apologism. One's skepticism should only increase when one considers that Omar not only obfuscates regarding Islamic terrorism, but pivots to engage in "whataboutism" by dishonestly claiming that white males present the *real* terrorist threat, and effectively that "terror has no religion"—as if violent jihad were not an Islamic concept.[92] As we will document in detail in a later chapter, Rep. Omar's extensive ties to Islamist organizations, individuals, and governments, her aping of their rhetoric, and support for their agenda, suggest something far more disturbing is at play.

Rep. Omar's Blame America First rhetoric reflects a distinctly radical political philosophy. In the next chapter, we will elucidate upon it.

CHAPTER 3

OMAR, INTERSECTIONALITY, AND IDENTITY POLITICS

Where Progressives and Islamists Intersect

At first glance, there appears to be an inconsistency in Rep. Omar's previously explored rhetoric. On the one hand, she espouses views that fit firmly within the secular progressive camp. But on the other, she seems to espouse views consistent with the Islamist camp. How can she serve two such seemingly opposite masters? Rep. Omar is able to do so because while these two schools of thought diverge in many areas, they align when it comes to their chief objective: to impose totalitarian designs anathema to America's founding principles and the Judeo-Christian values that underlie them. Progressives and Islamists align on nearly all the theoretical and practical grounds on which Rep. Omar fights—and where they do not, deviations may be justified on grounds of expedience.

Throughout this book, we will demonstrate how simpatico these movements are, driven by their common goal, and how Rep. Omar sits at their center. We will focus for the moment on the progressivism she proudly champions, and leave the evidence of her Islamist sympathies, and the impact they may have on her worldview, for later.

Omar's Intersectional Feminism

Rep. Omar describes herself as an "intersectional feminist." The concept of intersectionality derives from the work of critical race theorist and UCLA and Columbia Law School professor Kimberlé Williams Crenshaw. In a 1989 paper titled "Demarginalizing the Intersection of Race and Sex: A Black Feminist Critique of Antidiscrimination Doctrine, Feminist Theory and Antiracist Politics," Professor Crenshaw introduced the theory, writing that:

> ...Black women are sometimes excluded from feminist theory and antiracist policy discourse because both are predicated on a discrete set of experiences that often does not accurately reflect the interaction of race and gender. These problems of exclusion cannot be solved simply by including Black women within an already established analytical structure. Because the intersectional experience is greater than the sum of racism and sexism, any analysis that does not take intersectionality into account cannot sufficiently address the particular manner in which Black women are subordinated.[1]

In a recent interview, Crenshaw provided a more colloquial definition: "Intersectionality is a lens through which you can see where power comes and collides, where it interlocks and intersects. It's not simply that there's a race problem here, a gender problem here, and a class or LBGTQ problem there. Many times that framework erases what happens to people who are subject to all of these things."

Intersectionalism ought to be seen as a part of the critical race theory to which Crenshaw adheres, which views the law—and by implication our political institutions themselves—as tools of white supremacy.[2] Indeed, to the critical race theorist: "racism is endemic, not aberrational, in American society...liberal legal ideals of neutrality and color-blindness have replicated rather than undone racism...analysis should be informed by personal experience and contextual, historical studies; and...pragmatic and eclectic strategies should be pursued in the struggle for racial and social justice."[3]

The case of Justice Brett Kavanaugh's Supreme Court confirmation fight would seem to provide a real-life case study in what happens when such a theory permeates a political system—seeing as how "Believe all women" was the rallying cry against the nominee, who was treated as the archetype of white male elitism, and therefore assumed guilty until proven innocent and undeserving of due process.

The radical underlying premise held by critical race theorists and their comrades seems to be that America is an inherently immoral and evil land by dint of its systemic racism. This conforms to Rep. Omar's critique of the country. And if she has it her way, as she puts it, America "is not going to be the country of white people."[4] As an intersectional *feminist*, presumably it will not be the country of white males, like Justice Kavanaugh, specifically. In fact, in September 2019, Rep. Omar called for his impeachment.[5]

It is worth stopping and appreciating the lack of self-awareness embedded in such arguments, given the rampant bigotry that has marked most places and most times, compared with the reality that as historian Victor Davis Hanson has noted:

> …[M]ore than 243 years after its independence, the current longest-lived democracy [America] arguably is also the world's most racially, ethnically, and religiously diverse nation and unmatched in its efforts to promote equality.
>
> More exceptionally, the United States did not resort to a coercive political ideology such as Stalinist Communism to unite the diverse, or embrace an all-encompassing religious orthodoxy in the manner of the dramatic spread of Islam between the 8th and 16th centuries among widely disparate peoples.[6]

It was the Founders, now cast as inherently evil dead, white, European males who were responsible for this system. The Republic they left us—based in the spirit of the Declaration of Independence and letter of the Constitution—allowed the American people to realize a greater degree of liberty and justice than any other. The American founding contained within it the keys to overcoming the country's worst bouts of illiberalism and gravest injustices. The model proved so successful that at no other point in history have a people had the time or resources to spend their days creating such elaborate, revolutionary theories of national self-loathing. Our progressive academics do not seem to realize, on a relative and absolute basis, how good they have it. At the very least they do not seem to appreciate the country that has afforded them such opportunities. Instead, they wish to impose upon their fellow citizens a "coercive political ideology" as referenced by Professor Hanson that would necessarily undo the successes of the American experiment.

Intersectionality, it should also be noted, fits well with the aims and philosophy of community organizers, of which Omar was one. Writing back in 1988 in *Illinois Issues*, the most famous community organizer of all, Barack Obama, described community organizing as:

> a way to merge various strategies for neighborhood empowerment. Organizing begins with the premise that (1) the problems facing inner-city communities do not result from a lack of effective solutions, but from **a lack of power** to implement these solutions; (2) that the only way for communities to build long-term power is by organizing people and the money [they raise] around a common vision; and (3) that a viable organization can only be achieved if a broadly based indigenous leadership—and not one or two charismatic leaders—**can knit together the diverse interests of their local institutions.**[7] [Emphasis added]

At the heart of critical race theorists' views, those of their intersectionalist offspring, and the community organizers who apply them, is a belief that American life can be reduced to a zero-sum group political power struggle. Seemingly absent from their worldview is the primacy in a free nation of a robust civil society fueled by and comprised of empowered individuals, families, and voluntary associations.

What does Rep. Omar, as an intersectional feminist, seek? As is her wont, she expressed the goal in a tweet, writing in December of 2017:

> We need to have conversations about race and class, and we need to understand the linkage between those things to **dismantle ideas of patriarchy, misogyny, racism and capitalism**, and what autonomy and self-determination needs to look like for women.[8] [Emphasis added]

Setting aside the Marxian nature of this rhetoric, and the fact that Omar would likely define America's bedrock institutions themselves as pillars of "patriarchy, misogyny, [and] racism," the idea that in Omar's reading, intersectionalism is dedicated to, among other things, destroying America's relatively free-market economic system should clue us into the fact that it is really an organizing strategy for Leftist political revolution.

Omar's aforementioned mentor, Habon Abdulle, argues that intersectionalism has been a powerful political tool for the freshman representative, writing:

> In both elections [for both the Minnesota and U.S. Houses of Representatives] Omar won because she demonstrated that intersectionality can be used to mobilize for social justice, as she navigates identities that register the effects of otherness. This has allowed her to anticipate and enact new social relations grounded in multiple axes of intersecting. Omar deployed intersectionality as a means for getting through the various oppressive systems in society, but also as a way of collecting all her identities into a movement for social change… Social and gender equality requires challenging the very institutions and practices that uphold white male privilege and power. In Minnesota we have taken a collective action toward redistributing power…[9]

Stated differently, intersectionalism is about linking together various identity groups through shared victimology to overthrow the existing order, by imposing a progressive ideology that is antithetical to our founding values and principles. It is a means for seizing power to achieve radical ends or at least ginning up those who desire radical ends to seize power.

Even if Omar and her acolytes are solely able to accumulate power, rather than using it to impose their stated agenda, in the process they will be turning the American system of individual liberty, private property rights, and the rule of law on its head.

Man's lot throughout much of history has been one of oppression and misery, with the people serving as slaves or subjects, and their rulers omnipotent masters or kings—whether in the form of a man or the state. The Founders developed a system in which sovereignty would be vested in the citizenry, with every man a king, and the state subservient to the people.

Omar and her fellow *progressives* would, therefore, be taking us *backwards*. They would redistribute wealth and power from the people to the state while claiming to do the opposite—in the process taking control over our lives for themselves and others in the ruling political class. The aggrieved, on behalf of whom Omar and her acolytes claim to speak, would end up the most disenfranchised and hurt. This story has played out repeatedly in history. It is what the record shows from Mao's China, to Stalin's Soviet Union, to Chavez/Maduro's Venezuela. We see a far more benign example of this pattern in the failures of our own Great Society.[10] The progressive political elite, the ones promulgating the policies, would benefit most. It is for this reason that Rep. Omar's "progressivism" is in actuality "regressive."

The reason it is critical to understand the means and ends of the intersectionalist is that intersectionalism is integral to everything Ilhan Omar does in politics. As she put it herself in a June 2019 interview with the African-American publication, the *Minnesota Spokesman-Recorder*:

> I've always talked about the importance of having intersectionality in the center of the way we propose policy. Race and gender are compounding factors of discrimination or any sort of disparity. If we are not addressing the class issues, race issues, gender issues, then we are never going to have any just policies that are going to be helpful for all of us, equally...Intersectionality is the most valued lens that

leaders and policy advocates can use to make sure we have just policies. It's a layered way of looking at issues, but as someone who carries multiple identities, it's something I understand.[11]

Merriam-Webster Dictionary broadens the definition of intersectionality to: "the complex, cumulative way in which the effects of multiple forms of discrimination (such as racism, sexism, and classism) combine, overlap, or intersect especially in the experiences of marginalized individuals or groups."[12] What "intersects" are "identities."

Intersectionality, Identity Politics, and the Unmaking of American Identity

Identity politics is the mechanism by which the theory of intersectionalism is put into practice. Conservative scholar David Azerrad argues that identity politics:

> ...combine a focus on race, sex, sexual orientation, gender identity, and any other number of identitarian categories with a politics of victimization. The key to understanding identity politics is to realize that it is primarily a politics of oppression and victimization rather than identity. This is apparent in the first document to use the term, the 1977 Combahee River Collective Statement. As the black lesbian feminists who drafted it explain: "This focusing upon our own oppression is embodied in the concept of identity politics."
>
> The cornerstone of the identitarian worldview is the claim that America, contrary to its egalitarian professions of faith, is at its core a supremacist regime that oppresses certain groups. The oppressed groups vary according to the different identitarian movements—black people, women, Hispanics, homosexuals, transsexuals, etc.—although most

recognize the oppression of other groups and proclaim solidarity with them. This struggle between the oppressors and those whom they oppress on the basis of their identity is the most fundamental dimension of reality. Oppression of women and minorities, in this view, does not mark a departure from American republican ideals. Rather, it reveals the repressive nature of the regime.[13]

Outside of failed Georgia Democratic gubernatorial candidate Stacey Abrams, Ilhan Omar appears to be the model identity politics practitioner, and symbol, in today's American Left.

Beyond its underlying victimology, intersectionality's focus on the overlapping grievances of distinct identity groups is by its nature divisive. Squad member Ayanna Pressley (D-MA) perhaps best illustrated this divisiveness in July of 2019 at the premier annual progressive gathering, the "Netroots Nation" conference, when she stated: "We don't need any more brown faces that don't want to be a brown voice. We don't need black faces that don't want to be a black voice. We don't need Muslims that don't want to be a Muslim voice. We don't need queers that don't want to be a queer voice."[14]

But what of American voices? That is, of course, the point. The purpose of identity politics is to unmake the American identity. The Left does not strive for the "melting pot" ideal of yesteryear because dividing, agitating, and conquering serve its political ends. The circular firing squad that will naturally result with a constantly changing hierarchy of the oppressed, in which one day's victims can easily become the next day's victimizers, is of no concern when you are trying to effectuate a revolution—in fact, it may serve as a benefit as political tides and demographic trends change. As we will soon see, this is not hyperbole—what Rep. Omar seeks are revolutionary changes.

Intersectionalists implicitly reject Martin Luther King Jr.'s vision of a nation whose people judge one another on the content of their character, rather than the color of their skin. The intersectionalists instead make pigmentation primary. They further classify individuals as demoralized members of marginalized identity groups, rather than treating them as empowered individuals with agency. Left unasked is the question: Why strive to improve one's condition if the deck is rigged, and only politicians can make things right? This is of no concern to intersectional politicians, who leverage identity politics to build coalitions and reap the benefits of divide-and-conquer tribalism.

Another political benefit of wrapping oneself in an intersectional veil is that it protects the ideas of those who wear it from scrutiny. Identity is used as a shield against merit-based critiques and substantive discourse. The cost to society is inordinate. When in a debate skin pigmentation, or sexual preference, or immigrant status trump the substance of the competing ideas, the free exchange of views on which our system relies erodes.

In First Amendment vernacular, the poison of identity politics, and its debilitating cousin political correctness, serve as de facto "prior restraints" on speech. Rep. Omar has sought to portray herself, consistent with the victimology inherent to intersectionality, as the aggrieved party when she receives legitimate criticism for her positions, accusing her interlocutors of "Islamophobia." When challenged, we have witnessed Rep. Omar and her comrades in the Squad turn the shield of identity into a weapon against even fellow Democrats such as House Speaker Nancy Pelosi. They do so by proclaiming that to challenge the views or actions of the women of color who comprise the Squad is *a priori* racist. The constant inapt invocation of "racism," "sexism," and the other panoply of "isms," like falsely screaming "fire" in a movie theater over and over, simply devalues their statements and discredits the people making them. Sadly, their false protestations are to the detriment of actual victims of hatred and bigotry.

Rep. Omar takes the idea that "the personal is political" to heart. In a series of comments throughout the years, Omar has shown that she views her own life through an intersectional prism, consistent with the victimological chords she constantly plays. In an interview in *Vogue*—yes, that *Vogue*—without a hint of self-awareness, Omar bemoaned that: "When you're a kid and you're raised in an all-black, all- Muslim [sic] environment, nobody really talks to you about your identity. You just are. There is freedom in knowing that you are accepted as your full self. So the notion that there is a conflict with your identity in society was hard at the age of 12."[15]

This was telling on two levels: First, it would appear Omar was assimilated into an identity politics-centric America; second, the focus on identity colored her perspective from her earliest time in the country. As a politician, Omar has said: "I am not a Somali representative. I am not a Muslim representative. I am not a millennial representative. I am not a woman representative. I am a representative who happens to have all of these marginalized identities and can understand the intersectionality of all of them in a very unique way."[16] Note again Rep. Omar's focus on discrete identities rather than a unifying Americanism.

Thus Omar, in spite of her rapid rise to such commanding heights in American society, remains through it all the eternal victim. As she stated on the floor of the Minnesota House: "I think I know a little bit about discrimination. I face it every single day. I carry multiple identities that are constantly, constantly being discriminated against."[17] She said this while advocating *against* an anti-boycott, divestment, and sanctions (BDS) measure targeting Israel. The reality is that Omar uses her "marginalized identities" to create a veneer of virtue around her end goal of imposing a Leftist ideology on America.

A Recipe for Disunion

Suffice it to say, the idea that the U.S. consists in large measure of hapless groups of victims that must be banded together to overthrow the existing oppressive order to achieve power, rather than of unique individuals empowered by a system that enables them to pursue their dreams on their own merits, necessarily tears at the fabric of a country that is supposed to assimilate all peoples into a system of shared values and principles.

Intersectionality is about rubbing at the sores of society and inventing ones that might not otherwise exist. Those doing the agitating seek more power in the hands of the state—a state guided by those who claim to know what is best to vanquish the ills of others. Yet such politics are a recipe for discord, demoralization, and destruction—while also leading to illiberal outcomes.[18] By its very nature, intersectionality tears society apart in pitting not just blacks against whites, and gay people against straight people, but men against women. It is truly antisocial.

Operationally, again intersectionality and its politics of identity are mechanisms for achieving "social justice" by collecting wealth and power in the hands of the state, and redistributing it to the "oppressed" as the social justice warriors define them, domestically and internationally.[19] Yet in practice, the wealth and power inevitably trickle up, not down. It accrues to the ruling class, rather than the declared beneficiaries on whose behalf it claimed to rule. Those who benefit are the political elites and the foreign adversaries of freedom.

On a micro-level, Rep. Ilhan Omar's Minnesota's 5th Congressional district is illustrative. It has long been led at the national, state, and local levels by progressives. How have its residents fared? Rep. Omar's district was recently rated as the worst for black Americans in the nation, on the basis of numerous socioeconomic criteria. The report noted that "Black area residents are about four times more likely to live below the poverty line than white residents and three times more likely to be unemployed."[20]

Though they will not heed his words, Justice Clarence Thomas provides a most worthy rejoinder to the intersectionalists. He stated in a 1998 speech to a not necessarily sympathetic crowd at the predominately black National Bar Association:

> There now seems to be a broad acceptance of the racial divide as a permanent state. While we once celebrated those things that we had in common with our fellow citizens who did not share our race, so many now are triumphal about our differences, finding little, if anything, in common. Indeed, some go so far as to all but define each of us by our race and establish the range of our thinking and our opinions, if not our deeds by our color.
>
> I, for one, see this in much the same way I saw our denial of rights—as nothing short of a denial of our humanity. Not one of us has the "gospel," nor are our opinions based upon some revealed precepts to be taken as faith. As thinking, rational individuals, not one of us can claim infallibility, even from the overwhelming advantage of hindsight and Monday-morning quarterbacking.

This makes it all the more important that our fallible ideas be examined as all ideas are in the realm of reason, not as some doctrinal or racial heresy. None of us—none of us—have been appointed by God or appointed God. And if any of us has, then my question is why hasn't he or she solved all these problems?[21]

CHAPTER 4

OMAR'S PROGRESSIVE AGENDA

Socialism at Home

In keeping with her philosophical orientation, Rep. Omar seeks to upend an America that she sees as fundamentally unjust and oppressive. Accordingly, Rep. Omar's domestic platform appears to be lifted from President Franklin Delano Roosevelt's radical "Second Bill of Rights."[1] This agenda calls for treating all manner of goods and services as G-d-given guarantees that the government is to confer upon citizens through unbound powers. Such a schema flips on its head our constitutional system meant to protect individual rights while constraining the power of government. Though Omar has not publicly identified as such, a staffer referred to Omar as a "democratic socialist."[2] Omar maintains deep ties with the Democratic Socialists of America (DSA) and its coterie of fellow travelers. The DSA has released numerous statements in support of her.[3,4] Whether Rep. Omar considers herself a socialist or not, as we will show, her domestic agenda is synonymous with socialism. In fact, given Rep. Omar's rhetoric at a November 2019 campaign rally for socialist presidential candidate Bernie Sanders (D-VT) in which she called for a "mass movement of the working class," it may well be that socialism is too moderate a label for her program.[5]

As noted previously, Rep. Omar has tweeted of her desire to "dismantle" capitalism.[6] She has said: "The capitalist system has led to a concentration of wealth in a small handful of elites while working people suffer. We must stop the exploitation of working people to create a fair and just economy."[7] Rep. Omar detailed her agenda for achieving "a fair and just economy" in a July 2019 tweet that reads: "Medicare for All. Homes for All. Universal School Meals. A Green New Deal. We are fighting for policies that lift up all Americans. We are fighting for the many, not the few!"[8] Indeed, socialized medicine and the deindustrialization of our entire economy would represent the dismantling of capitalism. How it would "lift up all Americans" is less clear. Though the math is fuzzy, Rep. Omar seeks to fund her collectivist designs by imposing confiscatory tax rates for high-income earners of between 70 percent and 90 percent, presumably to be supplemented by dismantling America's military, as we will touch on shortly.[9,10]

Rep. Omar's "Homes for All" proposal represents an extreme departure even from the most radical of her colleagues on the national stage. The legislation, introduced in November 2019, calls for $1 trillion in government spending on 12 million housing units, 9.5 million of which would be public, and the remaining 2.5 million of which would be private but affordable.[11] According to her website: "We cannot simply trust that for-profit developers will invest in housing that is affordable to working people. We need to move towards publicly- and cooperatively-owned models of housing for all income-levels."[12]

Rep. Omar also seeks a federal jobs guarantee program for those who want one.[13] Such paternalism would have been deemed not only unacceptable but laughable by "liberal" politicians of even just a decade ago, if not less.

Last but not least regarding Rep. Omar's anti-capitalist program, she, alongside Sen. Bernie Sanders, introduced a bill in Congress to eliminate all student debt.[14] Rep. Omar asserts that student debt "is not the result of bad choices or behaviors. It is the result of a system that tells students to get an education, go to college in order to have a stable life, but then does not provide the resources so that they can afford that education."[15]

As noted earlier, Rep. Omar has a penchant for blaming "the system." As a proponent of criminal justice reform, she says Americans "must advocate for justice for the incarcerated, whom the system renders disenfranchised and voiceless."[16] Omar has called for "restoring the vote for felons."[17] And in order to close the "school-to-prison pipeline," which Omar believes stems from racism rather than individual misconduct, Omar claimed to introduce a bill in the Minnesota state legislature to block schools from hiring resource officers.[18,19] "Resource officers" are former law enforcement officials who work to protect students.[20] One would be hard-pressed to locate comments by Rep. Omar calling for the defense of innocent Americans against would-be criminals, or for harshly punishing those who commit heinous crimes.

As perhaps the ultimate measure of justice, in Rep. Omar's view, she appears to be in favor of reparations for the ancestors of slaves.[21,22]

On immigration, consistent with her rancorous rhetoric, Omar has called for abolishing ICE.[23] She has also clamored for putting the United Nations (UN) High Commissioner on Refugees in charge of dealing with the crisis on our southern border—notwithstanding the fact that such a move would directly violate U.S. sovereignty, and perhaps breach our Constitution.[24] We should also keep in mind that the stated aims of the UN High Commissioner are anathema to U.S. immigration law. In an August 2019 Facebook post, the Commissioner wrote: "It is never a crime to seek asylum in another country even if one enters a country *irregularly*."[25] [Emphasis added] For Rep. Omar, that likely only heightened her appeal.

It is therefore unsurprising that, like several of her House colleagues, in July 2019 Rep. Omar warned constituents of forthcoming ICE raids.[26] As a Minnesota state representative, she urged Democratic Governor Mark Dayton to issue an executive order preventing state resources from being used in so-called family separation policies with respect to asylum seekers.[27] She also sought to pass a sanctuary-state bill, perhaps missing the irony that she was engaging in modern-day nullification, echoing the white supremacists of yesteryear.[28,29] In spite of her Open Borders views, Rep. Omar has called for deportations—of those with whom she disagrees on Twitter.[30] Combining her radicalism on immigration with her radicalism on abortion, Omar has gone so far as to endorse the idea of taxpayer-funded abortions for illegal aliens.[31]

With respect to domestic terrorism, in keeping with her intersectional feminist bent, Rep. Omar does not believe we face a threat from jihadism, but rather, from white males. Rep. Omar claimed in an interview with Qatar-backed *Al-Jazeera* that: "our country should be more fearful of white men…because they are actually causing most of the deaths within this country…And so if fear was the driving force of policies to keep America safe – Americans safe inside of this country – we should be profiling, monitoring, and creating policies to fight the radicalization of white men."[32]

On a related note, when Rep. Omar served in the Minnesota State legislature, she was one of only two representatives to vote *against* a bill that would prevent insurance payouts to the estates of those committing acts of terrorism. The bill in question arose in response to the San Bernardino jihadist attack perpetrated by Syed Rizwan Farook and wife Tashfeen Malik, both of whom were killed in a shootout with police. The bill Omar voted against would give life insurance companies the right to deny payouts to beneficiaries of those who died in the process of committing jihadist acts.[33] Omar has never explained this vote, so we asked her if she would provide a rationale. Neither the congresswoman nor her office provided a response.

And with respect to her opposition to President Trump's anti-terror entry executive orders, and criticism of the Trump administration's reduced refugee resettlement caps, to the author's knowledge, she has never explained how she would propose strengthening our defenses against jihadists seeking to infiltrate the country through immigration, nor whether she considers it a problem in the first place.[34] We asked Rep. Omar about these issues as well. As with our other inquiries, neither Rep. Omar nor her office provided a response.

Finally, we would be remiss if we did not mention Rep. Omar's stated support for commencing impeachment proceedings against President Trump, as indicated in April 2019.[35] Her party's leadership would later fall in line.

Beyond her policy proclamations, another way to measure what really matters to Rep. Omar is to look at those issues about which she has spoken on the U.S. House floor. Through the summer of 2019, Rep. Omar's remarks appeared some sixteen times in the Congressional Record. Four times she delivered "had I been present" vote declarations. Once, she read a portion of Special Counsel Robert Mueller's Report on Trump-Russia. Yet included in the remarks she made during the eleven times she spoke on substantive issues, Rep. Omar:

- Attacked U.S. defense spending as "part of an outrageously bloated budget that lines the pockets of defense contractors;"[36]

- Castigated the U.S. government for sharing access to terrorist screening databases with regimes of which she disapproved;[37]

- Blamed America for the ongoing global refugee crisis—attributable to climate change to which the U.S. has disproportionately contributed, and for which U.S. citizens have an obligation to compensate the globe;[38]

- Smeared Christian pro-life advocates as "anti-choice," "religious fundamentalists" who are "criminaliz[ing] women simply for existing and…punish[ing] us when we don't conform to their attempts to control us;"[39,40]

- Advocated for ending solitary confinement, which she described as "torture;"[41] and

- Criticized the U.S. government and private industry—rather than the Chinese Communist Party (CCP)—for *our* policies towards China's Uighur Muslim minority. An estimated over one million Uighurs are being held in modern-day gulags by the CCP in China's Xinjiang province.[42] Omar noted that federal authorities had historically held nearly two dozen Uighur Muslims for twelve years in Guantanamo Bay, supposedly at the behest of the Chinese government. She called for an investigation into American firms purportedly benefiting from said Uighur persecution.[i,43]

---

i   On the former point, Rep. Omar's characterization is misleading. As *The New York Times* reported upon release of the last of the prisoners—several of whom were released well before the twelve-year timeframe Rep. Omar cited—"the United States could not repatriate them because the Chinese government has a history of mistreating Uighurs… Other countries were reluctant to take them, in part because of Chinese diplomatic pressure." The latter point is of course legitimate, but it is notable that Rep. Omar again was more focused on these matters than seeking to punish the Chinese regime for its extensive human rights violations.

Omar's domestic policies go hand in hand with her anti-Americanism: Since capitalism is fundamentally unfair and oppressive, America must dismantle it. Since America's past and present is one of victimization and marginalization, the victimized and marginalized are to receive just compensation through the redistribution of wealth and power. Since American society is at fault for criminality, on account of its fundamental injustice, like others in the hierarchy of victimology, criminals must receive "restorative justice." Since white males are the scourge of the Earth, not jihadis, they should be the ones profiled. Given the ills to which America has contributed across the globe, our sovereignty and the defense of our homeland is to be determined based on the needs of aggrieved non-Americans, not the citizenry. Rep. Omar's agenda fundamentally rejects and seeks to overturn the American system.

Surrender Abroad

Just as Rep. Omar's domestic agenda is based in a view that America must achieve social justice by redistributing wealth and power to the putatively oppressed, likewise, her foreign policy agenda is based in a view that America must achieve global social justice by redistributing America's wealth and power to the wronged adversaries we created, and other Third World victims. Stated differently, seeing America as the world's great oppressor, justice demands the reduction of American might.

Rep. Omar has skin in this game. She sees foreign policy not from the perspective of an American citizen seeking to promote U.S. national interest, but rather as "someone who has seen the United States from the perspective of a foreigner."[44] Based on her policies, the foreigner's perspective is not one of awe and appreciation. We know this because Rep. Omar seeks the end of "Western imperialism," to be achieved through "an overhaul of our foreign policy...from the standpoint of really thinking how it impacts those around the world, and where our values intersect with what's happening."[45] In a word, she wants to cut our military down to size, and shift military funds to domestic aims.

In Rep. Omar's explanation for her "Nay" vote on the 2019 federal budget, she wrote: "I cannot in good conscience support a bill that continues to throw billions of dollars at endless wars and Pentagon contractors. In order to pursue peace and prosperity at home, we must not continue to destabilize entire countries, fuel migration crises, and put American troops at risk. 'We must reduce Pentagon waste and reinvest that money into healthcare, education, housing, jobs, clean energy and infra-structure.'"[46] In her words, Rep. Omar has been working hard to achieve the "demilitarization of our foreign policy," to end "perpetual war and military aggression."[47,48]

While there are perfectly legitimate "guns-versus-butter" arguments to be made, Rep. Omar provides only the thinnest veneer for the idea that she is advocating based on the security and national interest needs of the United States.

Beyond the demoralizing and hostile nature of her rhetoric about America and its place in the world, one would be hard-pressed to find Rep. Omar expressing concern for the size, scope, and nature of the threats facing our nation, and how her favored policies would protect Americans from them. Rep. Omar provided the most detailed description of her ideal-istic foreign policy in a 2019 *Washington Post* editorial, in which she wrote:

> I believe in an inclusive foreign policy—one that centers on human rights, justice and peace as the pillars of America's engagement in the world, one that brings our troops home and truly makes military action a last resort. This is a vision that centers on the experiences of the people directly affected by conflict, that takes into account the long-term effects of U.S. engagement in war and that is sincere about our values regardless of short-term political convenience.
>
> This means reorienting our foreign affairs to focus on diplomacy and economic and cultural engagement.[49]

Rep. Omar's column is heavy on "universal values," and light on "national interest." While her message of inclusion must warm the hearts of the Chinese, the Russians, the Islamists and their allies, and diplo-macy, economic, and cultural engagement sound nice, in a world of brutal regimes acting out of self-interest, talk is cheap absent a robust military capability and the credible threat to use it.

One might argue, as we did before, that if one were truly interested in ensuring peace, one would seek to make the costs of war intolerably high for any and all adversaries, while vigorously defending the homeland. Yet Rep. Omar is not advocating such a peace through strength agenda. She wishes for the U.S. to demilitarize. She is not calling for securing the homeland. She wishes to increase immigration, legal and illegal alike. She is not calling for the military to be more prudent with its funds. She wants to slash the military budget across the board. Rep. Omar is simply calling for peace through disarmament and appeasement—peace through surrender.

It therefore follows that when Rep. Omar has asserted herself on issues of foreign policy, she has generally taken the positions favored by America's most ardent adversaries. She contends that these positions are good for the country. By her progressive logic, aiding and abetting those who challenge American's status quo will lead to mutually beneficial reform. A strategy of diplomatic appeasement will yield respect. A program of dropping our arms will lead others to drop theirs. This is the logic put forth.

How does Rep. Omar apply this view to the problems of the real world? As noted previously, she blames the crisis in Venezuela not on Chavismo/Maduro socialism, but rather on the U.S. To that end, she has called for "lift[ing] the economic sanctions that are inflicting suffering on innocent families, making it harder for them to access food and medicines, and deepening the economic crisis."[50] She has said, "We should support dialogue, not a coup!"[51] But again, this is a dishonest reading of America's Venezuela policy, the benefits of which accrue to Maduro and his global anti-American allies.[52] It would be different if Rep. Omar made the claim that the U.S. interest would be best served by extricating ourselves to the largest extent possible from complex geopolitical situations, but in each instance, as we will demonstrate herein, Rep. Omar seems to come down on the side of our adversaries, who violate the human rights and reject the values she claims to so cherish.

Moving to the Middle East, like President Obama before her, Rep. Omar seems to side with Islamic supremacist regimes over their foes. Omar is a major proponent of re-entering the Iran nuclear deal. In 2019, she blamed America's pressure campaign against the Khomeinist regime for Iran's hostile actions towards the U.S. and our allies, rather than pointing the finger at the Iranian regime itself. She condemned President Trump alone.[53] Consistent with her desire to disarm the U.S. military, the congresswoman co-sponsored the "Prevention of Unconstitutional War with Iran Act of 2019."[54] In a propaganda coup for the Iranian regime, Omar compared liberal and pluralistic Israel to theocratic Iran—falsely besmirching our closest ally in the region, while simultaneously placating an Iran dedicated to that ally's destruction.[55] She has also sought to delegitimize America's own government vis-à-vis Iran by endorsing the comparison of President Trump to Iranian President Rouhani, retweeting a propagandistic video produced by Qatar-backed *Al-Jazeera Plus* (AJ+) with the note: "He is ruining our country and it's (sic) reputation one stupid speech at a time #resist #ImpeachTrump."[56] Last but not least, in December 2019, just days before an Iran-backed militia in Iraq carried out a rocket attack killing an American contractor and injuring several others, and backers of that militia attempted to storm the U.S. Embassy in Baghdad following U.S. retaliatory airstrikes, Omar signed a letter challenging the Trump admin- istration's sanctions on the Central Bank of Iran (CBI).[57,58,59,60] According to the U.S. Treasury Department, CBI is "a crucial funding mechanism that the Iranian regime uses to support its terrorist network, including the Qods Force, Hizballah, **and other militants that spread terror and desta- bilize the region.**"[61] [Emphasis added]

Also like President Obama, Rep. Omar favors supporting Egyp- tian Islamists, having lobbied for the release of an imprisoned Egyptian Muslim Brotherhood leader.[62] Rep. Omar was outraged and perhaps saddened at the news of the death of deposed Egyptian president, and leader of its Muslim Brotherhood "Freedom and Justice" Party, Mohamed Morsi. Upon his June 2019 death while in detention, Omar promoted a conspiracy theory proliferating in the Islamic world, tweeting alarmingly: "None of this makes sense! We must call for an independent inquiry into the circumstances of President Morsi's death, his hastened burial and detention conditions. *Ala ya rahma…*"[63,64] Lest one thinks Rep. Omar took issue with Morsi's rule, back in July 2013, she retweeted a *BBC Africa* message that "Morsi has asked all citizens to abide by the constitution and the law, and not to respond to what he describes as a coup."[65] Did the retweet, in this case, equal an endorsement?[ii]

Then there is Rep. Omar's position on Turkey. In a move that simultaneously undermined her purported devotion to justice and upholding human rights, while illustrating her support for an authoritarian Islamist regime, Rep. Omar was one of only two Democrats not to affirm an October 2019 House resolution recognizing the Armenian genocide at the hands of the Ottoman Empire—a resolution that drew the ire of the Turkish government. Amazingly, in Omar's explanation for her "present" vote, she sought to draw moral equivalence between Turkey and America on grounds of "fairness," claiming "A true acknowledgment of historical crimes against humanity must include both the heinous genocides of the 20th century, along with earlier mass slaughters like the transatlantic slave trade and Native American genocide, which took the lives of hundreds of millions of indigenous people in this country."[66] Rep. Omar similarly bucked her Party as the sole Democrat to vote against the imposition of sanctions on Turkey for its incursion into northern Syria against Syrian Kurds, which passed the House with overwhelming bipartisan support.[67] As we will illustrate later in the book, Rep. Omar's staking out of positions favorable to the regime of Turkish Prime Minister Recep Tayyip Erdoğan on these two issues was no aberration.

Conversely, Rep. Omar has castigated the opponents of Shia and Sunni Islamic supremacists alike in the form of Gulf Arab powers like Saudi Arabia, an avowed adversary most notably of Iran and the Muslim Brotherhood. Rep. Omar's contempt for the Saudi regime is palpable. In what might qualify as her most hostile message to any government in the Middle East outside of Israel, in October 2018 she tweeted:

> The Saudi government might have been strategic at covering up the daily atrocities carried out against minorities,

---

ii   There in fact appears to be mutual admiration at play, as. Rep. Omar has won accolades from leading Egyptian Muslim Brotherhood figures such as Amr Darrag. See: https://twitter.com/jrossman12/status/1162061052131061761 and https://www.washingtoninstitute.org/policy-analysis/view/whos-who-in-the-muslim-brotherhood#AmrDarrag.

women, activists and even the #YemenGenocide, but the murder of #JamaKhashoggi should be the last evil act they are allowed to commit. #BDSSaudi #murderedjournalist.[68]

Rep. Omar has also called Saudi Arabia the "most oppressive country."[69] When being more diplomatic, she says, "Our alliedship (sic) with Saudi Arabia and the Emirates is immoral. I believe that it is one of the most absurd alliedships (sic); it doesn't fit with any of our values." She adds: "How can we make a decision to sell weapons to Saudi Arabia, knowing that they have been part of causing one of the most atrocious humanitarian crises in Yemen, when we know that they have a hand in what's happening right now in Sudan, what's happening in Libya, and the list can go on and on and on." She has made these claims, incidentally, on Qatar-backed outlet *Al-Jazeera*. Qatar has stood side-by-side with Iran and Muslim Brotherhood forces against the Saudis, Emiratis and their partners including Israel.[iii] In an inadvertent acknowledgment of the truly retrograde nature of Tehran's tyranny, she has sought to draw moral equivalence between Iran and its foes, writing that America's "criticisms of oppression and regional instability caused by Iran are not legitimate if we do not hold Egypt, the United Arab Emirates and Bahrain to the same standards."[iv,70]

While no American would want to live under any of these regimes, in terms of "oppression and regional instability," Iran is unrivaled, and most importantly, poses a major threat to the U.S. and our interests. As the author has written elsewhere:

> At home, the Khomeinist mullocracy is responsible for pervasive human rights abuses and violently suppressing political dissent (even taking Washington Post journalists hostage), and holds the dubious distinction of ranking number one in the world in per capita executions. It seeks to expand its Islamic Revolution and subdue rival

---

iii   We will extensively discuss Rep. Omar's views on Israel and Jews, and their broader significance, subsequently.

iv   We will put Rep. Omar's views on the Middle East in context of her Islamist ties in a later chapter.

regimes not only by threats, proxy wars and jihad, but also by cyberattacks and information warfare.

> "Death to Israel," followed closely by "Death to America," form the unifying ethos of Iran's Islamic totalitarian theocracy. Stated succinctly, Iran combines the brutal savagery and repression of the Saudis, with the subversion and destabilization emphasis of the Russians and the Jew-hatred of the neo-Nazis—with its hands drenched in the blood of hundreds of Americans dating back over the almost forty years since the overthrow of the Shah and the taking of U.S. hostages at our embassy in Tehran.[71]

In the Sunni-Shia, authoritarian versus Islamic supremacist battle, neither side favors Western values. That said, what ought to determine America's best course of action, to the extent there is one, is our national interest. Rep. Omar has not explained why coddling Iran and allowing the Muslim Brotherhood and its offshoots and fellow travelers to go unchecked in the Middle East serves U.S. interests. What she has said is that the likes of the Kingdom of Saudi Arabia, "are threatened, really, by Muslims who have now come to Congress who have the roots and understanding of the problems and can speak to solutions that do not involve them."[72] This is quite a statement from someone who advocates for a foreign policy based on "inclusion." Rep. Omar has not wavered from her position while in Congress. Upon her appointment to the House Foreign Affairs Committee (HFAC), she stated that one of her main priorities was "reign[ing] in arms sales to human rights abusers like Saudi Arabia."[73] She also co-sponsored the House resolution directing the removal of U.S. forces from Yemen that had not been authorized by Congress.[74] Again, there are real consequences to her being seated on such a vital House committee, and as we will explore later, major dangers to it.

Consistent with Rep. Omar's view that the U.S. fuels the world's fires, she slipped an amendment into the 2019 National Defense Authorization Act (NDAA) which stipulated that the U.S. establish no permanent bases or installations in Omar's native Somalia.[75] Given Rep. Omar's ties to the Somali regime, which we will discuss in detail in a later chapter, this action should raise serious alarm bells. Somalia was the only country for which such an amendment was applied in the NDAA. While Rep. Omar has called for keeping the U.S. military out of Somalia, America's adversaries—namely, China, Iran, and Turkey—have been taking advantage of the vacuum created there.[76]

Lastly, Rep. Omar is a proponent of subordinating U.S. authority to intergovernmental organizations. As mentioned before, she wishes to cede authority over the refugee crisis on America's southern border to the UN High Commissioner on Refugees. Relatedly, she has criticized the Trump administration for withdrawing from the UN's Global Compact on Migration, which the White House claimed, "could undermine the sovereign right of the United States to enforce our immigration laws and secure our borders."[77,78] Rep. Omar has also co-authored a letter challenging the Trump administration's decision to reject the visa of International Criminal Court (ICC) chief prosecutor Fatou Bensouda of Gambia, and other personnel involved, in the State Department's words, of engaging in "unjust investigation and prosecution [of Americans] by the international criminal court."[79,80] The ICC was reportedly seeking to investigate purported war crimes perpetrated by U.S. troops in Afghanistan. As former Trump National Security Advisor John Bolton describes it:

> In theory, the ICC holds perpetrators of the most egregious atrocities accountable for their crimes, provides justice to the victims, and deters future abuses. In practice, however, the Court has been ineffective, unaccountable, and indeed, outright dangerous. Moreover, the largely unspoken, but always central, aim of its most vigorous supporters was to constrain the United States. The objective was not limited to targeting individual U.S. service members, but rather America's senior political leadership, and its relentless determination to keep our country secure.[81]

The U.S. "unsigned" the Rome Statute under which the ICC was established under the George W. Bush administration precisely because of its illegitimacy in granting the ICC prosecutorial powers violating our sovereignty and threatening the rights of U.S. citizens. Why would Rep. Omar seek to defend an organization that so threatens Americans?

In total, as a result of her rhetoric and policies, progressive publications celebrate Omar as "one of the loudest voices challenging the hegemony of U.S. power," rising above her progressive peers. Writes one publication: "Alexandria Ocasio-Cortez and Bernie Sanders, stalwart on economic issues, have sometimes waffled on questions of imperial power and foreign relations, [while] Omar has remained stalwart as she faces the (predictable) consequences of touching American politics' long-standing third rails."[82] This begs the question: How can someone who seeks to challenge U.S. power serve in the House of Representatives, let alone on the HFAC?

PART II

*Omar as a Symbol of—
and Contributor to—
the Progressive
Transformation of the
Democrats*

CHAPTER 5

THE SPECIAL CASE OF ISRAEL AND THE JEWS

Anti-Semitism and the West

More than any other topic, Rep. Ilhan Omar's odious views regarding the Jewish state of Israel, and the Jewish people have come to define her first term in Congress. Her particular animus on these issues has far broader and deeper implications than we believe have been fully appreciated. As such, we will spend considerable time discussing them.

Rep. Omar's anti-Semitism masquerading as anti-Zionism is notable not just because she is a prominent representative with influence on U.S. foreign policy, but because such views have grown increasingly acceptable among the progressive Left in America and beyond. Notably, such Israel- and Jew-hatred is a key ingredient in the glue that holds the progressive-Islamist axis in the West together, an "intersectional" alliance in which Rep. Omar sits at the center. That the Democratic establishment has chosen to coddle Rep. Omar and her like-minded Squad mates, in spite of such positions, indicates consent out of both pusillanimousness, and political calculation.

Collectively, these realities foretell disaster for freedom. It is not solely that seeking to undermine and delegitimize Israel, a nation representing the first line of defense of Western civilization against Islamist tyranny, is decidedly antithetical to America's interest. It is that hatred of the Jewish state is indistinguishable from, and indeed a mask for, hatred of the Jewish people, and their values, which are foundational to Judeo-Christian Western values and Western civilization itself. This is why Rep. Omar's views, and the Left's willingness to kowtow to her over them—therefore legitimizing them—transcend matters of individual bigotry or international relations, and at their root concern the perpetual struggle between civilization and barbarism.

A Foreboding Intervention

Before Ilhan Omar was ever elected to Congress, politically aligned Minnesota Jews were alarmed over the nature and content of her views on Israel and Jews in general. Among the items that vexed them was a now-infamous tweet. In November of 2012, while Israel engaged in a retaliatory military operation in Hamas-controlled Gaza after Gazan jihadis launched some 100 rockets into Israel's south, a then-unknown Ilhan Omar tweeted: "Israel has hypnotized the world, may Allah awaken the people and help them see the evil doings of Israel. #Gaza #Palestine #Israel."[1] Needless to say, conjuring up images of scheming Jews engaged in a global conspiracy represented a loud and long-held anti-Semitic dog whistle.[2] Now a rising political force seeking a single-term jump from the statehouse to the U.S. Capitol, the Minnesota-based *Pioneer Press* reported of Omar that: "In local political discourse during the Democratic Party's endorsement process, Omar's phrasing as she spoke of Middle East policy troubled some."[3] Then-State Representative Omar generated unease strong enough such that Jewish political allies felt the need to hold an intervention. Following a lengthy discussion with Omar in which Jewish allies sought to disabuse her of her ignorant notions, the participants were left chastened. They "came out of that conversation very troubled by the answers…received."[4] The group's fears would prove well-founded.

Omar and BDS

In January 2016, state representative candidate Ilhan Omar expressed a desire for the University of Minnesota to divest itself of Israel bonds.[5] In February 2017, true to form, State Representative Omar rejected an anti-BDS measure.[i] In August 2018, U.S. House candidate Omar seemed to reverse herself, declaring at a Democratic primary debate held in a synagogue:

> I support a two-state solution…I believe right now with the BDS movement, it's not helpful in getting that two-state solution. I think the particular purpose for [BDS] is to make sure that there is pressure, and I think that pressure really is counteractive.[6]

Yet just days after her election, in November 2018, Congresswoman Omar's staff told the publication *Muslim Girl*:

> Ilhan believes in and supports the BDS movement, and has fought to make sure people's right to support it isn't criminalized. She does, however, have reservations on the effectiveness of the movement in accomplishing a lasting solution.[7]

This apparent flip-flop stunned many of her remaining Jewish supporters. Based on what was known about her past BDS positions, and the troubling comments she had made on social media, it should not have.

Subsequent to her tweet about Israeli hypnosis, months before the 2018 election in May of that year, Rep. Omar referred to Israel in a tweet as an "apartheid regime"—a characterization frequently invoked by BDSers and Jew-haters of all stripes—which she tried to distinguish from hatred of Jews.[8,9] Her statement harkened back to the notorious UN resolution effectively declaring "Zionism is racism," which stood from 1975 to the conclusion of the Cold War in 1991. It was supported by a coalition led by the Soviet Union and joined by various and sundry Arab and aligned non-Arab Third World nations.

---

i   It is worth noting that in opposing the anti-BDS measure, Rep. Omar invoked conversations she had had with her grandfather regarding apartheid South Africa, implying a false moral equivalence between the Israeli and Afrikaner governments.

How Rep. Omar could on the merits level this charge at the world's lone Jewish state when it guarantees its Arab citizens, and indeed all minorities, rights they would be unable to avail themselves of anywhere else in the Middle East—if not almost anywhere else in the world at large—is inexplicable.[10] That she would do so even though Israel was the first nation to recognize Somaliland's independence from the United Kingdom, makes it on the merits even more perplexing.[11] The only logical explanation is that Rep. Omar does not judge Israel on the merits. She does so out of ignorance and/or bigotry.

Further illustrating the anti-Jewish animus underlying her claim is Omar's silence regarding the deplorable treatment of Jews by other Middle Eastern regimes—not to mention in her native Somalia—given her stated desire for "balance" in perspective.[ii,iii] During and particularly towards the

---

ii   In Dr. Nancy Hartevelt Kobrin's *The Last Two Jews of Mogadishu*, based on her email correspondence with the last two Jews there, she writes: "The Somali society harbors extreme hatred of the Jew, who is used as a scapegoat to purge and project the Somalis' feelings of inferiority and low self-worth and serve as an outlet for unconscious rage to be concretized and acted out violently with bloodshed. Islamic anti-Semitism forces and coerces the Jews to go "underground" to hide who they are in order to protect themselves…Jews living in Muslim cultures at the very least unconsciously fall into the subjugated, "allegedly" protected, category of *dhimma*, whose Arabic root means to blame. Islam has a mechanism that maintains splitting into us vs. them, that promotes paranoia of the Other, conspiracy-think as well as Islamic anti-Semitism. This is what Rami [one of the two Jews] endured growing up in Mogadishu…
They [Somalia's crypto-Jews] were determined to live their lives in their own world, hiding their beliefs and their identity as they tried to blend in as good Muslims. Yet they always remained fearful and hyperattentive to what would happen if they were found out by the religious authorities who ruled Somalia or even by their neighbors, who had been brainwashed to think all Jews are Israelis and all Israelis are the hated Other…[Emails in the book] are the only documents that bear witness to the day-in and day-out attempts of Jewish survival in a hostile Somali environment under constant threat of attack by Al Shabaab." See: https://www.academia.edu/35681958/ The_Last_Two_Jews_of_Mogadishu_Living_Under_Al_Shabaabs_Fire.

iii   As an example of "balance," Rep. Omar defended her comments about Israeli hypnosis by noting that "I say the same things, if not worse, when it comes to the Saudi government. I've called for boycotts of Hajj and boycotts to Saudi Arabia because to me it is important when you see oppression taking place, when you see regressiveness happening, when you see our values being attacked as humans, you must stand up and it doesn't matter who the inhabiters of that particular region might be." The subtext however is that Islamists Sunni and Shia both lump the ruling Saudi regime under Mohammad bin Salman together with Israel given its anti-Khomeinist and anti-Muslim Brotherhood bent. See: https:// dailycaller.com/2019/01/16/omar-defends-anti-israel-tweet/.

end of the first half of the 20th century, hundreds of thousands of Jews residing in the Levant were forced to flee their generations-old homes, leaving their possessions behind because Islamic regimes imposed actual apartheid policies, persecuting Jews and in some cases expelling them altogether. Such countries today are de facto if not de jure *Judenrein*, and Jew-hatred among their peoples is overwhelming, notwithstanding national security-driven under-the-radar governmental contacts between Israel and several Sunni Arab regimes.[iv,v]

With respect to Rep. Omar's favored Arab opponents of Israel, as has been the case for decades, Palestinian Arab law—which is by nature theocratic since it ties legislative and judicial authority to Sharia—codifies the Nazi-esque apartheid policy of punishment by death for those who sell property to Jews.[12,13] Indeed, Sharia law itself imposes an apartheid system of sorts for those who refuse to submit to it.[vi,14] In the areas in which Arab authorities rule in Hebron, they apply apartheid policies against Jews.[15] Rep. Omar has never referred to such regimes that actually systematically discriminate against religious minorities, and specifically Jews, as "apartheid." Her application of this double standard is characteristic of anti-Semites, and, according to many governments including that of the United States of America, its usage is definitionally anti-Semitic.[16]

While her concordant rhetoric, views and past action as a state legislator indicated Rep. Omar's affinity for the BDS movement, it was only when Omar came to Washington that she proved her true BDS bona fides. In

---

iv   According to the Anti-Defamation League's worldwide survey of 100 countries, the sixteen countries exhibiting the highest levels of anti-Semitism were all in the Middle East, with levels of anti-Semitism ranging from 74 percent to 93 percent. See http://global100.adl.org/public/ADL-Global-100-Executive-Summary.pdf, page 25.

v   Israel's burgeoning governmental relations, notably with Saudi Arabia, Egypt, the United Arab Emirates (UAE) and Bahrain, are driven by the common threat they face posed by Iran and its proxies. This is in no small part a consequence of the Obama administration's effort to seek to make Iran—sworn enemy foremost of Israel and secondarily of several Sunni nations—the regional hegemon. It would appear Rep. Omar would support this policy, given her support of the Iran nuclear deal, as well as her friendly ties to Iran's partners in Turkey and Qatar. Conversely, Rep Omar has expressed her opposition to partners in the anti-Iranian alliance via her scathing criticism of Saudi Arabia and its proxy war with Iran's Houthis in Yemen, and her opposition to Egypt's Sisi regime, as well as her vitriol towards Israel.

vi   See the discussion on Jews as *dhimmis* in the following chapter.

July 2019, following several firestorms over classically anti-Semitic remarks, Congresswoman Omar was one of only sixteen House Democrats to reject an anti-BDS resolution passed with an overwhelming bipartisan majority, as part of a battery of ostensibly pro-Israel measures.[17] She went further by introducing her own pro-BDS resolution. Rep. Omar euphemistically cast her resolution (HR 496) as being about free speech, "Affirming that all Americans have the right to participate in boycotts in pursuit of civil and human rights at home and abroad, as protected by the First Amendment to the Constitution."[18] She divulged that the resolution was explicitly about championing BDS to the Middle Eastern publication *Al-Monitor*, stating that it provides an "opportunity for us to explain why it is we support a nonviolent movement, which is the BDS movement."[19] Such a resolution should have been unnecessary on its own terms, given that by law and legal precedent, no individual is prohibited from engaging in an economic boycott. Rather, it is organized economic boycotts—in particular those the U.S. government has classified as contrary to the U.S. national interest often in coordination with foreign adversaries—that do not constitute First Amendment protected speech.[20,21]

BDS has its roots in the Arab League's boycott of Israel, which began in the 1940s, built on earlier Arab boycotts of Jewish concerns, some of which were modeled on Nazi policies. Given the essential anti-Jewish nature of the Arab League boycott, the U.S. government condemned it rhetorically and challenged it statutorily.[22] In the present day, the Trump administration has argued that BDS is not an expression of free speech, but rather an anti-Semitic weapon of economic warfare wielded by Israel's would-be destroyers.[23] The House and Senate leaders of Omar's own party have respectively referred to BDS as one of a set of "bigoted or dangerous ideologies masquerading as policy," and "a reinvented form of anti-Semitism."[24,25] Notably, even the German government—which up until December 2019 had refused to outlaw Hezbollah—has formally declared that BDS is anti-Semitic.[26,27,28]

Rep. Omar dismissed this background and through her resolution gave her seal of approval to the BDS movement. Yet the subtext of her resolution was most repugnant of all. It presented economic boycotts as having been essential to combating Jim Crow, Imperial Japan, apartheid South Africa, the Communist Soviet Union, and last but not least, Nazi Germany. By inference then, Rep. Omar suggested that the world's sole Jewish state was equivalent to the world's most evil regimes, including the one responsible for slaughtering six million Jews, thereby forcing a grudging world to fulfill its legal if not ethical and moral commitment to allow the Jewish people to settle in their Biblical and historical homeland.

It is difficult to find a more offensive insinuation than that Israel is akin to the Soviet regime that engaged in widespread discrimination against and persecution of Jews while bolstering its mortal enemies. But Rep. Omar achieved it in her pro-BDS resolution by comparing Israel to the Third Reich while politicizing the systematic slaughter and attempted extermination of the Jewish people. It would appear that for the anti-Semites who created and propagated this narrative of "Holocaust inversion," their efforts have paid off in spades.[29]

Perhaps most evil of all regarding Rep. Omar's championing of BDS is the fact that since its inception, the movement has plainly been about destroying Israel. That a seated member of the House Foreign Affairs Committee (HFAC) would legitimize such a movement, and lie about its nonviolence, is beyond loathsome. Illustrating at best the projection of Omar and her fellow progressives, it is BDSers who wish to achieve a modern-day Holocaust by supplanting the Jewish state with an Arab one "from the river to the sea."[30] As the founder of the movement Omar Barghouti puts it, "we oppose a Jewish state in any part of Palestine," "Palestine" in his formulation being Israel. He argues that "Ending the occupation doesn't mean anything if it doesn't mean upending the Jewish state itself."[31] As'ad AbuKhalil, a professor at California State University is even more direct, stating, "The real aim of BDS is to bring down the State of Israel... this should be stated as an unambiguous goal."[32] AbuKhalil, incidentally, has fawned over Rep. Omar, calling her "the most formidable foe Israel has faced in US politics-ever. No exaggeration. She doesn't get intimidated by anyone. What a force."[33] Even reliably liberal critics of Israel like *The New York Times'* Roger Cohen concede that "Mellifluous talk of democracy and rights and justice masks the BDS objective that is nothing other than the end of the Jewish state."[34]

When Rep. Ocasio-Cortez (D-NY) told *Buzzfeed* that her support for BDS was predicated in part on her "concern with being overly punitive on nonviolent forms of protest...forc[ing] people into other channels...I would hate to be a part of..." she seemed to inadvertently be admitting the reality of the BDSers' deep-seated bloodlust.[35]

AOC's unintentionally perceptive statement proves accurate when one considers the BDS movement's deep ties to jihadist groups working to achieve their shared goal through genocidal violence. In February 2019, the Israeli Ministry of Strategic Affairs and Public Diplomacy published an investigation detailing:

> ...100 links between the terror organizations Hamas and the Popular Front for the Liberation of Palestine and anti-Israel BDS-promoting NGOs. In addition, 30 terror operatives were identified – most of whom served time in Israeli prisons, some even perpetrated deadly terror attacks against Israelis – serve (sic) in key roles within these NGOs. They have done so while concealing, or at least de-emphasizing, their past involvement in terrorist groups and activities.[36]

Similarly, in May 2019, the *Daily Caller* published an investigative report establishing that:

> Several groups in the anti-Israel boycott, divest and sanction (BDS) movement operating in the United States have ties to Palestinian groups on the U.S. State Department's list of designated terrorist organizations...Ties between BDS organizations operating in the U.S. and Palestinian terror groups include: BDS leaders coordinating with the Popular Front for the Liberation of Palestine (PFLP), officials in BDS groups whipping up public support for terrorists, and a U.S. nonprofit reportedly facilitating tax exempt donations to a Palestinian coalition that includes multiple terrorist organizations.[37]

The Samidoun Palestinian Prisoner Solidarity Network—whose ties to PFLP are legion, extending well beyond common leadership between the two organizations—has publicly supported Rep. Omar.[38,39,40] PFLP has been endorsed on social media by the US Campaign for Palestinian Rights (USCPR), a Virginia-based nonprofit that coordinates the efforts of 329 pro-BDS organizations, "working to advocate for Palestinian rights and a shift in US policy…bound by commonly shared principles on Palestine solidarity as well as our anti-racism principles."[41] As Jewish magazine *Tablet* reported however, in reality, the group subsidizes jihad.[42] Apparently for the USCPR to fulfill its mission of achieving "Freedom, justice, and equality for the Palestinian people in a world without racism and oppression," it must back Israel's genocidal foes.[43]

So again, when Rep. Omar told *Al-Monitor* that BDS was "nonviolent," she was dissembling.[44] As we will later show, such deception is consistent with that of her friends in the global Islamist movement. As is the mendacious way in which she defends her positions. As a case in point, Rep. Omar boldly compares BDS to the Boston Tea Party—simultaneously engaging in an ahistorical smear of colonial-era patriots, while seeking to elevate those dedicated to Israel's destruction to the level of American revolutionaries.[45] As we will soon explore, such an argument would only make sense part and parcel of the progressives' perversely Sophistic worldview on these matters. Progressives have come to frame opposition to Israel, like opposition to America, as worthy of reverence—casting opponents of the "Great" and "Little Satans" as freedom fighters seeking to overthrow racist, colonialist, occupying powers.

Targeting Israel Using Her Foes' Propaganda

Beyond BDS, Rep. Omar has co-sponsored other vindictive pieces of legislation targeting Israel. She and her three Squad mates are backers of Rep. Betty McCollum's "Promoting Human Rights for Palestinian Children Living Under Israeli Military Occupation Act," which claims that Israel tortures children. The bill's largely dishonest assertions originate from a terror-tied organization, Defense for Children International-Palestine (DCI-P), whose links to the aforementioned PFLP are extensive.

DCI-P is an organization with which Rep. Omar planned to meet during her ultimately canceled August 2019 trip to Israel, which she sought to use as an anti-Israel propaganda tour.[vii]

On the back of dubious claims from an even more dubious organization, Warren Henry writes in *The Federalist* that the Omar-backed bill "ultimately aims to prohibit 'U.S. assistance to Israel from being used to support the military detention, interrogation, or ill-treatment of Palestinian children in violation of international humanitarian law.' As federal law already bars U.S. aid to foreign security forces who commit gross human rights violations, **the bill is an exercise in singling out the Jewish state.**"[46] [Emphasis added] In other words, Rep. Omar and the bill's other sponsors seek to demonize Israel as an end in itself, rather than holding it to account for actual wrongdoing.[viii] While the bill focuses on Israel's purported mistreatment of Arab children, reports indicate that the DCI-P group has no problem with jihadists putting them in harm's way by recruiting, indoctrinating, and training them.[47] Rep. Omar must have missed the hypocrisy.

Attacking Israel for "Occupying" Gaza

At times, Rep. Omar has even been overtly sympathetic to Israel's attackers. The case of Gaza is illustrative. Israel captured Gaza in its defensive 1967 Six-Day War—a war in which the Jewish state, outmanned,

---

vii   A June 2018 *Jerusalem Post* article notes: "Defense for Children International-Palestine (DCI-P) is a Ramallah-based NGO meant to promote Palestinian children's rights, and tries to convince foreign governments and UN bodies that Israel is systematically abusing Palestinian children. Many of its officials and board members are linked to the Popular Front for the Liberation of Palestine (PFLP), designated as a terrorist organization in the US, EU, Canada and Israel.

    The PFLP is responsible for hijacking an Air France plane to Uganda in 1976, which led to the famous IDF raid on Entebbe; attacking a preschool on Kibbutz Misgav Am in 1980, killing two-and-a-half-year-old Eyal Gluska; and for massacring Jewish worshipers in a Jerusalem synagogue in 2014, among many other terrorist attacks." See: https://www.jpost.com/Arab-Israeli-Conflict/Rockefeller-Bros-Fund-gives-to-groups-funding-Palestinian-terrorism-559258.

viii   See NGO Monitor's debunking of the bill's claims here: https://www.ngo-monitor.org/reports/evaluation-of-the-promoting-human-rights-for-palestinian-children-living-under-israeli-military-occupation-act-hr-2407/.

outgunned, and surrounded by would-be invader armies amassing against it from Egypt, Jordan, and Syria, miraculously triumphed. In what has proven to be a costly gesture for a non-existent peace, in 2005, Israel unilaterally disengaged. Since, Gaza has been self-governed by Palestinian Arabs, who are currently represented by Hamas. The result is that post-disengagement, Israel has faced ongoing rocket attacks and other military assaults from Gaza. Nevertheless, according to Rep. Omar and other progressives, Israel is the primary party at fault, responsible for murdering innocent civilians, creating jihadists by way of its "occupation," and stoking a "humanitarian crisis."[ix] In May of 2019, after Israel was attacked from Gaza, Omar sided with the aggressors, tweeting:

> How many more protesters must be shot, rockets must be fired, and little kids must be killed until the endless cycle of violence ends?

> The status quo of occupation and humanitarian crisis in Gaza is unsustainable. Only real justice can bring about security and lasting peace.[48]

Rep. Omar fully disregards the fact that prior to her tweet, jihadists fired nearly 700 rockets into Israel from Gaza, killing four and injuring 234 more, which prompted an Israeli military response in the first place.[49] She ignores the fact that the vast majority of the twenty-three Arabs identified as killed were members of jihadist groups.[50] She fails to acknowledge the reality that Hamas, like other jihadist groups, embeds itself among civilians precisely so non-jihadists will be killed, serving its propaganda campaign. She also fails to recognize the inconvenient truth that Israel almost assuredly takes more extreme precautions than any other nation to avoid civilian deaths in military operations, and has developed some

---

ix   Regarding the "humanitarian crisis," it bears noting that Gaza is an economic basket case whose borders and economy are tightly controlled by Israel *and* Egypt precisely because Hamas—which frequently diverts aid to its jihadis—is in control of Gaza. Israel continues to provide substantial humanitarian assistance in spite of this fact. See: https://www.jewishvirtuallibrary.org/israel-s-quot-blockade-quot-of-gaza.

of the world's most sophisticated technologies to execute precision strikes that drastically reduce collateral damage—all while its adversaries aim their rockets, bombs, cars, guns, knives, and rocks indiscriminately.[51,52]

Gaza has been in Omar's sights for some time. As noted previously, in 2012 when Israel responded to Arab aggression emanating from Gaza, Rep. Omar spoke of "evil" Israel's "hypnosis" of the world. In a separate tweet, she said that "My heart aches for all the lives lost. Oh Allah protect the innocent! #Gaza #GazaUnderAttack."[53] She shared an Instagram link to her Twitter account featuring a picture of herself holding up a sign reading "Free Palestine," with the caption: "Standing in solidarity with the people of Gaza!"[54] In September of 2018, then-congressional candidate Omar headlined an event in her district raising funds "in solidarity with the Gaza strip" for victims of "Israeli oppression."[55]

Missing in all of this was any context—not only that Israel was responding to attacks on its civilians perpetrated by jihadists, but the history of the situation in Gaza. Several of the important facts notably absent from Rep. Omar's narrative are as follows: Again, the Gaza strip is controlled by a jihadist group dedicated to Israel's destruction—the Iran-backed, Palestinian Arab branch of the Muslim Brotherhood, Hamas. And again, contrary to the notion Israel is occupying Gaza, it has been wholly disengaged since September 2005, at great cost to the Israelis who were uprooted.[56,57] The so-called blockade exists, like checkpoints and other measures applied to Arab areas, precisely because of the jihad waged against Israel.

Ironically, as concerns the Palestinian Arab cause, the original Palestinian National Charter drafted in 1964 specifically noted that the organization, dedicated to fighting for its "homeland," did not consider Gaza to be part of it. Under the charter, the PLO asserted it "does not exercise any regional sovereignty over the West Bank in the Hashemite Kingdom of Jordan, on the **Gaza Strip** or the Himmah Area."[58] [Emphasis added] This might be in part because though the charter's drafters would be loath to admit it, Jews had had a constant presence in Gaza for more than 4,000 years. They were only displaced temporarily after Egypt occupied Gaza, following its illegal invasion of Israel at its founding in 1948.[59]

Seeing All of Israel as "Occupied Territory"

Rep. Omar's policy and rhetoric raise questions about whether she recognizes not just the legitimacy of the Jewish state, but the state itself. The congresswoman's scheduled August 2019 trip to Israel was canceled due to her being barred from Israel on the basis of its anti-BDS law and amid fears of incitement.[60] Regardless, Rep. Omar's draft itinerary referred to Israel as "Palestine."[61] Rep. Omar tweeted that the purpose of her trip was to "witness firsthand what is happening on the ground in *Palestine*."[62] [Emphasis added]

Consider this word choice against the backdrop of her constant hectoring of Israel over its "occupation," not just in relation to a Gaza that Israel does not occupy, but more broadly.[63] Rep. Omar may be referring to lands captured by Israel in 1967. But more likely, as with many of her fellow travelers, she may well see Israel's very existence as the real "occupation." Rep. Omar's rhetoric on the issue makes it difficult to discern her view. But it is telling that in a December 2019 vote, she and fellow anti-Zionist and anti-Semitic Squad mate Rep. Rashida Tlaib (D-MI) rejected a nonbinding resolution supported overwhelmingly by House Democrats in support of a two-state solution—concerning as she described it "Israel/Palestine"—in part on grounds that language about "occupation" was removed.[64] Rep. Omar asserted that "you are either for peace or you are for occupation. But you can't be for both. For this reason, I voted no."[65] In this regard, the views of the Palestinian Arabs, whose cause Rep. Omar supports, may be instructive.

Palestinian Authority (PA) leader Mahmoud Abbas reportedly stated in October 2013 that "All Palestinian land is occupied—Gaza is occupied, the West Bank is occupied, the 1948 lands [i.e. the original borders within which Israel was constituted] are occupied, and Jerusalem [Israel's Biblical, historic and U.S.-recognized capitol] is occupied."[66] As recently as August 2019, Abbas told an audience at the Jalazone refugee camp near Ramallah that "We shall enter Jerusalem—millions of fighters!" He added, in a statement that could have referred either to Israeli settlements or the state in toto, that "Every stone you have [used] to build on our land, and every house you have built on our land, is bound to be destroyed, Allah willing…They will all go to the garbage bin of history."[67]

A 2019 survey conducted by the Bethlehem-based Palestine Center for Public Opinion found that 47 percent of those polled in Judea and Samaria, and 48 percent of those polled in Gaza, listed as their "top Palestinian national priority during the coming five years" the "Regaining of all historical Palestine for the Palestinians, **from the river to the sea.**" [Emphasis added] Another 18 percent and 12 percent respectively listed "Achieving a one-state solution, in which Arabs and Jews have equal rights, from the river to the sea" as their top priority.[68] In practice, this means that the majority of Arabs polled ranked Israel's destruction as their highest aspiration—an end to its "occupation."

Finally, when the Arab world cries of the *nakba* or catastrophe, it is referring to Israel's creation in 1948, not lands conquered in defensive wars thereafter. Indeed, as Steve Frank writes in *Algemeiner,* "Understanding the Palestinians' view of the occupation helps explain their otherwise inexplicable rejection of numerous offers from Israel and the international community to create their own independent state living in peace, side-by-side with Israel (1937, 1947, 1967, 2000, 2008)."[x,69] Conversely, as Johns Hopkins University political scientist Michael Mandelbaum notes, the PA "has never put forward a counteroffer of its own or indicated the kind of settlement it envisions. It has done nothing to build the institutions of statehood other than deploying multiple police forces that repress political opposition. It has generated vile anti-Jewish propaganda that harks back to Europe in the 1930s and has sponsored the murder of Jews by publicly praising and paying the murderers."[70]

---

x   As William Voegeli notes in the Summer 2019 edition of the *Claremont Review of Books*: "…[I]f Palestinians are more determined to drive Jews out of Israel than to achieve statehood, then the opportunities—as early as the recommendation by Great Britain's Peel Commission in 1937 for an Arab state occupying 80% of the Palestine Mandate territory, and as recent as the 2008 offer by then-Israeli prime minister Ehud Barak of a detailed map that met every condition Palestinian negotiators had identified as vital to establishing their own new state—haven't been "missed." They've been rejected by people aiming at a fundamentally different resolution." See: https://www.claremont.org/crb/article/the-chosen-and-the-woke/.

While the likes of Rep. Omar would never admit it, the simple reality is that were Israel to lay down its arms tomorrow, it would be destroyed. Israel has no peace partner because its counterpart is not desirous of peace. The PLO's Yasser Arafat made this clear when in December of 1980 he declared: "We shall never stop until we can go back home and Israel is destroyed.... The goal of our struggle is the end of Israel, and there can be no compromises or mediations. We do not want peace; we want victory. Peace for us means Israel's destruction, and nothing else."[71]

Defending a False Narrative of Israel, the Arabs, and the Holocaust

Given the foregoing, it is unsurprising that Rep. Omar rushed to the defense of Rep. Tlaib after she made perhaps her most despicable and dishonest comment of all. Rep. Tlaib tried to cast the Palestinian Arabs as victims of the Holocaust. She conveniently ignored that many such people had engaged in horrific pogroms against the Jews, and later colluded with the Nazis, led by Hitler confidante Haj Amin-al Husseini, the Grand Mufti of Jerusalem. Tlaib made the asinine assertion, backed by a brazenly bogus revisionist history, that it gave her a:[72]

> calming feeling…that it was my ancestors—Palestinians—who lost their land and some lost their lives, their livelihood, their human dignity, their existence in many ways, have been wiped out, and some people's passports… And, just all of it was in the name of trying to create a safe haven for Jews, post-the Holocaust, post-the tragedy and the horrific persecution of Jews across the world at that time. And, I love the fact that it was my ancestors that provided that, right, in many ways, but they did it in a way that took their human dignity away and it was forced on them.[73]

The level of factual inaccuracy on every level is so great in this instance, that when considered in the context of Rep. Tlaib's associations with Islamists, it cannot be treated as anything other than Hamasian propaganda.[xi,74] Instead of condemning these remarks, or keeping quiet, the preternaturally victimological Rep. Omar cried Islamophobia in Rep. Tlaib's defense, claiming that her critics were attempting to, "eliminate the public voice of Muslims from the public discourse."[75] Of course, what Rep.

---

xi   The creation of the modern Jewish state can be traced to the 1917 Balfour Declaration—delivered by the British Government's foreign secretary during the first World War, decades before the Holocaust. The Declaration made clear the imperative to form "a national home for the Jewish people" in their ancestral homeland, rooted in the Jews' Biblical and historical claims to the land. In 1922 the League of Nations entrusted Great Britain with responsibility for the Mandate for Palestine—establishing the Jewish national home in Eretz Yisrael (Palestine) and specifying that their homeland would not apply to lands that would be reserved for Arabs east of the Jordan River (in a territory which was initially named Transjordan, and ultimately became the Hashemite Kingdom of Jordan). The British Mandatory government initially allowed Jews and Arabs to run their respective internal affairs, but was ultimately unable to uphold its commitment to respect free immigration and land acquisition. Under Arab pressure, the British Mandatory government withdrew their related commitment, restricting immigration and land acquisition by Jews through both 1930 and 1939 White Papers, and 1940 Land Transfer Regulations. After World War II, in November of 1947 the U.N. General Assembly approved a resolution to formally partition Palestine, leading Great Britain to terminate its Mandate over Palestine. In May of 1948 the Jews proclaimed the State of Israel in the land specified for this purpose by the United Nations resolution. The next day, Israel was attacked by the armies of five neighboring Arab states. Rep. Tlaib's ancestors, therefore, could not legitimately make her claim. Further, Arabs did not "provide" for the settlement of the Jewish homeland, nor help it become a safe haven. On the contrary, they explicitly sought to destroy it in 1948 and several times subsequently—and to attack Jewish inhabitants in pogroms prior to the establishment of the Jewish State. Specifically noteworthy is that over 400 Jews survived the Holocaust only to be killed by Palestinian Arabs and Jordanians prior to the settling of Israel on May 14, 1948. See: https://www.tabletmag.com/scroll/284748/rashida-tlaibs-unbelievable-lies. As Israeli émigré and member of Israel's First Knesset Shmuel Katz wrote in his 1973 book *Battleground: Fact & Fantasy in Palestine*, based on contemporaneous press accounts from anti-Zionist Western publications and statements from Arab leaders in the months leading up to Israel's founding in 1948, and free of any mention of displaced Arabs: "The Arab refugees were not driven from Palestine by anyone. The vast majority left, whether of their own free will or at the orders or exhortations of their leaders, always with the same reassurance that their departure would help in the war against Israel." This summary is corroborated in numerous news accounts from both Western and Arabic sources in the months that followed. See relevant excerpts here: https://www.theblaze.com/news/2014/07/25/the-one-passage-on-the-history-of-the-arab-israeli-conflict-that-the-mainstream-media-will-never-print.

Omar was trying to do by issuing this statement was eliminate the public voice of critics of those with such noxious views as Rep. Tlaib.

Attacking Israel for Not Being Democratic

Another assault leveled by Rep. Omar against Israel is that it is not a democracy. Rather, Rep. Omar suggests that Israel is on par with the Islamist Khomeinist regime of Iran, which is dedicated to Israel's destruction.[76] That is, Rep. Omar apparently considers Israel a tyrannical theocracy. Here she seems to have invented a new manifestation of "Holocaust inversion."[xii]

Given Israel's representative, democratically elected government—guarantor of rights to citizens of all races and religions—and its societal pluralism, such a claim is dumbfounding.[77] In fact, one could argue that Israel is democratic to a fault, since democracy is not a suicide pact, yet Israel seats in its Knesset proponents of a BDS movement that seeks the state's elimination.[78] Illustrating Israel's almost foolhardy devotion to democracy, aforementioned BDS leader Omar Barghouti is himself a permanent resident who has had the privilege of studying at Tel Aviv University.[79] Yet Rep. Omar has endorsed a series of since-deleted tweets from anti-Israel progressive activist Max Berger in which he claims that "Israel is like the [American] south before 1963…It's a democracy for Jews only." Rep. Omar added: "Many of them truly know this, but don't want to accept it. In the same way many Americans knew separate yet equal was immoral but remained silent until brave few were silent no more. They can attack, spin my words and vilify me, but they will not succeeded (sic) in silencing me."[80,81]

In justifying this shameful calumny, Rep. Omar has alluded to Israel's so-called "Basic Law," claiming a conflict between Judaism and democracy. That statute, which essentially recognizes and reinforces the reality that Israel is the Jewish homeland, in no way contradicts the country's

---

xii   Fatah had beaten Rep. Omar to the punch, however. As anti-Semitism historian Robert Wistrich writes: "Already in its 1974 National Covenant, Arafat's Fatah movement and the PLO as a whole had proclaimed the elimination of the 'racist' State of Israel as its central aim. Article 22 of the Palestinian Covenant denounced Zionism as 'a racist and fanatical movement in its formation [and] aggressive, expansionist, and colonialist in its aims, and **Fascist and Nazi in its means**.'" [Emphasis added] See: https://www.tandfonline.com/doi/pdf/10.1080/23739770.2015.1037579, pages 194-195.

Declaration of Independence, which says that Israel "will ensure complete equality of social and political rights to all its inhabitants irrespective of religion, race or sex; it will guarantee freedom of religion, conscience, language, education and culture; it will safeguard the Holy Places of all religions; and it will be faithful to the principles of the Charter of the United Nations."[82,83] One is, again, hard-pressed to find another country in the Middle East that guarantees such rights, let alone one that does not compel followers of other faiths to convert or face dire consequences.

And in practice, Israel has shown not only that it can exist as a Jewish state and a democratic one, but by any number of measures that it has thrived as one, literally and figuratively blooming in the middle of a desert. It has done so not in spite of Judaism, but precisely because of its ability as a Jewish state to blend faith and reason, tradition and modernity. Israel has grown increasingly liberal and dynamic in spite of the fact it could easily be a moribund military dictatorship, given the constant existential threats it has faced since before its birth. In the process, it has made remarkable contributions to the world in any number of vital areas.[84]

Contrary to Rep. Omar's fears about Israel's ethnonationalism, there is a real argument to be made in fact that it is its detractors in the region, on which Rep. Omar is mum, that cannot exist as Islamic states and democratic ones. Consider for example the aims of the Palestinian Arab cause. As renowned anti-Semitism historian Robert Wistrich notes:

> There is no doubt that the PLO ultimately envisaged transforming Israel into an **Arab Palestine in which Islam would be the dominant faith and only Palestinian Arabs would possess national rights.** It is clearly stated in Article 1 of the Palestinian National Covenant that "Palestine is the homeland of the Palestinian Arab people and an integral part of the great Arab homeland, and the people of Palestine is a part of the Arab nation." **This exclusivist nationalist vision of Fatah and the PLO has never been definitively repudiated**...This sleight-of-hand is all the more striking given the total rejection of any Jewish right to national self-determination in Israel exemplified by the

> Palestinian Hamas [which as noted controls Gaza]…the Palestinian offshoot of the viscerally anti-Jewish Egyptian Muslim Brotherhood, has been imbued from its very birth with a thoroughly toxic ideology of Jew-hatred based on the paranoid conspiracy theories contained in the *Protocols of the Learned Elders of Zion*.[85] [Emphasis added]

Other Muslim-majority states throughout the Middle East, whose constitutions generally subordinate manmade law to Sharia, also seem to demonstrate the incompatibility of Islam and democracy in any meaningful sense beyond perhaps holding elections, given their authoritarian qualities. One might ask, are there no other "startup nations" surrounding Israel because the West is oppressive, led by the New Jersey-sized "Zionist entity," or because of oppressive Islamic regimes and concomitant cultures that shun liberty, stifling societal vitality, and the economic vibrancy that flows from it?

Rep. Omar's mocking of Israel by putting in quotes that it is the "only democracy" in the Middle East in the days following her barred visit is particularly rich since her visa was denied on the basis of law voted on by a democratically elected parliament.[86] And of course, no nation has an obligation to invite those who seek to undermine it to its shores. The egregious double standard to which Rep. Omar holds Israel versus its Islamic neighbors on the matter of "democracy" betrays her true sentiments.

Rep. Omar proved this double standard over Israel and democracy in the days following her halted Israel trip. The congresswoman fashions herself a champion of gay rights. Israel is undeniably more tolerant of gay people than any nation in the Middle East. Yet in August 2019, when the PA announced it would be banning all LGBTQ activity in the West Bank, an apartheid-esque policy, Omar went to bat for it—because it opposes Israel.[87] She issued a "both sides" non-condemnation in which she strained to draw a (false) moral equivalence between Israel and its Arabs foes, defending the PA's bigotry by deflection. She tweeted: "LGBTQ rights are human rights and we should condemn any effort to infringe upon them. But we should also condemn any effort to equate this with the occupation or use this as a distraction."[88] She added: "Pretending that this act somehow balances or mitigates Israel violating the dignity & rights of Palestinians

– or undermines case for defending Palestinian rights – is deplorable!"[89] To bolster her position, Rep. Omar proceeded to share a tweet thread from the "alQaws" LGBTQ group whose activities had spurred the ban, in which the group made clear that its primary beef was not with the oppressive PA, but rather with the oppressor par excellence of Israel.[90] Echoing Rep. Omar's anti-Israel, intersectionalist rhetoric, alQaws wrote in part: "Singling out incidents of homophobia in Palestinian society ignores the complexities of Israel's colonization and military occupation being a contributing factor to Palestinian LGBTQ oppression…We ask that you situate Palestinian LGBTQ oppression within the larger context of Israeli occupation, colonialism, patriarchy and homophobia at large."[91] At core, it is always Israel, the collective Jew, at fault. And for Rep. Omar, when it comes to Israel, it is delegitimization and double standards all the way down.

Anti-Zionism Masking Anti-Semitism

Lest one thinks the anti-Zionist cause Rep. Omar has taken up is all about the Jewish state, and not the Jews who believe they were promised it as part of their Covenant with G-d, consider the sentiments of Hezbollah leader Sheikh Hassan Nasrallah when he says this:[92,93] "If we searched the entire world for a person more cowardly, despicable, weak and feeble in psyche, mind, ideology and religion, we would not find anyone like the Jew. Notice, I do not say the Israeli."[94]

Similarly, Hamas' 1988 charter contains these lines:

- "This Covenant of the Islamic Resistance Movement (HAMAS), clarifies its picture, reveals its identity, outlines its stand, explains its aims, speaks about its hopes, and calls for its support, adoption and joining its ranks. **Our struggle against the Jews** is very great and very serious…The Movement is but one squadron that should be supported by more and more squadrons from this vast Arab and Islamic world, until the enemy is vanquished and Allah's victory is realized."

- "…[T]he Islamic Resistance Movement aspires to the realization of Allah's promise, no matter how long that should take. The Prophet, Allah bless him and grant him salvation, has said:

"The Day of Judgement will not come about until Moslems fight the Jews (killing the Jews), when the Jew will hide behind stones and trees. The stones and trees will say O Moslems, O Abdulla, there is a Jew behind me, come and kill him. Only the Gharkad tree, (evidently a certain kind of tree) would not do that because it is one of the trees of the Jews." (related by al-Bukhari and Moslem).

- "The day that enemies usurp part of Moslem land, Jihad becomes the individual duty of every Moslem. In face of the **Jews' usurpation** of Palestine, it is compulsory that the banner of Jihad be raised."[95] [Emphasis added]

In 2017, Hamas sought to "rebrand" by issuing a new "Document of General Principles and Policies." Its substance was consistent with the 1988 charter, but it explicitly sought to frame Hamas' quarrel as with the "Zionist project not with the Jews."[96] This was a ruse. Beyond Hamas' (i) continued anti-Semitism, (ii) argument that the "Zionist project" is the "enemy of the Arabic and Islamic Ummah [world]," consistent with the 1988 charter, and (iii) propensity to dissemble, perhaps the best indicator the document was disingenuous and mainly intended for political purposes is that it did not replace or abrogate its founding charter.[97,98]

Even the infamously hostile-to-Israel United Nations has not been able to turn a blind eye to Palestinian Arab anti-Semitism—and not just Hamas's bile, but that of the more "moderate" PA. In August 2019, Chinsung Chung, special rapporteur for the PA's first ever review by the Committee on the Elimination of Racial Discrimination, asked of the PA's representatives: "Several NGO reports pointed out antisemitic and anti-Israel prejudice and incitement to hatred, especially in the [Palestinian Arab] media and speeches of state officials. Can the state party [the PA] provide any explanation in this regard?"[99] Another committee member raised the issue of copious anti-Semitism in PA textbooks. The PA effectively ducked the questions, asking the committee to cut it some "slack," while attacking "Israel's racist occupation," and "the presence of apartheid."[100,101] When Rep. Omar decries "occupation," again, one must pause and consider the meaning Arabs historically, and today, have ascribed to it: Jews living freely in their homeland.

Final Points on the Anti-Israel Non-Trip

Relatedly, Rep. Omar's aborted Israel trip was sponsored in part by a group called MIFTAH, which has: endorsed the age-old anti-Semitic libel that "Jews use the blood of Christians in Jewish Passover;" per *NGO Monitor* "promotes an intense anti-Israel agenda, with accusations of 'massacres,' 'apartheid,' 'summary executions' and of 'Judaizing' Jerusalem;" and according to the Israeli government supports the BDS movement and consists of members who have expressed support for jihadism against Israel.[102,103,104] The late Edward Said, who we will discuss at length subsequently, had served as a board member.[105] MIFTAH's founder, Hanan Ashrawi, a senior member of the PLO, and terror apologist was herself denied a visa to the United States only months prior.[106,107] Rep. Omar was reportedly scheduled to meet with her.[108]

Rep. Omar also reportedly planned to meet with the aforementioned DCI-P, which maintains ties to the BDS-linked PFLP terrorist organization.[109] Predictably, when Israel barred Rep. Omar from visiting on perfectly legal, national security-related grounds, she once again compared it to apartheid South Africa—as if keeping out devotees to a movement dedicated to a country's destruction constitutes apartheid.[110]

On cue, in the days following the trip kerfuffle, Reps. Omar and Tlaib would both share a cartoon on social media drawn by anti-Semitic Marxist-Islamist artist Carlos Latuff, a man who achieved the distinction of coming in as a runner-up in Iran's 2006 International Holocaust Cartoon Competition.[111] And when Reps. Omar and Tlaib held a press conference seeking to turn Israel's rejection of their trips—or in Rep. Tlaib's case, her rejection of Israel's offer for her to visit her family—into a propaganda coup, Rep. Omar fittingly introduced another "victim," a Minnesota resident denied entry to Israel who had trafficked in Jew-hatred and associated with numerous anti-Israel organizations.[112]

None of this is to mention the myriad ties, which we will document in a later chapter, between Rep. Omar and Jew-haters of all stripes, or her echoing of their rhetoric in ways large and small, such as her endorsement of the argument frequently invoked by those speaking on behalf of the Palestinian Arab cause that Jesus was a Palestinian.[113]

Omar's Outright Anti-Semitism

If neither Rep. Omar's hatred of the Jewish state, nor her support for anti-Semites masquerading as anti-Zionists is convincing enough, her rhetoric with respect to American Jews should remove all doubt regarding her anti-Semitic core. The congresswoman's modus operandi is to raise a classically anti-Semitic claim, feign ignorance, and then only when absolutely forced to address an issue, make a tacit non-apology apology—only to later double down while playing the victim.

So as concerns the anti-Semitism-laced tweet about Israeli "hypnosis," when Rep. Omar started to be faced with questions about it by national media in January of 2019, she explained away her tweet by telling a reporter: "You know, I have P.T.S.D. [post-traumatic stress disorder] around, like, guns and ammunition and bombs."[114] She also said, "those unfortunate words were the only words I could think about expressing at that moment."[115] One need not hold a medical degree to know that anti-Semitism is no symptom of PTSD. Yet more dishonestly still, Rep. Omar claimed, "I don't know how my comments would be offensive to Jewish Americans…I am clearly speaking about the way the Israeli regime was conducting itself in that war."[116] We know this is a disingenuous statement because reporting prior to these tortured rationalizations recounted Jewish leaders having staged an intervention for Omar over her rhetoric. One progressive Jewish leader described as sympathetic to Omar even "gave the candidate and her staff a long presentation that mentioned ways that progressives could express criticism of Israel without inviting charges of anti-Semitism."[117] Of course, what does it say about a person if he or she must be coached on how to avoid being perceived as anti-Semitic?

When the firestorm over these comments proved too great, Omar concurred with the hypothetical presented by *The New York Times*' Bari Weiss that the congresswoman was "sincerely befuddled and not simply deflecting," adding in a series of tweets that amounted to a faux *mea culpa* that would set the template for future faux *mea culpas*:

That statement came in the context of the Gaza War.

It's now apparent to me that I spent lots of energy putting my 2012 tweet in context and little energy is disavowing the anti-semitic trope I unknowingly used, which is unfortunate and offensive.

With that said, it is important to distinguish between criticizing a military action by a government and attacking a particular people of faith.

I will not shy away of criticism of any government when I see injustice—whether it be Saudi Arabia, Somalia, even our own government!

As a survivor of war, the acts of war justified or not will always be acts of evil to me…

It is important that when you see oppression taking place – when you see our values being attacked as humans – you stand up, and it doesn't matter who the inhabitors of that particular region might be…

There are many narratives of who and what I am, designed to demonize and vilify me.

It's being [sic] building since my early days as an organizer. A concussion didn't deter me and smears certainly won't [sic]. I fought for my seat at the table & will use it to fight a more peaceful world![118]

Rep. Omar might as well have said: "Sorry, I'm not sorry."

We also know Rep. Omar did not take any of this to heart because, in February of 2019, she trod into anti-Semitic territory once again. Left-wing journalist Glenn Greenwald used a tweet to castigate House Minority leader Kevin McCarthy (R-CA) for threatening to censure Reps. Omar and Tlaib for their anti-Zionist and anti-Semitic remarks, writing in part: "It's stunning how much time US political leaders spend defending a foreign nation [i.e. Israel] even if it means attacking free speech rights of Americans." In a since-deleted tweet, Rep. Omar retweeted Greenwald's words and added the note, "It's all about the Benjamins baby."[119] Batya Ungar-Sargon, the opinion editor of left-wing Jewish publication the *Forward*, replied: "Would love to know who @IlhanMN [Rep. Omar's Twitter handle] thinks is paying American politicians to be pro-Israel..."[120] Rep. Omar specified that she was referring to "AIPAC!"[121] By invoking the American Israel Public Affairs Committee, it is clear Rep. Omar was saying that the euphemistic "Israel Lobby," i.e., Jewish money, was buying off Congress to back Israel.[xiii]

The statement was not only bigoted, but ignorant in the sense that it proved a lack of knowledge, given that AIPAC does not donate to campaigns, and of course the myriad reasons why Israel has historically garnered widespread bipartisan support having nothing to do with political funding.[122] In fact, it is ironically J Street, the left-wing anti-Zionist Jewish organization that Rep. Omar herself has promoted, that contributed more money than any other Israel-focused group during the 2018 midterm election cycle. 98 percent of its campaign funds went to the congresswoman's fellow Democrats.[123,124,125,126]

Like her comment on Israeli hypnosis, Omar's AIPAC statement reflected an age-old anti-Semitic refrain, in this case about Jews using their money to control government on behalf of foreign interests. The backlash from Rep. Omar's own party was so strong that she was forced to again issue an apology—albeit of the same disingenuous, non-apology variety—reading:

> Anti-Semitism is real and I am grateful for Jewish allies and colleagues who are educating me on the painful history of anti-Semitic tropes. My intention is never to offend my

---

xiii   For a particularly strong debunking of the "Israel Lobby" argument of Professors Stephen Walt and John Mearsheimer, see: https://sites.hks.harvard.edu/research/working_papers/dershowitzreply.pdf.

constituents or Jewish Americans as a whole. We have to always be willing to step back and think through criticism, just as I expect people to hear me when others attack me for my identity. This is why I **unequivocally** apologize.

At the same time, I reaffirmed the problematic role of lobbyists in our politics, whether it be AIPAC, the NRA or the fossil fuel industry. It's gone on too long and we must be willing to address it.[127] [Emphasis added]

Typically, unequivocal apologies end at "This is why I unequivocally apologize." True to the form of her equivocal "unequivocality," mere hours later, the congresswoman was back on Twitter, retweeting a thread praising a former staffer on a failed congressional campaign who claimed his candidate accepted money from AIPAC in return for issuing pro-Israel statements. The retweeted thread contained explicit criticism of Speaker Pelosi, who had demanded Rep. Omar's apology.[128]

Omar's equivocation was further borne out just weeks later, when she raised the Jewish dual loyalty canard, telling a group of Leftists, "I want to talk about the political influence in this country that says it is okay to push for allegiance to a foreign country."[xiv,129] Polling shows that charges of dual loyalty represent the dominant anti-Semitic motif globally.[130] These comments were simultaneously conspiratorial, while offensively questioning whether pro-Israel Jews and their political representatives were patriotic Americans. On the latter point, this is particularly hypocritical—to again use Rep. Omar's favored word—given how involved she and her family have been in Somali politics.

Omar would just days later triple down, attacking Nita Lowey, a Democratic colleague from New York. In a series of tweets, Rep. Lowey wrote: "...Anti-Semitic tropes that accuse Jews of dual loyalty are...painful and must...be roundly condemned. Lawmakers must be able to debate w/o prejudice or bigotry. I am saddened that Rep. Omar continues to

---

xiv The dual loyalty canard consists of the accusation that one cannot be both a patriotic American and Jewish—i.e. that Jews swear allegiance first and foremost to the Jewish state of Israel.

mischaracterize support for Israel. I urge her [Rep. Omar] to retract this statement and engage in further dialogue with the Jewish community on why these comments are so hurtful."[131] Rep. Omar shot back: "Our democracy is built on debate, Congresswoman! I should not be expected to have allegiance/pledge support to a foreign country in order to serve my country in Congress or serve on committee..."[132]

If Rep. Omar's feelings were still not abundantly clear, a July 2019 interview on "CBS This Morning" removed all doubt. During an exchange in which host Gayle King practically begged Rep. Omar to show contrition for her past statements, the congresswoman confirmed she *did not* regret her previous comments and was, "grateful...for the opportunity to really learn how I made people feel." When King asked Rep. Omar multiple times explicitly whether she would like to make clear she was not being anti-Semitic in her rhetoric—in an almost surreal attempted rehabilitation almost no other politician, and certainly no Republican would or ever should be afforded—the best Rep. Omar could offer was: "Nothing I said, at least to me, was meant for that purpose."[133]

Notwithstanding many Americans' support for Israel—which stems from a belief that it is in the United States' national interest to support an ally in the Middle East with whom we share defense interests, historical, cultural, and economic ties, and political and religious values, Rep. Omar sees the relationship as nothing more than a product of untoward foreign influence. Yet Rep. Omar is quiet about a terror-tied foreign lobby that spends millions of dollars to influence Congress and American public opinion. While Rep. Omar frequently gives interviews to and endorses messages delivered by *Al-Jazeera* and its related properties, a network some in Congress wish to designate as a foreign agent, she has said nary a peep about the millions of dollars the Iran-aligned, jihad-supporting regime that backs it, Qatar, has been throwing at America.[134,135] Nor, unsurprisingly, has she criticized its network for the video its online channel, *AJ+*, ran and ultimately had to take down denying the Holocaust, or for revelations about the anti-Israel and anti-Semitic views of its staffers.[136,137]

In fact, two days after *AJ+* published the offending video regarding the Holocaust, Rep. Omar retweeted a tweet linking to another *AJ+* video. It celebrated a sixteen-year-old climate activist. The climate activist herself had tweeted it out, with a message ending in a heart emoji adjacent to "@ajplus," signifying love for the network. The activist who Rep. Omar retweeted was Omar's daughter, Isra Hirsi. Which is to say, AJ+ was promoting Omar's family. Later that day, Rep. Omar retweeted an article from AJ+ covering legislation she introduced challenging Brunei's anti-LGBT laws.[138,139] While refreshing to see Rep. Omar opposing a barbaric application of Sharia law, should she not refuse to appear on a network that is a foreign government mouthpiece, endorse its related outlets, and acknowledge the support given to her family from it, for purposes of evenhandedness and not favoring a foreign country? Is Rep. Omar not compelled by her own standards to speak out on Qatar's influence efforts more broadly? Or is it just that these standards do not matter when Rep. Omar sympathizes with the country in question?

Equating Anti-Semitism and "Islamophobia"

In Rep. Omar's non-apology apologies, she has sought to deflect from her own demonstrable Jew-hatred by equating "Islamophobia" with anti-Semitism. She has claimed critiques of her own bigoted remarks are based on bigotry towards Muslims. In other words, she has leveraged criticism of her own bigotry to transform herself from victimizer into victim. Following Rep. Omar's remarks on AIPAC, during an interview with Mehdi Hasan of Glenn Greenwald's publication, *The Intercept*, Omar seemed to wholly backtrack and flip the story of her anti-Semitic remarks on its head. Here is the relevant exchange:

> **Hasan**: So you since apologized unequivocally for the tweet. You said rightly, that anti-Semitism is real but just to be clear I mean, we're a few weeks on now. I mean, what were you apologizing for? Was it a badly worded tweet that you [were] apologizing for or was it for being anti-Semitic wittingly or unwittingly?
>
> **Rep. Omar**: Absolutely not, I apologized for the way that my words made people feel. Often times, you know,

we are in places where someone will say something and they might not know how it makes you feel and it's not acceptable that once you express to them that this is hurtful or that you have felt attacked by their words. They should acknowledge how you feel. They should speak to that. They should apologize. And you know figure out a way to remedy that situation.

Hasan: That's why you apologized.

Rep. Omar: That is why I apologized.[140]

Rep. Omar added: "I mean, it's no secret that money dominates the political discourse in this country…it's one of the dirty secrets that is not so secret. And so for me, it was really speaking to that…" The criticism Rep. Omar was sparking, in her mind, was attributable to America's bigotry. "I think the theme here is because I'm Muslim," said Rep. Omar.[141] Making oneself the victim of an Islamophobic witch hunt for receiving criticism over plainly anti-Semitic rhetoric is self-evidently chicanerous. In the months that followed, Rep. Omar—with the help of the Democrat Party—would continue this victimological pivot.

The Democrat Party aided her efforts by failing to issue a resolution condemning her bigoted rhetoric by name, replacing it with a broad-based resolution condemning multiple types of bigoted speech.

Omar herself claimed that criticism from President Trump and others over her flippant statement on the September 11, 2001 attacks that "some people did something," constituted an incitement to violence.

Then, following a shooting at the Chabad of Poway in California on the final day of Passover, killing one and injuring three, Rep. Omar had the nerve to claim that "when we are talking about anti-Semitism, we must also talk about Islamophobia; it's two sides of the same coin of bigotry… Just this week, when we've had the attack in California on a synagogue, it's the same person who's accused of attempting to bomb a mosque. So I can't ever speak of Islamophobia and fight for Muslims if I am not willing to fight against anti-Semitism."[142] By unabashedly turning herself and Islam into victims equivalent to Jews attacked on the High Holidays, Rep. Omar only further evinced her bigotry.

"Islamophobia" is Not Equivalent to Anti-Semitism

It is worth examining Rep. Omar's attempt to draw an equivalence between Jew-hatred and Islamophobia because it illustrates the pernicious game in which she is engaged. While anti-Semitism has been a fact of Jewish life since time immemorial, and across nearly every land where Jews have settled, the concept of "Islamophobia" itself was apparently spawned in recent decades and popularized by a Leftist British outfit called the Runnymede Trust in the 1990s.[143,144]

In a notable instance of useful idiots on the Left and Islamists uniting, the foremost global Islamic political body—encompassing fifty-seven Muslim member states—the Organisation of Islamic Conference (OIC), adopted the Runnymede Trust's definition of the term. It incorporated it into legal attempts to criminalize speech in the West flouting Sharia's speech codes prohibiting slander, talebearing, blasphemy, and lying, while related civil society institutions used Islamophobia to chill criticism of, or dissenting views on, Islam.[xv] Notably, in October 2019, it was reported that three leaders within the collective Islamic world, Turkey's Recep Tayyip Erdoğan, Pakistan's Imran Khan, and Malaysia's Mahathir Mohamad according to Khan had agreed to "jointly start an English language channel dedicated to confronting the challenges posed by Islamophobia and setting the record strait (sic) on our great religion."[145]

Now of course, since man set foot on Earth there has been bigotry. But if there was an epidemic of irrational fear about Islam, one would think it would be reflected for example in U.S. hate crime statistics. Thankfully, such crimes are blissfully few in a country as large and diverse as America, totaling 7,120 in 2018 according to the Federal Bureau of Investigations (FBI).[146] This illustrates the fundamental goodness of the American people, contrary to the claims of the likes of Rep. Omar. Religion-based hate crimes

---

xv   This is an argument that requires acquaintance with theology, law, and politics beyond the scope of this book. See chapters V and VI of Stephen Coughlin's *Catastrophic Failure* for a comprehensive explanation.

resulted in 1,550 offenses. Of these offenses, an astounding 57.8 percent were driven by anti-Jewish animus, versus 14.5 percent by anti-Muslim animus, indicating the predominance of Jew-hatred on an absolute and relative basis over not just anti-Muslim but all other religious bigotry.[147] Annual FBI statistics year after year show that it is not Muslims, but Jews who are the victims of a *majority* of all such attacks.[148] Contrary to what one might think listening to Rep. Omar, anti-Muslim hate crimes *fell* by 11 percent from the last year of the Obama presidency through the first year of the Trump presidency.[149] A report from California State University at San Bernardino indicates that anti-Muslim hate crimes in ten of the largest U.S. cities declined in both 2017 and 2018.[150] Meanwhile, many of the most heinous alleged hate crimes against Muslims have proven to be hoaxes.[151,152]

Relatedly, Jew-hatred predominates to an astounding degree in the Muslim world, which consists of an estimated 1.8 billion people. Even before considering Jew-hatred among non-Muslims, to put the sheer mass of Islamic Jew-haters relative to Jews into perspective, there are under 15 million Jews worldwide, period.[153] Stated differently, Jews are outnumbered by Muslim Jew-haters alone by several orders of magnitude, with Israel being a Jewish oasis in a region dominated by anti-Semites. It is virtually mathematically impossible that Jew-hatred and "Islamophobia" could be comparable in pervasiveness, and certainly not in terms of the extent of the threat.

British writer Melanie Phillips has made an even more provocative fundamental argument. She writes that "The stifling effect of the Islamophobia-equals-anti-Semitism trope…means few appreciate that the concept of Islamophobia is itself fundamentally anti-Jew." She continues:

> That's because Islamophobia, like much Muslim discourse, is based on an appropriation and inversion of Jewish experience and precepts.
>
> The Islamists invented "Islamophobia" because they wanted to gain what they (wrongly) thought were the benefits to the Jews of anti-Semitism—protection from criticism. That's why they claim an equivalence between the two.

But the great difference is that anti-Semitism is true prejudice because the Jews are innocent of the grotesque misdeeds attributed to them. By contrast, while many Muslims are decent people who wouldn't harm a fly, Islam is an all-too real, historic source of oppression, fanatical violence and colonialist wars.

...The Jews are the only people for whom the land of Israel was ever their national kingdom, hundreds of years before Islam was even founded. Yet Muslims say (preposterously) that they are the indigenous people of the land.

...Jews were ethnically cleansed from Arab lands; yet Muslims claim Israel is ethnically cleansing the Palestinians, a ludicrous assertion given that the Arab population in the disputed territories and Gaza has increased more than fourfold since 1948.

...Anti-Jewish appropriation and inversion are fundamental to Islam. One reason why the existence of Israel as a Jewish state is anathema is that Islam teaches that the real, authentic Jews are ... the Muslims. Thus, Osama bin Laden declared in his Letter to the American People:

"It is the Muslims who are the inheritors of Moses (peace be upon him) and the inheritors of the real Torah that has not been changed. ... If the followers of Moses have been promised a right to Palestine in the Torah, then the Muslims are the most worthy nation of this."

...All espousing the Palestinian cause go along with this surreal appropriation and inversion agenda.[154]

Finally, as previously noted, the charge of "Islamophobia" has been used to chill dissent against Islamic supremacists. There is no Jewish equivalent of jihadists or Jewish supremacists seeking to impose *halachic* speech codes on the world. Nor is there any effort among Jews to chill dissent by screaming "anti-Semitism," contrary to Rep. Omar's claims.[155] On the contrary, Jews themselves are uniquely self-critical.[156] In the Islamic world, such self-criticism could literally get one killed. Are not the real Islamophobes those afraid of grappling with Islamic ideology and its manifestation in the world?

Rep. Omar's comparisons of Israel to apartheid South Africa, and, even more despicably, Nazi Germany; her holding of Israel to a dishonest double standard while supporting those who wish to destroy it; her unapologetic musings about global Jewish conspiracies and invocation of the dual loyalty canard; and her attempt to draw equivalence between Jew-hatred and "Islamophobia" both to obfuscate from the preeminence of the former and protect herself from criticism using the defense of the latter—not to mention her associations, as we will detail, with individuals and organizations who daily do all of these things and more—leave one wondering if Omar is deliberately trying to act out every example of anti-Semitism cited in the U.S. State Department's definition of the term.[157] She passes former Soviet dissident and Israeli politician Natan Sharansky's "3D test" of anti-Semitism with flying colors, engaging repeatedly in all three forms of Jew-hatred that his test encompasses: delegitimization of Israel, demonization of Israel, and subjecting Israel to double standards.[158]

It is ironic that Rep. Omar has likened her motivations in politics to those that drove Martin Luther King Jr., speaking of a common belief in "radical love."[159] What makes it ironic is that Dr. King's words tell us that Omar's positions towards Israel and the Jews represent nothing less than radical hate. He is said to have stated: "When people criticize Zionists, they mean Jews. You're talking anti-Semitism!"[160] The author would put it this way: If you hate the Jewish state, champion those who wish to destroy it, and constantly invoke the language of Jew-haters—all while associating with Leftists and Islamists who share these views—you are a Jew-hater yourself.

CHAPTER 6

EMBODIMENT OF THE PROGRESSIVE-ISLAMIST AXIS

The Intersection of Progressivism and Islamist Thought

All Jew-haters merit scorn and opprobrium. What makes Rep. Omar's anti-Semitism especially noteworthy is its centrality to the two groups to which she most appeals: Progressives and Islamists. As noted previously, these two cohorts seemingly have little in common. The former is largely anti-religious, while the latter is religiously fundamentalist. The former accepts lifestyles and condones conduct that the latter considers intolerable and blasphemous. But they are able to set aside their differences and partner in a bid to triumph over common foes who stand in the way of their respective totalitarian visions. The biggest stumbling block for each has been traditional, Judeo-Christian Western civilization, of which Judeo-Christian America is the "Great Satan," and Jewish Israel is the "Little Satan." As we will demonstrate in this chapter, anti-Americanism has always gone hand in hand with anti-Semitism masquerading as anti-Zionism.

Based on Rep. Omar's rhetoric, philosophy, policy positions, and as we will show subsequently, the like-minded company she keeps, she personifies and sits at the intersection of this progressive-Islamist partnership.[1]

When considered in historical context, Rep. Omar would indeed seem to be a product of it.

We see the intersection of progressive and Islamist ideology most clearly in Rep. Omar's positions concerning the Islamic world. Consider her benign neglect, if not overt support for Islamic supremacist regimes and groups, and apologism on behalf of jihadism, contrasted with her attacks on the mortal enemies of Islamic supremacism, namely America and Israel. Such views can be justified by Leftism, and seen as part and parcel of her intersectional Blame America First-ism. Yet these are also positions justified by and shared with Islamists, whose rhetoric Rep. Omar apes and champions—and with whose adherents we will show she consorts and colludes to a dizzying degree.

What makes Rep. Omar such a significant a figure then, as one very junior member of a 435-member House, is that there has never been a U.S. representative so perfectly positioned at the intersection of these two ideologies aimed at undermining our country, who has garnered such widespread support, not only from her Squad but from the Congressional Progressive Caucus (CPC) and the Democratic Party itself. Party leadership, as I will chronicle, has shown it is gutless in the face of Rep. Omar and her odious views.

This is a leading indicator that the party will wave the white flag in the face of a fundamentally anti-American regressive progressive movement. Stated differently, we are potentially witnessing the takeover of one of America's two major parties by anti-Americanism, even if it takes time for this to be reflected in representation in Congress. The existing players, including Rep. Omar, have already achieved outsized influence. Reliably progressive popular culture figures have elevated them, echoing the cheerleading of the party.

But before we expound upon these points, herein, we will provide the missed historical context behind them. In particular, we will look at the seminal role that anti-Semitism masquerading as anti-Zionism has played in binding the Left-Islamist alliance that Rep. Omar personifies. We will consequently show that she is the heir to an inherently anti-American project.

The Ideological Basis for Anti-Zionism and Anti-Semitism

Legitimate criticism of a government does not constitute hatred of the people it represents.[i] Anti-Zionism, however, seeks to legitimize hatred of Jews under the guise of targeting the Jewish nation-state. It manifests itself in the harassment of and holding of Israel to an unreachable double standard to which no other nation is held. This double standard proves ruinous by privileging and effectively sponsoring those who seek its destruction. At root, it denies to the Jewish people their theological, legal, and historical claims to the homeland in which they have maintained a continuous presence—bases on which other claimants cannot compete. This in spite of the fact that Jews have been a maligned minority since antiquity, which would otherwise seem to have made them a favored cause of "progressives."

Anti-Zionists do not criticize Israel in good faith, but rather out of prejudice, which separates them from critics whose positions in the author's view may well be wrongheaded and naïve, but who genuinely wish to see Israel not only survive but thrive. And what is best for Israel—living in peace and prosperity in a part of the world marked by hostility towards it, and the West that it represents—would indeed be best for the U.S. and all free nations, given the dangers in the region, Israel's strategic importance, and the remarkable contributions Israel has made to the world's progress in spite of the perilous position in which it finds itself. Anti-Zionism in actuality plays out as a cudgel not only against Jews and Israel, but against all Americans, and the West itself, who, even setting aside moral and spiritual considerations, richly benefit from its existence.[ii]

---

i   As concerns Israel, its policies have been susceptible to criticism from the "right," specifically on the basis of a belief that, as an essential ally in working to preserve Western civilization, Israel can take further measures to strengthen its security—the benefits of which will accrue not only to Israel but to its allies. See for example: https://www. claremont.org/crb/basicpage/israels-lamentable-temple-mount-appeasement/.

ii   Some foreign policy realists, and establishmentarians have challenged this view, claiming that the Israeli-Arab conflict—with emphasis on *Israel*—is the central cause of regional strife. The thinking goes that if Israel is the primary regional irritant, then it is not in America's national interest to partner with her. Leaving aside the intelligence, military, technological, and geopolitical stability benefits that accrue to the U.S. due to the Israel relationship, and taking into account the fact that anti-Semitism has historically been a defining feature of the Islamic world, for centuries before Israel's declaration of independence, there was widespread infighting among Muslims. This continues today most notably in the sectarian Sunni-Shia battle playing out between expansionist Iran, and its proxies and partners, versus several Arab states and Israel. That select Sunni Arab states and Israel are part of a delicate partnership in and of it itself undermines the Israel-centric Middle East turmoil narrative.

The historical roots of anti-Zionism are integral to understanding today's Islamo-Left of France, "Corbynization" in the United Kingdom, and its Ilhan Omar incarnation here in America.[iii,2,3] The original purveyors of anti-Zionism introduced it to make anti-Semitism viable in a post-Holocaust world, as part of a broader anti-Western project. It appealed to and linked the Left and the Islamists, who again share sometimes-overlapping worldviews and ambitions, but perhaps most importantly today, common enemies. They will stay allied in their mutual quest to overcome their enemies at least until the point at which they collectively triumph when they will logically turn on each other given their multiple points of departure.

Marxist historian Eric Hobsbawm made the connection between anti-Zionism and anti-Semitism, and the Left and the Islamists, several decades ago, predicting the threat that has now metastasized. Professor Alan Johnson's 2019 report on anti-Semitism in the British Labour Party notes that Hobsbawm:

> …issued a warning in 1980 that a new form of antisemitism was emerging. Across huge tracts of the world, he noted, antisemitism had never gone away, surviving in two major regions in the post-war years – 'under Islam and, unfortunately, in some countries committed to an ideology which rejected racism, notably the Soviet Union.' Today, almost all the cases of antsemitism (sic) are Islamist or Stalinist in inspiration, whether the perpetrator knows it or not. Though he was a lifelong member of the Communist Party, Hobsbawm pointed out that in Stalinist Eastern Europe, 'antisemitism … was … tolerated and sometimes encouraged' after the Holocaust, 'albeit now dressed up as anti-Zionism' in the era of the Jewish state. Hobsbawm predicted that this 'new' form of antisemitism – antisemitism 'dressed up' as anti-Zionism as a camouflage in a post-Holocaust world – would grow in influence.[4]

---

iii Of note, Rep. Omar has retweeted support from Jeremy Corbyn. See: http://archive.is/v5irC. So has Squad mate Rep. Ocasio-Cortez. See: https://jewishinsider.com/2019/02/daily-kickoff-meet-trumps-pick-amb-south-africa-lana-marks-aoc-responds-corbyn-critics-julian-edelman-first-jewish-super-bowl-mvp/. In fact, AOC went so far as to effectively endorse Corbyn in the run-up to his ultimately failed 2019 bid for prime minister. See: http://archive.is/XsEhU.

This "dressing up" of anti-Semitism as anti-Zionism conforms to the rhetoric of modern Leftists, Islamists, their mutual admirers and defenders, and the subject of this book. Writes Professor Johnson:

> ...Antisemitism 'dressed up' as anti-Zionism has three components: (i) a political programme to abolish the Jewish homeland (and no other homeland); (ii) a discourse to demonise it as evil and 'Nazi' (and only it); and (iii) a movement to make it a global pariah state so it can be 'smashed' (an anathema applied to no other state in the world). The old antisemitism – which has not gone away, but is co-mingled with the new form – believed 'the Jew is our Misfortune'. The new antisemitism proclaims 'the Zionist is our misfortune'. The old antisemitism wanted to make the world 'Judenrein' – free of Jews. The new antisemitism wants to make the world 'Judenstaatrein'– free of the Jewish State, which all but a tiny sliver of world Jewry either lives in, has family members living in, or treats as a vitally important part of their identity.[5]

As several scholars have argued, Israel has come to represent the collective Jew, with all that this entails. How did the Left and the Islamists coalesce around the "new anti-Semitism?"

Left-Wing Anti-Semitism

Jew-hatred has a long history on the Left. The cruel irony is that this is true in spite of the fact that Jews have often been leading Leftist thinkers and proponents of Leftist causes.[iv,6] Karl Marx himself was the descendant

---

iv   As Robert Wistrich, a premier historian of anti-Semitism writes: "Modern Socialism, whose initial raison d'être was the overthrow of capitalism, owed much...to militant Jews who were among its initial creators, leading practitioners, and most fervent apostles. Jewish intellectuals, in particular, brought to the Socialist ranks their acute critical intelligence, unabashed rationalism, devotion to justice, and high ethical ideals...Their secularized heritage of Hebraic messianism enabled Jewish intellectuals to provide a new sense of urgency to the fashionable liberal ideals of modern Progress." See Wistrich's *From Ambivalence to Betrayal*, page 4.

of a long line of Rabbis, yet vacillated between virulent anti-Semitism and mere antipathy towards Judaism—himself personifying this seeming paradox.[7] Beyond self-hating Jews like Marx, for others, revolutionary socialism became their religion. This is akin to more secular Jews today who effectively equate their faith with progressivism, in large part on the basis of a flawed view of the concept of *tikkun olam*, which they translate as "healing or repairing the world one central planner at a time."[v] Socialism was also—seemingly ironically given the dominant strain of Jew-hatred in Leftism—bound up in the Zionist cause.[vi] Haters of Jews justified their views on any number of bases, often varying by country.[8] Those who espoused universalist materialist ideologies like socialism may have rationalized their hostility to Jews based on their predominance in "capitalist" fields—ones to which they were ironically relegated due to discriminatory policies—or at a far more fundamental level on the basis of envy of and hatred towards achievement, combined with Jewish particularism. And of course, as an often insular minority community, Jews could easily be scapegoated and attacked on secular grounds as easily as Jews' great tormenters of yesteryear had done on religious ones. Regardless of how Jew-haters justified their views, the key point is that as Adolf Hitler explained in 1920: "If we are

---

v   See the author's interview with Jonathan Neumann at: https://benweingarten. com/2018/08/how-leftism-supplanted-judaism-and-subverted-israel-and-zionism-under-tikkun-olam-social-justice-with-a-perverse-and-baseless-religious-veneer/, and Neumann's book *To Heal the World*.

vi   As Robert S. Wistrich notes, Zionist socialists primarily consisted of "secularists driven by a quasi-religious pioneering fervor to transform the 'Promised Land' into a Jewish 'national home.' The essence of the Zionist Revolution in their eyes was to turn Diaspora Jews away from their traditional middlemen occupations or petty commerce into becoming primary producers on the land. They revolted against the bourgeois cult of individual success in favor of building up a national society. From a condition of virtual powerlessness they aspired to one where Jews could again become sovereign masters of their own fate. In the Zionist socialist dispensation, this drive for Jewish national self-determination had a pioneering dimension that demanded physical rootedness in the land of Zion (Palestine). Zionism was intended to be a social, spiritual and political revolution against the very condition of Jewish Exile, against the predominant current of Jewish history for 2,000 years and against the 'yoke of the Gentiles.' Only by redeeming the Jewish people in their own homeland could Jews hope to 'normalize' their status among the nations and fully participate in transforming the destiny of mankind." See Wistrich's *From Ambivalence to Tragedy*, page 9.

socialists, then we must definitely be anti-Semites—and the opposite, in that case, is Materialism and Mammonism, which we seek to oppose."⁹

If indeed there is a correlation between Leftism and Jew-hatred, it would follow that anti-Semitism would be a primary feature in the world's preeminent Leftist regimes. Paul Johnson tells us in his essential *A History of the Jews* that "anti-Semitism corrupts the people and societies possessed by it."¹⁰ According to Johnson, "nowhere were its corrosive effects more apparent than in Russia"—the world's great (terrible) incubator and executor of Leftism.¹¹ Johnson's explication of this point is particularly poignant in light of what we are seeing with today's anti-Semitism on the Left:

> The ubiquitous petty corruption engendered by the Tsarist laws against the Jews has…been noted. More important in the long run was its moral corruption of state authority. For in harassing the Jews, the Tsarist Russian state became habituated to a close, repressive and highly bureaucratic system of control. It controlled the internal movements and residence of the Jews, their right to go to school or university and what they studied there, to enter professions or institutes, to sell their labour, to start businesses or form companies, to worship, to belong to organizations and to engage in an endless list of other activities. This system exercised monstrous, all-pervading control of the lives of an unpopular and underprivileged minority and a ruthless invasion of their homes and families. **As such, it became a bureaucratic model, and when the Tsars were replaced first by Lenin, then by Stalin, the control of the Jews was extended to the control of the entire population, and the model became the whole.**¹² [Emphasis added]

None of this is to mention the Jew-hatred in the national *socialist* Nazi regime, or in contemporary Islamist-aligned Leftist regimes like those of Chavez and Maduro in Venezuela, or Islamist regimes that have blended Marxism into their ruling ideologies, like Khomeinist Iran.¹³ We will return to this point momentarily.

Islamic Anti-Semitism

The history of Jew-hatred in the Islamic world predates Marxism by many centuries, deriving in no small part from the Islamic canon, and manifesting itself across Muslim societies worldwide in pervasive Jewish repression.[14] Jews have historically lived in Islamic states at very best as *dhimmis*, oppressed second-class non-citizens with limited rights and limitless burdens. At worst, they have found themselves massacred.[15] This fate is consistent with Koran 9:29, which as noted earlier instructs Muslims to:

> Fight those among the People of the Book [Christians and Jews] who do not believe in Allah nor the Last Day, nor forbid what Allah and His Messenger have forbidden, nor embrace the religion of truth, until they pay the jizya [tax on non-Muslims] with willing submission and feel themselves subdued. [vii,16]

Islam's sacred texts contain many such passages, which contemporary Islamic scholars reiterate in their commentaries.[viii,17,18]

The proof of this poisonous legacy is in the pudding of the present-day Islamic world, something the Trump administration's U.S. Special Envoy for Monitoring and Combating Anti-Semitism, Elan Carr has openly acknowledged.[19] According to the Anti-Defamation League's (ADL) 2014

---

vii   Dr. Andrew Bostom, an expert on Islam who has published a number of books on its theology and history, writes: "The 'contract of the jizya', or 'dhimma' encompassed… obligatory and recommended obligations for the conquered non-Muslim 'dhimmi' peoples…imposed upon non-Muslims—Jews, Christians, as well as Zoroastrians, Hindus, and Buddhists—subjugated by jihad. Some of the more salient features of dhimmitude include: the prohibition of arms for the vanquished dhimmis, and of church bells; restrictions concerning the building and restoration of churches, synagogues, and temples; inequality between Muslims and non-Muslims with regard to taxes and penal law; the refusal of dhimmi testimony by Muslim courts; a requirement that Jews, Christians, and other non-Muslims, including Zoroastrians and Hindus, wear special clothes; and the overall humiliation and abasement of non-Muslims. It is important to note that these regulations and attitudes were institutionalized as permanent features of the sacred Islamic law, or Sharia." See: https://www.andrewbostom.org/2011/08/bernard-lewis-pied-piper-of-islamic-confusion/.

viii   For a comprehensive treatment of the roots of Islamic Jew-hatred and how it has manifested itself over many centuries, see Andrew Bostom's *The Legacy of Islamic Antisemitism*.

worldwide survey of 100 countries, the sixteen countries exhibiting the highest levels of anti-Semitism were all in the Middle East, demonstrating staggering levels of anti-Semitism at rates ranging from 74 percent to 93 percent.[20] 49 percent of all Muslims worldwide were shown to harbor anti-Semitic attitudes. Writing on the massive increase in anti-Semitic violence in France, coinciding with the swelling of its Muslim population, *The New York Times* noted that in "16 surveys conducted over the last 12 years in Europe, 'anti-Semitism is significantly higher among Muslims than among non-Muslims,'" per the work of Indiana University German historian Gunther Jikeli.[21] Predictably, such anti-Semitic attitudes correlate with anti-Israel views among new Muslim migrants, as illustrated for example by Germany's recent arrivals.[22] Even among American Muslims, per a 2016-2017 ADL survey of 5,100 interviewees, 34 percent were shown to hold extreme anti-Semitic views, versus 14 percent of the general non-Muslim U.S. population.[23] According to Omar Jamal, a self-described Somali community activist in St. Paul, such Jew-hatred also festers among Somalis in Rep. Omar's Minnesota.[24] Anti-Semitism pervades mosques both globally and in the United States.[25] It has been and remains ubiquitous in Islamic media, schools, and culture.[26,27]

Though barely a footnote in coverage of the Arab Spring, two poignant examples of Islamic Jew-hatred emerged during its revolutionary days. In a sort of macabre comedy, Islamist opponents of deposed leaders Ben-Ali of Tunisia, Muammar Gaddafi of Libya, and Hosni Mubarak of Egypt referred to them pejoratively as "Jews."[28] Too, in one of the Arab Spring's more horrifying episodes, as the Muslim Brotherhood ascended to power in Egypt, a mob beat and gang-raped then-CBS reporter Lara Logan in Tahrir Square. Though it was not widely reported at the time, the perpetrators of the brutal crime reportedly chanted "Jew!" "Jew!" "Jew!"[29] In other words, these savage men assailed their victim with what they deemed the most vile slur.[30]

These anecdotes are the rule, not the exception in the Muslim world. As the courageous ex-Muslim Brotherhood member-turned-outspoken-apostate, and Somali-born Ayaan Hirsi Ali—who on account of her apostasy and public positions lives under the constant threat of death from jihadists—put it in a speech to the American Jewish Committee:

Ladies and gentlemen I have a confession to make, if you are Jewish. It's a testimony to my dark past when I lived in ignorance. I used to hate you. I hated you because I thought you were responsible for the war that took my father from me for so long. When the Soviet Union allied with our home-grown dictator in Somalia, I was told the Jews were behind that.[ix] In Saudi Arabia I saw poor people from a place called Palestine. Men, women, and children huddled together in despair. I was told you drove them out of their homes. I hated you for that. When we had no water I thought you closed the tap. I don't know how you did it, but you did it. If my mother was unkind to me I knew you were definitely behind it. Even when I failed an exam I knew it was your fault. I don't know how you did all these things. But then I didn't need proof. You are by nature evil. And you had evil powers and you used them to evil ends. Learning to hate you was easy. Unlearning it was difficult. Even after I had learned about The Holocaust in Europe, the terrible outcome of centuries of Antisemitism, I still found it difficult to take a stand against it. When my half-sister told me The Holocaust was the best thing that had happened to Jews, I refrained from arguing with her because I did not wish to risk breaking the family ties. When she showed me holy [Koranic] verses to support her hatred of Jews I feared arguing with Allah for Allah would burn me. Isn't it ironic that the American Jewish Committee decided to give me the Moral Courage Award? I am ashamed of my prejudices against you in the past. The good news is I am not alone in learning not to blame you for my misfortunes. Many others who are taught in the name of Islam to hate you have stopped hating you. **The tragedy is however that those unlearning to hate are far fewer in number than those who still do. As we sit here thousands, perhaps millions**

---

ix   As will soon become clear, the Soviets must have gotten a chuckle out of this, seeing it as an unintentional affirmation of their efforts.

are learning to blame you and wishing to destroy you.[31]
[Emphasis and footnote mine]

Anti-Semitism Binds the Left and the Islamists

During the Cold War, the Soviet Union rebranded anti-Semitism as "anti-Zionism," consistent with today's Jeremy Corbyns and Ilhan Omars.[x] As Paul Johnson writes:

> The Soviet campaign against the Jews, after 1967 a permanent feature of the system, was...conducted under the code-name of anti-Zionism, which became a cover for every variety of anti-Semitism. Soviet anti-Zionism...was in turn grafted on to Leninist anti-imperialism.
>
> ...From the early 1950s, Soviet anti-Zionist propaganda, growing steadily in intensity and comprehensiveness, stressed the links between Zionism, the Jews in general, and Judaism.[32]

If the prevalence of Islamic Jew-hatred in the 20th century is even remotely comparable to the levels of today, then Soviet anti-Semites would seem to have had a natural partner in the Islamic world. In fact, its prevalence today almost assuredly reflects that the Soviets had a more than willing partner. Indeed, according to several accounts, "anti-Zionism" provided a bridge between Communists and the Islamists of the strategically

---

x   As Professor Alan Johnson notes in his aforementioned report on modern left-wing anti-Semitism: "Dave Rich, author of The Left's Jewish Problem: Jeremy Corbyn, Israel and Antisemitism, explains contemporary antisemitism in the clearest terms: 'Nowadays antisemitism often appears in discourse relating to Israel, either by targeting Israel itself as a proxy for Jews or by repeating old antisemitic slanders with "Israel" or "Zionist" swapped in for the word "Jew".' He goes on: 'Antisemitism in today's Labour Party ... usually involves language that draws on old racist lies about Jews, but reframes the bigotry in a modern, "anti-Zionist" setting that has nothing to do with what Zionism is, or with how Israel actually behaves.'"

important Middle East during the Cold War.^{xi} In a 2014 email interview the author conducted with Lt. Gen. Ion Pacepa, the highest-ranking Soviet bloc intelligence officer ever to defect, Gen. Pacepa recounted how:

> In 1972, during a breakfast in his office, KGB chairman [Yuri] Andropov told me that "our" disinformation machinery should ignite a campaign aimed at transforming Arab anti-Semitism into an anti-American doctrine for the whole Muslim world. The idea was to portray the United States as a war-mongering, Zionist country financed by Jewish money and run by a rapacious "Council of the Elders of Zion" (the KGB's derisive epithet for the U.S. Congress), the aim of which was to transform the rest of the world into a Jewish fiefdom. Andropov made the point that one billion adversaries could cause far greater damage than could a mere 150 million.

> The KGB boss described the Muslim world as a waiting petri dish, in which we could nurture a strain of hate-America. The Muslims had a taste for nationalism, jingoism and victimology. We had only to keep repeating, over and over, that the United States was a war-mongering, Zionist country financed by Jewish money, with the goal of taking over the whole world.

---

xi   However, these ties predated the Cold War. As Robert Wistrich writes: "Since the late 1920s Islamists and Arab nationalists had violently opposed Zionism (as well as imperialism)—regarding it as the prime enemy of the Muslim *umma* [collective]. In their agitation, they owed not a little to the Communists (especially in Palestine) who had taught them the fine arts of agitprop and indoctrinated them in Marxist-Leninist techniques of denouncing colonialism and Western imperialism." Wistrich adds that on top of the Bolshevik's frequent invocation of the Islamic concept of "Holy War" in rhetoric and documents rallying Communists against imperialist Britain, its messaging to the Arab world was typified by the following propaganda message, deployed to the Muslim East in 1920: "Peoples of the East! . . . What has Britain done to Palestine? There, at first, acting for the benefit of Anglo-Jewish capitalists, it drove Arabs from the land in order to give the latter to Jewish settlers. Then, trying to appease the discontent of the Arabs, it incited them against the same Jewish settlers." See Wistrich's *From Ambivalence to Betrayal*, pages 567-568.

The KGB community threw millions of dollars and thousands of people into that gigantic project, as described in our book.

...The grisly decapitation and dismembering of Wall Street Journal reporter Daniel Pearl in 2002 symbolizes Andropov's legacy. The mastermind of the Sept. 11, 2001, attacks, Khalid Sheikh Mohammed, gruesomely murdered Pearl because he was an American Jew.[33]

Paul Johnson relates that: "The quantity of anti-Zionist material flooding into the world, from both the Soviet bloc and the Arab states, was augmented first by the 1967 Six Day War, which acted as a powerful stimulant to Soviet propaganda against Israel, then the oil-price revolution following the 1973 Yom Kippur War, which greatly increased Arab funds made available for anti-Zionist propaganda."[34]

In a 2003 *Wall Street Journal* op-ed, Lt. Gen. Pacepa revealed the extensive ties between the KGB, and Fatah founder and PLO chairman Yasser Arafat. In essence, Pacepa claims that the KGB made Arafat. It trained him in the Soviet Union in the 1960s, groomed him to be a PLO leader, adorned him with an invented Palestinian Arab personal narrative, and bolstered his credibility by carefully crafting and widely disseminating propaganda under his name. As Pacepa writes:

Arafat was an important undercover operative for the KGB. Right after the 1967 Six Day Arab-Israeli war, Moscow got him appointed to chairman of the PLO. Egyptian ruler Gamal Abdel Nasser, a Soviet puppet, proposed the appointment. In 1969 the KGB asked Arafat to declare war on American "imperial-Zionism" during the first summit of the Black Terrorist International, a neo-Fascist pro-Palestine organization financed by the KGB and Libya's Moammar Gadhafi.[xii] It appealed to him so much, Arafat later claimed

---

xii   The irony was clearly lost on Qaddafi's previously discussed opponents, who had derisively referred to him as a "Jew" during the Arab Spring.

to have invented the imperial-Zionist battle cry. But in fact, "imperial-Zionism" was a Moscow invention, a modern adaptation of the "Protocols of the Elders of Zion," and long a favorite tool of Russian intelligence to foment ethnic hatred. **The KGB always regarded anti-Semitism plus anti-imperialism as a rich source of anti-Americanism.**[35] [Footnote and Emphasis added]

Arafat is not alone. The corrupt and Jew-hating Mahmoud Abbas, now in the 15th year of his four-year term as president of the PA, exemplifies in real time the legacy of Left/Islamist anti-Zionism/anti-Semitism in which he was indoctrinated. As the Kennan Institute's Izabella Tabarovsky details in a *Fathom* piece titled "Soviet Anti-Zionism and Contemporary Left Antisemitism:"

Arab-language anti-Zionist literature was an important part of Soviet propaganda directed at the Middle East. According to [Israeli investigative journalist Ronen] Bergman, it served as source material for Mahmoud Abbas's 1982 Ph.D. dissertation. In the early 1980s, Abbas was enrolled at Moscow's Patrice Lumumba University, a school established to train future Third World elites in Marxism-Leninism and prepare them to become pro-Soviet influencers (Hazan 2017: 87-88). He defended his dissertation at Moscow's Institute of Oriental Studies – an important institution within the Academy of Sciences, which regularly churned out 'scholarly' works demonizing Zionism and Israel. During Abbas's tenure, the Institute was headed by Yevgeny Primakov, an Arabist with lifelong connections to Soviet intelligence in the Middle East, who would eventually head the Soviet foreign intelligence agency SVR. That Primakov personally appointed Abbas's dissertation advisor shows the importance that the Soviet foreign policy and intelligence establishments attached to the educational output of this already prominent Palestinian leader.

Abbas's dissertation was published as a book in 2011 in Arabic under the title *The Other Side: The Secret Relationship between Nazism and Zionism*. Several passages from the book reproduced in Bergman's article, replicate some of the mainstays of the Soviet anti-Zionist campaign, including those concerning the alleged Zionist collaboration with the Nazis during the Holocaust and casting doubt on the number of Holocaust victims.

A particularly curious piece of historical falsification that made it into Abbas's book concerned Adolf Eichmann's capture by the Mossad. According to Bergman, Abbas wrote that the Mossad abducted Eichmann in order to prevent the high-ranking Nazi from revealing the secret of Zionists' role in the Final Solution.[36]

As Tabarovsky summarizes it in a separate piece:

> Many of the core tropes that animate the anti-Zionist left today are carbon copies of ideas that the KGB and the Department of Propaganda's ideologues developed, weaponized, and popularized with particular intensity in the wake of the Six-Day War. It is there, not among the Nazi oeuvre, that the direct precursors to the *New York Times* cartoon [its anti-Semitic cartoon caricaturing Israeli Prime Minister Benjamin Netanyahu as a dog with a Star of David on its collar leading a blind, yarmulke-wearing President Donald Trump] and similar such efforts, in which the European press has been awash for the past two decades, are to be found.[37,38]

Paul Johnson adds: "In the twenty years after the 1967 Six-Day War, the Soviet propaganda machine became the main source for anti-Semitic material in the world. In doing so it assembled materials from virtually every archaeological layer of anti-Semitic history, from classical antiquity to Hitlerism."[39]

Tabarovsky and Johnson's focus on the Six-Day War is important because—as several historians compellingly argue—this is the demarcation point at which the international Left, and specifically the New Left, broadly broke from Israel and adopted an anti-Zionism in common with the Islamists.[40] Up to that point, Israel, which for many early Zionists represented the founding of a potential socialist Utopia—realized in the form of the kibbutzim—had been treated as David to the Arab world's Goliath. But after its miraculous victory over the mighty Arab forces surrounding it, the New Jersey-sized state, under siege from the day it declared independence, lacking in natural resources, diplomatic and trade partners, was transformed into a global pariah because it had the temerity to stand up and fight a defensive war against Soviet proxies—in the process gaining territory.[xiii] Israel was no longer the underdog. It was the "strong horse." It was an oppressive occupier, the victimizer to the Arab victim. The Palestinian Arabs, led by Yasser Arafat, could conjure up a narrative consistent with other anti-Western, Soviet-backed Third World "national liberation"

---

xiii   University of Maryland-College Park Professor Jeffrey Herf writes: "For the Soviet Union, it was infuriating and embarrassing to see its Arab clients fail so miserably. It was a severe blow to its efforts to drive out Western influence in the Middle East and gain control over oil supplies so vital to the global economy. Yet the leftist Holocaust inversion did rest on very old and false attributions of enormous power and great evil which religious and secular antisemites had attributed to the Jews in Europe. Rather than acknowledge that the Jews, like any other nation with a state of its own, had defended itself against a real threat and won a war, the Communists and the radical Left applied the negative attributes once applied to the Jews of Europe to the State of Israel. While antisemites before 1945 had described the Jews as the center of a powerful international conspiracy, the anti-Zionists of the Cold War era described Israel as the spearhead in the Middle East of a conspiracy led by the US and supported by West Germany. Rather than describe the war for what it was, a war of self-defence in the face of serious threats, Israel's leftist antagonists during and after 1967 tried to delegitimate its victory as an act of aggression. In the aftermath of the Six-Day War, the idea of the powerful and evil Jew, so familiar in the history of European antisemitism, assumed a new form of a powerful and evil Israel. The Communists and the radical Left in the West blinded themselves with such hatred they were unable to understand why and how a people threatened with destruction less than a quarter of a century after the Holocaust could have fought and won a war against great odds." See: https://www.meforum.org/6644/the-global-left-and-the-six-day-war.

movements to justify their war to destroy the Jewish state under the guise of anti-Zionism.

Thus, as Joshua Muravchik highlights in a particularly pertinent section of his seminal *Making David Into Goliath*, in January 1969 Fatah's central committee declared:[41] "Fatah, the Palestine National Liberation Movement, is not struggling against the Jews as an ethnic and religious community. It is struggling against Israel as **the expression of colonisation based on a theocratic, racist and expansionist system and of Zionism and colonialism.**"[42] [Emphasis added] It linked this cause to other revolutionary movements around the world, including most notably the anti-American sympathizers with the North Vietnamese, stating: "The struggle of the Palestinian people, like that of the Vietnamese people and other peoples of Asia, Africa and Latin America, is part of the historic process of the liberation of the oppressed peoples from colonialism and imperialism."[43] Muravchik records that as Arafat would put it: "Our struggle is part and parcel of every struggle against imperialism, injustice and oppression in the world…It is the part of the world revolution which aims at establishing **social justice** and liberating mankind."[44] [Emphasis added]

George Habash, the founder of the Marxist counterpart to Arafat's Fatah, the previously discussed PFLP—which similarly has engaged in martyrdom, hijackings, and murder—would later write that: "Many have been surprised…that we, as Marxists, should be on the side of a religious movement like Khomeini's [revolutionary Islamic ideology]. But beyond ideology, we have in common anti-imperialist, anti-Zionist and anti-Israeli elements."[45] This unlikely marriage of Islam and Marxism to varying degrees would manifest itself in the philosophies of Islamic supremacists on both the Sunni and Shia sides, from Sayyid Abul Ala Maududi's Jamaat-e-Islami and Sayyid Qutb's Muslim Brotherhood, to again, Iran's Khomeinists.

Naturally, the Palestinian Arab cause would prove irresistible for the Left. It remains so. Just consider Arafat's words: "Social Justice." "Theocracy." "Racism." "Oppression." "Colonization." "Imperialism." Is this not the very rhetoric Rep. Omar and her intersectionalist partners on the Left employ today regarding both Israel and America?

Of course, justice needs no modifier, and the steps needed to administer the supposed panacea of "social justice" would deprive us of the latter, while destroying the former.

Israel and America are not theocratic but rather liberal and pluralistic because of their liberal, respectively Judeo and Judeo-Christian, Western roots. The two nations are more racially diverse than almost any others on the planet and have achieved remarkable degrees of racial harmony and equality. Israel and America are not oppressors, colonizers, and imperialists, but rather nations concerned primarily with protecting and preserving the freedoms of their peoples. On the Israeli side, what makes this argument at its core completely illegitimate is that Zionism was itself an anti-colonial liberation movement against Great Britain and the Islamist forces with which the British colluded to oppress Jews residing in today's Israel while denying them previously promised statehood.[46] The idea that any of these adjectives describe America is equally fatuous.

Consider on the other hand the purest expression of Arafat's ideology in our time, that of the Islamic State. If we were to revise Arafat's formulation, replacing "Zionism" with "Islamic supremacism," would the Islamic State not fit perfectly as "the expression of colonisation based on a theocratic, racist and expansionist system and of Islamic supremacism and colonialism?" From Yasser Arafat to Ilhan Omar, exponents of this view of Israel and America, the West's leading lights, are again engaging in projection on a grand scale.

Left-Islamism From Edward Said to Ilhan Omar

A pseudo-intellectual framework would develop that also echoes in the modern progressive-Islamist axis, and particularly its focus on victimology, as reflected by Rep. Omar. Perhaps the strongest force behind it was Edward Said. Said was an academic-activist who personified the links between the Leftist intelligentsia and the Islamist world as an Ivy League professor and member of the Palestinian National Council. As Joshua Muravchik writes in *Making David Into Goliath*:

Said's objective [in his most famous work, *Orientalism*] was to expose the evil worm at the core of Western civilization, namely, its inability to define itself except against an imagined "other." That "other" was the Oriental, a figure "to be feared...or to be controlled." Ergo, Said claimed that "every European, in what he could say about the Orient, was...a racist, an imperialist, and almost totally ethnocentric." Elsewhere in the text, he made clear that what was true for Europeans held equally for Americans.

This echoed a theme of 1960s radicalism which was forged in the movements against Jim Crow and against America's war in Vietnam, namely that the Caucasian race was the scourge of humanity...to the New Left, of which Said was an avatar, the lines of conflict were demographic: young against old, female against male, and above all black against white. The Marxist notion of class struggle had never resonated in America, which lacked Europe's history of hereditary social position. Race was a different matter. For Europe, colonialism and imperialism were the original sins. But in America the victimization of blacks through slavery and segregation was the running sore, the great stain on the nation's honor, the excruciating counterpoint to the proclaimed ideals of the founding fathers.

Said rolled American racism and European colonialism into one ball of wax: white oppression of darker-skinned peoples. He was not the only thinker to have forged this amalgam, but he made a unique contribution in portraying "Orientals" as the epitome of the dark-skinned; Muslims as the representative Orientals; Arabs as the essential Muslims; and, finally, Palestinians as the ultimate Arabs. Abracadabra, Israel, in conflict with the Palestinians, was transformed from a redemptive refuge from two thousand years of persecution to the very embodiment of white supremacy.[xiv,47]

This view clearly had staying power. In May 2019, San Francisco State University Arab and Muslim Ethnicities Professor Rabab Abdulhadi reportedly remarked, in the retelling of a witness, "that those who support Israel want to ethnically cleanse the Middle East and those affiliated with Israel and pro-Israel organizations are white supremacists."[48]

Amazingly, today's prominent Democrats parrot such propaganda. Leading 2020 Democratic presidential candidate and 2016 Democratic presidential primary runner-up Senator Bernie Sanders calls the Israeli government "racist." His contemptible campaign surrogate Linda Sarsour, another representative of the progressive-Islamist axis on whom we will dwell later, says Israel is built on Jewish "supremacy"—an analogue to American white supremacy—a position she tried in vain to clarify when called on it.[49,50] Beto O'Rourke says Israeli Prime Minister Benjamin Netanyahu is a "racist."[51] Rep. Omar calls Trump administration official Stephen Miller, who is Jewish, a "white nationalist," which amounts to the same charge.[52] The sickening irony is that the Zionist movement was antithetical to racism, and indeed a response in part to longtime discrimination against Jews at the hands of both Europeans and Arabs.[xv]

---

xiv   According to sociologist Yiannis Gabriel, "Othering is the process of casting a group, an individual or an object into the role of the 'other' and establishing one's own identity through opposition to and, frequently, vilification of this Other." See: https://www.claremont.org/crb/article/the-chosen-and-the-woke/. Rep. Omar has frequently invoked this concept, stating that she confronts "otherness" as a black person and Muslim, and has linked "*othering* and xenophobia" as a driving force behind Islamophobia. See: https://www.nytimes.com/2018/12/30/us/politics/ilhan-omar-minnesota-congress.html and https://www.thenation.com/podcast/ilhan-omar-next-left-politics/.

xv   As the doyen of anti-Semitism Robert Wistrich wrote in his final essay, posthumously published in July 2015: "Far from being based on 'race,' the Zionist movement arose in part as a political answer to the racist, nationalist, and religious antisemitism created by deeply reactionary forces in European and Middle Eastern societies. European racist antisemitism in particular was a major force in pushing Jews to seek their own path toward auto-emancipation. It was the decisive factor in bringing more acculturated secular Jews such as Pinsker, Herzl, and Nordau to Zionism. Their search for a cure to antisemitism could also build on much older Biblical visions of redemption that linked all Zionist groups—secular and religious—to the Land of Israel." See: https://www.tandfonline.com/doi/pdf/10.1080/23739770.2015.1037579, page 193.

Note too that the idea behind the transmogrification of Jews into white supremacists, in addition to once again reflecting a form of Holocaust Inversion, is congruent with today's focus on "privilege," and in particular white privilege. To extend Muravchik's soliloquy regarding Edward Said and "Orientals" to their counterpart: white Europeans are the epitome of the light-skinned; Jews are the representative white Europeans; Ashkenazis are the essential Jews, and Israelis are the ultimate Ashkenazis. If white Europeans are the *privileged*, in the modern vernacular, then Ashkenazi Israelis are the most privileged of them all. Consequently, Jews, as the ultimate victimizers, cannot be victims of Jew-hatred, at least from the Left or the Left's favored minorities, including Muslims. Jews' disproportionate fealty to progressivism, belief in a justice akin to social justice, and historic devotion to championing minority underdogs is no defense. It does not absolve them of their *a priori* sins given their place in the privilege pyramid. As William Voegeli puts it in the *Claremont Review of Books*:

> ...the Holocaust established Jewish victimhood only temporarily. Among the Woke, writes [PhD candidate in Political Science at Georgia State University Zach] Goldberg [in *Tablet*], "Jews are perceived to be privileged—at least in comparison to other historically victimized groups."
>
> *Having made a full recovery from the Holocaust, Jews are no longer the downtrodden collective that white liberals can readily sympathize with. Other groups lower on the privilege hierarchy and less tainted by association with whiteness now have priority.*
>
> In particular, these victimier victims have come to include the Palestinians. In the belief that Palestinians have, as a rule, darker complexions than Israel's Ashkenazim (Jews whose ancestors lived in Europe for centuries), the Woke apply the implicit rule of their privilege hierarchy, which holds that melanin is the most reliable proxy for moral worth.[53]

This explains why Rep. Omar's intersectional feminists, for example in the Women's March, reject progressives otherwise in good standing, should they be at all pro-Israel. Its leaders' virulent Jew-hatred was so overwhelming that the Democratic Party had to sever ties with its Farrakhanites altogether.[54,55] Yet Rep. Omar remains pals with, among others, the now-former Islamist Women's March co-chair Linda Sarsour. Sarsour, a purported Muslim feminist, wrote in a since-deleted tweet that the aforementioned Ayaan Hirsi Ali, a victim of female genital mutilation, was "asking 4 an a$$ whippin'," and of Ali and prominent female counterjihadist Brigitte Gabrielle, "I wish I could take their vaginas away – they don't deserve to be women."[56,57,58] Rep. Omar has also appeared at events with and been publicly supported by a short-lived replacement Women's March board member, the similarly Islamist and virulently anti-Semitic Zahra Billoo, whom we will discuss subsequently. Anecdotal evidence suggests pro-Israel progressive Jewish women are being harassed on social media first and foremost by fellow progressives.[59] "Progressive" tech executives at leading companies refer to politically conservative Jews like Dennis Prager and Ben Shapiro as "Nazis."[60] Conversely, jihadist groups—prior to recent crackdowns at the urging of lawmakers—have freely proliferated social media accounts, and Muslim Brotherhood-aligned groups have freely deployed apps allegedly disseminating Jew-hatred.[61,62]

Meanwhile, what is Rep. Omar's takeaway from the various controversies she has embroiled herself in due to her anti-Semitic bigotry? Ever the victim, according to a *Huffington Post* interview: "the lesson she has learned since she took office is just how far people will go to '*other*' those that they find discomfort in."[63] [Emphasis added]

On account of their shared ideology, reflected in their common rhetoric and positions, it should be clear that Ilhan Omar and her acolytes are the heirs of the historical Left-Islamist axis. They connect a worldview of a West dominated by privilege, racism, and "othering," to a victimological historical narrative of occupation, oppression, and colonization, necessitating a revolutionary overthrow of the existing order to achieve social justice. In the June 2019 issue of *The New Criterion*, columnist Dominic Green further linked the history of Leftist anti-Semitism masquerading as anti-Zionism to the present:

[T]he modern Left has always been predisposed to hostility towards nationalism in general, Jews in particular, and Jewish nationalism most of all. The rational case for irrational loathing, and the revolutionary case for eliminating class enemies, are foundational left-wing principles. The Western Left has frequently rejected the very existence of a Jewish state, and started even before Israel's alleged turn to tyranny after 1967. Since 1967, the Left has consistently denied Jewish rights in the historical Land of Israel, choosing instead to pander first to terrorists and now to Islamists in a foolish and cynical campaign to mobilize the wretched of the postcolonial earth. As in earlier variations of the Left's war for the future, the Jews are condemned as proxies of "imperialism" and "capitalism."[64]

Robert Wistrich connected these dots with profound clarity in his *From Ambivalence to Betrayal*, writing that: "Anticapitalist antisemitism underpinning radical antizionism is an integral part of the Marxist-Islamist ideological axis which seeks to redeem the contemporary world from the sinister 'plots' of American imperialism and the yoke of Zionist oppression." Of the Holocaust Inversion to which Rep. Omar and her precursors subscribe, he explains their perverse logic as follows: "capitalism begat fascism which begat imperialism which begat Israel and its proxy Zionism—the ultimate form of racist domination—sponsored, of course, by the 'Great Satan'—the United States of America."[65]

That is, the shared anti-Semitism of the progressives and Islamists is a proxy for anti-Americanism and opposition to the West. To defend Rep. Omar is to defend this historical legacy and its present mutation. To refuse to purge one's political party of anti-Semitism masquerading as anti-Zionism is to legitimize if not accede to this anti-Western view. At the very best, it is to begin the slide down the slipperiest of slopes. The Democratic Party's succumbing to anti-Semitism by way of anti-Zionism in its defense of Rep. Omar is an indicator of an impending takeover of the party by a radicalism that, if implemented, would result in national self-immolation. The consequences are playing out on the streets of America's Leftist urban areas. There, religious Jews find themselves weekly, if not daily under attack—often by minorities who tower above them in the victimological hierarchy—without any sign their purported representatives will do anything to defend them, while progressives perversely blame them for being assaulted.[66,67,68,69,70]

CHAPTER 7

THE DEMOCRATS' CAVE ON ISRAEL AND THE JEWS

A Dangerous Embrace

The Democrat establishment's relationship with Rep. Ilhan Omar, like its relationship with her Squad colleagues, has gone from arm's length to bear hug in under one year.[1] Symbolically, this represents a shameful and disastrous embrace, legitimizing these figures, with all of their baggage, including their positions on Israel and the Jews. Such positions are proxies for where the Party of Jefferson—that has already begun to disavow him by name—is headed on all manner of issues.[2] The fight over Israel and Jews is a microcosm of, but also essential to, the broader fight between the Left Democratic establishment, and the even further Left progressives. Anti-Zionism is a façade for anti-Semitism, as the Democrats' own leaders have acknowledged. It follows that if anti-Semitism masquerading as anti-Zionism is inextricably intertwined with anti-Americanism, that the Left is effectively accepting an ethos of national self-hatred. This ideology and its associated policies would be consistent with Rep. Omar's desire, compelling in effect the eventual overthrow of the American system of government under the guise of "helping it live up to its principles."

The Democrats' embrace of Rep. Omar, therefore, has a symbolic meaning with substantive implications. Regarding Israel and the Jews, we should be perfectly clear: While the majority of the Democratic electorate, and its current representatives may not have swung to the Left to the same extent as Rep. Omar, and her compatriot Rep. Tlaib, the party's willingness to defend these figures reflects a shift in the Overton Window.[i] Once shifted, and in light of the ideological trends on the Left directionally consistent with Rep. Omar and her comrades, it is unlikely the window will shift back. This anti-Semitism and concomitant anti-Americanism is a grave danger to our republic. For as Paul Johnson argues, Jew-hatred (and presumably its derivatives) "corrupts the people and societies possessed by it."[3]

Prelude to the Cave

Before they were ever sworn in, Ilhan Omar, Alexandria Ocasio-Cortez, and to a lesser extent their Squad mates Rashida Tlaib and Ayanna Pressley, were hailed by the media and in popular culture as Resistance rock stars. Consequently, at the start of the 116th Congress, leading House Democrats happily graced magazine covers with them in the hopes of co-opting their supporters, while in actuality dismissing the radical freshmen as a small, powerless minority. The Squad was to be seen, but not heard; if heard, it was not to be taken seriously. Rep.

---

i   The Overton Window is a theory on the viability of ideas and their impact on the positions taken by politicians developed by the late Joseph P. Overton of the Mackinac Center for Public Policy. The Mackinac Center describes the Overton Window as follows: "The Overton Window is a model for understanding how ideas in society change over time and influence politics. The core concept is that politicians are limited in what policy ideas they can support—they generally only pursue policies that are widely accepted throughout society as legitimate policy options. These policies lie inside the Overton Window. Other policy ideas exist, but politicians risk losing popular support if they champion these ideas. These policies lie outside the Overton Window.

But the Overton Window can both shift and expand, either increasing or shrinking the number of ideas politicians can support without unduly risking their electoral support. Sometimes politicians can move the Overton Window themselves by courageously endorsing a policy lying outside the window, but this is rare. More often, the window moves based on a much more complex and dynamic phenomenon, one that is not easily controlled from on high: the slow evolution of societal values and norms." See: https://www.mackinac.org/OvertonWindow.

Tlaib would later rightly recognize that she and her colleagues were being used as political props, playing to the party's identity politics predilections. When in April 2019 she angrily tweeted in part: "They [the Democratic establishment] put us [including Rep. Omar] in photos when they want to show our party is diverse…," she was right. Why the patronizing attitude? Because from the perspective of the party's establishment, not only was the Squad out of the mainstream, thereby imperiling the just-won House and perhaps the White House in 2020, but given the fact its members like AOC showed they could primary longtime members like Joe Crowley, they represented a threat to establishment authority.

On the issues of Israel and Jews, the Democratic establishment sought to maintain a tricky balance, which in and of itself says something. On the one hand, for decades it claimed support for the U.S.-Israel alliance, though it was conservatives specifically and the Republican Party more broadly that had grown increasingly more pro-Israel and philo-Semitic. Jews—specifically the non-Orthodox Jews who make up the vast majority of American Jewry—were an important constituency for the Democrats, having voted solidly blue since their arrival in America. Indicative of this fact is that since 1916, the highwater mark for the Jewish popular vote for a Republican presidential candidate was 45 percent. The beneficiary was Charles Evan Hughes…in 1916.[4]

On the other hand, the energy in the Democratic Party was increasingly with its progressives, who were more hostile to Israel and Jews supportive of her. Even though views on Israel and views on Jews are theoretically separable, as we have shown, anti-Zionism and anti-Semitism in practice represent a distinction without a difference. Meanwhile, though American Jews do not necessarily prioritize Israel at or near the top of their policy list, particularly among the vast majority of non-devout Jews, they almost unanimously view Israel favorably outside of the most radically Leftist cadre.[5]

How would Democratic Party leadership appear reasonable to the liberal bicoastal professional class and more moderate middle American voters—Jews included—while at least tacitly courting their progressive urban and suburban constituencies with 2020 on the horizon? How could the Resistance Party pragmatically deal with its most radical elements? Well, in short, on the matters of Israel and left-wing anti-Semitism, it caved to its increasingly anti-Semitic progressive wing, headlined by Rep. Omar and her colleague Rep. Tlaib. It tried to have its proverbial cake and eat it too by paying lip service to Israel while tsk-tsking its party's anti-Semitic freshmen congresswomen—only to then ardently defend them. This is illustrative of how the Democratic Party has moved on a variety of other matters, proving the point that Israel and the Jews are proxy issues, a leading indicator, and that the coddling of Rep. Omar represents an inflection point.

The Craven Cave

The evolution of the Democrats' position with respect to Rep. Omar's documented bigotry matches the fallacious historical narratives of victimology to which she subscribes. Paralleling her favored narrative regarding the Arab nations versus Israel, Rep. Omar has managed to turn herself from victimizer into victim—the anti-Semite suddenly the victim of the "Islamophobes." She attacks Jews, and then when condemned on a bipartisan basis, and most notably by Jews within her own caucus, she claims she was the one truly harmed—with her party's leaders ultimately blessing this preposterous inversion.

The first sign that the Democrats had no stomach for opposing Rep. Omar, and might ultimately embrace her, anti-Semitic warts and all, was that in spite of her known comments about Israeli hypnosis, in January 2019 she was appointed to the House Foreign Affairs Committee (HFAC).[6] One might chalk this decision up to the Democratic establishment's making good on its promise to provide progressives representation on key committees as a means of appeasing them, without ceding actual power.[7] This was foolish because the HFAC provided Omar a unique platform for her Blame America First-ism, inextricably intertwined with her anti-Semitic anti-Zionism. Her appointment also sent a signal to her fellow progressives that their radicalism would be tolerated with the party's blessing. Tellingly, just days before the announcement of the assignment, Rep. Omar defended her comments about Israeli hypnosis during a CNN interview.[8] That Speaker Pelosi did not rescind the assignment in spite of Rep. Omar's inflammatory defense indicates Pelosi was willing to look the other way rather than antagonize the freshman representative.

When on top of her remarks regarding Israel hypnosis, Rep. Omar raised the Jewish dual loyalty canard, suddenly it appeared the Democrats had awoken to the bigotry in their midst. On February 11, 2019, party leadership put out a statement reading in part that "…Congresswoman Omar's use of anti-Semitic tropes and prejudicial accusations about Israel's supporters is deeply offensive. We condemn these remarks and we call upon Congresswoman Omar to immediately apologize for these hurtful comments."[9] Speaker Pelosi and other senior members were joined by the chairs of the HFAC, the House Judiciary Committee, and the House Intelligence Committee—all Jews—who each issued statements criticizing Rep. Omar by name, and recognizing explicitly the anti-Semitic nature of her comments.[10] As would be shown later, non-Jews in the Democratic Party would prove comparatively quiet. Yet ardent Leftists who share Rep. Omar's sympathies with respect to Israel, like *The New York Times'* Michelle Goldberg, understood Rep. Omar's remarks for what they were, if only grudgingly because they threatened to harm their shared cause.[11] Goldberg wrote:

> …I certainly have no problem with denunciations of Aipac [The American Israel Public Affairs Committee], which plays a malign role in pushing American policy in the Middle East to the right.

> But at a moment when activists have finally pried open space in American politics to question our relationship with Israel, it's particularly incumbent on Israel's legitimate critics to avoid anything that smacks of anti-Jewish bigotry. And the idea of Jews as global puppet masters, using their financial savvy to make the gentiles do their bidding, clearly does.[12]

As chronicled earlier, Rep. Omar proceeded to equivocate on her "unequivocal" apology for these remarks, spurred by criticism in her party. She doubled and then tripled down while adding accusations of dual loyalty to her charge about the undue influence of unsavory Jewish money in American politics. In early March 2019, establishment Democratic leaders rushed to draft a resolution condemning Rep. Omar's anti-Semitism. Seemingly sensitive to the line they were walking, the party floated what appeared to be a trial balloon resolution condemning anti-Semitism, including the usage of the dual loyalty canard. However, the resolution refused to call out Rep. Omar by name, already indicating weakness.

Yet even this language did not satisfy the Left. Within hours of the release of the draft resolution, at the urging of the Congressional Progressive Caucus (CPC), Speaker Pelosi vowed to expand its language to condemn not just anti-Semitism, but anti-Muslim expressions. Later, the language would widen still more—thereby further watering it down—to include condemnation of "bigotry against minorities" as well.[13]

Leadership's inability or unwillingness to maintain the original resolution stemmed from an uproar from party progressives, who commenced their pivot to the victimhood narrative, and played the race card, as they would later do in defense of the entire Squad against Speaker Pelosi. As *The New York Times* reported: "Alexandria Ocasio-Cortez, Democrat of New York, and liberal groups like Justice Democrats and IfNotNow, a movement of young Jews dedicated to ending the Israeli occupation of the West Bank…accuse Democratic leaders of singling out a woman of color…A coalition of [leftist] Muslim and Jewish groups, including IfNotNow and Jewish Voice for Peace, intend to deliver a letter of support for Ms. Omar to Ms. Pelosi…And there is a rising backlash from the Left on social media, where a slew of left-leaning journalists and activists are posting under the hashtag #IStandWithIlhan."[14]

The day before the House resolution came to the floor, the Congressional Black Caucus emerged from a meeting with Rep. Omar, reportedly forming a circle around her. Rep. Marcia Fudge stiff-armed reporters, protecting Omar from questioning. Then, several members proceeded to hug her.[15] This would prove to be a metaphor for the party itself.

When the resolution made it to the House floor the next day, Speaker Pelosi had cravenly acquiesced to the purportedly powerless progressives. House Democrats passed a resolution that refused to condemn Rep. Omar by name and refused to solely condemn her offending anti-Semitic rhetoric.[16,17,18,19]

On the day the House passed the resolution, Speaker Pelosi stated: "I don't think that the congresswoman [Omar] perhaps appreciates the full weight of how it [her statement] was heard by other people, although I don't believe it was intended in an anti-Semitic way…But the fact is, if that's how it was interpreted, we have to remove all doubt."[20] The only doubt Speaker Pelosi removed was whether the party would stand up to its Jew-hating progressives.

In subsequent comments, Pelosi further excused and defended Rep. Omar, stating: "The incident that happened with [Omar], I don't think our colleague is anti-Semitic…I think she has a different experience in the use of words, doesn't understand that some of them are fraught with meaning."[21] Again, we know this is bogus because Jewish Minnesotans had confronted Rep. Omar on this very issue months earlier. Omar knew exactly what she was doing.

Meanwhile, Rep. Eliot Engel, the chairman of the HFAC who had rightly condemned Rep. Omar's "vile anti-Semitic slur [regarding dual loyalty]…following so closely on another instance of Ms. Omar seeming to invoke an anti-Semitic stereotype [regarding AIPAC]," indicated there would truly be no consequences for Rep. Omar's actions.[22] When asked if he would remove her from the HFAC, Rep. Engel said he could not since leadership makes such decisions, would not, and was only "looking to get rid of anti-Semitism, not…to punish anybody."[23] But if you do not punish bigots, are you not likely to get more bigotry?

The resolution, Speaker Pelosi's pathetic excuses for Rep. Omar, and Rep. Engel's falling in line with his party had the impact of freeing Rep. Omar from blame while minimizing the focus on the Jew-hatred she had unleashed into the national discourse—a Jew-hatred as we have argued intrinsic to the progressive-Islamist alliance. By expanding the resolution to condemn anti-Semitism, anti-Islamic rhetoric, as well as bigotry towards minorities—when it was Rep. Omar's Jew-hatred that had spurred the resolution in the first place—Omar achieved a coup. House Democrats treated her as the victim rather than the aggressor while furthering her narrative that Islamophobia is equivalent to anti-Semitism.

Presidential candidates Senators Bernie Sanders (D-VT) and Elizabeth Warren (D-MA), along with then-candidate Senator Kamala Harris

(D-CA), came to Rep. Omar's defense, further elevating her profile.[24] Long-time Congressman Jim Clyburn (D-SC), the Democrats' Whip, presented the most sickening rationalization of all for Rep. Omar's comments:

> …lamenting that many of the media reports surrounding the recent controversy have omitted mentioning that Omar, who was born in Somalia, had to flee the country to escape violence and spent four years in a Kenyan refugee camp before coming to the United States.
>
> **Her experience, Clyburn argued, is much more empirical—and powerful—than that of people who are generations removed from the Holocaust, Japanese internment camps during World War II and the other violent episodes that have marked history.**
>
> **"I'm serious about that. There are people who tell me, 'Well, my parents are Holocaust survivors.' 'My parents did this.' It's more personal with her," Clyburn said…[25]**
> [Emphasis added]

At the end of March 2019, following the Democrats' fig leaf resolution, Speaker Pelosi told AIPAC that "We must…be vigilant against bigoted or dangerous ideologies masquerading as policy, and that includes BDS." She added that "to be anti-Semitic is to be anti-American. It has no place in our country."[26] Fresh off her victory in the anti-Semitism resolution battle, and feeling liberated, Rep. Omar, like any bully who goes unpunished, fired back: "A condemnation for people that want to exercise their First Amendment rights is beneath any leader, and I hope that we find a better use of language when we are trying to speak as members of Congress that are sworn to protect the Constitution."[27]

Apparently, she would face no consequences. By May, Speaker Pelosi was telling a group of Reform Jews that "We have to be sure that as we fight it, we don't label everything as antisemitism, if it is not."[28] Democratic leadership further indicated it had no stomach for taking Rep. Omar to task when it refused to condemn her words trivializing the attacks of

September 11, 2001, at an April 2019 Council on American-Islamic Relations (CAIR) fundraiser. Instead, it turned to attack President Trump, this
time for his loud condemnation of her remarks, claiming he was inciting
violence. Next, in May 2019 when Rep. Rashida Tlaib peddled her historically illiterate, Hamasian hagiography on Israel's founding, the Holocaust,
and the Arabs' role in relation to both, Speaker Pelosi and House Majority
Leader Steny Hoyer responded fecklessly, defending Rep. Tlaib, as Rep.
Omar had done.

Then, in July 2019, the Democrats compounded the travesty of their
initial series of caves to Rep. Omar and her ilk with a move that would
set the tone for the rest of the Congress, and perhaps the party's future.
The House passed a resolution condemning the President of the United
States *by name* for comments Democrats cast singularly as "racist." President Donald Trump had implored certain "Progressive…Congresswomen
who originally came from countries whose governments are a complete
and total catastrophe, the worst, most corrupt and inept anywhere in the
world (if they even have a functioning government at all)" to "go back
and help fix the totally broken and crime infested places from which they
came."[29] Unlike Rep. Omar's comments, which have a long anti-Semitic
provenance, an observer would have had to read bigotry into President
Trump's words. Presumably, he was referring most of all to Rep. Omar, as
he later added that "Democrats [were] sticking up for people who speak
so badly of our Country and who, in addition, hate Israel with a true and
unbridled passion."[30] By censuring Trump individually, and condemning
his speech specifically—in contrast with the way the Democrats had
treated Rep. Omar—they delivered a clear message: Politics would trump
principle. The Democrat Old Guard had shown it would no longer engage
in even muted criticism of its party's rising radical progressive provoca-
teurs. Rather, it would wholeheartedly defend them while condemning
their condemners, including Americans, and the Israeli government.[31]
Understandably feeling empowered, in the wake of the president's tweets,
the Squad held its own nationally televised press conference challenging
him. The cave to the Blame America Firsters on the related matters of
anti-Zionism, anti-Semitism, and to an extent, jihadism appeared to be

complete.[32,33,34] To the progressives, it signaled they could act with impunity, as their future words and actions would reflect.

Progressives Are Winning the Race to the Bottom on Israel and the Jews

Why did the Democratic establishment cave? Beyond the fact that Democrats are attempting to play the racism and Islamophobia cards against critics of their young progressives for partisan political purposes, party veterans are likely seeing the writing on the wall. Even though they are right that in terms of actually moving legislation, Rep. Omar and the Squads' power is limited, the Party is trending in the Squad's direction ideologically, both generally, and on the related matters of the Jewish state and the Jewish people.

Consider the words and actions of the Democrats' 2020 presidential candidates, who presumably have a better feel for where their party's base is than anyone. Even if we were to discount their positions for the fact they are trying to appeal to their more partisan voters in primaries, while shifting later towards the "median voter" in the general election, the early returns reflect this thesis. In February 2019, every Democrat U.S. Senator at that point running for president, including Cory Booker (D-NJ), Kirsten Gillibrand (D-NY), Kamala Harris (D-CA), Bernie Sanders (D-VT), and Elizabeth Warren (D-MA) voted *against* an anti-BDS bill that passed with seventy-seven votes, including almost half of the Democratic caucus.[35] They voted as such again in spite of the BDS movement's raison d'être of Israel's destruction, and its inextricable links to the jihadist groups working to achieve it.

If one considers *The New York Times* a bellwether of Democratic opinion, then both the question it posed to every primary candidate excluding Joe Biden, and the candidates' answers, proved instructive. Of the eighteen questions the *Times* proffered across a broad array of policy issues, the *Times* chose to use one to single out Israel, inquiring: "Do you think Israel meets international standards of human rights?"[36] Rep. Omar might as well have been drafting the questions. Of the candidates who arguably gave the strongest, most unequivocal "Yeses," as of September 2019 only one was polling above 4.5 percent in the *RealClearPolitics* polling average for Democratic presidential candidates—California Senator Kamala Harris at 7 percent.[37] Senator Harris described Israel as a "democracy" with "shared values and priorities," and when prodded regarding Israel's respect for human rights "overall," she said, "Overall, yes." By December 2019, Sen. Harris had dropped out of the race. Senators Sanders and Warren, who at the same time garnered a plurality of support in the Democratic field, both essentially skirted the question. South Bend, IN Mayor Pete Buttigieg, stated outright: "Israel's human rights record is problematic and moving in the wrong direction…"

When pressed by the anti-Zionist Jewish progressive group IfNotNow to condemn the "occupation," presidential candidates Biden and Buttigieg expressed varying degrees of sympathy to the position. Biden, the purported moderate and frontrunner of the field, called the occupation "a real problem, a significant problem." Asked if he would "pressure Israel to end the occupation as president," Biden replied: "You know I have."[38] The aforementioned Buttigieg, portrayed as a moderate midwestern small-city mayor in spite of his increasingly overt Leftism, and elite pedigree and backing, said, "The occupation has to end."[39,40] Candidates Bernie Sanders and Elizabeth Warren went even further. Senator Sanders posed for a picture holding a sign reading "Jews Against the Occupation."[41] In July 2019, Sanders said he would "absolutely" consider leveraging foreign aid to entice Israel to bend towards his more pro-Arab position.[42] Senator Warren assented to a statement from IfNotNow that "We'd really love it if you…pushed the Israeli government to end occupation."[43,44] In October 2019, Warren indicated that "everything is on the table" when it comes to pushing Israel towards a two-state solution.[45] It is Warren who perhaps best illustrates just how significantly the Party has shifted on the Jewish state. As Erielle Davidson of *The Federalist* writes:

> Those curious about the direction of the Democratic Party on Israel need not look any further than Warren's campaign for a blueprint of the anti-Israel pivot. In 2014, Warren defended the right of the Israeli military to shoot at rocket launchers in self-defense against Hamas, even if

Hamas placed those rocket launchers in Palestinian hospitals and schools. Now she is hiring those who admire Hamas.[46]

Indeed, as Davidson chronicled:

Warren's recent moves follow a linear trend that the 2020 hopeful has been following since she first boycotted Israeli Prime Minister Benjamin Netanyahu's address to Congress in 2015. She was a vocal critic of the embassy move and recognition of Israel's capital in 2017 and joined Bernie Sanders in chastising Israel during the March 2018 Gaza protests without one critique of Hamas, despite Hamas' role in orchestrating the protests.

…Warren recently hired anti-Israel radical Max Berger, who helped to found the IfNotNow organization, a group that has devoted itself to damaging Israel's reputation in America under the guise of seeking an end to Israel's "occupation" of Judea and Samaria and East Jerusalem.

In doing so, IfNotNow routinely ignores Palestinian terrorism against Jews, promotes the "scholarship" of noted terrorist spokespersons, and even harasses young Jews attending Birthright trips. Berger's co-founder, Simone Zimmerman, previously served as the Jewish outreach coordinator for Bernie Sanders, until she was fired for writing a profanity-filled Facebook post directed at Benjamin Netanyahu.

Like Zimmerman, Berger has a[n] unsavory social media past. In 2013, he posted on Twitter that he "would totally be friends with Hamas…"

…It is likely Warren sees an opportunity to remain silent about Berger as a way of offering tacit support to the far-left, anti-Israel progressives of her base…[47]

Candidates like Senator Booker of New Jersey have had similar "evolutions" with respect to Israel.[48]

Unsurprisingly, Democratic presidential contenders have generally condemned the Trump administration's major policy moves with respect to Israel. While no candidate is on record as stating he or she would move the U.S. Embassy in Jerusalem back to Tel Aviv, leading candidates such as Senators Sanders and Warren were critical of the move.[49] *Axios* reported that there was an emerging consensus among leading Democrat national security and foreign policy advisors—some of whom were advising candidates at the time of the report—that a Democratic president should freeze the process of building the new embassy there, in addition to reversing a host of other Trump administration policies with respect to Israel and the Palestinian Arabs.[50] Though most candidates have remained mum on the matter, Mayor Buttigieg said in August 2019 that U.S. recognition of Israeli sovereignty over the Golan Heights "would not have come about [were he president] as part of an intervention in Israeli politics."[51] Setting aside Buttigieg's editorialization, the mayor skirted the question of whether he would have ever supported such a decision. A broad spectrum of candidates in the Democratic field from former Vice President Biden to Senators Sanders and Warren all condemned the Trump administration's November 2019 decision to no longer deem Israeli settlements in Judea and Samaria illegal.[52]

Democrats have even gone so far as to stake out positions antithetical to Israel's government on hypotheticals, that is, questions politicians generally wish to avoid. Mayor Buttigieg threatened that were he president, the U.S. would curtail aid should Israel seek to annex any of Judea and Samaria, as Prime Minister Benjamin Netanyahu had intimated he might do in the run-up to Israel's September 2019 election.[53] Buttigieg, it should be noted, hired Ned Price as one of his chief foreign policy advisors. Price was a deputy of Ben Rhodes—Iran Deal echo chamber creator and Obama administration Deputy National Security Advisor for Strategic Communications. Coincidentally, or not, Buttigieg's positions on Israel have grown significantly more hostile since commencing his run for the presidency, and he has endorsed a return to the Iran nuclear deal.[54] Of Buttigieg's threat to Netanyahu regarding annexation, J Street President Jeremy Ben-Ami was thrilled, tweeting: "Really important comments from @PeteButtigieg

[Mayor Buttigieg's Twitter handle]. Annexation would be a game-changer - and the US has every right to exert control over how its money is spent. #NoMoreBlankCheck."[55] Matt Duss, a radical anti-Zionist foreign policy advisor to Senator Bernie Sanders highlighted its significance, tweeting: "Conditioning U.S. aid to Israel to stop settlements and end occupation quickly becoming the mainstream Democratic position. This is good."[56]

Duss, it bears noting, met with aforementioned terror apologist and senior PLO official Hanan Ashrawi in May 2019.[57] In fact, all of these data points add up to a coup for among others, Ashrawi's PLO. In June 2019, Ashrawi—with whom Rep. Omar again had planned to meet during her canceled August 2019 trip—noted in public remarks:

> People who are running for office [in America] now are beginning to understand that they are going to be judged, not by how much money they take from AIPAC, that's not the issue, but by what kind of position they have, vis-a-vis issues that are important to their electorate – and their electorate is now becoming…more aware of the Palestinian question and it has become a test for many people…
>
> It's not just Rashida [Tlaib] and Ilhan [Omar] and so on who raise the issue—but Bernie Sanders in the last election spoke up, and before that there were others. But now it is becoming, I don't want to say critical mass (sic), but there is sort of greater confluence of voices (sic) approaching from different angles, but understanding they need to stop the excesses of the Israeli occupation and the need to bring justice to the Palestinian people as a right.[58]

And regarding Rep. Omar's August 2019 Israel non-trip, not one candidate in the Democratic field defended Israel's right to deny her entry to the country. Sen. Gillibrand, who has since suspended her campaign, and had replied with an unequivocal "Yes" to the *Times*' question about Israel's respect for human rights, threatened the U.S.-Israel alliance altogether in response to the Omar episode, stating:

Congress has a duty to make decisions about whether we give aid, how we protect allies such as Israel with qualitative military edge...I don't know why Netanyahu would want to deny members of Congress to come to Israel if they expect us to be that never-ending partner and friend.[59]

Even factoring in that Gillibrand has waffled on all manner of positions during her time in federal office, that a senator from a state with a large, disproportionately pro-Israel Jewish population would stake out such a position shows just how radically the Democratic Party has moved.

Last but not least, and relatedly, in contrast with a Democratic Party that consisted of notable skeptics and outright opponents at the time of President Obama's Iran Deal, like Buttigieg, most every Democratic presidential candidate supports re-entering it today.[60]

When looked at in its totality, a Democratic presidential field has likely never been as far to the Left as this one with respect to Israel, and its adversaries at home and abroad. While its less extreme candidates robotically repeat traditional lines about the historic U.S.-Israel alliance—granting several of its most irrelevant ones in the polls seem to genuinely mean it—such words have never held less weight. Sensing the impending challenges for those who are pro-Israel in the Democratic Party, in early 2019, prominent establishment Democrats set up a group called Democratic Majority for Israel. Such a group had never before been seen as needed. Whether they wish to admit it or not, that traditional Democrats felt compelled to create this outfit to combat the progressives pushing the party ever further leftward, reveals a palpable sense of panic, and peril.

At the congressional level, while House Democrats did in the summer of 2019 issue a package of putatively pro-Israel resolutions, including one combating BDS, contra Rep. Omar and her Squad mates—notwithstanding the fact that the two-state language likely undermines the resolutions' purportedly pro-Israel nature—it is instructive that this was only a *non-binding resolution*.[61] It was symbolic. As of December 2019, Speaker Pelosi had continued to refuse to bring to the House floor the anti-BDS *law* passed by a 54-vote margin in the Senate.[62] Her actions, or lack thereof, speak for themselves.

Illustrating the weakness of Democrats in the face of Rep. Omar and her colleagues, Democratic Rep. Brad Schneider, co-sponsor of the House's anti-BDS resolution, provided an unbelievable, as in literally not believable, alibi for his party's BDSers, stating: "Very simply, the fact that they support this movement, I believe they have an understanding of what they believe the movement does *without fully understanding the impact of it.*"[63] [Emphasis added]

Democrats representing the progressive and establishment wings, including Congressional Progressive Caucus chair Rep. Pramila Jayapal (D-WA), and Sen. Chris Van Hollen (D-MD) told the audience at J Street's 2019 national conference gala that they supported the inclusion of language in the Democrats' 2020 platform concerning the "occupation."[64] Regarding the previously mentioned Trump administration decision no longer to deem Israeli settlements in Judea and Samaria illegal, nearly half of all House Democrats, including Rep. Omar, signed a letter to Secretary of State Mike Pompeo expressing "strong disagreement" with the move, and urging the administration "to reverse this policy decision immediately."[65,66]

The Democrats' tolerance for hostility to the Jewish state is also reflected by its countenancing those who overtly hate it. In May 2019, at the invitation of Democratic Congresswoman Bernice Johnson of Texas, Imam Omar Suleiman delivered the opening invocation for an afternoon session of Congress.[67] As Republican Rep. Lee Zeldin of New York noted on Twitter, Suleiman "compares Israel to the Nazis & calls them terrorists, supports [the] Muslim Brotherhood, incites violence calling for a Palestinian antifada & the end of zionism, etc." Suleiman has also called homosexuality a "disease."[68] There was no outcry from the Democrats. Rep. Omar endorses his work on social media.[69]

Meanwhile, it would appear that progressives smell blood in the water when it comes to pro-Israel congressional Democrats. Activists associated with the Squad and Bernie Sanders are seeking to primary those they might call "soft-on-Israel" incumbents. For example, the aforementioned Rep. Eliot Engel of New York is facing two progressive challengers in 2020, one of whom is backed by the group behind AOC's successful run for Congress, Justice Democrats.[70] Rep. Engel too is being targeted by the Bernie Sanders-backed group Roots Action, which is also seeking to unseat other relatively pro-Israel colleagues including Josh Gottheimer of New Jersey, Steny Hoyer of Maryland, Brad Schneider of Illinois, and Juan Vargas of California, among other relative moderates.[71] Longtime New York Democrat Representative Nita Lowey, one of the more pro-Israel members of her party who as noted had previously been involved in a skirmish with Rep. Omar, decided not to run for re-election in 2020. She too was facing an ideologically Squad-like progressive primary challenger—the first such challenge in three decades—though she scoffed at the idea that the challenger prompted her decision not to seek re-election.[72,73,74]

Returning to Gottheimer, he—a pro-Israel Democrat from a previously red New Jersey district, who, like Rep. Engel, is Jewish—has been hard hit by the progressive publication, *The Intercept*, for being insufficiently "Woke," notably regarding the Jewish state.[75,76,77] Gottheimer has also been the subject of apparent dirty tricks intended to damage his re-election efforts.[78] The second-term representative seemed to be paying a price for having challenged Rep. Tlaib for comments similar to Rep. Omar's smacking of "dual loyalty," when she tweeted in January 2019 that pro-Israel and anti-BDS congressmen "forgot what country they represent."[79]

In March 2019, following the Democrats' cave on the non-Omar Omar "hate speech" resolution, freshman Rep. Max Rose, a Democrat from New York, who is also Jewish and represents a purple district, apologized to Jewish constituents at a town hall for "failing" them "Because I know that Congresswoman Ilhan Omar's comments really caused you all a lot of pain by bringing up anti-Semitic tropes." Rep. Rose continued: "I am not satisfied with what I've seen thus far [from Rep. Omar], I'm not…To equate Jewish organizations with the NRA, of course I'm upset. Of course I'm not satisfied and I don't know any who are either. That's why the first thing that I said is that 'I'm sorry,' I'm sorry because I couldn't protect you from this. And that takes a lot to say."[80] Ignoring the dig at the National Rifle Association, Rep. Rose's comments were telling.

One is left to wonder: Can any Democratic representative but one who is Jewish and/or who resides in a district with a sizable Jewish constituency dare challenge Rep. Omar and her Squad mates? If not, what does it say about the Democratic Party now, and in the future?

In Rep. Omar's own district, there were stirrings among those who had conducted her anti-Semitism intervention about a potential primary challenge. While visiting the district in fall 2019, the author heard rumblings that former Senator Al Franken, who resigned amid #MeToo furor, which he seems to regret, might be up to the task—though any victory would qualify as a demotion.[81] As of December 2019, though several candidates had filed to run against Rep. Omar in the 2020 primary, no such serious challenge had materialized.[82] Omar was likely perceived as too strong by prominent Democrats, a reality borne out in unreleased polling of primary voters that the author reviewed.[83]

Progressive-backed Jew-hatred has also seeped into state-level politics. In this Hall of Shame, an honorable mention must go to California, the bright blue state with more votes in the electoral college than any other. At the Democratic Party's 2019 State Convention, progressives—like Ilhan Omar had done implicitly in her pro-BDS resolution—put forth a resolution monstrously seeking to portray Israel as being Nazi-esque by claiming it was complicit in the Tree of Life Massacre in Pittsburgh.[84] But this was not all. As Aaron Kliegman wrote in the *Washington Free Beacon*:

> ...one resolution demanded a Palestinian "right of return," which mandates that the Arabs—and *each and every one* of their descendants—who fled what is now Israel during the failed Arab war of 1948 to destroy the Jewish state, should be allowed to return to the land. The two other resolutions called for returning the Golan Heights, a strategic region on Israel's northern border, to Syria, which previously controlled it.
>
> Taken together, these resolutions comprise a call to destroy Israel.[85]

Democrats' positions on Israel and anti-Semitism did not emerge spontaneously after the 2018 midterm elections. Party leaders have been trending this way for some time. Consider the symbolic if not substantive acts taken by Democrats at their last two national conventions. During the 2016 Democratic National Convention (DNC), some of Bernie Sanders's delegates were seen waving Palestinian flags on the convention floor. Sanders's fans, as well as protesters, were seen burning Israeli flags outside the convention while crying "Long live the intifada," and "Death to the U.S. empire!"[86,87] The senator had appointed at least three anti-Israel appointees to the party's platform committee, including the aforementioned then-Rep. Ellison, academic Cornel West, and Arab American Institute head James Zogby.[ii,88] All three of these men have defended Rep. Omar, and hold like-minded positions on Israel and Jews. West's glowing words are perhaps most representative, having spoken of his "deep and profound admiration for Sister Ilhan's [Omar's] courage and willingness to speak truth from her heart as it relates to the suffering of precious Palestinians."[89] The 2012 DNC presaged what was to come in 2016. At the previous confab, DNC delegates booed loudly over presiding then-Los Angeles Mayor Antonio Villaraigosa's attempt to re-incorporate G-d, and Jerusalem as the capital of Israel, to the party platform. Villaraigosa embarrassingly rammed the changes through over the apparent objections of the party establishment—with President Obama at pains to take credit for the reversal.[90] Nevertheless, the party removed several pro-Israel planks from the platform, while omitting language with respect to the Palestinian Arabs it had included historically, including in its 2008 iteration, that effectively made the document more pro-Palestinian Arab.[91,92]

Democrats broke against Israel on pivotal policy matters as well. During President Obama's push to clinch the Iran nuclear deal, Israeli Prime Minister Benjamin Netanyahu came to America to deliver a plea to Congress in March 2015 arguing against the non-binding commitment, which the Trump administration would later vacate. Prime Minister Netanyahu said the deal would threaten "the very survival of the State of Israel." According to *Reuters*, up to sixty House Democrats boycotted the speech in protest.[93] During the heat of the debate, in an implicit nod to

---

ii   West, it bears noting, previously served on an advisory council of prominent black figures convened by Barack Obama during his 2008 campaign, though he would ultimately become a harsh critic of the president—in part for not fulfilling his radical expectations. See: https://www.nytimes.com/2008/02/12/us/politics/12obama.html and https://www.theguardian.com/commentisfree/2017/jan/09/barack-obama-legacy-presidency.

the dual loyalty canard, in September 2015 *The New York Times* issued an infographic breaking down Iran Deal opponents on the Democratic side by whether they were Jewish or not.[94] Among the few outspoken Democrat opponents of Iran Deal was Senator Bob Menendez of New Jersey. He appeared to pay a dear price for his heresy. The Obama administration's Department of Justice filed an indictment against Sen. Menendez implicating him in bribery and underage prostitution that coincided with his criticism of the deal.[95] Was this political punishment for crossing the leader of the party on a deal the Jewish state believed imperiled its existence?

Democratic Politicians Are Following Their Increasingly Leftist Constituents

The question of why Democrats running for president, in Congress, and at the state level have swung so far to the Left on Israel, and related matters requires an explanation. Politicians go where the votes are. All of the data points we have highlighted heretofore must be weighed against the backdrop of a changing Democratic electorate. The Democratic Party is no longer the Party of John F. Kennedy or Bill Clinton—at least that is not where its energy lies. Rather, it is far closer to the Party of Jimmy Carter and Barack Obama. With respect to Israel and Jews, as left-wing publications like *Vice* argued explicitly in February of 2019, these have become "wedge issues" for Democrats.[96] The irony is particularly rich here given that just months before *Vice* ran that headline, former Democratic National Committee (DNC) chair Rep. Debbie Wasserman-Schultz of Florida had told *The New York Times*: "Anyone trying to use Israel as a political wedge and football doesn't have Israel's best interest at heart and should be ashamed of themselves."[97]

Rep. Wasserman-Schultz was perhaps ignoring mounting evidence in her caucus. The colleague who came in second in the race to serve as her successor, landing the position as Deputy Chairman of the DNC—the number two person in the party establishment—was none other than then-Rep. Keith Ellison. The Islamist-tied, anti-Israel radical who now serves as Minnesota's state attorney general, assumed his current position after vacating his congressional seat. His replacement was none other than Ilhan Omar.

In March of 2019, *The New York Times Magazine* ran a feature titled "How the Battle Over Israel and Anti-Semitism is Fracturing American Politics."[98] But as the article itself illustrated, the fractures are all on Rep. Wasserman-Schultz's side. The Democratic Party's recent actions and polling numbers bear this out.

Per Pew, in 2001, only 29 percent of Democrats identified as "liberal;" by 2018, 44 percent did, a 15 percent jump.[99] In 2001, liberal Democrats sympathized with Israel over Palestinian Arabs at a rate of 48 percent—11 percentage points higher than "Conservative/Moderate Democrats;" by 2018, liberal Democrats sympathized with Palestinian Arabs over Israel at a rate of 35 percent to 19 percent. "Conservative/Moderate Democrats" sympathized with Israel over the Palestinian Arabs at the same rate that liberals sympathized with Palestinian Arabs over Israel.[100] A February 2019 Gallup poll found that "Liberal Democrats are [the] only party/ideology group not partial to Israel." Its results showed that among this group, net sympathy towards Israel is today only plus 3 percent, whereas going back to the 2001-2004 time period, it was plus 15 percent.[101] Summarizing an October 2018 YouGov/Economist poll on American views on Israel, the left-wing *Haaretz* wrote that "support for Israel is directly co-related to gender, age, economic status, and political outlook. It is strongest among older, well-to-do, conservative white men and weakest among young, liberal, minorities and women."[102]

So the Democratic Party has grown increasingly Leftist; the Left has grown increasingly pro-Palestinian Arab; and its demographically most-favored, growing voter segments represent the least pro-Israel cadre of the U.S. voting population.[103]

As *The New York Times Magazine* described this constituency in the aforementioned March 2019 feature:

> Members of the Democratic Party's progressive activist base...find themselves light years from their representatives in Washington. The Movement for Black Lives, the racial-justice coalition that includes the Black Lives Matter network, has called for supporting divestment campaigns with the goal of ending American military

aid to Israel; the Democratic Socialists of America has endorsed B.D.S. Kate Gould, a lobbyist for the Friends Committee on National Legislation, a Quaker group dedicated to peace, justice and environmental steward-ship, told me that generally even progressive members of Congress frame development aid for the Palestinians merely as help for people who are suffering. There is rarely any acknowledgment, she says, "that they are suffering because we are funding their oppression. Hello! You do know that we are funding the occupation?"[104]

And as mentioned previously, these organized groups, including Rep. Omar's "intersectional feminists," are increasingly anti-Israel if not full-on pro-*Judenrein*. As *The New York Times* noted, "Jewish organizers of the 2017 Women's March were deliberately sidelined, excluded and attacked by some of its founders, at least one of whom, activist Tamika Mallory, is an unapologetic admirer of Louis Farrakhan, the Nation of Islam's unapologetically anti-Semitic leader." Mallory had called Farrakhan the "GOAT [greatest of all time]," and the Women's March had reportedly used individuals linked to Farrakhan's Nation of Islam to provide security.[105,106] Unsurprisingly, Mallory has defended both Reps. Omar and Tlaib in the wake of the various controversies they created with their rhetoric.[iii,107,108]

In recent years, organizers of the related so-called "Dyke Marches" in Chicago and Washington D.C. have barred Israeli and Jewish symbols from their events.[109,110,111] Two self-proclaimed Jewish anti-Zionist leaders of the 2019 D.C. Dyke March stated that a rainbow flag with the Star of David represents "violent nationalism," and "does not fit with our vision of queer liberation…we need the march to be a space that is as welcoming to Palestinian Dykes as it is to Jewish Dykes."[112] Joel Kotkin summarizes the political state of play in *City Journal* thusly:

---

iii Perhaps not coincidentally, it appears Ms. Mallory and Rep. Tlaib shared an affinity for Farrakhan, as Rep. Tlaib herself had published an article in one of the Nation of Islam's publications back in 2006. See: https://www.foxnews.com/politics/rashida-tlaib-once-wrote-column-for-nation-of-islams-publication-reprinting-farrakhans-anti-semitic-comments.

Much of the Democratic Party coalition—the progressive Left, minorities, and millennials—has turned decisively against Israel. The most anti-Israel members of Congress tend to come not from the backwoods of Alabama but from "progressive" inner cities, coastal tech-burbs, and academic communities. In polls, minorities and millennials are consistently less sympathetic to Jews and Israel than older, generally white Republicans. According to the Anti-Defamation League (ADL), African-Americans are twice as likely to be anti-Semitic than the general population; roughly 12 percent of blacks express anti-Semitic views. The attitudes of native-born Americans of Hispanic descent track fairly closely with those of other Americans, but Hispanics born abroad are three times as likely to dislike Jews. Equally disturbing, notes Pew, warm feelings toward Jews are strongest among seniors, at 74 percent, but drop to 62 percent among millennials.[113]

That Israel is increasingly becoming a one-party issue, as less-progressive Democrats openly lament, reflects the party's leftward shift, which began well before the presidential election of even Barack Obama.

Among Republicans, there has been no "fracturing." They have demonstrated this by concrete actions, including the Trump administration's: doggedly defending Israel at the infamously hostile United Nations—even seeking to challenge the prior president's anti-Israel resolutions prior to being seated;[114] cutting hundreds of millions of dollars in funding to the anti-Israel, so-called UN Relief and Works Agency (UNRWA);[115,116] withdrawing from the anti-Israel UN Human Rights Council; voting against an annual resolution over which the Obama administration had historically abstained condemning Israel's "occupation" of the Golan Heights;[117] condemning the International Criminal Court over its targeting of Israel;[118] formally recognizing the Golan Heights as part of Israel by presidential proclamation;[119] removing language referring to the West Bank, Golan Heights, and Gaza as "occupied" territories in State Department documentation;[120] closing the PLO's Washington, D.C. office over its unwillingness to enter negotiations with Israel;[121] slashing hundreds of millions of dollars more in aid that would have been directed to Palestinian Arabs in Judea and Samaria, and Gaza;[122] expanding the State Department's working definition of anti-Semitism to include examples such as Holocaust inversion, in accordance with the International Holocaust Remembrance Alliance (IHRA);[123] applying the IHRA definition and examples—which focus on anti-Semitism masquerading as anti-Zionism—within the Education Department for use in adjudicating cases involving alleged discrimination against Jewish students implicating Title VI of the Civil Rights Act of 1964;[124,125] issuing a related executive order on combating anti-Semitism calling for "the executive branch to enforce Title VI against prohibited forms of discrimination rooted in anti-Semitism as vigorously as against all other forms of discrimination prohibited by Title VI," including applying the IHRA definition and examples;[126] reversing the Obama administration's position on Israeli settlements in Judea and Samaria in declaring their establishment no longer "per se inconsistent with international law;"[127] and moving the U.S. Embassy to Jerusalem, fulfilling a (at least formerly) bipartisan U.S. commitment that all prior administrations had failed to keep.[128] The Trump administration took these actions while concurrently exiting the Iran nuclear deal, and seeking to squeeze the Iranian regime with a multifaceted policy of maximum pressure. Republicans in Congress overwhelmingly back these efforts, and similar ones, including opposing BDS.

The policies of President Trump and Republicans in Congress reflect the GOP electorate. According to the aforementioned Pew poll, since 1978, Republicans have never shown greater sympathy for Israel over Palestinian Arabs, at a rate of 79 percent to 27 percent for Democrats, with conservative Republicans most sympathetic of all. The spread with Democrats has never been greater during that period. The aforementioned February 2019 Gallup poll similarly showed Republicans sympathizing more with Israel over the Palestinian Arabs at a rate of 76 percent to 43 percent for Democrats—for the Republicans albeit down from an all-time high of 87 percent in 2018.[129] When the Left points to a scourge of "far-right" anti-Semitism—while either ignoring or falsely attributing the accelerating attacks on the most pro-Israel and politically conservative Jews (the Orthodox) in the bluest of areas (like New York City) to the "right"—they not only obfuscate the truth, but wittingly smear conservatives and Republicans, who demonstrate by word and deed that they are America's preeminent philo-Semites.[130]

The Elephant in the Room: Democrats are Trading Jewish Votes for Muslim Votes

Consider these political and ideological trends along with the fact that American Muslims, an increasingly powerful and growing political cohort, identify as Democrats at a rate of nearly 70 percent.[131] In the 2018 election cycle, a record number of Muslim Americans ran for state or national office, the most in nearly two decades.[132] The U.S. Muslim population is expected to double by 2050.[133] Presumably, the number of Muslim voters and candidates will only increase. They may well support those with views akin to Reps. Omar and Tlaib, who are themselves representatives of heavily Muslim districts. It would appear that Muslims will grow ever more important to the Democratic Party due to the confluence of these political factors.

There is a philosophical basis for this assumption as well. As the Democrats continue their leftward march, the imperative to champion Muslims, and especially Muslim immigrants, should only increase given their commanding position atop the progressive identity politics hierarchy. Bernie Sanders's 2016 strategy in the Michigan Democratic primary, which he won by a small margin partially attributable to his extensive courting of Muslim voters, may prove to be the model for the Democratic Party.[134] In a sign of the times, at the August 2019 gathering of the Islamic Society of North America (ISNA), touted as the largest such gathering of Muslim Americans, the Hamas/Muslim Brotherhood-linked group hosted its first-ever U.S. presidential forum. Sanders and former Obama Housing and Urban Development Secretary Julián Castro attended.[135] In future presidential elections, expect the number of candidates participating to grow.

By contrast, the American Jewish population, which also votes reliably Democrat, is expected to decline from 1.8 percent to 1.4 percent by 2050. The only growing segment of Jews, the Orthodox, tend to vote majority

Republican.[136] Ideologically, one might expect that the views of the likes of Ilhan Omar would repulse Jewish voters, threatening Democrats' hold on a prominent longtime constituency. But polling on any number of issues indicates otherwise.[137] Among less religious Jews, which is the majority of American Jews, progressivism predominates.[138] An August 2019 Gallup poll indicates that Jews identify as liberal at a rate of 19 percent above the total U.S. population, making Jews the most liberal religious group of all that Gallup measures.[139] This is particularly true among younger Jews, who tend to be more left-leaning, and thus less pro-Israel, if not overtly anti-Israel.[140,141] These are the people who staff and support the likes of IfNotNow.[142] Even if a mass "Jexodus" were to miraculously materialize, with Jews exiting the Democratic Party en masse—a highly unlikely but not totally impossible to imagine phenomenon given the Jewish exodus from the Corbyn Labour Party in Great Britain—they are likely going to represent a declining share of the voting public.[143,144] Last but not least, in the eyes of the progressive faithful, Jews are likely to continue to be downgraded within the Democratic Party given their "privileged" place in the progressive hierarchy of identity politics. In the years ahead, Jews are therefore likely to prove ever less relevant to the Democrats' designs, and thus ultimately find themselves ignored, supplanted by Muslims.

American Politics on Israel and the Jews Reflects the Progressivism of our Institutions

Politics is downstream from culture. It would stand to reason then that the decline in sympathy towards Israel and the Jews in our political class reflects increasing progressivism in our culture. That this has occurred is almost self-evident.

Consider the modern college campus. Edward Said's shadow looms over it. Institutions of higher education have become hotbeds of anti-Semitism masquerading as anti-Zionism.[145,146] This view prevails among academics broadly, who tend to be disproportionately on the Left.[147] While in the past it may have been most visible in Middle East studies departments, this sentiment has transcended academic disciplines.[148,149] As a testament to this, anti-Semitism masquerading as anti-Zionism has increasingly become an essential component of the Woke ideology developed by black nationalist academics.[150] The extent to which U.S. college campuses have been corrupted is reflected in the way BDS has prevailed over them. According to *The New York Times Magazine*:

> Since 2005, resolutions to boycott or divest from companies tied to Israeli settlements, occupation or violations of Palestinian human rights have been introduced at dozens of American campuses, including Stanford and Berkeley, Oberlin and Barnard, George Washington and the University of Chicago. Of these, about two-thirds voted for divestment at some point, though at only one, Hampshire College, did administrators agree, in 2009, to divest endowments from companies connected to human rights violations in Israel.[151]

Teachers bear substantial responsibility for this phenomenon, as they are some of the strongest BDS advocates.[152] According to Mitchell Bard, a foreign policy expert and Executive Director of the Jewish Virtual Library, more than 2,000 professors support BDS.[153,154,155,156] In September 2018, one such University of Michigan Professor reneged on a commitment to write a letter of recommendation in support of a student when he discovered that the pupil was seeking the letter to study abroad in Israel.[157] Bard reports that over 1,000 professors signed a petition in support.[158,159]

Schools across the country today feature definitionally anti-Semitic "Israel Apartheid" weeks, replete with a bevy of radical Leftist and Islamist speakers, and fake walls constructed in the middle of campuses meant to symbolize Israel's security barriers.[160] These events have been co-opted as part of the intersectional cause, with *The New York Times* reporting that they are now led in some instances by "black, Latino and Native American students." At one University of Michigan event, a Latino campus group member reportedly shouted, "We have the same goal: fighting white supremacy and xenophobia." Others yelled: "From Palestine to Mexico, all the walls have got to go!"[161]

In this cauldron of Jew-hatred, according to House testimony delivered by Mort Klein, chairman of the Zionist Organization of America (ZOA), in April 2019, the number of attacks on Jewish students on campus is swelling. The perpetrators are almost universally Rep. Omar's progressive-Islamists, not the "far-right." Says Klein:

> During more than 15 years that ZOA has been combating campus antisemitism, ZOA has never received a single complaint about antisemitic discrimination, harassment or intimidation perpetrated by neo-Nazis or white supremacists. By contrast, ZOA's Center for Law and Justice and campus professionals receive hundreds (sic) calls from students about antisemitic harassment, discrimination and intimidation perpetrated by the hate group "Students for Justice in Palestine"(SJP) —which reportedly has approximately 200 chapters on campuses across the country —and SJP's allies. It's always about the Muslims and left attacking, verbally abusing, and threatening Jewish and pro-Israel students. The Amcha Initiative database list of almost 2,600 incidents confirms that SJP and its allies are the perpetrators in most incidents on U.S. campuses...[iv,162,163]

As Attorney General William Barr summarized it in a July 2019 conference on combating anti-Semitism: "On college campuses today, Jewish students who support Israel are frequently targeted for harassment, Jewish student organizations are marginalized, and **progressive Jewish students are told they must denounce their beliefs and their heritage in order be part of 'intersectional' causes.**"[164] [Emphasis added] Writer Daniella Greenbaum Davis notes that the effort to drive pro-Israel students from campus life extends beyond "intersectional causes," to virtually all types

---

iv   This fact is reflected outside of the campus as well. According to a fall 2018 report in *The New York Times*, in New York, which has seen a disturbing increase in anti-Jewish attacks on the disproportionately Jewish community in recent years, "not one person caught or identified as the aggressor in an anti-Semitic hate crime has been associated with a far right-wing group, [per] Mark Molinari, commanding officer of the police department's Hate Crimes Task Force..." See: https://www.nytimes.com/2018/10/31/nyregion/jewish-bias-safety-nyc.html.

of activism.[165] As noted previously, groups like the Marxist-Leninist Palestinian terrorist group Popular Front for the Liberation of Palestine have increasingly become cause célèbres on college campuses.[166]

This incendiary view of Israel and the Jews also trickles down to lower levels of education. In August 2019, California was considering instituting an ethnic studies curriculum in public schools with an Arabist, anti-Zionist, and anti-Semitic bent, pushed by education department personnel who hold views much the same.[167]

Turning to another pivotal American institution, if, as anti-Semitic conspiracy theorists suggest, Jews control the media, one wonders how they might explain that such an anti-Israel and anti-Semitic bias pervades it. In this regard, Matti Friedman, a Jerusalem-based Israeli-Canadian reporter formally of the *Associated Press* (AP) is worth quoting at length. In a landmark 2014 exposé of journalists who cover Israeli-Arab matters, Friedman wrote that in such circles:

> …a distaste for Israel has come to be something between an acceptable prejudice and a prerequisite for entry. I don't mean a critical approach to Israeli policies or to the ham-fisted government currently in charge in this country, but a belief that to some extent the Jews of Israel are a symbol of the world's ills, particularly those connected to nationalism, militarism, colonialism, and racism—an idea quickly becoming one of the central elements of the "progressive" Western zeitgeist, spreading from the European left to American college campuses and intellectuals, including journalists. In this social group, this sentiment is translated into editorial decisions made by individual reporters and editors covering Israel, and this, in turn, gives such thinking the means of mass self-replication.[168]

More pointedly, as he put it in *Tablet*:

> When the people responsible for explaining the world to the world, journalists, cover the Jews' war as more worthy

of attention than any other, when they portray the Jews of Israel as the party obviously in the wrong, when they omit all possible justifications for the Jews' actions and obscure the true face of their enemies, **what they are saying to their readers—whether they intend to or not—is that Jews are the worst people on earth. The Jews are a symbol of the evils that civilized people are taught from an early age to abhor.** International press coverage has become a morality play starring a familiar villain.

…You don't need to be a history professor, or a psychiatrist, to understand what's going on. Having rehabilitated themselves against considerable odds in a minute corner of the earth, the descendants of powerless people who were pushed out of Europe and the Islamic Middle East have become what their grandparents were—the pool into which the world spits. The Jews of Israel are the screen onto which it has become socially acceptable to project the things you hate about yourself and your own country. The tool through which this psychological projection is executed is the international press.[169] [Emphasis added]

The New York Times, the preeminent representative of the overwhelmingly Left news media, has proven so hostile and in some cases ignorant on matters regarding Israel and Judaism, that the English language Jewish newspaper, *Algemeiner*, has a columnist, Ira Stoll, dedicated to correcting and critiquing the "paper of records'" rampant errors, and deeply rooted biases on these issues. This is to say nothing of the *Times*' printing of the previously described virulently anti-Semitic cartoon featuring President Donald Trump and Prime Minister Netanyahu, and the graphic it published flagging Democratic opponents to the Iran nuclear deal by whether they were Jewish or not.

Small examples from other sources reflect these greater biases in the media as well. In 2015, the *AP* described the Palestinian Arab jihadists who took hostage and murdered eleven members of the Israeli Olympic team at the 1972 Munich games as "terrorists." By 2019, the *AP* was calling them "guerrillas," which the news source then softened to "gunmen."[170]

Networks welcome television personalities with a history of making anti-Semitic comments like Al Sharpton and Temple Professor Marc Lamont Hill. And naturally, Reps. Omar and Tlaib have been media darlings from the start. Outlets have not only sung their praises but have ignored, if not actively suppressed, numerous newsworthy stories that might damage them politically while attacking those who cover them.[171,172] This is to say nothing of the individuals at major media organizations whose anti-Semitic remarks have been exposed just in recent months.[173,174]

In the related area of pop culture, the message rings the same. As Victor Davis Hanson chronicles:

> Rap and hip-hop music now routinely incorporate anti-Semitic lyrics and themes of Jews as oppressors—note the lyrics of rappers such as Malice, Pusha T, The Clipse, Ghostface Killah, Gunplay, Ice Cube, Jay-Z, Mos Def, and Scarface. More recently, LeBron James, the Los Angeles Lakers basketball legend, tweeted out the anti-Semitic lyrics of rapper 21 Savage: "We been getting that Jewish money, everything is Kosher." LeBron was puzzled about why anyone would take offense, much less question him, a deified figure. He has a point, given that singling out Jews as money-grubbers, cheats, and conspirators has become a sort of rap brand, integral to the notion of the rapper as Everyman's pushback against the universal oppressor. The music executive and franchise owner is the new Pawnbroker, and his demonization is often cast as no big deal at best and at worst as a sort of legitimate cry of the heart from the oppressed.[175]

The artists who engage in boycotts of Israel rarely if ever pay a price for it. One can also detect a bias given the cynical way in which Israel and its security authorities are portrayed in major network programs. On the other hand, the likes of Reps. Omar and Tlaib are feted on late-night television, lobbed softball questions to the extent they are ever forced to account for their anti-Semitic bigotry.[176]

There is no stigma around purveyors of such hate. Needless to say, from the academy to the media, and pop culture, we are not talking about the realms of Tea Party conservatives. Where progressives predominate, so too does anti-Semitism masquerading as anti-Zionism. We live with and will rue its consequences in our political system. One of the great contributors to the present peril is a figure who preceded Rep. Omar, and arguably paved the path for her success, yet who she has ironically maligned. Now, we turn to his unappreciated role.

CHAPTER 8

HOW BARACK OBAMA MADE ILHAN OMAR POSSIBLE

Introduction

President Barack Obama is the missing link in the story of Rep. Ilhan Omar's rise, and its relation to what is transpiring in the Democratic Party. Though he has not received credit for it, President Obama created the precedent for and the conditions that enabled Rep. Omar to enter the American political scene. His policies and rhetoric derived from a radical worldview and reflected a set of associations substantially similar to those of Rep. Ilhan Omar. The two longtime community organizers, influenced by their roots in the global Left-Islamist milieu, are fellow travelers.[1]

Their views had previously been treated as fringe, and in the recent past would have been dismissed. Obama helped make them mainstream. He created a "safe space" for Omar's unsafe, unabashed radicalism by presenting his own in a polished manner, under cover of soaring rhetoric and an aesthetic of moderation, with the help of a pliant and sycophantic media.[2] Through his superficial moderation, President Obama shifted the national Overton Window leftward, opening a Pandora's Box of progressivism. Rep. Omar, and the rise of her fellow Squadmates, are but one consequence of President Obama's success in normalizing such radicalism. And as with Rep. Omar, the great proxy for President Obama's views on

170

America and the West concerned Israel, the Jews, and their enemies—
and ours.

Obama's Canary in the Coal Mine

In the waning days of the Obama presidency, facing few political
constraints and about to relinquish power to a figure who threatened to
upend his entire agenda, the lame-duck administration focused on its true
priorities. Among them: Settling one last score with Israel by way of a
devastating action that could not be undone.

On December 23, 2016, the United Nations Security Council (UNSC)
adopted Resolution 2334. In contravention of long-standing U.S. policy to
veto such measures, America abstained. The jackals frolicked. This would
be a fitting epigraph for the Obama years. While the administration's critics
often equated inaction with feebleness, the reality was that as with UNSCR
2334, President Obama acted at times with restraint, and other times quite
forcefully—but always in relentless pursuit of his detrimental global goals.
What critics saw as weakness, he saw as strength when measured by fealty
to social justice. The Simon Wiesenthal Center saw something else altogether: Anti-Semitism. It ranked the Obama administration's abstention as
the number one such act of 2016.[3]

Indeed, UNSC Resolution 2334 was a classic of the Israel-hater
genre. The headline of the UN press release, summarizing the resolution,
understated its significance: "Israel's Settlements Have No Legal Validity,
Constitute Flagrant Violation of International Law, Security Council Reaf-
firms."[4] The resolution went far beyond so-called "settlements"—legitimate
residences in the heart of the Jews' Biblical homeland in Judea and Samaria
that for years had drawn Obama's ire.[5] It cast Israel as an "occupying
power." It deemed illegitimate Israel's construction on its own land, and
treated the lands surrendered by the Arabs who sought to destroy Israel,
including East Jerusalem, as "Palestinian territory." It threatened Israel's
right to its holiest sites in Jerusalem. It opened the door to lawfare in international courts against the Jewish state and paved the way for increased
BDS activity.[6] Perhaps most importantly, it overturned the United Nations
resolution stipulating that in a future peace negotiation, Israel would only

cede some portion of lands claimed in response to the impending 1967 invasion, consistent with its security needs. As American-turned-Israeli writer-turned-politician Caroline Glick described it in the *Jerusalem Post*:

> Resolution 2334 asserts that Israel has no right to any of the lands it took control over during the war. From the Western Wall to Shiloh, from Hebron to Ariel, 2334 says all Israeli presence in the areas beyond the 1949 armistice lines is crime.

> Given that Israel has no right to hold territory under 2334, it naturally follows that the Palestinians have no incentive to give Israel peace. So they won't. The peace process, like the two-state solution, ended…to the raucous applause of all Security Council members.[7]

Glick, who incidentally grew up in the same Hyde Park neighborhood in Chicago where Obama began his political rise, and likewise attended Obama's alma mater of Columbia University, concluded in a separate column that:

> Resolution 2334 serves to criminalize Israel and its people and to undermine Israel's right to exist, while embracing Palestinian terrorists and empowering them in their war to annihilate Israel.

> America's historic refusal to countenance such actions at the UN Security was never a purely altruistic position. It was also a stand for American power and the inherent justice of American superpower status and global leadership.

> …Obama is not leading the war against Israel at the Security Council simply to advance the PLO's war for the annihilation of Israel. He is acting in this manner to undermine the legitimacy of American power.[8]

"Undermining the legitimacy of American power" might be the most concise formulation of Rep. Omar's foreign policy agenda. That President Obama "accomplished" this feat so acutely by way of Israel policy underscores its outsized significance as a measure of America's steadfastness to its principles. Though he would not go so far as to praise the Obama administration's resolution machinations, President Obama's Arabist friend, and a former Arafat mouthpiece, Rashid Khalidi—the *Edward Said* Professor of Arab Studies at Columbia University—did acknowledge that it, and a related speech from Secretary of State John Kerry: "offer[ed] an opening for an overdue global response to the arrogance of the Israeli and American enablers of the denial of the inalienable rights of the Palestinian people."[9,10] What did it say about the direction of the Democratic Party that its leaders were becoming enablers of the denial of the inalienable rights of the Israeli people? This was global social justice in action.

The administration's abstention was at once both brazen and cowardly—brazen in that the Obama team undermined the Jewish state to an unprecedented degree at the world's preeminent forum of anti-Zionism and anti-Semitism, and cowardly because it refused to "vote its 'conscience'" by affirming the resolution.[11] Its unwillingness to quash the measure was so outrageous and out of line with long-standing U.S. policy that it drew bipartisan condemnation across the U.S. political establishment.[12,13]

And it gets worse. Unbeknownst to observers at the time, the Obama administration allegedly did more than merely abstain. With the benefit of several years of distance, in March 2019 *The New York Times* reported that according to an anonymous former Obama administration official, the White House was not an innocent bystander in resolution deliberations.[14] It had cynically pushed for the resolution not to be brought to the UN Security Council prior to the 2016 presidential election—knowing full well it would pass—lest its position rankle Democratic donors, and force Hillary Clinton to take a politically fraught stand on the issue.[15] In the context of the resolution ruse, the aforementioned Ben Rhodes, President Obama's Deputy National Security Advisor for Strategic Communications—with whom he was said to have a "mind meld"—seemed to channel Rep. Omar in the *Times* article referenced, stating: "The Washington view of Israel-Palestine is still shaped by the donor class…The donor class is profoundly to the right of where the activists are…" Rhodes indicated that some members of the Obama administration wished to, according to the article's author, "adopt a more assertive policy toward Israel," but felt constrained.[i,ii,16] There are conflicting accounts as to the full extent of the Obama administration's role in the drafting, lobbying, and bringing of the resolution to the floor, and seemingly there were fissures within the administration over how to approach it. Israeli Prime Minister Benjamin Netanyahu was adamant that the Obama team led the effort to see it passed.[17] Regardless, that the Obama administration decided to abstain, and was adamantly opposed to casting a veto, reflected a sea change in the Democratic Party. Its left-most wing was winning.

Even before UNSCR 2234, President Obama had normalized unseen levels of Democratic "anti-Zionism." As the leader of the party for eight years, he had audaciously put the screws to Israel, and elevated its sworn enemies, with a litany of words and deeds.[18] The abstention and passage of UNSCR 2234 was merely the apotheosis of his efforts—one final act in an international forum devoted seemingly above all else to legitimizing tyranny while delegitimizing Israel and the West, representing the culmination of Obama's work to reorient U.S. foreign policy towards his "progressive" worldview.[19] Its latent anti-Semitism was a proxy for the administration's broader progressive-Islamist ethos.[20]

---

i   Rep. Omar would endorse Rhodes's condemnation of Israel in July of 2019 when it was reported that Israeli authorities would be demolishing certain structures in East Jerusalem. U.S. Ambassador to Israel David Friedman challenged Rhodes and Omar's portrayal of the demolition as racist, tweeting: "Real News: Demolition authorized as to some but not all illegal structures on national security grounds by the highly regarded Israeli High Court of Justice after seven years of legal proceedings. Yet another phony charge of racism." See Rep. Omar's tweet here: https://twitter.com/IlhanMN/status/1153427369497153541?s=20, and Amb. Friedman's response with context here: https://www.jpost.com/Israel-News/Former-Obama-advisor-bashes-Wadi-Hummus-demolitions-Ilhan-Omar-retweets-596576.

ii   The Trump administration's efforts to thwart this concluding act of hostility towards Israel would later imperil President Trump's pro-Israel, counterjihadist National Security Advisor Lt. Gen. Michael Flynn.

The Obama Worldview

What drove the resolution and the rest of the Obama agenda was a worldview consistent with that of Rep. Omar. It was a worldview that President Obama showcased on the international stage, when, in one of the first acts of his administration, the newly elected president set out on a global apology tour, begging forgiveness for America's transgressions.[21] The tour would extend the length of his presidency.[22] We might summarize Obama's spin on the Obama-Omar narrative as follows: The U.S. is an immoral, oppressive, occupying force. It is only exceptional insofar as all nations' countrymen believe their homelands to be exceptional. Global social justice demands that we not only repent for our national sins on the domestic and international stages but that we redistribute wealth and power to our victims at home and abroad—on the latter point coddling our adversaries (among others, Islamists) and cudgeling our friends (among others, Israel).[23] Therefore, Islamists such as the Muslim Brotherhood are to be partnered with and engaged.[24,25,26,27] Lest we inflame the Islamists, Islamic terror is to be treated as non-Islamic;[28] rather, the process of becoming a jihadi is to be thought of as like being infected by a virus. The bug is to be referred to by the nondescript name "violent extremism"—which by its general nature lumps jihadis with the real menace of radical right-wing "bitter clingers" in flyover country. America must adhere to political correctness so as not to lend legitimacy to the ideology jihadis tell us they hold dear or risk inciting them.[29] As such, jihadis are not to be defined as they define themselves, as the most pious of Muslims, but rather as nihilists. Attacks on Israel and Jews by Islamic terrorists are to be referred to as "random," or ignored altogether since Islamic supremacism must not be tied to Islamic Jew-hatred.[30] The federal government is to elide references to Islam pertaining to Islamist terror, even in transcripts of jihadists' own 911 calls, lest we lend credence to their misinterpretation of religion—according to experts with no expertise in Islam, and the Islamists advising us on national security.[31,32,33,34,35,36] Terrorists are to be treated not as singularly responsible for their actions. Society, and particularly Western society, is culpable. Stated differently, we create terrorists by blowback, and not just from military actions but even the inequality our capitalism causes.[37,38] Therefore, we must stop attacking jihadis, and instead focus on ameliorating root cause material conditions of terror by focusing on providing good jobs, an education, and political enfranchisement.[iii] While the damage America has done to the Islamic world is profound, of all Western powers, Israel is most responsible for Islamist violence as the "occupying," neocolonialist oppressor of the Middle East.

Most perversely, President Obama justified the anti-Israel aspect of his agenda, backed by the foregoing narrative, with Judaism. He argued in his hostility towards Israel that he merely sought to ensure the Jewish state was living up to its own values, like any good friend. He effectively equated Judaism with progressivism, cynically pandering to like-minded Jews on the Left who do the same. He condescendingly asked Israelis and American Jews to engage in "self-reflection."[39] Through it all, he maintained the same pose as Ilhan Omar regarding America. He could just as well have said, "I probably love Israel more than Israelis do"—to the same disingenuous effect. Consider a representative sampling of President Obama's record.[40]

---

iii   It is striking to juxtapose then-State Senator Barack Obama's words, released seven days after the September 11, 2001 attacks, with those of then-State. Rep Omar who asked for leniency for terrorists in her district. Obama wrote in part: "We must...engage...in the... difficult task of understanding the sources of such madness. The essence of this tragedy, it seems to me, derives from a fundamental absence of empathy on the part of the attackers: an inability to imagine, or connect with, the humanity and suffering of others. Such a failure of empathy, such numbness to the pain of a child or the desperation of a parent, is not innate; nor, history tells us, is it unique to a particular culture, religion, or ethnicity. It may find expression in a particular brand of violence, and may be channeled by particular demagogues or fanatics. **Most often, though, it grows out of a climate of poverty and ignorance, helplessness and despair.**

We will have to make sure, despite our rage, that any U.S. military action takes into account the lives of innocent civilians abroad. We will have to be unwavering in opposing bigotry or discrimination directed against neighbors and friends of Middle Eastern descent. Finally, we will have to devote far more attention to the monumental task of raising the hopes and prospects of embittered children across the globe-children not just in the Middle East, but also in Africa, Asia, Latin America, Eastern Europe and within our own shores." [Emphasis added] See: http://web.archive.org/web/20111025013123/http://blogs.telegraph.co.uk/news/tobyharnden/5213537/Barack_Obama_and_John_McCain_on_911_Statements_then_and_now/.

Cudgeling Israel

The Obama administration sought to cajole, and where unable, alienate, threaten and punish Israel at every turn, while privileging its enemies. President Obama described his policy as one of creating "daylight" with Israel, so as to impose upon it a "peace" in his terms—terms satisfactory to Israel's worst enemies.[41] He made his philosophy clear from the start in his much-bandied 2009 Cairo address. There, in front of a representative audience of the Sunni Islamic world—that per the wishes of the Obama White House included Muslim Brotherhood officials—Obama declared: "The Jewish people were persecuted. …anti-Semitism …culminated in an unprecedented Holocaust…. Six million Jews were killed…. On the other hand, it is also undeniable that the Palestinian people—Muslims and Christians—have suffered in pursuit of a homeland."[42] At the close of his presidency, Obama would again engage in such Holocaust inversion, stating at the Israeli Embassy in the U.S. that among the "lesson[s] of the Holocaust" is the need "to make common cause with the outsider, the minority, whether that minority is Christian or Jew, whether it is Hindu or Muslim, or a nonbeliever; whether that minority is native born or immigrant; **whether they're Israeli or Palestinian**."[43] [Emphasis added] Throughout his tenure in the Oval Office, President Obama sought to draw a false moral equivalence between Israel and Palestinian Arabs dedicated to Israel's destruction.[44]

Obama marked his Cairo speech with other indicators that Israel and the Jews would be downgraded, and Palestinian Arabs and Muslims generally elevated. Consistent with his speech, during President Obama's first UN General Assembly address, he pointedly dedicated a large portion of his remarks to the Israeli-Arab conflict. He seemed to blame Israel for creating the conditions that drove people to jihad—as if poverty causes people to take up arms and kill innocents, and as if the plight of the Palestinian Arabs was not a direct function of their own behavior. Point blank, he said that "America does not accept the legitimacy of continued Israeli settlements." This was no small matter—President Obama was saying Jews should no longer be able to build in the Biblically and historically vital Judea and Samaria. Regarding settlements, the Obama administration proceeded to unmercifully browbeat the Israeli government, and publicly so.[45] But the administration went still further. The Obama White House and State Department repeatedly referred to Jerusalem itself as being separate and apart from Israel.[46] Consistent with the sentiment underlying UNSCR 2234, regarding Israel and the Arabs, President Obama referred to the pre-1967 Armistice Line as a "border," which appeared to make the 1949 lines the non-negotiable outline for a new Palestinian Arab state, a literally and figuratively indefensible position.[47,48,49] Further consistent with UNSCR 2234, the Obama administration coyly sided with the BDS movement by signing into law anti-BDS legislation but indicating its intent *not* to apply its provisions to enterprises in Judea and Samaria.[50] In fact, to the delight of BDSers, the Obama Department of Homeland Security (DHS) would later stipulate that goods produced in the West Bank or Gaza *not* be marked as made in Israel.[iv]

The Obama administration also issued related threats against Israel—some veiled, others more direct. Secretary of State John Kerry indicated that if Israel refused to commit to the Obama administration's vision for "peace" with the Palestinian Arabs, it could be faced with boycotts, and even a Third Intifada—that is, another jihadist war on Israel.[51,52] President Obama also put the onus on Israel to "make peace" with Mahmoud Abbas, or find itself "more isolated internationally," and repeatedly framed Israel as being the more responsible, intransigent party in conflict with those committed to its destruction.[53,54] The message was clear, and it was not one delivered by an ally: "Nice country you've got there. It'd be a shame if something happened to it."

On top of its threats, the Obama administration repeatedly urged the Netanyahu administration to show "restraint" when it came to combating jihadists and defending itself against Iran and its nuclear program.[55] It forced such restraint by refusing to deliver weapons to Israel in a timely fashion while engaged in battle with Hamas in August 2014. President Obama made

---

iv   The January 23, 2016 directive read in part: "It is not acceptable to mark…goods [produced in the West Bank or Gaza Strip] with the words "Israel," "Made in Israel," "Occupied Territories-Israel," or any variation thereof. Goods that are erroneously marked as products of Israel will be subject to an enforcement action carried out by U.S. Customs and Border Protection." See: https://csms.cbp.gov/viewmssg. asp?Recid=21420&page=129&srch_argv=&srchtype=&btype=partner&sortby=&sby=.

arms requests go directly through him, adding an additional layer of bureau-cracy described as unprecedented by national security officials.[56,57]

That President Obama harbored real animus towards Jews came through in the course of his lobbying for his central foreign policy "achievement," the Iran nuclear deal. In order to summon Jewish support for the disastrous pact, the administration's Iran Deal echo chamber, led by the aforemen-tioned Ben Rhodes, engaged in a campaign of vicious Jew-baiting. In accordance with rhetoric later employed by Rep. Omar, Team Obama tried to browbeat recalcitrant American Jews into backing the deal by raising the classically anti-Semitic dual loyalty canard.[58,59,60] Meanwhile, in the years leading up to the Iran Deal, the Obama-controlled National Security Agency spied on Israeli leaders, including Prime Minister Netanyahu, in contradiction of its stated policy not to surveil allied heads of state. Its main reason for doing so was to ensure Prime Minister Netanyahu would not scuttle the deal.[61] Secretary Kerry threatened that Israel would be blamed if Congress opposed the Iran Deal.[62]

The Obama administration further demonstrated its malice towards Israel by leaking sensitive information about its military and intelligence activities and capabilities, including breaking the several decades-old prac-tice of not publicly discussing Israel's nuclear program. The Obama White House declassified a 1987 Pentagon document that referred to the program, as it stewed over the revelation that Prime Minister Netanyahu would be taking his case against the Iran nuclear deal to Congress.[63,64] To curry favor with the Iranians in order to preserve deal negotiations, while concurrently sticking a finger in Israel's eye, in the run-up to the nuclear deal the Obama administration repeatedly leaked damaging information about Israeli attacks on Iranian assets, as well as intelligence meant to dissuade Israel from striking additional targets.[65,66] As Israel's former Ambassador to the United States and Knesset member Michael Oren wrote in the *Wall Street Journal* in June 2015, "parallel to the [Iran Deal] talks came administration statements and leaks—for example, each time Israeli warplanes reportedly struck Hezbollah-bound arms convoys in Syria—intended to deter Israel from striking Iran pre-emptively."[67]

Given the Obama administration's enmity towards Prime Minister Netanyahu's administration, it may be unsurprising that he used U.S.

taxpayer dollars to fund efforts to defeat Netanyahu in his 2015 race.[68] A State Department official intentionally deleted emails pertaining to this effort.[69] When Netanyahu was re-elected, the administration congratulated the Israeli people on the election, not Netanyahu for his victory. President Obama did not call the Israeli prime minister to recognize his victory for two days. This is in stark contrast with the effusive and quickly delivered congratulations President Obama extended anti-Israel and anti-American strongmen including Turkey's Recep Tayyip Erdoğan, Egypt's Mohamed Morsi, and Iran's Hassan Rouhani.[70]

Philosophically, the Obama administration made it popular among progressives to challenge the notion that Israel could be both Jewish and Democratic.[71]

All along the way, the media, the Democratic Party, and disproportionately Leftist Jews rarely asked the question the Obama administration begged of them: "Cui bono?"

In short, Obama delegitimized, demonized, and held Israel to a double standard relative to actually regressive states, passing Natan Sharansky's 3D Test of anti-Semitism with flying colors. Following the rejection of her visa by Israel, Rep. Omar stood alongside her colleague, Rep. Tlaib, and declared she would "fight...the oppressive Netanyahu administration until we take our last breath."[72] In President Obama, she had a kindred spirit.

Coddling Israel's Foes

At the same time President Obama bludgeoned Israel, he also took actions that strengthened her enemies—and America's. With respect to Israel's Palestinian Arab foes, they were the immediate beneficiaries of his attacks. While in Obama's rhetoric and policies, Israel was treated as the aggressor and thus the true roadblock to "peace," Israel's antagonists, the Palestinian Arabs, were portrayed as hapless victims with legitimate grievances and claims.[73] As a fitting coda to his efforts, in the waning hours of his administration, he ordered the release of 221 million dollars to the Palestinian Authority.[74] Perhaps it should have told us something that during the 2008 presidential election, Hamas endorsed President Obama, and advisor David Axelrod said he was "flattered" by Hamas' glowing praise of the candidate.[75]

But the Palestinian Arabs were not the only ones to benefit from Obama's Israel obsession. So were their backers. After a dogged campaign of Chamberlainian appeasement, President Obama consummated the Iran nuclear agreement, flooding the mullocratic regime's coffers with well over 100 billion dollars, while guaranteeing that the U.S. would protect Iran's nuclear infrastructure. The Obama administration's single-minded pursuit of this deal led it to ignore if not become complicit in major malevolent Iranian acts. These included: Spiking an investigation into Hezbollah's cars-for-cocaine money laundering scheme;[76] refusing to faithfully enforce sanctions, enabling the Turkey-Iran gas-for-gold trade that generated billions for the mullahs;[77] and reportedly refusing to respond to an Iran-sanctioned plot to blow up a tony Washington, D.C. restaurant in a bid to murder then-Saudi Ambassador to the United States Adel al-Jubeir.[78]

President Obama permitted such behavior to proceed unchallenged, all in an effort to consummate a deal that effectively sought to bribe the Iranian regime into going nuclear after President Obama left office. Thereby, America became the world's greatest sponsor of the world's greatest sponsor of jihad. Iran proved that with progressives in power, aggression begets appeasement; that terror is an effective tactic for those willing to pay for a false "peace" at any cost.

But stunningly, the Obama administration went still further. It sought to make Iran the pillar of regional stability, and our chief partner—the same mullocratic Iran that as noted previously has been at war with America since its Islamic revolution in 1979, resulting in hundreds of American deaths from Lebanon to Iraq.[79,80,81,82,83,84,85]

Regarding Sunni Islamists, President Obama reflexively supported the Arab Spring. In so doing, he helped destabilize the already sectarian Middle East, directly benefiting Islamic supremacist groups that threatened Israel's existence. These included Iran's proxy Hezbollah, the Muslim Brotherhood, and the myriad of jihadist offshoots it spawned—including Iran-funded Hamas, and ISIS.[86] The Obama administration supported the collapse of relatively authoritarian dictators that kept some semblance of order in the region, thereby enabling the growth of Iran's Shiite Crescent, while unleashing Sunni Islamist political forces with which Iran sometimes partners, and other times wars.[87]

The administration's support was in spite of the fact that as the man who ran U.S. Central Command from 2010-2013, and no conservative ideologue, General James Mattis put it: "From my first day at CENTCOM, I knew we faced two principal adversaries: stateless Sunni Islamist terrorists and the revolutionary Shiite regime of Iran, the most destabilizing country in the region...Iran was by far the more deadly of the two threats."[88] The Obama administration would even go so far as to whitewash the radical views of its chosen partners, including the Jew-hatred of the late Mohamed Morsi, the short-lived Muslim Brotherhood potentate of Egypt—whose demise Rep. Omar would seemingly lament.[89]

Consistent with Islamists who we will profile in Part III of the book, President Obama sought to draw moral equivalence again between jihadists and Israeli forces, providing a propaganda coup for Israel's enemies.[90]

From the start, President Obama promised to extend an open hand to the West's enemies via a tactic similarly favored by Rep. Omar's favored: Diplomatic engagement.[91] By extending his hand as he did to our enemies, President Obama provided the back of his hand to the West itself. All of these words and acts were in keeping with a worldview consonant with Rep. Omar's.

The consequence of these policies was that American forces were increasingly imperiled and thrust into disastrous situations from Iraq and Syria, to Libya—with different U.S. government agencies in select instances incoherently funding opposing sides in conflicts, neither of which were pro-American.[92] Israel naturally bore the greatest brunt of President Obama's intentional follies. It found itself facing mounting jihadist forces armed with thousands of missiles and rockets, while situated in a region that could increasingly be characterized as a bubbling cauldron of Islamist chaos that threatened to tip over and scald the Jewish state.

The threats to America, Israel, and our allies manifested themselves most notably in Iran's land-bridge across the Middle East, and the creation of the Islamic State. The silver lining was that by siding with Iran, the Muslim Brotherhood, and their proxies, the Obama administration inadvertently brought together Israel and historically adversarial Arab regimes in a previously unimaginable partnership against the greater existential threat of America's new, but mercifully short-lived Iranian partners.

Homeland Insecurity

The Obama administration treated domestic jihadism not as a matter of war, but as one of law enforcement. Like Rep. Omar, the White House sought to, in its own words, "rehabilitat[e] and reintegrate[e] violent extremists."[93] It obstinately refused to refer to them as "jihadists," or "Islamic terrorists." In fact, out of a suicidal devotion to political correctness, it purged our national security lexicon of the very language jihadists use to describe themselves, their ideology, and their goals.[94] It sacked experts in Islamist ideology altogether, removing them from the ranks of our national security apparatus.[95] It replaced the "War on Terror"—itself euphemistic given one cannot be at war with a tactic—with a see-no-Islam "countering violent extremism" (CVE) paradigm whereby ostensible counterjihadist work was outsourced to Muslim Brotherhood-tied Islamic supremacists themselves.[96,97] Under CVE guidelines, those tasked with keeping America safe from jihadists were told to avoid ventur[ing] too deep into the weeds of religious doctrine and history," or studying the "role of Islam in majority Muslim nations." Homeland security officials were also forbidden from:

> ...us[ing] training that equates radical thought, religious expression, freedom to protest, or other constitutionally protected activity, with criminal activity. One can have radical thoughts/ideas, including disliking the U.S. government, without being violent; for example, trainers who equate the desire for Sharia law with criminal activity violate basic tenets of the First Amendment.[98]

In other words, "Don't study the enemy's threat doctrine or investigate anyone who espouses it until he or she starts planning an attack."

At the same time, the Obama administration protected jihadists from scrutiny under the guise of free speech. Like Rep. Omar, it also sought to shut up those critical of Islamists, even threatening to prosecute them. In so doing, it held counterjihadists to a standard to which it would not hold jihadists themselves. The Obama administration endorsed the UN Human Rights Council Resolution 16/18. The Organisation of Islamic

Conference-drafted resolution, the result of a more than decade-long effort to get other nations to criminalize "Islamophobic" speech—that is, to impose de facto Sharia-based speech codes—required "combating intolerance, negative stereotyping and stigmatization of, and discrimination, incitement to violence, and violence against persons based on religion or belief."[99],[100] Relatedly, Obama Attorney General Loretta Lynch warned that while:

> this is a country that is based on free speech…when it edges towards violence, when we see the potential for someone lifting that mantle of anti-Muslim rhetoric -- or, as we saw after 9/11, violence directed at individuals who may not even be Muslims but perceived to be Muslims, and they will suffer just as much -- when we see that we will take action.[101]

She later attempted to walk back these comments, but the administration's sentiment was clear.[102]

How a nation could combat an enemy it would not name, imbued with an ideology it would not define—under the belief that not speaking let alone recognizing the truth would prevent Islamists from "radicalizing"—is beyond incomprehensible. It is a proposition that makes no sense if one is seeking to protect one's nation from a perceived threat. Yet it is what guided policies like the CIA's deleting of hundreds of law enforcement records containing critical information on individuals connected to the Muslim Brotherhood—records essential to preventing terrorist attacks in America.[103],[104] It arguably contributed to the intelligence failures that culminated in the Boston Marathon bombing and the Orlando nightclub shooting.[105],[106] We should note that Rep. Omar was a critic of the policy of CVE. However, her criticism was that the policy went *too far* in the way of targeting jihadists.[107],[108] Nevertheless, through its policies, the Obama administration empowered the Islamists with whom Rep. Omar, as we will explore in Part III of the book, consorts and colludes.

Obama's Related Panoply of Progressive Policies

As we have argued, one's treatment of Israel and the Jews, as well as their mortal enemies, is a good proxy for one's views in any number of other areas. Oppose the Jewish state and Jewish people, and you likely oppose the West. The Obama policies discussed heretofore, and the worldview they illustrate, are, consistent with Rep. Omar's, of a piece with a progressive-Islamist ideology dedicated to undermining the West, implying support for a number of commensurately anti-Western policies.

Contrary to what Rep. Omar argues, one does not browbeat his or her country out of love. One does not seek to "fundamentally transform" a great nation out of love. But President Barack Obama dedicated his presidency to achieving just that end. Consistent with Rep. Omar's desire, he worked day and night to push the country as far Left as politically possible. Social justice demanded it. His signature foreign policy "achievement," the Iran nuclear deal, and his signature domestic policy "achievement," Obamacare, were fitting bookends to this effort.

The latter law, it bears noting, led to the hyper-regulation of one-sixth of the U.S. economy. It gave the U.S. government unprecedented control over Americans' most personal and intimate decisions—ones regarding their own health. It set the country on a path towards the collapse of private medicine, and laid the groundwork for current progressive calls for "Medicare for All." It led the Supreme Court to do incalculable damage to its own legitimacy, the rule of law, and perhaps liberty itself, by deeming a government mandate to purchase a good or service a "tax," making the unconstitutional constitutional. Obamacare was arguably the single greatest progressive policy measure since the Great Society.

If President Obama resigned the day after Obamacare passed, he could have legitimately claimed he had fundamentally transformed the country. But he kept going. In between recapitalizing the mullocracy and setting it on a path to nuclear armament, while putting the U.S. healthcare system on a glide path to socialism, President Obama shepherded a raft of policies borne of a similar ideology. These included the trillion-dollar "stimulus," Dodd-Frank, the Paris Climate Accord, Deferred Action for Childhood Arrivals (aka DACA), his gutting of workfare, and the dramatic expansion of the administrative state and hyper-regulation of the economy, just to name a few. The values and principles underlying these policies were consistent with those of Rep. Omar.

For good measure, his administration weaponized the Internal Revenue Service, Department of Justice, and seemingly the entire national security apparatus in a bid to sideline his political opponents, and ultimately undermine if not destroy a successor who threatened his policies.

That progressive movements such as Occupy Wall Street and Black Lives Matter were advents of the Obama years should come as no surprise given the political environment he created.[109,110,111] And as a skilled practitioner of identity politics, President Obama's legacy lives on in today's Democratic Party.[112]

Some progressives have expressed disappointment in President Obama, arguing he did not go far enough to achieve their priorities. But the reality is that he sacrificed everything he could to achieve his agenda—most importantly for Obamacare, the consequences of which we will likely be dealing with for decades. President Obama's commitment to the progressive cause can be measured not only by his policy victories, and the intractable challenges he created for the Trump administration, but also the more than 1,030 legislative seats Democrats lost up and down ballot during his tenure.[113,114,115] Barack Obama spent nearly every penny of political capital he had to achieve what he could. The price was Democrat control of the executive branch, majorities in both Houses of Congress, and control over the majority of state legislatures and governorships across the country.

Creating a Safe Space for Radicalism

President Obama, like Rep. Omar, has maintained associations with those deeply inculcated in the Left, Islamist, or Left-Islamist milieu, almost all of whom are hostile to Israel and Jews. Race-baiter Al Sharpton visited the Obama White House over 100 times.[116] President Obama rehabilitated Sharpton in spite of the fact he is unrepentant about his anti-Semitic rhetoric that inspired two fatal events: The Crown Heights Riot, and the firebombing of Freddy's Fashion Mart. The former resulted in the killing of a Jewish man named Yankel Rosenbaum.[117] The latter led to the deaths of eight people, including the attacker, while damaging the Jewish-owned

Harlem retailer.[118] Senior Obama advisor Valerie Jarrett lauded Sharpton's efforts on behalf of the administration.[119]

Though suppressed until after he was out of office, Barack Obama, like many prominent Democrats, apparently had consorted with the Jew-hating head of the Nation of Islam, Louis Farrakhan. A media dedicated to protecting Obama suppressed a 2005 picture showing a smiling Obama alongside the Nazi-praiser until after he departed the White House.

Perhaps most infamously, President Obama sat in anti-American, anti-Semitic, Marxist Reverend Jeremiah Wright's pews for two decades. His views on America, Israel, and Jews are so venomous as not to be worthy of reprinting here. As with Farrakhan—with whom Rev. Wright also consorted—President Obama sought to alibi this relationship, knowing that the views espoused by Rev. Wright were unacceptable to the American electorate.[120]

Similar figures abound in Obama's background, from Bill Ayers and Bernadine Dhorn, to Father Pfleger and Frank Marshall Davis.[121,122]

Leaning towards the Islamist side of the Left-Islamist axis are individuals such as Rashid Khalidi. During the 2008 presidential election, the *Los Angeles Times*, which would endorse President Obama, obtained but refused to release a videotape of then-State Senator Barack Obama reportedly delivering a toast to his Arabist friend at an event in his honor in 2003. The newspaper did report that Obama had been a fixture at Palestinian Arab events in America, for example attending a 1998 speech delivered by none other than Edward Said in which Said reportedly called for a nonviolent campaign "against settlements, against Israeli apartheid," along with numerous functions with Ali Abunimah, co-founder of the notoriously anti-Israel, Chicago-based *Electronic Intifada* publication. Obama reportedly left the impression among some in the Palestinian Arab cause that he was "more receptive to their viewpoint than he is willing to say."[123] Khalidi himself refused to criticize Obama for taking more "moderate" positions publicly, out of an understanding Obama was required to do so in order to win politically.[124] Khalidi has, incidentally, lauded Rep. Omar for her support of BDS, and having "demonstrated that things can be said today about Israel and Palestine in Congress...

that were simply unsayable in American public discourse only a few years ago."[125]

Perhaps more disturbingly, an extensive report by the *Investigative Project on Terrorism* (IPT) published in October of 2012 revealed a laundry list of Islamist organizations and individuals who received entrée to the Obama White House through numerous meetings with senior officials. As the investigation noted:

> Among the [White House] visitors were officials representing groups which have:
>
> - Been designated by the Department of Justice as unindicted co-conspirators in terrorist trials; Extolled Islamic terrorist groups including Hamas and Hizballah;
>
> - Obstructed terrorist investigations by instructing their followers not to cooperate with law enforcement;
>
> - Promoted the incendiary conspiratorial allegation that the United States is engaged in a "war against Islam"— a leading tool in recruiting Muslims to carry out acts of terror;
>
> - Repeatedly claimed that many of the Islamic terrorists convicted since 9-11 were framed by the U.S government as part of an anti-Muslim profiling campaign.[126]

Many of the individuals *IPT* identified had been tied to Islamists, and made public statements consistent with the Islamist line on matters from jihad and counterterrorism, to Iran and Israel.

Also instructive are the backgrounds of President Obama's like-minded appointees. We will discuss but a few of them.

Obama's CIA Director John Brennan voted Communist during the height of the Cold War and is by all accounts an Islamophile.[127,128] He refers to Jerusalem by its Arabic name, 'Al-Quds,' and says jihad is about "purifying oneself or one's community," not killing infidels.[129,130]

Rob Malley had to be publicly fired from the 2008 Obama campaign—after it originally denied he was a part of it—once it became public that he had met with Hamas leaders and remained in regular contact with them, only to later land on his feet as Obama's ISIS czar.[131,132]

Chuck Hagel, President Obama's Secretary of Defense from 2013-2015, said in 2006 that "the Jewish Lobby intimidates a lot of people up here [on Capitol Hill]," for which he later apologized. This view, however, was consistent with many of his past votes in relation to Israel, and its adversaries.[133]

Imam Mohamed Magid, president of the Muslim Brotherhood-tied Islamic Society of North America (ISNA), which, like CAIR, was an unindicted co-conspirator in the largest terrorist financing case in history, was appointed to Barack Obama's DHS Countering Violent Extremism Working Group. There, he was largely responsible for the purging of the study of jihadist ideology from America's putative counterterrorism policies.[134,135]

The Obama administration also appointed like-minded Mohamed Elibiary to the DHS's Advisory Council. Elibiary is an outspoken Muslim Brotherhood supporter who has publicly declared that it is "inevitable that [the] 'Caliphate' return[s]," and that America is "an Islamic country with an Islamically compliant constitution." He was also involved in leading U.S. counterterrorism policy.[136,137]

Dalia Mogahed was one of President Obama's most influential advisors on Islamic affairs by dint of her appointment to his Advisory Council on Faith-Based and Neighborhood Partnerships. Mogahed has been a consistent apologist for Islamic supremacism. She ensured that the views of prominent Islamists and Islamist groups, including a veritable alphabet soup of Muslim Brotherhood-tied American organizations, were represented in the White House.[138,139] Mogahed sits firmly in Rep. Omar's orbit today, as we will discuss later in the book.

As economist, social theorist, and philosopher Thomas Sowell wrote in July 2008, President Obama "is a man who has consistently aided and abetted people who have openly expressed their contempt for this country, both in words and in such deeds as planting bombs to advance their left-wing agenda."[140] The same can be said of Rep. Omar. Yet while Obama felt the need to explain away if not actively hide such relationships, Rep. Omar shares no such compunctions with appearing onstage with the likes of Angela Davis, or Linda Sarsour. By doing so, she demonstrates that President Obama created a safe space for her.

Similarly, President Obama was often careful or intentionally vague in rhetoric so as to make his radical positions appear more moderate. Yet Rep. Omar feels free to flaunt her radicalism.

President Obama played an unappreciated role in making Ilhan Omar possible. For the Left, this qualifies as progress. The great irony is that Rep. Omar is not grateful for what Obama did for her. Following her election as Minnesota state representative in December 2016, when asked at an event for her thoughts on the idea that President George W. Bush did some admirable things with respect to the Muslim world, she replied:

> If we are to be honest, as a Muslim there's a lot more policies that negatively impact those that I care about that came through the Obama administration [than the Bush administration].[141]

As a U.S. congresswoman, she further criticized President Obama in context of his "caging of kids" at the U.S.-Mexico border and "droning of countries around the world," noting:

> We can't be only upset with Trump. ... His policies are bad, but many of the people who came before him also had really bad policies. They just were more polished than he was ... And that's not what we should be looking for anymore. **We don't want anybody to get away with murder because they are polished. We want to recognize the actual policies that are behind the pretty face and the smile.**[142] [Emphasis added]

One wonders, if Rep. Omar is ungrateful towards the America that gave her unparalleled opportunities, and the former president who made it possible for a politician like her to rise to power, is there anything or anyone for whom she is actually grateful?

The reality is that her harsh words for President Obama aside, Obama anticipated Rep. Omar and the other progressives ascendant in the Democratic Party today. His hostility towards the Jewish state, and Jews themselves, was a leading indicator, and again served as a proxy for like-minded views on a range of other issues. That Rep. Omar is and always has been unabashedly radical, where President Obama had to be more cunning, is a testament to his success. What ensued in the wake of Obama's success is a simmering civil war to which we will now turn—one that Obama's heirs stand poised to win.

CHAPTER 9

THE PROGRESSIVE TAKEOVER OF THE DEMOCRATIC PARTY

Progressivism in the Era of Trump

President Donald Trump is a human trigger for progressives across the nation. His presidency has coincided with, among his critics, an endless array of temper tantrums, media meltdowns, and public displays of unrest. But while the president has indeed built massive Trump Towers in the heads of his Resistance foes—perhaps most of all because he fights them like no other Republican would—the reality is that Trump did not create the rabid progressives. In fact, he can be seen as a consequence of their rise. President Trump was elected in no small part as a counterpunch by traditional Americans, against progressives, who felt that for far too long they had been living under assault on their deeply held values.

Progressive orthodoxy prevails across our core institutions. In nearly every aspect of American life, one will find oneself bombarded with progressive narratives, from our schools to our tv screens, to our workplaces. Political correctness is rampant. Comedy has become humorless. Americans are condemned to constantly walk on eggshells.

Our progressives seek to rewrite our founding so as to delegitimize the entire American project. They seek to abolish core parts of our political system when an election does not go their way. And they seek to exorcise from civil society anyone who dares disagree with them or tries to thwart their aims.

President Trump may have pushed the progressives over the edge, but they had walked up to it before he arrived at 1600 Pennsylvania Avenue.

The Democratic Party in the Era of Trump

Against this backdrop of discontent, division, and demoralization on the Left during the Trump era, the Democratic Party is embroiled in a civil, and at times less-than-civil war. Its divides are generational, ideological, and tactical: The old establishmentarians represented by Speaker Nancy Pelosi, versus the new Young Turks represented by Rep. Alexandria Ocasio-Cortez; the Bolsheviks versus the Mensheviks; the incrementalists versus the maximalists. The Democratic Party's response to Rep. Omar and her colleagues' positions on Israel and the Jews is a leading indicator and proxy for where it is headed on a raft of other issues. To that end, the party's caving to Omar foretells a broader cave that will ensure the Squad triumphs more broadly. What would its triumph entail? Omar has called for her supporters to "continue to mobilize for a movement that will get many Ilhans, many Ilhans."[1] The inevitable consequence of such a movement need not be that Speaker Nancy Pelosi hands over her Speaker's gavel to AOC in 2020, though it bears noting that Pelosi owes that gavel in no small part to the party's progressives, who agreed to back her in exchange for significant concessions. What it is to say is that in terms of where the party is headed philosophically, it is moving to the Left. Consequently, it is the Squad and its disciples who stand to inherit the scorched Earth that will result from their efforts.[2] Progressive ideas and candidates will increasingly dominate the Democratic Party. Ultimately, the shrewder radicals, having buttoned-up their rhetoric and presentation, will become the establishment themselves—like Barack Obama, and Nancy Pelosi did before them. We can measure the validity of this theory in several ways.

Polls Show Our Leftward March

First, consider that the Democratic electorate has been trending inexorably leftward for nearly two decades—that is, commencing well before President Obama. According to Pew, 41 percent of Democrats identified as "Liberal" in 2018—a 15 percent jump from where the party was in 2001.[3] A 2018 Gallup poll showed an even greater percentage—half of all Democrats—identifying as "Liberal."[4] When broken by race, and education, it is whites, and those with college or postgraduate degrees, who rate most Liberal among all demographics. Americans increasingly accept the idea of socialism, with several recent polls revealing upwards of 40 percent support—disproportionately among Democrats' most-favored constituencies.[5,6]

An August 2019 survey reveals an even more startling fundamental shift.[7] An *NBC News/Wall Street Journal* poll asked of respondents whether they considered a series of topics "very important," including among them questions about G-d, family, and country. Between 1998 and 2019, the importance those surveyed attached to each of these pillars of American life has declined precipitously. In 1998, 62 percent of respondents rated religion as "very important." By 2019, that number had fallen to only 48 percent. In 1998, 59 percent of respondents considered having children "very important." By 2019, that number had fallen to just 43 percent. In 1998, 70 percent of respondents considered patriotism "very important." By 2019, that number had fallen to 61 percent.

The polling data is even more troubling when parsed by age cohort. Millennials and members of Generation Z—which includes Ilhan Omar—who are eighteen to thirty-eight years old, rate far lower than those over fifty-five in all three categories. A mere 30 percent of such individuals rank religion as "very important." Alarmingly, only 32 percent consider having children "very important." And only 42 percent consider patriotism "very important."[8]

On this last point, the data is consistent with a 2018 poll conducted by YouGov on behalf of The Foundation for Liberty and Greatness that found that one in five millennials believe the U.S. flag is "a sign of intolerance and hatred," while nearly half of millennials and Generation Z-ers do *not* agree that "America is the greatest country in the world."[9] A 2017

Pew Research Center survey similarly found that those who say the "U.S. stands above all other countries in the world," rather than that "There are other countries that are better than the U.S.," breaks by age and political orientation. Those under thirty rate other countries as superior to the U.S. by a 16-point margin. While conservatives rate America as superior by a ten-to-one rate, liberals rate it as inferior to some other countries by a two-to-one rate.[10]

The decline in religiosity, devotion to building families, and love of country among the next generation of voters and leaders indicate America is going the progressives' way.

The Significance of the "Great Awokening"

Above all other issues, and among all other cohorts, it is opinions on race held by white elites on the Left, arguably the most politically influential group, that have shifted perhaps most dramatically of all.[i] Recall that race is intrinsic to the "intersectional feminism" by which Rep. Omar defines herself. Also, recall that her race-centric view tends to link one to the kaleidoscope of social justice causes, all of which go hand in hand with Blame America First-ism. Educated whites on the Left have come to define themselves by the same views as those held by Omar. This political segment has undergone what has been termed a "Great Awokening." "Wokeness" denotes one's hyper-sensitivity towards, or "heightening of the consciousness" about, racism and the fact that it is present, even if imperceptibly, in nearly every matter. *Vox*'s Matthew Yglesias writes of this "awokening" that "In the past five years, white liberals have moved so far to the left on questions of race and racism that they are now, on these issues, to the left of

---

i   Regarding the political power of white elites on the Left, as Zach Goldberg writes in *Tablet*: "A wealth of research shows that elected officials are most responsive to the voices (and campaign contributors) they hear from the most; and, by many measures, white liberals and Democrats are the most politically active group on their side of the partisan aisle. White liberals make up 20-24% of the general population but, for a multitude of reasons, exert an outsize political and cultural influence. They are more likely to consider themselves activists, are more active on social media, and, significantly, they are one of the most affluent groups in the country." See: https://www.tabletmag.com/jewish-news-and-politics/284875/americas-white-saviors.

the typical black voter."[11] Writing in the *Claremont Review of Books*, William Voegeli shares one particularly striking data point illustrating the magnitude of this change:[ii]

> Since 1994 the National Opinion Research Center's General Social Survey has asked respondents whether they agreed or disagreed with this statement: "Irish, Italians, Jewish, and many other minorities overcame prejudice and worked their way up. Blacks should do the same without special favors." Dissecting the results…white liberals were only half as likely as blacks to reject that proposition in 1994. By 2016, after white liberals' opposition to that statement had increased and blacks' opposition to it had declined, the former were half-again as likely as the latter to disagree with it. That is, **white liberals have come to believe that blacks don't fully appreciate how burdened they are by white racism.**[12] [Emphasis added]

In fact, white liberals are the only group in America that views other groups more favorably than themselves.[13]

As Zach Goldberg chronicles, these changing views have resulted in explosive growth in support for affirmative action, government spending based on race, a belief in government-backed income equalization by race, and a variety of similar positions. But changing perspectives on race have also manifested themselves in—or at a minimum correlated with—trends in areas only tangentially related. They are linked only when viewed through the prism of identity politics and its victimological hierarchy, or privilege pyramid. As Goldberg observes:

> …[B]etween 1965 and 2000, the percentage of white liberals preferring increased immigration levels never deviated far from 10%. From the mid-2000s to roughly the end of President Obama's term in office, this figure

---

ii   Disclosure: The author is a Fellow of the Claremont Institute, publisher of the *Claremont Review of Books*.

gradually ascended into the 20-30% range. As of 2018, it sits at over 50%. Then, there is the marked shift [as noted previously] in attitudes toward Israel. Between 1978 and 2014, white liberals consistently reported sympathizing more with Israel than the Palestinians. Since March of 2016, this trend has turned on its face: Significantly more white liberals now report greater sympathy for the Palestinians than for Israel.

Some of these changes arguably stem from Trump's rhetoric and policies on immigration. But a glance at the data shows that, as with their attitudes toward blacks, the percentage of white liberals perceiving "a lot" or "a great deal" of discrimination against immigrants more than doubled between 2000 (29%) and 2013 (57%)—i.e., well before Trump arrived on the scene.[14]

Conversely, Goldberg writes:

...[B]lack and Asian Democrats *and* liberals are significantly *more* supportive of restrictive immigration policies and *less* positive toward racial/ethnic diversity than their white counterparts. Black and Hispanic Democrats and liberals are more sympathetic toward Israel than the Palestinians (likely due in part to the fact that they tend to be more religious). They are also more likely to part ways when it comes to contemporary social and gender-identity issues, including views of the #MeToo movement. **In all, though they do converge on some issues, the attitudes and policy preferences of the woke white left are unrepresentative of the "marginalized communities" with whom they are supposed to be allies. And as woke liberals play a leading role in party politics, the Democrats, who are increasingly defined by their embrace of diversity and progressive stances on issues of racial**

justice, appear to do so, at least partly at the direction of a small white elite. [15] [Emphasis added]

Goldberg perhaps inadvertently illustrates that in contrast with Rep. Omar's view that her progressive policies will empower the groups comprising her intersectional coalition, it is actually the white elite social justice warriors who will be empowered by imposing their vision on us all. The idea of moralistic white elites dictating victimology-based policies to minorities because the elites know best seems at core to be rooted not in a desire for justice, social or otherwise, but rather in a condescending paternalism justified by narcissistic virtue-signaling. As Goldberg concludes: "The woke elite act like white saviors who must lead the rest of the country, including the racial minorities whose interests they claim to represent, to a vision of justice the less enlightened groups would not choose for themselves." Progressivism, in short, proves to be a power grab for those putting the progressive agenda into action, driven by a perverse kind of postmodern noblesse oblige.

Rep. Omar's rise can be seen as symptomatic of the "Great Awokening."[16] Her overwhelmingly progressive congressional district is comprised not only of thousands of fellow Somali immigrants, but upwards of 60 percent whites—including among them, college students, urbanites, and suburban professionals.[17] If elite opinion ultimately represents ruling class opinion, then the ruling class stands with her.

Whether it is a reflection of the fact that the race-centric worldview has come to define the Left or an indicator that we are still only part of the way down this road, it is notable that the most reliable predictor of elite liberal (or illiberal) opinion, *The New York Times*, vowed in the summer of 2019 to make race its seminal issue in a post-Russiagate world.[18] The beginning of this project can be seen in the *Times'* ambitious attempt to rewrite our past via its "1619 Project." The *Times* aims to "reframe the country's history, understanding 1619 [when it dates slavery as having come to the English colonies] as our true founding." The editor's note to the project reveals its core argument:

Out of slavery – and the anti-black racism it required – grew nearly everything that has truly made America exceptional: its economic might, its industrial power, its electoral system, diet and popular music, the inequities of its public health and education, its astonishing penchant for violence, its income inequality, the example it sets for the world as a land of freedom and equality, its slang, its legal system and the endemic racial fears and hatreds that continue to plague it to this day.[19]

In other words, America was conceived in the ultimate racist sin, which toxifies all else including the Declaration of Independence, Constitution, and all that has followed. In a leaked transcript from a *New York Times* town hall convened by top executives in the midst of a particularly acrimonious week in August 2019, one staffer posed a question to executive editor Dean Baquet that crystallizes the state of the Left, exclaiming:

I just feel like racism is in everything. It should be considered in our science reporting, in our culture reporting, in our national reporting. And so, to me, it's less about the individual instances of racism, and sort of how we're thinking about racism and white supremacy as the foundation of all of the systems in the country. And I think particularly as we are launching a 1619 Project, I feel like that's going to open us up to even more criticism from people who are like, "OK, well you're saying this, and you're producing this big project about this. But are you guys actually considering this in your daily reporting?"[20]

Baquet replied in part that "one reason we all signed off on the 1619 Project and made it so ambitious and expansive was to teach our readers to think a little bit more like that."[21] The editorial thrust of the paper, as represented by its 1619 Project, management, and the staffer quoted, reflect the very race-centric worldview to which Rep. Omar subscribes. Again, Omar's opinion is elite opinion—ironically, white elite opinion.

The Number of Progressives in Congress Has Swelled

The second major indicator that progressivism is ascendant flows from the first in the form of Washington D.C. representation. If white elites are disproportionately politically influential and have grown significantly more progressive, we would expect Americans to elect more progressives. They have, in spades. At the founding of the Congressional Progressive Caucus in 1991, there were a mere six Democratic members.[22] Speaker Nancy Pelosi ironically was one of the early joiners, only departing in 2003 when she was elected minority leader.[23] Fast-forward to 2010, the highwater mark for the CPC during Barack Obama's presidency, and there were seventy-seven such House members.[24] Today, in the 116th Congress, there is an all-time high of ninety-eight CPC members, including Rep. Omar, who serves as Whip.[25] The CPC now represents more than 40 percent of all House Democrats. It has enjoyed a 15-fold increase in membership in a single generation. Beyond the numbers, the fact that Congress has transformed can be proven anecdotally as well. In 1993, then-Senator Joe Biden and Rep. Bernie Sanders, the two leading candidates representing the left and further left poles of the 2020 Democratic presidential field, both supported the Religious Freedom Restoration Act when it came up for a vote.[26] They would be tarred and feathered for taking such a position today.

Progressivism Has Been Overwhelmingly Embraced by Democratic Presidential Aspirants

The third major indicator of progressive strength can be found in their performance and the criticality of their ideas to the last two Democratic presidential primaries. In 2016, in spite of a primary process skewed against him by the Democratic establishment, Senator Bernie Sanders, the past and present candidate best-aligned with the CPC in general, and the Squad in particular, was still able to win approximately 40 percent of all delegates.[iii,27] Senator Sanders personifies the ascendancy of progressivism,

---

iii   It bears noting that Justice Democrats, the group that recruited Alexandria Ocasio-Cortez to run for the House, spun out of an organization led by organizers from Bernie Sanders's 2016 presidential run. See: https://truthout.org/video/democratic-divide-new-progressives-in-the-party-at-odds-with-the-establishment/.

not just because of his success in the 2016 race, but because he spawned the CPC himself nearly three decades ago.

With respect to 2020, Democrats are embracing the ideas of Sanders and the Squad, as well as the person of the octogenarian and his ideological progeny. As liberal comedian and political observer Bill Maher pithily describes it, his fellow Leftists are "coming across as unserious people who are going to take away all your money so migrants from Honduras can go to college for free and get a major in 'America sucks.'"[28] While the author disagrees with Maher on any number of issues, he wholeheartedly concurs with this synopsis.

Beyond the fact that the most competitive progressives in the field, the aforementioned Sanders and Senator Elizabeth Warren, polled collectively in the 30-plus percent range in the Democratic primary during the second half of 2019, it is the progressive agenda that has dominated on the campaign trail. Whether on healthcare, immigration, the environment, education, abortion, or impeachment, the field has been pulled Left to an unimaginable extent even relative to 2016, as some Democrats lament.[29,30] The candidates have overwhelmingly embraced "Medicare for All" or slightly moderated versions thereof—including for illegal aliens.[31,32] They portray support for anything less than open, "decriminalized" borders as heartless, immoral and un-American.[33] Democrats have by and large endorsed AOC's Green New Deal, and the decarbonization and therefore deindustrialization of our economy, believing that absent the abolition of capitalism and the redistribution of its remaining fruits, the Earth will end in about a decade.[34,35] They wish to cancel student debt post-haste by government fiat, and heavily subsidize it.[36] The Democratic Party now also supports third-trimester abortions—if not outright infanticide upon delivery—for all who seek it, including illegal aliens.[37] Some even find intersectionality in abortion and climate change, like Senator Sanders, who advocates Malthusian population control to ensure the climate does not destroy us.[38] That such policies harken back to the original progressives' eugenicist roots is certainly lost on today's Democrats, though perhaps not on the octogenarian Senator Sanders. Prior to Speaker Nancy Pelosi's announcement that the House would begin an impeachment inquiry into President Trump, nearly half the Democratic field had already backed impeachment, including top candidates Warren and Sanders, and former candidate Senator Harris.[39]

As a result of the rising progressive tide, candidates have been forced to flip their positions on all manner of issues.[40] The presumptive favorite, former Vice President Joe Biden, had to recant his past support of the Hyde Amendment.[41] He has also had to change his rhetoric after coming under fire for past positions regarding busing, criminal justice, working with Dixiecrats, as well as daring to compliment Vice President Mike Pence.[42] Senator Elizabeth Warren, who was once described as a "diehard conservative," has morphed into a Sandersian progressive avatar.[43] The formerly tough-on-crime prosecutor Senator Kamala Harris had, like Biden, softened her positions to curry favor with a party in thrall to the belief that the criminal justice system is the problem, not the criminals.[44] She waffled several times on the degree to which she wished to socialize healthcare.[45] Far from running from the Squad, she even teamed up with AOC on legislation geared towards making herself seem more sympathetic to criminals, in the form of the Fair Chance at Housing Act.[46] Perhaps the defining characteristic of failed candidate Senator Kirsten Gillibrand's career has been her metamorphosis from upstate New York Blue Dog, to the ardent progressive we saw on the debate stage briefly in 2019.

Those candidates refusing to sing progressive paeans, like Maryland Congressman John Delaney, his colleague from Ohio Tim Ryan, and Colorado Governor John Hickenlooper, have been complete nonentities—their campaigns being over before they ever got started. Rep. Ryan dropped from the race in October 2019. Governor Hickenlooper had suspended his run in August. But before he did so, he got a taste of the Democratic electorate's progressive demands. At the 2019 California Democratic Party organizing convention, Governor Hickenlooper was booed loudly after reciting each of the following lines: "Socialism is not the answer." "We shouldn't try to achieve universal coverage by removing private insurance from 150 million Americans." "We shouldn't try to tackle climate change by guaranteeing every American a gov[ernment] job."[47] And still, the so-called moderates like himself, and fellow Coloradan Senator Michael Bennet, largely toed the progressive line, arguing for example that "health care is a human right."[48] One would be hard-pressed to find a single candidate who has not moved leftward since the start of the campaign or a single issue on which the Democratic field collectively has not moved significantly more left than any such field to precede it. The issues of emphasis on the campaign trail and in debates alone reveal the triumph of progressivism.

One of the issues with which the candidates seem most obsessed is race. The racial angle has been ever-present during the campaign, and as the author alluded to earlier in context of the 1619 Project, if the likes of *The New York Times* has its way, the racial angle will take on ever-greater focus once we enter the general election. The Manhattan Institute's Heather Mac Donald captures the race-obsessed 2020 climate among those on the Left in citing a smattering of headlines from their media cheerleaders and quotes from candidates:

> As race dominates the political conversation, 10 white Democratic candidates will take the stage" (the Washington Post); Mr. Trump's rally audiences are "overwhelmingly white" (multiple sources); your son's "whiteness is what protects him from not [sic] being shot" by the police (Sen. Kirsten Gillibrand); white candidates need to be conscious of "white privilege" (South Bend, Ind., Mayor Pete Buttigieg); "white supremacy manifests itself" in the criminal-justice, immigration and health-care systems (Sen. Cory Booker); " Michael Brown was murdered by a white police officer in Ferguson, Missouri" (Sen. Elizabeth Warren); whiteness is "the very core" of Mr. Trump's power, whereas his "predecessors made their way to high office through the passive power of whiteness" (Ta-Nehisi Coates in the Atlantic).[49]

To this list we can add another item: In September 2019, "moderate" frontrunner Joe Biden warned of "the domestic terrorism of white supremacy."[50] In a nod to the power of these views in the party, several candidates have backed a study of slavery reparations as the first step towards developing and implementing such a plan.[51] How did we get here? As Yglesias chronicles in his article on the "Great Awokening:"

[President] Obama's 2012 observation that **"if I had a son, he'd look like Trayvon"** is just one small example of how elite actors have helped push a shift in whites' perception of race. And the shift, once underway, became mutually reinforcing. Liberal white audiences became increasingly interested in black intellectuals' conceptions of race and racism in America. Back in April 2015, the social justice group **Race Forward produced a series of videos starring Jay Smooth trying to explain the concept of "systemic racism"** to a mass audience. **Hillary Clinton used the term in a February 2016 speech.**

…[Political scientist Brian] Schaffner observes that "Clinton talked a lot more about racial justice issues during the 2016 campaign than Obama did during his campaigns"—further priming the minority of white Americans who supported her to adopt a more sweeping view of racial justice. Key to this view, as **Adam Serwer wrote in the Atlantic in November 2017,** is that we should see racism as a question of "institutional and political power" rather than being "about name-calling or rudeness."

The extent to which that model has become mainstream among Democratic Party leaders is now evident. Just this March, Beto O'Rourke told an overwhelmingly white audience in Iowa that American capitalism is "racist." The previous summer, Elizabeth Warren called the criminal justice system "racist." Even Joe Biden— who in the mid-1970s was a leading political opponent of aggressive school integration measures—in a January 2019 speech called on white America "to admit there's still a systemic racism" in American life. Mainstream Democratic Party politicians, in other words, are beginning to take for granted that their constituents

will embrace the more institutional understanding of racism.[52] [Emphasis added]

Meanwhile, rather than running from the Squad, candidates across the ideological spectrum of the Democratic field have leaned into it. This is reflected not just in the face of failed candidate Senator Harris's embrace of AOC legislatively, or in various candidates defending Rep. Omar for her inflammatory comments. 2020 Democrats have gone much further. Joe Biden says the Squad is "an example of exactly what makes America great."[53] Bernie Sanders says the Squad is "speaking up for what America is supposed to be about."[54] Mayor Pete Buttigieg calls the Squad "very healthy for our party."[55] The candidates are kissing the ring. Why? Progressivism is where the energy in the Democratic base lies. And the Squad is progressivism's most powerful symbol.

The Congressional Transformation

Fourth, consider the Squad's activities in, and impact on Congress since its arrival. The Squad has feuded with and flouted the Democratic establishment while causing it to move leftward and even threatening to primary its members. If the inmates are not running the asylum, at the very least like Andy Dufresne in "The Shawshank Redemption" they have locked themselves in the warden's office and turned the music up. Brian Fallon, national press secretary for Hillary Clinton's 2016 presidential campaign, summarized well what we have witnessed in a July 2019 tweet regarding Speaker Pelosi's repeated attempts to marginalize the Squad. Fallon wrote: "The four house Freshmen whom Pelosi dismisses…have done more to define the vision and moral center of today's Democratic Party than all of the message bills pushed by the party leadership combined."[56] We have already discussed such trends in the context of Israel and Jews. They are reflected in myriad other areas in Congress as well. Consider just a sampling of what has transpired since the 2018 midterm election illustrating the Squad's power:

- Before 2019 even began, Rep. Alexandria Ocasio-Cortez joined the Sunrise Movement and the Justice Democrats activist group she led, in a climate change sit-in held at Speaker Pelosi's office. This was the first sign of the insubordination to come—an insubordination based in a belief that the establishment was no match for the freshmen insurgents.[57]

- In February 2019, Pelosi mocked AOC's Green New Deal, and her Squad, posing the rhetorical question: "The green dream or whatever they call it, nobody knows what it is, but they're for it right?" The Squad would get the last laugh. Far from treating the initiative glibly like Speaker Pelosi, all six Democratic presidential candidates who served in the Senate co-sponsored a resolution in support of it.[58] Speaker Pelosi has halted a floor vote on the companion House resolution, likely believing it to be a political non-starter. Nevertheless, that (i) the trial balloon exists, (ii) progressives are working on individual pieces of legislation geared towards achieving its goals, and (iii) conceptually, the Green New Deal has gained traction among the party's would-be leaders, signifies it is not merely a pie-in-the-sky effort, but one that has changed our politics.[59] As AOC's former chief of staff was later reported to have said in conversation with the climate director for former Democratic presidential candidate Governor Jay Inslee (WA): "The interesting thing about the Green New Deal…is it wasn't originally a climate thing at all…Do you guys think of it as a climate thing?…Because we really think of it as a how-do-you-change-the-entire-economy thing."[60] The stakes, in other words, could not be higher.

- Later, during an April 2016 interview for CBS' "60 Minutes," Lesley Stahl spoke to Speaker Pelosi of "AOC, and her group" as constituting one wing of the Democratic Party. Pelosi replied, "That's, like, five people."[61] This came on the heels of a thinly veiled dig from Pelosi at AOC et al., as reported in *USA Today*, that: "While there are people who have a large number of Twitter followers, what's important is that we have a large number of votes on the floor of the House."[62] She should not have had to belittle the Squad if it was really such a powerless group, and she would shortly pay a political price for so doing.

- In the summer of 2019, the Squad sought to scuttle Speaker Pelosi's plan to agree to the Senate-led bipartisan emergency border package, defying her demand to vote in favor of the legislation in an embarrassing rebuke to party leadership.[63] As Speaker Pelosi described it, "A vote against this bill is a vote for Donald Trump and his inhumane, outside-the-circle-of-civilized attitude toward the children."[64] Ultimately the progressive revolt prevented the Democrats from uniting behind an alternative to the Senate's package in what *The New York Times* called a "striking defeat" for Speaker Pelosi.[65] After the bill passed, the Squad attacked her, with Rep. Omar tweeting: "A vote for Mitch McConnell's border bill is a vote to keep kids in cages and terrorize immigrant communities." AOC declared: "Hell no. That's an abdication of power." This triggered another major spat between Pelosi and the Squad.[66] That such in-fighting festered again illustrated that Pelosi was unable to exert control over the four "powerless" freshmen. During the ensuing scrum, things got so bad that the Squad, and AOC's aforementioned chief of staff, played the race card against Pelosi, and more moderate Democrats.[67] AOC told the *Washington Post* that the Speaker was "explicit[ly] singling out…newly elected women of color."[68] Her then-chief of staff went much further, comparing Democratic opponents of the Squad to segregationists.[69] In a most telling Twitter thread, Karen Attiah, Global Opinions editor at the *Washington Post*, unleashed on Speaker Pelosi, reflecting the view of other Leftist activists enraged at her belittling of the Squad. She equated Speaker Pelosi with President Trump, in response to his tweet directing Squad members to "go back and help fix the totally broken and crime infested places from which they came," writing:

> Make no mistake: Nancy Pelosi's dogwhistling snipes at @ AOC [Rep. Ocasio-Cortez's Twitter handle], Ilhan Omar, @ RashidaTlaib [Rep. Tlaib's Twitter handle] and @RepPressley [Rep. Pressley's Twitter handle] helped pave the way for this vicious, racist attack from the president.

> See how quickly we have moved from two powerful white women, @maureendowd [*The New York Times* op-ed columnist Maureen Dowd's Twitter handle] and @SpeakerPelosi [Speaker Pelosi's Twitter handle] helping each other to attack women of color over a nice box of chocolates... ..to the president telling them to leave the country.

> What people need to see in this newly formed @maureendowd /@SpeakerPelosi/@realDonaldTrump [President Trump's Twitter handle] axis of shevil is that white supremacy relies on dismissing, silencing, and undermining women of color. Putting them in their place by any means necessary.[70]

Attiah sought to clarify her argument with a final tweet: "I never said Speaker Pelosi was the cause of Trump's general racism. What I *did* note was that we are witnessing in real time are (sic) the attempts to marginalize @AOC, @RashidaTlaib @IlhanMN and @RepPressley, who all are outspoken in defense of America's marginalized groups."[71]

- Shortly thereafter, in a "CBS This Morning" interview with the Squad, AOC and Rep. Tlaib seemed to suggest that Speaker Pelosi was responsible for threats of violence against them.[72] That the putatively most powerful elected Democrat in the country could be called a racist, and accused of inciting people to violence by freshmen in her own party once again showed a lack of respect for her power or fear of repercussions.

- Around the time of this spat, Democrats leaked an internal poll showing that AOC, Rep. Omar and the Squad were viewed very negatively by swing voters.[73] But that swing voters nationally knew of the Squad, and had strong feelings about it, indicated its prominence. That leadership leaked the poll in a bid to undermine the Squad indicated it recognized the Squad's prominence too.[74] Party officials also leaked other news seemingly meant to marginalize progressives, such as when word came out that Pelosi had told them "do not tweet" in a closed-door meeting.[75] Again, if the Squad was just a trifling concern, Speaker Pelosi would ignore it. Her actions indicate she believes it is a powerful enough phenomenon to sink the Democratic House majority in 2020.

- Meanwhile, Speaker Pelosi evidently sees risk in going too far in her attempts to strong-arm the Squad, which could enrage progressives. She demonstrated the criticality of the Squad to her party when in late July 2019, after months of in-fighting, she hosted a meeting with AOC in which the two emerged arm in arm, smiling in a picture for public consumption as one happy Democratic family.[76] Soon after, during a congressional delegation to Africa that included Speaker Pelosi and Rep. Omar, Rep. Omar would post a picture of herself leading a smiling Speaker Pelosi by the hand through Ghana's "Door of Return," with a caption expressing her solidarity with the Speaker.[77] These images of kumbaya, of course, follow on the heels of the numerous controversies already noted— such as the party's protecting AOC and her Squad for referring to U.S. immigration detention centers as "concentration camps;" protecting Rep. Omar in the wake of a variety of anti-Zionist, anti-Semitic, and anti-American comments; running interference for Rep. Tlaib in her discussion about Israel, the Holocaust, and the Arabs; and a host of similar matters. It is a tricky balancing act for Speaker Pelosi, but more and more it seems to hinge on assuaging concerns of party progressives, and specifically Rep. Omar and her companions.

- On several occasions, illustrating the Squad's refusal to stand in the shadow of party leadership, its members have in whole or in part delivered nationally televised press conferences expressing their positions.[78,79] In doing so, they are afforded the kind of coverage rarely if ever given to purported naïve neophyte backbenchers, or any freshman House members for that matter.

- Reflecting the Squad's audacity, again its members and supporters have been tied to numerous primary challenges against incumbent Democratic members in good standing, including even members of the Congressional Black Caucus, much to the House leadership's chagrin.[80]

- Regarding race-based legislation, as of this writing, there are 122 cosponsors of Rep. Sheila Jackson Lee's bill to create a commission to study and develop reparation proposals.[81]

- The race-centric focus of the Squad, and the progressive movement it represents, have also come to play an outsized role even in the Democrats' internal operations. Under fire from black and Latino lawmakers over a lack of diversity among its senior leaders, the Democratic Congressional Campaign Committee's top staffers, including its executive director, were all forced to resign in late July of 2019 in what *Politico* described as a scene of "full-blown turmoil."[82,83]

- In spite of the potentially catastrophic political repercussions to pursuing impeachment, and the prior failure of Special Counsel Robert Mueller's Report to corroborate the Democrats' damning allegations about a treasonous Trump-Russia conspiracy, House Democratic leaders originally appeared to pursue impeachment in contradiction of Speaker Pelosi's long-held anti-impeachment position.[84,85,86,87] Why? Likely in no small part out of fear of enraging progressives and being primaried themselves in 2020. Finally, in September of 2019, Speaker Pelosi herself relented, seemingly throwing up her hands and fully giving in to her party's progressives, announcing Democrats would indeed commence an impeachment inquiry into the president.[88] This charade of a process would result in the House approving two articles of impeachment on a party-line vote, with several Democrats voting against one or both of the articles—one of whom would ultimately switch parties altogether.[89,90,91] Speaker Pelosi would then bizarrely delay the transmission of the articles of impeachment to the Senate, out of a hypocritical stated concern that the Republican-led upper chamber would not run a fair process, thereby throwing Congress into chaos.[iv,92] As 2020 dawned, the Democrats' impeachment gambit appeared to be an unmitigated disaster for the party politically, and the American political system generally.[93,94]

It is important to remember that the Squad has been able to accumulate power both tangible and intangible in part because it has been ensconced in the Democratic Party since it emerged on the political scene. The Squad's pull is about more than large social media followings. The party has long embraced its young "rock stars," and the Squad fits the bill in this time of intersectionalism and identity politics. In Rep. Omar's case, on top of having been regaled on the covers of national magazines, and featured in glowing profiles, any number of prominent Democrats have sought to bask in her glow over the years—or at minimum gladly posed for photos with her. They include politicians and political figures from Hillary Clinton to Bernie Sanders, from John Lewis to Keith Ellison, and from Donna Brazile to Cecile Richards.[95,96,97,98,99,100,101] Perhaps most notably of all, according to its program, at the 2018 United State of Women Summit, Rep. Omar shared the stage with President Obama's consigliere Valerie Jarrett, among other political stars.[102] Jarrett, President Obama's senior advisor, and right-hand woman from his early political days in Chicago would tweet in celebration of Rep. Omar's victory in her run for the House that: "You are the change in Congress we have been waiting for. Thank you, @IlhanMN, for your willingness to jump with both feet into the arena! Many around the country are both counting on you and will have your back."[103]

Following President Trump's facetious call for Squad members to go back from whence they came, the late longtime Democratic Representative Elijah Cummings of Maryland, the Chairman of the House Oversight Committee, said of the Squad:

---

iv   On the matter of hypocrisy, Speaker Pelosi and her fellow congressional Democrats seemed to believe that the political remedy of impeachment ought to be pursued via a purely political process in the Democrat-controlled House, and a purely legal process in the Republican-controlled Senate. This "heads I win, tails you lose" procedural paradigm is consistent with the—in the author's view—meritless substance of the farcical impeachment case.

> These are folks and women who love their country, and they work very hard and they want to move us towards that more perfect union that our Founding Fathers talked about…these are some of the most brilliant young people that I have met and I am honored…to serve with them.[104]

Such effusive praise from a Democratic icon in the House may well indicate that Speaker Pelosi and the establishment see the writing on the wall. They have been unable to stymie the Squad. Now they have to coddle it, and where necessary co-opt it, and its ideas, to keep a precarious coalition together. But on top of the political risks of embracing the Squad, leadership cannot trust it. The Squad poses an existential threat because it is anathema to the establishment. Beyond its willingness to buck party authority, AOC made this clear when she primaried longtime Representative Joe Crowley, landing on Capitol Hill before she was thirty.

That Squad-aligned groups are planning more primary challenges against the Democratic establishment in 2020 suggests the problem for the Democratic leadership is not going away. Absent unforeseen primary challenges against the Squad itself, its members may soon outflank the establishment. Certainly, they should outlast it.

Either way, the civil war is destined to rage on. Following one of the major flare-ups between the Squad and leadership in July 2019, Rep. Omar stated: "There is a constant struggle with people who have power about sharing power and we're not in the business of asking to share that power, we're in the interest of grabbing that power."[105] Speaker Pelosi has internalized what Rep. Omar made concrete: The Squad does not wish to coexist with the establishment. It seeks to defeat it.

Rep. Omar and the Squad symbolize the ascendance of progressivism. Progressive ideas, and progressive figures, have never been more widely represented in our national politics. While traditionalists may argue that it would be a boon to our country for the Democratic Party to embrace its Scoop Jacksons rather than its Sheila Jackson-Lees, the simple fact is there are no more Scoop Jacksons. Were today's progressives to Google who Scoop Jackson was, they would be more likely to rush to erase his name from the history books than to embrace his philosophy. So when President

Trump casts Rep. Omar as "the face of the Democrat Party," even if driven by politics, there is truth to it. As more moderate older Democrats are replaced by Squad-like younger ones, what little moderation still remains within the party will evaporate.[106] America stands to suffer accordingly.

PART III

The Threat of Ilhan Omar to
U.S. National Security

CHAPTER 10

COLLUSION: OMAR'S TROUBLING TIES TO AMERICA'S ENEMIES

Troubling Questions

Would it concern Americans to know that an elected official with power over U.S. national security and foreign policy, and unfettered access to classified information related thereto, keynoted fundraisers on behalf of, and received remuneration from, organizations implicated in major terrorism financing conspiracies?

How about if the organizations spawned from subversive, theocratic, murderous foreign movements comprised of like-minded Jew-haters and terror whitewashers—with whom the elected official frequently palled around, and from whom the official received campaign contributions?

Would it add to these concerns if the elected official maintained ties to like-minded adversarial and/or corrupt foreign governments?

Would it worry Americans all the more if the elected official not only maintained such problematic ties but often aped these entities' rhetoric and endorsed their agendas?

Ilhan Omar's ascent to congress raises these questions of concern. The answers to them reveal why Rep. Omar—the personification of the progressive-Islamist axis—even independent of her destructive ideology presents a national security threat to America.

"Some People Did Something"

On March 23, 2019, Rep. Ilhan Omar delivered a speech at the Council on American-Islamic Relation's Los Angeles (CAIR-LA) annual fundraising banquet. CAIR bills itself as an Islamic civil rights organization, but as we alluded to previously and will demonstrate in this chapter, in practice it aims to subvert the civil rights of Americans of all religions. In the speech, she declared that her fellow Muslims should:

> raise hell; make people uncomfortable. Because…here's the truth: Far too long, we have lived with the discomfort of being a second-class citizen (sic), and frankly, I'm tired of it, and every single Muslim in this country should be tired of it. CAIR was founded after 9/11 because they (sic) recognized that some people did something, and that all of us were starting to lose access to our civil liberties.[1]

Americans were rightly outraged at the flippant manner in which she described the jihadist attacks of September 11, 2001—adding insult to injury by specifically focusing on and portraying Muslims as the victims of an attack perpetrated by their coreligionists. That Rep. Omar's Democratic colleagues rushed to her defense did little to assuage the shock and disgust of much of the American public.

Among the outraged was Nicholas Haros Jr., whose mother Frances went to work at the World Trade Center that fateful morning, never to return. On the eighteenth anniversary of the attacks, during the annual name-reading ceremony held at Ground Zero, Haros Jr. arrived clad in a t-shirt quoting Rep. Omar's flippant comment with an accusatory question mark at its end: "SOME PEOPLE DID SOMETHING?" He stepped up to the lectern and unleashed on Rep. Omar's statement. Mr. Haros shot back at her nebulous, yet abundantly clear words that the perpetrators of the attacks were not just "some people," but "19 Islamic terrorists, members of Al-Qaeda." As for the "something" they did, Haros exclaimed that they had "killed over 3,000 people and caused billions of dollars of economic damage." As to the victims of the jihad, Haros Jr. told the crowd of fellow mourners: "I was attacked. Your relatives and friends were attacked… Our constitutional freedoms were attacked and our nation's founding on Judeo-Christian principles was attacked."[2]

Remarkably, when confronted with these words, Rep. Omar doubled down, telling CBS' Margaret Brennan that while she "certainly could not understand the weight of the pain that the families of the victims of 9/11 must feel," after September 11th "many Americans found themselves… having their civil rights stripped from them." As is her wont, Omar reminded Americans that *she too was a victim*. She added, "as a Muslim, not only was I suffering as an American who was attacked on that day, but the next day I woke up as my fellow Americans were now treating me as suspect."[3] For Rep. Omar, the narcissist, the cynic, and most of all the perpetual victim, the focal point of 9/11 was not the jihadist attacks, but how America responded to jihadis, and how Americans' reactions impacted her!

The Minnesota congresswoman was factually incorrect when she said CAIR was founded after the 9/11 attacks. CAIR was in actuality founded years before in 1994. As she has done in the past, and undoubtedly will do in the future, Rep. Omar misstated the facts in order to fit her desired narrative—while obscuring a far more nefarious context.

CAIR, the Holy Land Foundation, and Hamas

As shameful as Rep. Omar's original offending statements were, the very fact that she delivered them at CAIR-LA should have troubled the nation even more.

Though rarely discussed, among other anti-American actions, CAIR, the purported "Muslim civil liberties organization," helped raise funds supporting a terrorist group that has killed Americans.[4,5]

CAIR was most brazen in its support. In the weeks following the 9/11 attacks, CAIR made an appeal on its website to support the relief effort by

"Donat[ing] through the Holy Land Foundation [(HLF)]."[6] What was the HLF? As the U.S. Department of Justice (DOJ) would later prove in court, the HLF was a "charitable organization" that in actuality existed to support Hamas. CAIR, in other words, used 9/11 to solicit money, in effect, for Al-Qaeda's Palestinian Arab cousin.[i]

CAIR had a history of making such appeals on behalf of HLF. According to an *IPT* dossier, months before the most deadly attack on the homeland in U.S. history, at a rally outside of the Israeli consulate in Los Angeles, a prominent CAIR member implored the crowd to "make sure to send our donations" to the HLF.[7] The individual making the appeal was Hussam Ayloush, the current Executive Director of CAIR-LA. Ayloush was not only in attendance during Rep. Omar's keynote speech but delivered one of his own.[8]

A couple of weeks later, Rep. Omar would be pictured with Ayloush and several other CAIR leaders on Capitol Hill.[9] Among them was CAIR-Florida Executive Director Hassan Shibly, another scheduled speaker at the CAIR-LA banquet.[10,11] Ayloush and Shibly, as we will shortly document, have made numerous incendiary comments about America, Israel, and Jews while obfuscating on the matter of Islamic terror.[ii,12]

By December 2001, the HLF was no longer accepting contributions from CAIR, Ayloush's allies, or anyone else for that matter. The U.S. Treasury Department classified the then-largest Muslim charity in the U.S. as a Specially Designated Terrorist, shuttering it. As the DOJ would later write at the conclusion of the largest terrorist financing prosecution in American history, which resulted in convictions for HLF and five of its senior members:

---

i   Though Al-Qaeda leaders have criticized Hamas in recent years, in the past the two terrorist groups have partnered. See for example: https://www.washingtonexaminer.com/weekly-standard/the-hamas-al-qaeda-alliance. More broadly, they are both Sunni jihadist organizations with ideological—and in Hamas' case direct—roots in the Muslim Brotherhood. See footnote (iii).

ii   In Ayloush's case, he is also plugged into Democratic politics, as of 2019 serving as an Assembly District Delegate to the California Democratic Party, and having previously served as a delegate at the 2012 DNC. He visited the Obama White House on multiple occasions. See: https://www.cadem.org/our-party/adem/assembly-district-meetings/ad-60 and https://www.investigativeproject.org/3777/a-red-carpet-for-radicals-at-the-white-house.

From its inception, HLF existed to support Hamas…The government presented evidence at trial that, as the U.S. began to scrutinize individuals and entities in the U.S. who were raising funds for terrorist groups in the mid-1990s, the HLF intentionally hid its financial support for Hamas behind the guise of charitable donations. HLF and these five defendants provided approximately $12.4 million in support to Hamas and its goal of creating an Islamic Palestinian state by eliminating the State of Israel through violent jihad.

…The defendants provided financial support to the families of Hamas martyrs, detainees, and activists knowing and intending that such assistance would support the Hamas terrorist organization.[13]

During the trial, CAIR was named as an unindicted co-conspirator with the HLF. As it turns out, the two organizations were linked from the very beginning. CAIR, like HLF, was listed as a member of the Palestine Committee. The Palestine Committee was a creation of the Muslim Brotherhood (MB) in the U.S. tasked with supporting Hamas, MB's Palestinian Arab wing.[iii,14] Its job, according to internal MB documents, was to provide the "Palestinian cause…media, money, [and] men."[15] The Palestine Committee's Islamic Association for Palestine (IAP), which was dedicated to "serv[ing] the cause of Palestine [on behalf of Hamas] on the political and media fronts," birthed CAIR.[16] If HLF was Hamas' U.S. fundraising arm, CAIR was to be its U.S. information warfare, or, "public affairs" arm. Its job was to serve as a front for Hamas that Americans would not identify with jihad.[17]

---

iii   Per Article Two of the Hamas' Charter: "The Islamic Resistance Movement is one of the wings of Moslem Brotherhood in Palestine. Moslem Brotherhood Movement is a universal organization which constitutes the largest Islamic movement in modern times. It is characterised by its deep understanding, accurate comprehension and its complete embrace of all Islamic concepts of all aspects of life, culture, creed, politics, economics, education, society, justice and judgement, the spreading of Islam, education, art, information, science of the occult and conversion to Islam." See: https://avalon.law.yale.edu/20th_century/hamas.asp.

We know this in part because members of the Palestine Committee, including senior leaders of Hamas, the HLF, and the IAP said so. In 1993, the Palestine Committee convened a meeting of senior operatives in a Philadelphia hotel that, unbeknownst to its members, the FBI recorded.[18] Former HLF executive director Shukri Abu Baker captured the tenor of the conference well when he stated, on tape, that "War is deception." The Committee convened the meeting, according to prosecutors, so members could "decide how to conceal their activities from the scrutiny of the United States government." They acted surreptitiously during the gathering itself, with some participants, for example, referring to Hamas as "Samah," and using pseudonyms to protect their identities.[19]

U.S. government litigators noted that among the items the Islamists discussed was "redefining the perception of…sub-organizations due to their work for the Palestinian cause…"[20] For his part, Abu Baker urged the group to form entities "whose Islamic hue is not very conspicuous."[21] Thankfully, Baker's own acts in support of terrorism proved conspicuous enough that he was sentenced to sixty-five years in prison during the HLF trial. Another attendee counseled, "We must form a new organization for activism which will be neutral, because we are placed in a corner…. It is known who we are. We are marked."[iv]

Two attendees demonstrated how to be inconspicuous and appear "neutral." As Andrew C. McCarthy, the former federal prosecutor responsible for leading the investigation and prosecution of the jihadist cell behind the 1993 World Trade Center attack, recounts:

> Omar Ahmed, the IAP's president…gave his confederates thoughtful advice [at the Philadelphia meeting] that underscored the extent to which communications strategy was weighing on his mind. It would be better, he counseled,

---

iv   This unidentified speaker also seemed to channel Rep. Omar, declaring, in context of the group's political posture with respect to Israel and "peace:" "[O]ur approach or our policies in the arena are: non-opposition to peace as a statement. I mean, someone will ask you: 'Are you against peace?' Tell him 'No. We are not opposed to peace as a peace but we are against hypocrisy because this peace is not just. We are with all just peace. Justice with peace', Without justice … Even the African-Americans have this title, that there is not justice without peace … No peace without justice. It is always a principle of peace with justice." See: https://www.investigativeproject.org/documents/misc/185.pdf.

to say, "I want to restore the '48 land" (i.e., return Israel to its original, indefensible 1948 boundaries) than to make crude (i.e., honest) statements like, "I want to destroy Israel." In the same vein, he warned that a new organization in the U.S. could not afford to admit publicly that "We represent Samah [i.e., Hamas]," or to tell a congressman that, say, "I am Omar Yahya [Ahmed's pseudonym]. . . and Yasser Arafat doesn't represent me but [Hamas founder] Ahmed Yassin does."

McCarthy also wrote that Ahmed was joined by:

Nihad Awad, then the IAP's public-relations director... [T]he FBI's recordings showed him to be an active participant, though he...later testified to a bout of amnesia about the meeting. No wonder: He had ardently concurred in Ahmad's suggestions about adopting "different but parallel types of address." "When I speak with the American," he elaborated, "I speak with someone who doesn't know anything. As for the Palestinian who has a martyr brother or something, I know how to address him, you see?"[22]

In 1994, the IAP executives—and listed members of the Palestine Committee—Ahmed and Awad, along with the former head of IAP's Chicago office, Rafeeq Jaber, developed the vehicle by which they would put these principles into practice: CAIR.[23,24] A Palestine Committee Meeting Agenda from July 1994 made this more explicit, listing CAIR as one of the Committee's working organizations, alongside IAP, HLF, and several other groups.[25]

Awad would go on to become CAIR's Executive Director, a position he holds today. He is an ardent defender of Ilhan Omar, whom he has praised for "shaking off the old mindset with regard to the Palestine question."[26,27,28,29] Awad is gleeful that Omar is "not trying to fit into the historical Washington mindset, which has been unjustly pro-Israel for decades...[T]hey [Reps. Omar and Tlaib] represent a whole new generation of progressive activists nationwide."[30]

CAIR was also linked directly to HLF by dint of a check it received from the Hamas fundraising arm dated just a handful of months after the IAP officers founded it. The aforementioned Awad tried to conceal this fact. In sworn testimony, he denied receipt of the check as seed money, and when presented with a copy of it, was at pains to distance the two organizations.[31] In future years, CAIR would solicit still more donations on the HLF's behalf, in spite of mounting public evidence of its fundraising on behalf of Hamas. On the basis of the findings in the HLF trial, in 2009 U.S. District Judge Jorge Solis declared that "The Government has produced ample evidence to establish the associations of CAIR…with HLF, the Islamic Association for Palestine…and with Hamas."[32] He quashed CAIR's plea to have its name expunged from the HLF's lengthy list of co-conspirators.[33] The FBI declared that it would cease all formal contacts with CAIR.[34]

Of course, that CAIR had ever been an FBI "liaison partner," with which it engaged in "outreach efforts" for years, illustrated CAIR's success, in effect, of aiding terrorism. Its engagement seemed to be a one-way street. Steve Pomerantz, former assistant director to the FBI who led its counter-terrorism efforts during the 1990s, has said that CAIR had "a consistent, long history of being antagonistic toward law enforcement," reflected in campaigns purportedly educating American Muslims on knowing their rights, but which implicitly, and sometimes explicitly, called for nonco-operation with the FBI.[35,36] Indeed, as the lawyers representing the estate of the late former FBI counterterrorism officer John P. O'Neill wrote of CAIR and CAIR-Canada, in a class action lawsuit the estate lawyers filed on behalf of the victims of 9/11:

> [B]oth organizations have actively sought to hamper governmental anti-terrorism efforts by direct propaganda activities aimed at police, first-responders, and intelligence agencies through so-called sensitivity training. Their goal is to create as much self-doubt, hesitation, fear of name-calling, and litigation within police departments and intelligence agencies as possible so as to render such authorities ineffective in pursuing international and domestic terrorist entities.[37]

O'Neill was one of the victims. After spending years investigating Al-Qaeda and other jihadist groups, he tragically lost his life while serving as head of security at the World Trade Center. In congressional testimony, former Rep. Frank Wolf (R-VA) noted that "After dozens of Somalian Americans disappeared…in 2009, CAIR attempted to drive a wedge between the Muslim community and the FBI, which was seeking to track down the missing men." The missing men Rep. Wolf highlighted had disappeared from Minneapolis—Rep. Omar's territory, a hotbed of jihadist activity.[38,39]

Incredibly, even today, law enforcement officials continue to partner with CAIR as a representative of the Muslim community, as do many elected officials.[40,41] In this regard, Rep. Omar, who has spoken in front of CAIR on numerous occasions, been paid for some of her talks, and consorted with its officers, is not alone. This was illustrated in late 2018 when—in spite of just the small portion of CAIR's history thus far detailed—more than 100 predominantly Democrat lawmakers—including current and former presidential aspirants Senators Booker, Harris, and Klobuchar—delivered letters of support to CAIR in connection with its annual national banquet and fundraiser.[42]

The Case for Ilhan Omar's Islamist Collusion

A single event with a single organization involving a single-digit number of individuals does not a case make, but it can certainly present a fertile area for inquiry. In this case, one quickly finds that the connections between Rep. Omar and Islamist organizations are numerous and quite close. Yet these relationships have gone ignored in public discourse. Ignorance, or still worse knowing silence on these matters, is a direct indictment of Congress, law enforcement officials, and the media. And what makes their collective lack of curiosity, or candor, all the more scandalous is the context of the present-day political environment.

Since before the wee hours of November 9, 2016, Americans were subjected to theories purporting that Donald Trump was engaged in a treasonous conspiracy with the Russian government. The DOJ empowered Special Counsel Robert Mueller with almost limitless resources to investigate "any links and/or coordination" between the Russian government and members of the Trump presidential campaign.[43] The media too devoted an army of journalists and nearly endless airtime to the case. Government officials and the press put under the microscope every meeting, utterance, and action of anyone and everyone in the president's orbit. They leveled all manner of outlandish and unfounded allegations and accusations at the president and his associates. To those who saw through the fog of political war, it became clear months in advance of Special Counsel Mueller's report that there was no "there" there.[44,45,46,47] The goal was to undermine and perhaps collapse a presidency independent of the fact pattern. In that regard, the House Democrats' impeachment effort seemed to represent still more of the same.[48]

Conversely, if one were to apply the Special Counsel's mandate to examine any "links and/or coordination" between the global Islamist network and Rep. Omar, the case for collusion would be beyond compelling. This poses a significant national security threat to our nation. That there are any number of credible allegations about Rep. Omar's personal criminality and ethics violations, as we will discuss in the next chapter, only adds to the peril she poses from her perch on Capitol Hill.

The Muslim Brotherhood as the Tip of the Sunni Islamist Spear

Before making the case for collusion, it is necessary to have some background on the global Islamist network with which Rep. Omar is linked. The Muslim Brotherhood is the tip of the Sunni Islamic supremacist spear. It has spawned jihadist groups from Al-Qaeda to Hamas, all of which are united by a desire to impose Sharia law.

The MB's motto is worth repeating because it so clearly elucidates its goals, strategies, and tactics: "Allah is our objective; the Prophet is our leader; the Quran is our law; Jihad is our way; dying in the way of Allah is our highest hope."[49] While the motto makes explicit the MB's violence— violence reflected most recently in its short-lived control of Egypt under Mohamed Morsi—violent jihad is not the only way by which its adherents, and other Islamists, pursue their theopolitical totalitarian ends.[50,51] As warriors for their cause, Brotherhood members are strategic thinkers, understanding they must tailor their means to practical realities, including their relative strength, and the nature of the societies they are targeting. This, they believe, is not only prudent but consistent with Islamic doctrine, beginning with the example set for them by Muhammad.

When the MB says "the Quran is our law; Jihad is our way," that implies that it can employ a broad array of weapons—not just physical ones like rockets, bombs, and knives. Islamists tell us that jihad goes hand in hand with *dawa*—ideological warfare, and the panoply of other non-violent tools at their disposal.[v,52] The MB has concluded that this last realm is particularly suitable for targeting the West, and its nonviolent organizations here can be

---

v   *Dawa* is often defined as Islamic proselytization, but it encompasses a much broader range of activities than proselytization entails as understood in the Western vernacular. In the Islamic canon, *dawa* is treated as an invitation to submit to Islam, or face jihad. See *Catastrophic Failure*, for example pages 127-147. As its author, Stephen Coughlin—who was recognized as the Pentagon's leading expert on Islamic law as it relates to national security and served in a variety of governmental capacities including on the Joint Staff, J-2 (Intelligence) for the Chairman, Joint Chiefs of Staff at the Pentagon—notes, *dawa* efforts relate to both Muslims and the societies over which the Islamists intend to triumph, garnering followers who will undertake revolutionary efforts. In leading MB scholar Sheikh Yusuf al-Qaradawi's *Islamic Education and Hassan al-Banna*, Qaradawi wrote: "The greatest responsibility [of the MB] is to train [the] Muslim, because he is the foundation stone of revolution. He is the axis of welfare and rectification of deeds, without which, the establishment of Islamic society or the enforcement of Islamic laws or establishment of government cannot be imagined." Coughlin notes that "Under Banna's leadership, the Muslim Brotherhood would become an exemplar for what would later be known as local 'community organizing.' He preached not only in mosques but also in community spaces, such as coffee shops. The group became creating the basic infrastructure of social services that soon won the loyalty of hundreds of thousands of Egyptians." In the HLF trial, federal prosecutors presented an exhibit showing a Hamas organization structure consisting of "Political," "Military," and "Social / Dawa" efforts, reflecting testimony in which they explained how "grass-roots" organizing and fundraising by *dawa* enabled it to fund its terror activity (through entities like HLF and its co-conspirators). Coughlin concludes that "For the Brotherhood, outreach is focused on two objectives: (1) inviting everyone to Islam and (2) subverting those who choose to remain infidels. In other words, *dawah*." See *Catastrophic Failure* pages 164-189. Contemporary Islamist "thought leaders" reflect classical Islamic doctrine, making clear that *dawa* and jihad work together. The late Grand Mufti of Saudi Arabia for example declared in 1998: "The aim of *da'wah* and jihaad is not to shed blood, take wealth, or enslave women and children; these things happen incidentally but are not the aim. This only takes place when the disbelievers (non-Muslims) refrain from accepting the truth and persist in disbelief and refuse to be subdued... The truth has been spread through the correct Islamic *da'wah*, which in turn has been aided and supported by jihad whenever anyone stood in its way... It was jihaad and *da'wah* together which helped to open the doors to victories." See: https://www.hsdl.org/?view&did=807409. The aforementioned Qaradawi has said: "We will conquer Europe, we will conquer America, not through the sword but through *dawa*." See: https://docs.house.gov/meetings/GO/GO06/20180711/108532/HHRG-115-GO06-Wstate-JasserMDM-20180711.pdf. For a primer on *dawa*, see aforementioned former Muslim Brotherhood member Ayaan Hirsi Ali's *The Challenge of Dawa: Political Islam as Ideology and Movement and How to Counter It* at https://www.hoover.org/sites/default/files/research/docs/ali_challengeofdawa_final_web.pdf.

thought of as *dawa* entities. Warring in this more deceptive manner, using the pen and the voice rather than the sword, takes advantage of America's devotion to freedom of speech, religion, and association, exploiting its political, legal, and civil society institutions. This is the same path pursued by Communists during the Cold War, the effects of which we are still dealing with to this day, as demonstrated by this book. And while true that violent jihadists continue to carry out attacks in the West, and Islamists do have internecine squabbles over strategy, tactics, and timing, in effect, they complement each other because violent jihadists make nonviolent jihadists appear to be a "moderate" alternative, which can be engaged. Since nonviolent Islamists use the institutions of free societies against them instead of attacking by force, it is they who are arguably more effective at advancing the shared long-term goal of ensuring that Islam triumphs.

Like the Left, Islamists have been engaged in a "long march" through our institutions for decades. The MB made clear this modus operandi in a document discovered during an FBI raid of a home in Virginia in 2004, which was submitted as evidence at the HLF trial. The document was prepared by a senior U.S. MB leader, Mohamed Akram, aka Mohamed Akram Adlouni. Akram was a member of the U.S. MB's Shura Council, its central committee, and listed in government exhibits as a member of the U.S. MB's Board of Directors, its Executive Office, and as its Office Secretary, which in the context of MB organizations, connotes that he was a chief or head. This was in addition to his leadership positions in a number of other key committees.[vi,53] Akram drafted the document in 1991 as a supplement to a long-term plan approved by the MB in 1987. He titled it "Explanatory Memorandum on the General Strategic Goal for the Group in North America." It begins:

The general strategic goal of the Group in America… is "Enablement of Islam in North America, meaning: establishing an effective and a stable Islamic Movement led

vi   As of February 2019, Adlouni was listed as the General Secretary of the Al-Quds International Foundation, which the U.S. Treasury Department classified as a Specially Designated Global Terrorist Entity for its ties to Hamas. Records indicate that at least as late as 2008, Adlouni shared the stage with fellow Palestine Committee member, and current Executive Director of CAIR, Nihad Awad.

by the Muslim Brotherhood which adopts Muslims' causes domestically and globally, and which works to expand the observant Muslim base, aims at unifying and directing Muslims' efforts, presents Islam as a civilization alternative, and supports the global Islamic State wherever it is."[54]

That the Brotherhood had a toehold in America at all is disturbing enough. But the way it sought to advance its position was particularly devious. The Memorandum described "Enablement of Islam," or "Settlement," as making "Islam and its movement become a part of the homeland it lives in." This meant that Islam must be firmly established, stable and enabled "within the souls, minds and the lives of the people of the country in which it moves," and "rooted…in the soil of the spot where it moves…"[55] To that end, members of the MB were instructed to internalize that:

> The process of settlement is a "Civilization-Jihadist Process" with all the word means. **The Ikhwan [Muslim Brothers] must understand that their work in America is a kind of grand Jihad in eliminating and destroying the Western civilization from within and "sabotaging" its miserable house by their hands and the hands of the believers so that it is eliminated and God's religion is made victorious over all other religions.**[56] [Emphasis added]

Needless to say, there was nothing "moderate" about the MB's aims.

Those readers familiar with the MB have likely seen this quote before. But what many may be unaware of is the crucial argument that follows regarding operationalization. The Memorandum speaks of the imperative to set up Islamic centers in each city as the "'axis' of our Movement, the 'perimeter' of the circle of our work, our 'balance center,' the 'base' for our rise…" It adds, critically, that Muslim organizations are to be developed and work in conjunction with each Islamic center. This, per Akram, is consistent with Muhammad's establishing of "the mosque, which truly became 'the comprehensive organization,'" as well as MB founder Hassan al-Banna, who "when he and his brothers felt the need to 're-establish'

Islam and its movement anew...establish[ed] organizations with all their kinds: economic, social, media, scouting, professional and even the military ones." Akram continued:

> ...[I]n order for the process of settlement to be completed, we must plan and work from now to equip and prepare ourselves, our brothers, our apparatuses, our sections and our committees in order to turn into comprehensive organizations in a gradual and balanced way that is suitable with the need and the reality. What encourages us to do that - in addition to the aforementioned - is that we possess "seeds" for each organization from the organization we call for [See attachment number (I)]...All we need is to tweak them, coordinate their work, collect their elements and merge their efforts with others and then connect them with the comprehensive plan we seek...The big challenge that is ahead of us is how to turn these seeds or "scattered" elements into comprehensive, stable, "settled" organizations that are connected with our Movement and which fly in our orbit and take orders from our guidance. This does not prevent - but calls for - each central organization to have its local branches but its connection with the Islamic center in the city is a must.[57]

It is critical to note that among violent jihadists in the West, virtually all of them have been linked to one or several Islamic centers and/or mosques, including those who have hailed from Rep. Omar's district. But what of the organizations in their network? Akram linked to his document an "Attachment number (1)" that listed a series of entities, described as "our organizations and the organizations of our friends." These were, in other words, the foot soldiers for the MB's process of civilizational jihad. They included among others: Islamic Association for Palestine (IAP), Islamic Society of North America (ISNA), and the Occupied Land Foundation (OLF)—later to be renamed the Holy Land Foundation.[58]

During the HLF case, ISNA, IAP and its derivatives like CAIR, were all named as unindicted co-conspirators. These organizations, and the like-minded groups that have proliferated around them, are the very ones with which Rep. Ilhan Omar has been working since before she was ever an elected official. And if we zoom out to a global perspective, those governments with which she has most closely consorted are wedded to these groups or their foreign equivalents and affiliates.

Some have challenged the weight of the Memorandum as seminal to the MB's aims. Yet leaving aside its author's senior position in the MB, one need merely consider that several of the groups referenced in the Memorandum were linked to the MB and Hamas in federal court. Further, these relationships and activities were corroborated by dozens of other exhibits presented by the U.S. government—all of which a federal judge found to be dispositive of the U.S. government's HLF case.

The historical record shows in the backgrounds, words, and actions of these groups, and their leaders, that the Memorandum prevailed. That a sitting U.S. congresswoman on the House Foreign Affairs Committee (HFAC) like Ilhan Omar would have inextricable links to these organizations, their members, and fellow travelers—as well as foreign governments to which they are tied—poses a significant threat to America's national security interests. Herein, we will examine Rep. Omar's ties.

Ilhan Omar's Ties to Domestic Islamist Organizations
Council on American-Islamic Relations

Background and Activities
We have established CAIR's roots in the MB, as well as its attempts to hamper U.S. law enforcement by turning American Muslim communities against American law enforcement authorities. CAIR's officials have also made numerous statements over the years: Alibiing, serving as apologists for, and whitewashing Islamic supremacism; attacking as "Islamophobes" those who dare challenge Islamic supremacism; haranguing Israel rhetorically, including comparing the Israel Defense Forces to ISIS, and engaging in Holocaust inversion; lobbying for causes like opposition to counterterror

training materials forthrightly dealing with jihadist ideology; and engaging in lawfare against policies like the maintenance of a terror watch list.[59,60,61,62] CAIR officials have also crossed the line from facially legal *dawa* activities, to plainly illegal jihadist ones. As Andrew C. McCarthy notes:

> Numerous CAIR figures have been convicted of federal felonies, including terrorism offenses. For example, when…[HLF co-founder and brother-in-law of Hamas leader Musa Abu Marzook, Ghassan] Elashi, the founder of CAIR's Texas chapter, was found guilty in the HLF case, it marked his third time around the block. He'd been convicted in 2006 for funneling money to Marzook and Hamas, and in 2005 for illegal transactions with Libya and Syria. Randall Royer, a CAIR communications specialist and civil-rights coordinator whose sideline was recruiting would-be jihadists for terrorist training in Pakistan, is now serving a 20-year prison sentence after his conviction on explosives and firearms charges in the "Virginia Jihad" case. Bassem Khafagi, CAIR's community-affairs director (and a founder of the Saudi-subsidized, al-Qaeda-promoting Islamic Assembly of North America), also makes this dishonor roll: He was deported to Egypt after convictions for visa and bank fraud. And then there's Rabih Haddad, a fundraiser for CAIR's Ann Arbor chapter who was deported to Lebanon after a "charity" he founded, the Global Relief Foundation, was designated as a terrorist facilitator by the Treasury Department for providing support to al-Qaeda.[63]

In all, wrote the *Middle East Forum*'s Daniel Pipes in a 2014 CAIR exposé: "At least seven board members or staff at CAIR have been arrested, denied entry to the U.S., or were indicted on or pled guilty to (or were convicted of) terrorist charges."[64]

CAIR is designated as a terrorist organization by the United Arab Emirates (UAE). Why? The UAE bars political Islamist groups, including the Muslim Brotherhood and its offshoots. Yet, in an homage to the progressive-Islamist axis, the Obama administration lobbied on CAIR's behalf to get the UAE to remove it from its list of terrorist organizations. These efforts failed. But CAIR was able to chalk up a victory in that it received, and made public, a letter from Secretary of State John Kerry reading in part: "Let me reiterate, first, that the U.S. government clearly does not consider CAIR to be a terrorist organization…the Department of State rejected this allegation immediately after the UAE designations were announced in November, and we will continue to do so…U.S. officials have raised the issue of CAIR's inclusion on the UAE's terror list with UAE officials on multiple occasions…."[65] Talk about sabotage by our own hands.

Rep. Omar and CAIR

Tactically, CAIR focuses on saying it promotes "justice" as a cover for its activities geared toward silencing counterjihadists through the charge of "Islamophobia." It seeks to thwart and delegitimize the counterjihadist efforts of the jihadist's "unjust" mortal enemies—including the United States and Israel—through portraying Muslims as their eternal victims.[66] This dubious claim fits well within the social justice-infused worldview of Rep. Omar. Consequently, her ties with CAIR are legion, covering speaking engagements, financial relations, and mutual support of numerous CAIR officials. Given their simpatico views, it should come as no surprise that Omar lists in an old biography on her website that she was a former Advisory Board member for Minnesota's CAIR chapter (CAIR-MN).[67] Herein we detail Rep. Omar's CAIR connections:

- **Speaking Engagements**: In addition to the aforementioned CAIR-LA event, Rep. Omar has spoken in front of CAIR audiences on many other occasions, including in:

  - October 2019, when Rep Omar keynoted CAIR-Florida's 19th Annual South Florida Banquet, alongside the aforementioned Hassan Shibly.[68] More on Shibly shortly.

  - May 2019, when Rep. Omar headlined a Ramadan Fundraiser at CAIR's Washington branch (CAIR-WA).[69]

- March 2019, when, while Rep. Omar was in town for the CAIR-LA keynote, she also participated in a "meet and greet" fundraiser sponsored by CAIR-CA PAC.[70]

- August 2018, when, as touted by the aforementioned Hussam Ayloush, CAIR-CA PAC also hosted three fundraising events with then-State Rep. Omar in connection with her congressional run.[71]

- December 2017, when State Rep. Omar spoke at CAIR-San Francisco Bay Area's (CAIR-SFBA) annual banquet.[72] CAIR-SFBA's Executive Director is Zahra Billoo, who we will discuss momentarily.

- June 2017, when State Rep. Omar keynoted an event at CAIR's Arizona chapter.[73]

- March 2017, when State Rep. Omar spoke in front of CAIR-MN.[vii,74] Omar's ties with CAIR-MN's Executive Director, Jaylani Hussein, date back to college. We will discuss that relationship shortly.

- February 2017, when State Rep. Omar delivered the keynote at CAIR Chicago's annual banquet.[75] Zahra Billoo served as emcee.

---

vii   CAIR-MN has regularly invited anti-Jewish speakers to its events, including the aforementioned Hussam Ayloush, and Hatem Bazian. Bazian tweeted two images accusing "Ashke-Nazis" of engaging in rape, murder, and organ-trafficking. We will come to meet Bazian shortly. See: https://www.haaretz.com/us-news/palestinian-uc-berkeley-professor-apologizes-for-retweeting-anti-semitic-cartoons-1.5626988. In April 2019, it was uncovered that Abubakar Osman, aka Saddiqq Abu Osman, who described himself on social media as "CAIR Minnesota's Government Affairs Coordinator," wrote back in 2008 "fuc* isreal!! (sic) stupid Jewish motherfuc*ers!!! man I wish hitler was alive to fuc* up the jewish ppl and add more jewish casualties to the 6 million he killed in the holocaust…" See: https://www.meforum.org/islamist-watch/58246/cair-official-i-wish-hitler-was-alive-to-f-up. CAIR-MN shared a statement apologizing for what "one of our former employees…" said "when he was a teenager." See: https://www.facebook.com/CAIR.Minnesota/posts/2154426041331788.

- **Organizational Pecuniary Ties:**

  - Between January 1, 2017, and June 30, 2018, Rep. Omar received $5,000 in personal income for speeches delivered to CAIR chapters.[76]

  - During her run for the House in 2018, CAIR-CA PAC contributed $5,000 to Rep. Omar.[77]

- **Individual Links:**

  - **Nihad Awad** – Awad's Islamist reputation precedes him. Unsurprisingly, he has historically defended Hamas.[78] He has also defended individual jihadis. According to remarks he gave to a Saudi Arabian source in 2012, Awad lobbied extensively on behalf of Aafia Siddiqui, who was sentenced to eighty-six years in jail for her efforts to assault and murder American officers in Afghanistan.[79] While testifying in the U.S. Senate in 2003, Awad defended the IAP, calling it a "grassroots organization which continues to function legally and has only been 'linked' through allusion and no charge of criminality has been brought against the organization." He sought to alibi the activities of terrorist financing entities including the IAP-tied HLF.[80] Awad has complained of Jewish influence over U.S. government policies.[81] From a policy perspective, like many at CAIR and in the Islamist movement, Awad has portrayed U.S. government officials as illegally spying on Muslims, and engaging in Islamophobic policies. He has supported, for example, the recent litigation that resulted in a federal judge ruling that the terror watchlist unconstitutionally violates due process rights—a ruling Rep. Omar cheered.[82,83] He has been a frequent defender of Rep. Omar, and they have worked on shared policies.[84] For example, he has supported her effort to probe the governments with which the U.S. shares its terror watchlist, as well as the criteria used for determining how such information is shared, citing concerns over names being exchanged with Saudi Arabia. Omar put out a press release quoting extensively from Awad in support of the probe.[85] In 2018, Awad took to Twitter to endorse then-State Rep. Omar in the DFL primary, which she ultimately won.[86] He also praised Glenn Greenwald for defending Rep. Omar on "Criticizing Israeli Lobby & AIPAC" as "Not Anti-Semitic."[87] As we will soon detail, Awad and Rep. Omar also share a common bond with a foreign MB-aligned regime.

- **Hussam Ayloush** – In 2018 Ayloush called for Israel to be "terminated," tweeting "Iran's regime calling Israel a 'cancerous tumor' is like the pot calling the kettle black. All the people of that region will be better off once both murderous regimes are terminated."[88] In an email sent years earlier in 2002, Ayloush referred to Israelis as "zionazis …a bunch of nice people; just like their nazi brethren!"[89] On election night 2016, he tweeted "Ok, repeat after me: *Al-Shaab yureed isqat al-nizaam* (Arab Spring chant)," which translates to "The people wants to bring down the regime"— that is, the newly elected Trump administration.[90] When asked to condemn Hamas in November 2013, he sought to obfuscate as many such Islamists do, by attacking the interlocutor, calling the question "not acceptable," and decrying that it "proves that you have nothing but bigotry in you."[91] Also consistent with others in CAIR like Awad, and across the Islamist movement, Ayloush has portrayed the FBI as seeking to entrap hapless Muslims. In a May 2015 Facebook post regarding the arrest of two Anaheim, CA men on terrorism charges, Ayloush lamented that "FBI-paid informants [were] hired to entrap feeble-minded young Muslim men."[92] Meanwhile, in a July 2014 tweet, he found a way to link his criticism of U.S. counterterror policies with his "anti-Zionism," writing, "Is the FBI now going to send informants to entrap, radicalize, then arrest young Jewish

Americans joining Israel's terrorist army?"[93] Last but not least, it bears noting that Ayloush, like other CAIR officials, cheered the rise of Egyptian Muslim Brotherhood leader Mohamed Morsi after he issued a decree placing himself above the judiciary.[94] Upon Morsi's death, Ayloush wrote: "Egypt's legitimate President Morsi wasn't merely killed by bloody coup leader Sisi. He was murdered by UAE and Saudi/UAE rulers who funded the coup and immoral Egyptians who supported the criminal coup and Sisi. There will be justice in this life and on the Day of Judgment."[95] Ayloush's conception of "justice" would seem to conform to the Brotherhood conception of "justice." This is a man who Rep. Omar has appeared alongside at multiple events, and who has vigorously defended her.[96] During her 2018 congressional run, Ayloush contributed $1,200 to her campaign.[97]

- **Zahra Billoo** – Billoo was brought into the new Women's March board in September 2019, after anti-Semites Linda Sarsour and Tamika Mallory, among others, stepped aside—only to be replaced within days because of her own anti-Semitic bigotry.[98] Representative of the CAIR-SFBA Executive Director is a tweet from December 2014 in which she said "will not renounce jihad, khilafah, or sharia. #MPAC14."[99] Billoo was a speaker that December at MPAC's annual convention—MPAC being the Muslim Public Affairs Council.[100] It was founded by MB followers and Hezbollah sympathizers and has historically advanced a progressive-Islamist agenda.[101] As recently as November 2018, the civil rights lawyer tweeted, "From the river to the sea, #Palestine will be free," a genocidal call for Israel's destruction.[102] Like her colleague Hussam Ayloush, she has repeatedly compared Israel and its IDF to ISIS, tweeting messages like "Who has killed, tortured, and imprisoned more people: Apartheid Israel or ISIS?" and that she "doesn't see any difference between American youth leaving the country to join ISIS or the IDF. Both are murderous, war crime committing, terrorist entities." She has repeatedly called Israel a "terrorist state."[103,104,105] Billoo was among the CAIR signers of a 2014 statement in support of BDS on grounds that—echoing the language of the Soviet's Arabist allies at the UN, and Rep. Omar today—"funding racism and **Apartheid** is un-American."[106] [Emphasis added] Billoo has tweeted that she is "waiting for everyone who demands that Muslims everywhere condemn 9/11 to now condemn US funded terrorism in #Palestine."[107] She has endorsed attacks on Israel from Hamas and Hezbollah.[108,109] In spite of the litany of such comments from Billoo, politicians from Senators Warren and Sanders to Rep. Tlaib have appeared alongside her with wide smiles.[110] Of course, Rep. Omar has appeared at events with her too. This is in fitting with their shared worldview. Billoo, echoing Awad, praises Rep. Omar for "help[ing] broaden the conversation about how we can criticize the state of Israel, and that is not inherently anti-Semitic. And we need to be able to distinguish the two."[111]

- **Jaylani Hussein** – Like Ayloush, when confronted with a question asking if he denounced Hamas, as well as the Muslim Brotherhood, Hussein has sought to deflect, by playing the victim. He claimed in part "I understand that my organization comes under threat and know why we come under attack. It's not because of our silence. It's because we carry a big stick, we remind people of the Constitution. We remind people that American Muslims are exactly like everyone else. And we're not gonna allow anyone to threaten us, or create the fact that Muslims have to hide, and so we are an organization just like any other organization. We get audited. We get reviewed, we are a state-accredited organization and so if you think we are a terrorist organization then call the FBI and let them know, and let them investigate." He proceeded to accuse the individual asking the question of using "talking points" of "anti-Muslim organizations."[112] Characteristic of Hussein, and CAIR, was his reaction when a Somali-American security guard at a St. Cloud, MN shopping mall went on a stabbing rampage, reportedly shouting "Allahu akbar" during the attacks, and asking potential targets if they were Muslim before seeking blood.[113] ISIS took credit for the attack.[114] Before the perpetrator of the crime was officially identified, Hussein got out what he perceived to be the most important message: "we are definitely concerned about the potential for backlash in the community, both in the immediate run and the longer term."[115] As with Omar, Hussein treats Muslims as the real victims of jihad perpetrated against non-Muslims. Before joining CAIR, Hussein led the Muslim Students' Association (MSA) at a community college he attended. He and Rep. Omar were classmates at NDSU, where he recalls that she was a bright student.[116] The two have appeared together at several events and lobbied together against President Obama's Countering Violent Extremism policy, which was piloted in Minnesota, on grounds that it constituted racial profiling unfairly targeting Muslims.[117] Hussein has been a frequent defender of Rep. Omar, and has referred to her as "an inspiration to members of our community to not only vote but to become active in politics."[118,119]

- **Hassan Shibly** – Like his colleagues, Shibly has been standoffish when asked whether Hamas is a terrorist organization. He also has attacked the U.S. government for supposedly entrapping American Muslims convicted in terrorism cases, and for pressuring Muslims to become informants. Shibly defended HLF founder and head Ghassan Elashi, claiming that the sixty-five-year sentence handed down to him during the HLF trial was "for giving…to zakat [Islamic charitable] committees, which are not even designated as terrorist, in the theory they're somehow controlled by Hamas…"

Shibly has also engaged in Holocaust inversion, writing: "They ['extremist groups…'] promote the same types of lies against the Muslim community that was being promoted against the Jews before the Holocaust," and equating Israelis with Nazis.[120] Reminiscent of Rep. Omar's own tweets, Shibly once tweeted "God as my wittiness (sic), Israel & it's supporters are enemies of God and humanity! How many more children must Israel kill 4 U 2 C?#Gaza."[121] Shibly has been a prominent public defender of Rep. Omar.[122]

Muslim American Society

Background and Activities

In a December 2007 federal court filing, the U.S. government described the Muslim American Society (MAS) as having been "founded as the overt arm of the Muslim Brotherhood in America."[123] A prior FBI file obtained by Judicial Watch indicated "MAS is controlled by HAMAS sympathizers and they are known to conduct firearms and other military type training."[124] Its own senior leadership has acknowledged MAS was founded by Muslim Brotherhood members.[125] An archived history page from the MAS Minnesota (MAS MN) website tells the story of its parent's origin. MAS sprung from ISNA, which was an outgrowth of the MSA, an advent of the "Islamic Movement" used interchangeably to describe the Muslim Brotherhood and the Islamic supremacist effort it leads.[viii,126] Both ISNA and MAS were listed as MB, or MB-friendly organizations in the previously discussed Explanatory Memorandum, and ISNA was, again, cited as an unindicted co-conspirator along with CAIR in the HLF case. As with CAIR, the UAE has designated MAS as a terrorist organization.[127] Bringing MAS' story

---

viii   Stephen Coughlin argues based upon the words of numerous Brotherhood leaders from founder Hassan al-Banna to Sheikh Yusuf al-Qaradawi, the modern intellectual leader of the Muslim Brotherhood, that the Islamic Movement is a term of art that transcends the Brotherhood to encompass the struggle to make Islam supreme, using means violent and nonviolent, for which the Brotherhood is the vanguard. Worth noting given our earlier discussion of the Left-Islamist axis is that Sayyid Qutb's writings specifically refer to the need for an Islamist "vanguard," in language echoing Vladimir Lenin. See *Catastrophic Failure* pages 142-143, 155-162.

up to the present day, readers may recall that in April 2019, its Philadelphia chapter posted a video from its "Ummah Day" celebration (*ummah* being the Muslim world), in which children performed a skit glorifying the beheading of Jews, and extolling the virtues of martyrdom in connection with their wish to "liberate" the Al-Aqsa Mosque in Jerusalem.[128]

Rep. Omar and MAS

Rep. Omar's ties to MAS MN are well-established and long-standing, though more in the way of mutual admiration than monetary support.[ix] As invaluable counterterrorism researcher and writer Patrick Poole wrote in a May 2019 piece in *The Federalist*:

> Omar's support for MAS goes back years. Her deep ties to the group were on display when she had the MAS-Minnesota chapter President Asad Zaman stand with her as she was ceremonially sworn into the Minnesota House of Representatives in January 2017 with her hand on an enormous Quran. MAS held a reception in honor of her inauguration.
>
> Just a few months later, Omar spoke at the 2017 MAS "Muslim Day" at the state capitol, acknowledging that she had previously participated in the group's annual event…
>
> The MAS-Minnesota chapter…Omar…ha[s] supported has a long history of controversy. The group gained national attention in 2007 when they issued a fatwa authorizing Muslim taxi cab drivers at the Minneapolis-St. Paul International Airport to deny service to non-Muslim passengers with seeing-eye dogs or who were carrying alcohol.

---

ix   In the way of pecuniary ties, MAS board member Hisham Abdallah has made several nominal campaign contributions to the congresswoman. See: https://www.meforum.org/islamist-watch/money-politics/recipient/682/.

As I reported in May 2009, the MAS-Minnesota's Vice President Hassan Mohamud had published a YouTube fundraising video decrying the "hell of living in America," and had defended Palestinian suicide attacks. When questioned by the local Minneapolis Fox News affiliate about his remarks, Mohamud claimed that he didn't mean anything anti-American by describing the United States as "hell." When asked about his statements in support of suicide bombings, he had to stop the interview on three separate occasions and consult with his attorney.

That incident was shortly after a local Somali reporter had identified Mohamud and his mosque as radicalization incubators following the disappearance of dozens of young Somali men, who left the country for Somalia to join the Al-Shabaab terrorist group. In an interview with USA Today, Mohamud denied any radical preaching or that any of the terror recruits had been involved in his mosque.

Yet Mohamud was again tied to a terror recruiting case after five men from the Twin Cities were arrested attempting to fly to Turkey to join the Islamic State in Syria. In March 2016, Justice Department prosecutors asked the court to disqualify Mohamud from the defense team of one of the men, telling the judge that they intended to introduce testimony during the trial of a witness claiming Mohamud had been preaching jihad and making other extremist statements. This disclosure prompted another member of the defense team to move to withdraw from the case.[129]

Rep. Omar hosted MAS MN president Asad Zaman on Capitol Hill for an April 2019 meeting, per pictures posted on the chapter's Facebook page.[130] Sam Westrop, director of the *Middle East Forum*'s "Islamist Watch," writes that Zaman's social media postings are "replete with anti-Semitism, apologism for Hamas and support for convicted war criminals." Westrop cited Zaman's posts endorsing the concept of the "Israel lobby," saying that "It is Israel, not Hamas, that uses human shields...," and sharing notes in support of Jamaat-e-Islami figures, an Islamist group that represents an Asian incarnation of the MB.[131,132]

It bears noting that MAS MN, like CAIR and its offshoots, presents itself as a social justice-oriented organization that fits perfectly in the progressive-Islamist axis that Rep. Omar personifies.[133,134] A 2019 event co-sponsored by the chapter entitled "Claiming Our Voices 2019" is instructive in this regard. The event calls for commemorating, and redoubling efforts to engage political officials to ensure:

- Radical civic inclusion by getting driver's licenses for all and restoring the vote to our disenfranchised residents;

- Creating a caring economy with quality and affordable childcare and eldercare, and paid family leave and sick time;

- Climate justice and right stewardship of the planet we've been entrusted with; and

- Quality, affordable and accessible Healthcare for all.

The coalition of "constituencies of our organization" includes not only Muslim groups but black, LatinX, and like-minded Christian partners as well.[135] This is intersectionality and community organizing in action.

Like Rep. Omar, some of MAS' local chapters seem to share her antipathy towards the Kingdom of Saudi Arabia (KSA) and its leader, Saudi Crown Prince Mohamed bin Salman (MBS).[136,137] Why? Most likely because the MBS regime has engaged in a crackdown on Sunni Islamist figures. In 2014, KSA designated the Muslim Brotherhood as a terrorist organization.[138] Relatedly, like Rep. Omar, in June 2019 MAS called for an investigation into the death of Egyptian Muslim Brotherhood leader Mohamed Morsi, which it insinuated was based in Egyptian human rights violations akin to those engaged in by the Saudis.[139]

United States Council of Muslim Organizations

Background and Activities

The United States Council of Muslim Organizations (USCMO) was established in 2014. In keeping with the thrust of the Explanatory Memorandum, USCMO aims to "build an active, integrated American Muslim Community," and "mobiliz[e] the Muslim populations of our local communities and that of our fellow Americans for the good of all." To accomplish this task, USCMO serves as an umbrella organization for other Muslim American groups—namely, MB-linked ones. These include the likes of CAIR and MAS, as well as others we will soon come to meet such as American Muslims for Palestine (AMP).[140]

USCMO's leader is Secretary General Oussama Jammal. Jammal also serves as the director of MAS' Public Affairs and Civic Engagement arm. As vice president of the Mosque Foundation, in 2003 Jammal raised money on behalf of Sami al-Arian, who was later convicted on one count of contributed services to or for the benefit of the Palestinian Islamic Jihad, a Specially Designated Terrorist Organization. That foundation has also hosted a series of foreign Islamists for functions, including a delegation from the Lebanese branch of the MB.[141]

USCMO's board includes among others the previously discussed Nihad Awad, as well as Imam Siraj Wahhaj, an unindicted co-conspirator in the 1993 World Trade Center bombing, who served as a character witness for its mastermind, the "Blind Sheikh," Omar Abdel-Rahman.[142,143] Wahhaj is an outspoken proponent of jihad and has espoused various other radically revolutionary and subversive anti-American views.[144,145] Mazen Mokhtar is another notable board member, as he is the executive director of MAS. In the past, Mokhtar was accused of fundraising on behalf of the Taliban and Chechen mujahideen by way of a website he operated.[146]

Unsurprisingly, speakers at USCMO's first annual banquet included the likes of the aforementioned Zahra Billoo and Omar Suleiman.[147] It is the sponsor of the Annual National Muslim Advocacy Day on Capitol Hill, bringing together its MB-linked member groups and representatives such as Ilhan Omar.[148] Naturally, it espouses the same views as its member organizations.[149] As we will discuss shortly, it represents them in dealing with ideologically like-minded governments—one in particular with which Rep. Omar has frequently consorted.

Rep. Omar and USCMO

Rep. Omar has spoken at USCMO events and garnered the organization's public support both in press releases and social media posts by its senior leadership. She was pictured on stage with her predecessor and ideological compatriot former Rep. Keith Ellison at the USCMO's Annual Ramadan Iftar in 2018, which was keynoted by the aforementioned Rob Malley.[150] When Reps. Omar and Tlaib won their respective primaries during the 2018 election cycle, USCMO celebrated their collective victory as "an important step in the right direction for the Muslim American community."[151]

USCMO Secretary General Oussama Jammal has tweeted in support of Rep. Omar, including one article from *The Nation* declaring "The Democratic Party Attacks on Ilhan Omar Are a Travesty," and another questioning whether "AIPAC [is] Too Powerful?"[152,153] He, like Nihad Awad, and Zahra Billoo, has also lauded Reps. Omar and Tlaib for bringing "to the fore the Palestinian cause that many believed is far from ever become (sic) a mainstream television debate."[154] Secretary General Jammal was pictured meeting with Rep. Omar on Capitol Hill during Muslim Advocacy Day in April 2019 when she also met with CAIR leaders.[155] We will soon discuss the links between the USCMO, Rep. Omar, and a Muslim Brotherhood-tied foreign regime.

Other Organizations

While CAIR, MAS, and the umbrella organization under which they sit, the USCMO, are the most powerful Islamist organizations to which Rep. Omar has been tied, two other connections are noteworthy as well:

- **Islamic Relief USA (IR-USA)** IR-USA is the U.S. branch of Islamic Relief Worldwide, which has raised hundreds of millions of dollars for purported humanitarian causes globally, and at least 80 million dollars from Western governments and international bodies, including the U.S. federal government.[156] Consistent with other organizations we have discussed, its leaders past and present—both representing its U.S. and foreign arms—have been tied to the MB, and groups implicated in the HLF trial. They have expressed virulently anti-Israel and anti-Semitic views. More disturbingly, several of its branches located internationally have been accused of serving as charitable fronts for financing jihad. Consequently, Israel and the UAE have both designated Islamic Relief as a terror-financing organization.[157] In January 2018, the U.S. government's Office for Personnel Management suggested IR-USA could be the subject of a criminal investigation, writing that it was withholding records associated with Islamic Relief under a Freedom of Information Act (FOIA) request "as they were compiled for law enforcement purposes and their disclosure could reasonably be expected to interfere with ongoing enforcement proceedings, by—for example—suggesting the scope of an investigation and alerting potential subjects as to the nature of the Government's evidence and strategy."[158,159] In February 2019, Rep. Omar delivered a keynote address at a private event hosted by Islamic Relief USA. Originally, she had come under fire when it emerged that one of the other scheduled speakers was Yousef Abdallah, the organization's operations manager. Abdallah has posted vehemently anti-Israel and anti-Semitic propaganda on social media. He was quickly dropped from the event, but Rep. Omar's communications team dishonestly claimed reports he would be speaking at it were "inaccurate...Abdallah will not be speaking or attending the event with Rep. Omar **and was never scheduled to do so.**" [Emphasis added] The original flyer associated with the event had pictured Abdallah as a speaker.[160] Whether Rep. Omar should have spoken at IR-USA at all was beyond questionable in the first place.

- **Muslim Legal Fund of America (MLFA)** According to the *IPT*, MLFA "boasts of its close ties to CAIR and has defended numerous Islamist terrorists and other radicals, including Palestinian Islamic Jihad governing board member Sami Al-Arian, Hamas operative Muhammad Salah, and Shain, Eljvir and Dritan Duka, brothers who…plotted [to] kill soldiers at New Jersey's Fort

Dix Army base."[161] MLFA is one of the members of the USCMO umbrella organization, and its executive director James "Khalil" Meek sits on its board. In October 2017, Rep. Omar delivered a paid speech to the Muslim Legal Fund of America for $6,000.[162,163]

Ilhan Omar's Ties to Other Domestic Islamists and Fellow Travelers

There are a number of additional prominent Islamists and fellow travelers with whom Rep. Omar has consorted, some of whom have, like others we have named, contributed to the nearly $22,000 that had flowed into her campaign coffers from Islamists as of December 2019. Notable supporters, financial and/or otherwise, include:[164]

- **Hatem Bazian** – Dr. Bazian currently teaches in the Department of Ethnic Studies, specifically in Asian American and Asian Diaspora Studies, at the University of California Berkeley (UC Berkeley).[165] A former president of the MB-spawned UC Berkeley MSA, Bazian is also credited with co-founding the virulently anti-Israel and anti-Semitic campus group Students for Justice in Palestine (SJP), and AMP, where he currently serves as chairman.[166] The Anti-Defamation League (ADL) describes AMP as "the leading organization providing anti-Zionist training and education to students and Muslim community organizations in the country. Founded in 2005, AMP promotes extreme anti-Israel views and has at times provided a platform for anti-Semitism under the guise of educating Americans about 'the just cause of Palestine and the rights of self-determination.'"[167] AMP's board has reportedly consisted of numerous MB-tied alumni from organizations including IAP and HLF.[168] Bazian is also considered a leader in the BDS movement.[169] He has tweeted radical comments attacking Jews in support of Islamist causes, and deflecting from jihadist attacks by harping on the real scourge of Islamophobia. He has also made frequent speaking appearances in front of MB-tied groups.[170,171] Bazian has been an outspoken supporter of Reps. Omar and Tlaib. In December 2018, the self-described "de-colonial Islamic thinker" wrote: "Rashida

247

[Tlaib], [Ilhan] Omar, and others created their fundraising path and garnered support from diverse grassroots communities across the country, which has immediately translated into two crucial positions, the BDS front of Ilhan and Rashida opting to challenge AIPAC's funded junkets to Israel. The days and months ahead will illustrate the erosion of AIPAC's and Israel's standing among the US public. I do believe that the recent shifts are irreversible. Israel's brand in the US has run its course and already is beginning to reverse course after reaching the pinnacle."[172] For President Trump's criticism of Rep. Omar, Bazian has compared him to Gestapo member Hermann Wilhelm Goring.[173] Bazian has cut several campaign checks to Ilhan Omar.[174]

- **Linda Sarsour** – Sarsour, as previously mentioned, has a long, disreputable record of Israel-bashing, Jew-hatred, jihad apologism, and borderline incitement to violence—on top of her deep connections within the Islamist world mirroring those of Rep. Omar.[175,176] In another telltale sign of the progressive-Islamist axis's strength, Sarsour is again serving as a campaign surrogate for Senator Bernie Sanders in his 2020 presidential run.[177] Sarsour has praised Omar as: "the best that our community has to offer: She's black, she's Somali, a former refugee…She's bold, she's unapologetic, she's anti-war and anti-imperialist…She's a supporter of the boycott, divestment, sanction movement…She stands with poor people. She stands with the most marginalized people in America. And she represents everything that is beautiful about Islam."[178] The feeling is mutual. Rep. Omar has referred to Sarsour as her "sister," who is "holding it down unapologetically for all of us."[179] They have been pictured together on several occasions, including from the very first day Rep. Omar assumed office on Capitol Hill.[180]

- **Debbie Almontaser** – Almontaser resigned from the Brooklyn-based Arab-language academy at which she taught over furor at her having worn a t-shirt that read "Intifada NYC." In classic Islamist doublespeak, she characterized "Intifada" as symbolic of "shaking off oppression."[181] Who were the oppressors, and what does shaking them off entail? Whether she was calling for jihad *in* New York, or just indicating her support for jihad *from* New York, Almontaser definitively partnered with CAIR to counter the New York Police Department's counterterrorism efforts.[182] She has taken similar positions to other figures mentioned here regarding the supposed scourge of Islamophobia, most notably opposing President Trump in his criticism of Rep. Omar by way of her stint as board secretary of the Yemeni American Merchants Association (YAMA). YAMA launched a bodega boycott after the *New York Post* published a cover responding to Rep. Omar's comment that "some people did something" on 9/11, with a headline reading, "Here's your something: 2,977 people dead by terrorism," superimposed over a picture of the Twin Towers in flames.[183,184] Rep. Omar has referred to Almontaser, in a tweet in which the two were pictured together at an event hosted by CAIR-MN, as a "SHERO."[185] Almontaser and her husband, who serves with her on YAMA's board, have both made campaign contributions to Rep. Omar.[186,187]

- **Dalia Mogahed** – Mogahed, a longtime defender of CAIR and ISNA, served on the Obama administration's Council on Faith-Based and Neighborhood Partnerships. From that position, she allegedly worked to ensure the administration engaged such groups, and other MB-tied organizations previously discussed, including MAS and MPAC. As the *Middle East Forum* summarizes her obfuscation regarding jihad: "Mogahed has two major themes: that only a small percentage of Muslims are radicalized, and that any radicalism that does exist results from perceptions that the West is 'hostile' to Muslims, as demonstrated by support for Israel, the war in Iraq, or a tough stance against Iran's nuclear weapons efforts." When questioned about Sharia law in a 2007 television appearance, she claimed that Sharia is primarily about "law that is going to make society more just, and that cannot be co-opted or thrown out at the whim of a despotic leader…"[188] Like others, Mogahed's definition of "justice" may not be the same as yours and mine. In Rep. Omar's tweet referring to her "SHEROs," pictured between herself and Debbie Almontaser is Dalia Mogahed.[189] Mogahed, like Almontaser, has also contributed to Rep. Omar's political coffers.[190]

- **James Zogby** – Zogby's ties to Islamist organizations, individuals, and acts are long-standing and well-documented. According to one report, the leader of the hostile-towards-Israel Arab American Institute, and chair of the similarly situated Palestine Human Rights Campaign has: "falsely accused Israel of committing a 'Holocaust' against Palestinians, called Israelis 'Nazis,' campaigned to prevent the extradition to Israel of a Fatah terrorist who killed two Israeli teenagers and wounded 36 other Israelis, called Cuban-American Congresswoman Ileana Ros-Lehtinen an 'Israel-firster' (an antisemitic trope implying dual loyalty), praised the intifada as a 'good story,' and was a leading architect of propaganda themes used to pry progressive Jews away from supporting Israel."[191] During Rep. Omar's 2018 congressional campaign, Zogby donated a total of $3,700 to Rep. Omar.[192]

- **Zaki Barzinji** – Barzinji has served as a board member of ISNA, and previously was president of Muslim Youth of North America (MYNA), an offshoot of ISNA. He comes from a family deeply rooted in the MB movement. His father was a founding member of MYNA, and his grandfather played a critical role in founding numerous U.S.-based organizations, including the aforementioned ISNA, MSA, the North American Islamic Trust (NAIT, another unindicted co-conspirator in the HLF case), and the International Institute of Islamic Thought (IIIT, frequently cited in the HLF trial and listed in the Explanatory Memorandum).[193,194] Remarkably, Zaki also served as a staffer to former Virginia Governor Terry McAuliffe, a Democrat, and was appointed as outreach liaison for Muslim Americans to the White House Office of Public Engagement in 2016 by President Barack Obama.[195] Barzinji pledged a nominal amount to Rep. Omar's 2018 congressional campaign.[196]

- **Various Imams** – In 2018, Rep. Omar posted an endorsement to Facebook featuring a number of Minnesota imams.[197] Among them were: (i) The presumed Mohamed Omar ("Mohamed Omar (Arab)" in the endorsement list), who according to a report "has posted videos about 'apartheid Israel,' along with rants by the fringe [Iran-supporting] Neturei Karta sect, claiming that Jews in Israel rape and pillage;"[198] Shaykh Dr. Walleed Al Meneese, Vice Chairman of the MB-linked North American Imams Federation;[199,200] and Hassan Dhooye, Executive Director of the Islamic Association of North America—formerly known as the North American Council of Somali Imams—which has backed BDS efforts against Israel.[201,202,203] Dhooye received a Turkish delegation featuring Turkish Consul General Umut Acar—with whom Rep. Omar too has met, as we will soon discuss—in which they chatted about "advancing the Muslim Community in America and strengthening our ties with our Turkish brothers."[204,205] Another notable imam endorser was Shaykh Shabaan Aboubadria, who once delivered a sermon in which he claimed "Western civilization is built on shedding blood, killing, and terrorism, and yet they accuse you – oh peaceful Muslims – of being terrorists," and declared that Egypt's President al-Sisi is "carrying out the Zio-crusader agenda."[206]

- **Al-Shabaab Members** – Perhaps most disturbingly yet least-noticed of all, is this nugget from a 2015 article per *Minnesota Public Radio*: "Omar...was friends with some of the young men who joined the Somali terror group al-Shabab several years ago...'They were happy young men,' she said. 'And then at some point, something happened. And that is what needs to be researched and studied. What is happening to make them feel disconnected from a community that has birthed them, that has nurtured them?'"[207] The passive voice here is all too telling—"Something happened," just like "Some people did something…" We asked Rep. Omar if she would detail such relationships, but as with our other inquiries, neither she nor her office provided a response.

Given that the Sunni Islamic Movement spearheaded by the Muslim Brotherhood is transnational, and bent on subverting American liberty and imposing an alien, theopolitical totalitarian ideology on us in its place, Rep. Omar's close relations with U.S. MB-tied organizations, individuals, and fellow travelers alone could be seen as a form of foreign collusion, if not treachery. But Rep. Omar also maintains explicit ties with foreign governments run by and/or closely partnered with Islamic supremacists, who seek to ensure Islam's global conquest.

Ilhan Omar's Ties to Islamist and/or Corrupt Foreign Governments

Turkey

Though largely unnoticed outside of conservative media, then-Minnesota State Representative Ilhan Omar participated in a closed-press meeting in fall 2017 with Turkish President Recep Tayyip Erdoğan, supposedly invited at the behest of the Turkish consulate in Chicago.[208] According to a curiously now-deleted article from a Somalian-language periodical based in her district, the *Tusmo Times*, Omar and the Islamist potentate met during his UN General Assembly (UNGA) visit to New York.[209] Per one account, they discussed:

> ...issues involving Omar's native Somalia and issues for Somalis in Minnesota. She [Omar] thanked Erdogan for Turkey's support for the Rohingya people in Myanmar. The two also discussed investment and trade between Turkey and Somalia. The meeting ended with Erdogan asking Omar to voice her support for Turkey. The report concludes by adding that Omar not only met with Erdogan, but also with the Turkish prime minister and other senior Turkish officials.[210]

Another news account indicated that the meeting "focused on Turkish/Muslim relationships, and how to be a better advocate for Somalia."[211]

One might think federal government officials or media members might have been stunned by the revelation of this meeting, given rampant concerns about foreign influence in the wake of the 2016 presidential election. Some questions that might have immediately come to mind about the Omar-Erdoğan meeting include: Why did a foreign head of state care to set it in the first place, given Omar was a mere Minnesota state representative? Was it appropriate for Omar to be discussing Turkish-Somali relations as such a representative? On whose authority was she speaking? Did anyone bless this meeting at the federal level, and on what grounds? Was she briefed and debriefed by U.S. officials? Did Omar have any reservations about meeting with Erdoğan given the totalitarian, bellicose, and bigoted nature of his regime?[212,213,214]

How could this social justice warrior and fierce opponent of human rights violators (almost) everywhere meet with and thereby legitimize an Erdoğan regime that has engaged in severe repression of its political foes, and routinely jailed more journalists than any other regime in the world?[215,216] Rep. Omar's fellow Democrats including Sens. Markey and Schumer, and Reps. Engel and Schiff had all at times spoken out against Erdoğan and his government's malevolent acts—including its attack on protesters in Washington, D.C. outside the Turkish ambassador's residence, and even on Sen. Schumer himself, with a Turkish prosecutor announcing he was investigating the Senate Minority Leader. Yet none of them spoke out about then-State Rep. Omar's meeting with President Erdoğan, nor did the mainstream media do any reporting on the curious meeting.[217]

Beyond Omar meeting with Turkey's Erdoğan, we should note that the congresswoman—before and after joining the House—has met with other high-ranking Turkish officials. Several months before her 2017 meeting with the Turkish president, Rep. Omar and then-husband Ahmed Hirsi met with Consul General Umat Acar. In a Facebook post on the meeting, Hirsi wrote: "Turkey has been a friend to Somalis everywhere and I look forward helping (sic) expanding our friendship for decades to come."[218]

Earlier that year, Omar traveled to Istanbul with Hirsi for a "Human Rights Defenders" conference that, according to a crude translation, was focused on fighting "gender-based discrimination."[219,220] *The Middle East Media Research Institute* (MEMRI) reports that the conference was organized by Istanbul's Şişli municipality.[221] A Turkish-language news account seems to indicate that while there, Rep. Omar criticized the Trump administration's so-called "travel ban."[222] That is, she attacked U.S. policy on foreign soil.

One month after the 2017 UNGA, on the sidelines of which State Rep. Omar and Erdoğan spoke, Omar took to Twitter to praise Turkey for providing airlifts serving injured Somalis, writing in part: "This is the most humane way anyone can show they #standwithMogadishu."[223]

In September 2018, after she had won the DFL nomination for the U.S. House, per social media, Consul General Acar hosted State Rep. Omar.[224]

In addition to interfacing with Erdoğan and Acar, Turkey seems to have been following Rep. Omar dating back to 2016, when its Foreign Minister reportedly congratulated her on her victory for state representative, as he would do again in 2018 when she was elected to Congress.[225]

In January 2019, the Diyanet Center of America (DCA) published a post reporting that several of its board and community members attended CAIR's Community Congressional Reception, in which they met with, among others, Reps. Omar and Tlaib. It stated that it "congratulates the two new Muslim members of Congress and is looking forward to fostering a relationship between our institutions."[226] The DCA is a U.S.-based, Turkish government-backed, Islamic center. Per its website, its Lanham, MD campus is a sprawling "small village," which recently underwent a 110 million dollar expansion.[227,228] More on the significance of the DCA shortly.

In April 2019, a Turkish pro-government, AKP-supporting newspaper posted an article soliciting campaign contributions for the Minnesota congresswoman, which was also reprinted in a series of other Turkish outlets. The article, a defense of Omar's comments about the "Israel Lobby," read in part that "donating money to Omar's campaign fund would be an adequate way of denying powerful organizations the power to censor alternative voices."[229,230] Leaving aside the illegality of foreign campaign contributions, that an Erdoğan house paper would publish such an article is beyond telling. In fact, *MEMRI* reports that Turkish state-owned broadcasting network *TRT* has published numerous videos featuring Rep. Omar, including an interview with her, on top of hundreds of news articles similar publications have run about Omar.[231]

In October 2019, it was revealed that Halil Mutlu, co-chairman of the Turkish American Steering Committee (TSAC) donated $1,500 to Rep. Omar's campaign. Mutlu is reportedly a cousin of President Recep Tayyip Erdoğan.[232] Relatedly, TSAC, as we will soon detail, is a Turkish government-linked organization. As noted previously, in October 2019 Rep. Omar took a series of votes favorable to the Turkish government regarding both the Armenian genocide and sanctions.

Now, it is true that Turkey is ostensibly a North Atlantic Treaty Organization (NATO) ally. Yet many have noted that Ankara has increasingly been violating the letter and spirit of the Treaty, from its internal repression, to its backing of jihadism, to its purchases of military hardware from Russia.[233,234,235,236,237] Moreover, it is not as if Rep. Omar has articulated a rationale for pulling punches with respect to Turkey on the basis of real-politik and a desire to thwart our foes in the region and beyond, rooted in devotion to U.S. national interest—as some conservative foreign policy hands have done.[238,239,240] She betrayed her true feelings when in an October 2019 *Washington Post* editorial, she claimed imposing sanctions on Turkey in connection with its incursion into northern Syria against Syrian Kurds would prove ineffective and perhaps harmful—without explaining why she supported employing such measures against Israel.[241] To be fair to Rep. Omar, there was one instance in which she did take a position that could have rankled Turkey. In December 2019, she delivered a letter to the Trump administration's Special Representative for Syria Engagement, Ambassador James Jeffrey, expressing concerns for and demanding a classified briefing on an alleged October 2019 chemical attack perpetrated by Turkish forces against Syrian civilians.[242] Of course, one cannot ignore the political context in which this still relatively mild poke at Turkey occurred—namely that Democrats have taken a far more adversarial stance towards Turkey as the Trump administration has undertaken efforts to re-establish positive relations with it. Therefore, Omar's letter could be seen more as a hit on Trump than Erdoğan.

Irrespective of these facts, at the very least Rep. Omar had no standing to be freelancing in foreign policy as a de facto representative of the U.S. government when she met with Erdoğan in 2017—and particularly concerning relations between foreign regimes, notably ones with significant

Islamist elements. Her additional contacts with Turkish officials and institutions only add to concerns.

What makes the tie that binds the Erdoğan regime and Rep. Omar even stronger is their shared affiliation with MB organizations. Erdoğan has publicly defended the MB, and vice versa, as he and the group share a common Sunni Islamic supremacist ideology, with Erdoğan fashioning himself a caliph-in-waiting for the Islamic world.[243,244,245]

Of related interest, as noted previously, in April 2019 Rep. Omar lobbied via Twitter on behalf of a jailed female leader of the Egyptian Muslim Brotherhood. As it turns out, the woman Omar defended had spoken fondly of Erdoğan during a visit he made to Cairo following the fall of President Hosni Mubarak in September 2011. The Muslim Brotherhood leader said: "I came here today to pay the Turkish prime minister the respect he earned. He stood in the face of Israel and was not afraid to speak the truth…I liked his reference to the Islamic identity…"[246] The Turkish dictator, like Rep. Omar, mourned the death of Morsi, declaring in its wake: "May Allah rest our brother Morsi, our martyr's soul, in peace."[247] Likewise, Erdoğan's Turkey has been a staunch supporter of Hamas.[248,249] Erdoğan has also launched into invective against the Jewish state, and Jews themselves, as he has tightened the Islamist noose on the formerly relatively secular and modern Atatürkian country.[250,251]

Erdoğan has consorted with a number of characters we have already discussed, and related organizations. Perhaps most prominent are his ties to CAIR, and its umbrella organization, the USCMO. In September 2019 when, while President Erdoğan visited New York in advance of the UNGA, he met with, among others, CAIR Executive Director Nihad Awad and Imam Siraj Wahhaj—both USCMO board members—and USCMO Secretary-General Oussama Jamal.[x,252] This was the third such annual meeting sponsored by the aforementioned TASC, a group whose leaders FBI officials had interviewed on suspicion of espionage back in 2016.[253]

---

x   During the UNGA proceedings, it was reported that Erdoğan, like many U.S. Islamists, engaged in Holocaust inversion, stating: "When we look at the genocide Nazis committed against Jews, we should look at the massacre happening in the Gaza Strip from the same point of view." See: https://jewishjournal.com/news/israel/304938/turkey-president-compares-israel-to-the-nazis-over-gaza/.

The American officials' glowing statements about Erdoğan following their most recent meeting illustrated the burgeoning relationship between the Turkish regime and U.S. Islamist groups. Imam Wahhaj, again an unindicted co-conspirator in the 1993 World Trade Center bombing who served as a character witness for the "Blind Sheikh" who masterminded it, praised Erdoğan during the meeting. He stated: "We need a **centralized leadership**…I have a feeling that the leadership is coming from Turkey… We love you here in New York." [Emphasis added] Secretary General Jammal said of Erdoğan: "You give us a sense of pride, an honor to meet a president and a leader and […] a wonderful human-being with **patience, love, worries and cares for Muslim ummah**…You set the bar so high. Many of today's Muslim leaders will fail to attain. Mr. President, we can see how your country is hosting, supporting and helping other Muslims in Turkey and around the world."[254] [Emphasis added] Esam Omeish, the former president of MAS, took to Facebook in effusive praise of Erdoğan, noting the meeting represented: "A tremendous exchange with a **leader of the Islamic world and a great nation** about our vision and aspirations as Muslims and Americans. We asserted our role in building our American society with the virtues of Islam, **defending the issues of the greater ummah** and facing the challenges of Islamophobia, xenophobia and racism. We also reaffirmed our role as civilizational bridge builders between East and West."[255] [Emphasis added]

For his part, Erdoğan, a man who has indicated an ambition to represent the Islamic world in toto, stated: "We are part of the Islamic Ummah of 1.7 billion people. The difference between us should never hinder our brotherhood and communication." Beyond the praise from leaders of the umbrella organization for, and others associated with, the leading Islamist groups in the U.S., and Erdoğan's relishing the opportunity to portray himself as a representative of the collective Islamic world, he punched home one more main point: "I am seeing that (sic) U.S. Muslim community is becoming more organized every passing day and trying to act in cooperation."[256] He should know—his regime has been working with those doing the cooperating, on behalf of the *ummah*.

As reflected in Erdoğan's first annual meeting with U.S. Islamist leaders during the UNGA, back in 2016—also attended by Awad and Jammal, among other Islamist notables—the *IPT* reported:[257]

> Political leaders affiliated with the AKP [Erdoğan's AK Party] and members of an Islamist Turkish business group have established deep relationships with the Brotherhood network in America, including with think tanks and academic centers affiliated with CAIR, USCMO, and other Islamist groups.[258]

Regarding CAIR, with which Rep. Omar has been most closely linked, its ties to Erdoğan are extensive. On top of UNGA-related meetings, Awad and Erdoğan, and/or members of the Turkish government, have met on several occasions. In September 2016, a Turkish delegation of parliament members from Erdoğan's AKP visited CAIR's offices. Awad seemed to advocate on behalf of the regime immediately thereafter. When speaking with Turkey's *Anadolu* news agency following the meeting, per an *IPT* translation, Awad stated that the gathering was important because it demonstrated the:

> …support of the Muslim community for democracy and the rule of law in Turkey…We believe in the need for more Turkish visitors and delegations to come to the United States to talk about their experiences and explain their views… because there is a view against them and a pathological fear of Turkey here. The Turkish government must be aware of the need to employ more efforts to explain what is happening (in) Turkey to American public opinion.[259]

A month prior, Awad had traveled to Turkey on the heels of Erdoğan's crackdown in the face of a purported coup. Awad tweeted a picture of himself from Turkey's Taksim Square reading in part: "People are out at weeknight guarding democracy. Supporting rule of law. #TurkeyCoup."[260] Earlier that year, Awad participated in a rally sponsored by TASC at the White House against the purported Turkish coup, at which he reportedly spoke.[261,262] In other words, he parroted the AK Party line—a party led by an Erdoğan regime that would arrest 77,000 people, purge 130,000 more from public service, and shut down almost 200 media organizations while jailing over 140 journalists in the purported coup's wake.[263]

CAIR had stood with the Erdoğan regime publicly on other occasions as well. For example, in April of 2015 CAIR signed on to a statement issued by the USCMO opposing calls for labeling the Armenian genocide, perpetrated by the Turks, as "genocide."[264] Later that year, Awad cheered on the AKP's victory, describing it as "tantamount to a global Islamic wedding, which was a delight for all, especially those who believe in Islam, and that Islam is not only a status but a leader upon the international and humanitarian scene."[265] Also in 2015, CAIR amazingly presented Turkey with its 2015 Humanitarian Award, for its work with Syrian and Iraqi refugees—an award received by Turkey's Ambassador to the U.S. CAIR is not registered as a foreign agent, but in this Age of Trump, one would think the past words and actions of its leaders might merit some questions from the DOJ's Foreign Agent Registration Act unit.

Another notable instance in which Erdoğan saw the "U.S. Muslim community…becoming more organized…and…act[ing] in cooperation" came in December 2017. When President Trump declared that the U.S. would recognize Israel as Jerusalem's capital, Turkey—leading the Organisation of Islamic Conference, again the world's preeminent collective Islamic governance body—CAIR, the USCMO, and related U.S. Islamist organizations banded together in opposition.[266,267] As the Center for Security Policy reported, Erdoğan, Awad, and USCMO Secretary General Jammal all gave parallel statements condemning the president's move. The USCMO organized a rally on Capitol Hill featuring, among numerous other Islamist groups, CAIR, and the aforementioned TASC. Hilal Mutlu, TASC's Director, and Erdoğan's rumored cousin, who as noted contributed to Rep. Omar's campaign in 2019, declared: "We said before, Al-Quds [Jerusalem] is our redline," invoking the language Erdoğan used in his own statement. During his address to the crowd, Mutlu reportedly referred to Erdoğan as "president of the ummah," with audience members reportedly chanting back, "Recep Tayyip Erdoğan, true leader of Ummah."[268]

Like its member CAIR, the USCMO's ties to the Turkish regime were also long-standing, and transcend the several statements and events already mentioned. As noted, dating back to at least 2016, Erdoğan has made a point during his annual UNGA pilgrimage to meet with U.S. Islamist leaders. These have included not just USCMO Secretary Jammal and CAIR Executive Director Awad, but USCMO board members Mazen Mokhtar, President of MAS, and James "Khalil" Meek, Executive Director of MLFA—in addition to representatives from other Islamist organizations we have previously mentioned, such as IR-USA Chairman Khaled Lamada.[269,270]

USCMO's links to the Turkish regime in fact date back to 2014, the year of its founding. Just months after it opened its doors, USCMO Secretary General Jammal visited Turkey on behalf of, and along with, several other USCMO representatives to witness elections and attend a conference held by the AKP in celebration of Erdoğan's election.[271]

As referenced in the aforementioned *IPT* report, the USCMO has also been tied to the Turkish regime by way of an Islamist business group—the AKP-allied and MB-associated Independent Industrials and Businessmen's Association (MUSIAD). Its former U.S. chapter spokesman was previously listed on USCMO's board.[272]

Turkish government officials have also attended USCMO-hosted events. In a gushing account of the 1st International Conference of Muslim Councils in the West hosted by USCMO in February 2016, AKP Member of Parliament Yaskin Aktay wrote in part:

> It should be noted that Turkey has a very special significance and value to everyone who attended the conference. Even the mention of President Recep Tayyip Erdoğan's name is enough to cheer people. On the first evening of the conference, Yaşar Çolak, the head Turkey's Presidency of Religious Affairs Center in Washington, hosted the entire delegation at the center's newly built magnificent mosque and complex [Diyanet Center of America].
>
> Even the existence of this mosque alone seems to have built a path between Turkey and the hearts of the 8 million

Muslims living [in] the US. **A majority of the participants of the conference with whom we were able to meet felt the need to state that they were ready for all calls to turn this connection into an opportunity, a political coalition for Turkey and the Muslim world.** Of course, after sharing all these good intentions, they wanted us to pass on their regards and sincere love to President Erdoğan and Prime Minister Ahmet Davutoğlu.

This organization has raised promising and charismatic leaders, who attract attention in US politics with their intelligent and well-balanced behaviors. **USCMO President Oussama Jammal and Council of American Islamic Relationship (CAIR) President Nihad Awad, whom I met years ago, are the ones that coordinated these activities.**[273] [Emphasis added]

Later that year, USCMO Secretary General Jammal reportedly spoke at the same TASC-sponsored protest regarding the failed purported Turkish coup at which Nihad Awad had spoken.[274]

As the Center for Security Policy has documented in great detail, the USCMO and Turkish government have coordinated on mutually beneficial projects in subsequent years using Turkey's aforementioned Diyanet Center of America.[275] DCA has served as an "axis," if you will, in Explanatory Memorandum parlance.

Again, it is critical to keep in mind that the USCMO is the umbrella organization for most all of the leading Islamist organizations in America. The MB-aligned Erdoğan sees himself as vying for leadership of the *ummah*, something at least some of the senior leadership members of the USCMO seem to endorse. Such ties, then, are extremely significant and must be considered in the context of Rep. Omar's own ties to both such entities.

Islamist Turkish President Recep Tayyip Erdoğan rules an MB-tied adversarial regime with an iron fist. Indications are that he seeks to be a modern-day caliph. In connection with his ideology and ambitions, his government appears to be cultivating ties with Rep. Omar, while increasingly coordinating with America's leading MB-aligned Islamist groups—groups with which Rep. Omar herself has been extensively tied. There are an inordinate number of national security concerns arising from this fact pattern. The fundamental question is, how great is America's risk exposure for any member of Congress, let alone one who sits on the HFAC, to maintain such relationships? And then, how much greater is the peril when one considers that Turkey's regime is not the only Islamist-tied one with which Rep. Omar has been linked. Now we turn to another such regime: that of her native Somalia.

Somalia and Its Partners

When President Trump scoffed at Squad members, directing them back to their countries of origin to fix "governments [that] are a complete and total catastrophe, the worst, most corrupt and inept anywhere in the world (if they even have a functioning government at all)," he may have most directly been speaking to Rep. Omar.

Since the fall of the Barre regime, Somalia has descended into violence and lawlessness, with the growth of Al-Qaeda affiliate Al-Shabaab adding to the tumult of the clan-based sectarian warring that preceded it. Somalia has failed to develop a stable, effective government. One could argue that its modern regimes have more often than not resembled organized crime syndicates—ones engaging in rampant human rights abuses against perceived rivals.[276] Transparency International has rated Somalia as the most corrupt country in the world for more than a decade running.[277]

It is a country that combines such corruption with the dominance of Islam. As we will show, Somalia's government is not only Islamist-tied, but the country is definitionally Islamist. The Constitution stipulates that not only is Islam the state religion but that "No law can be enacted that is not compliant with the general principles and objectives of Shari'ah."[278] Article 3 of Somalia's Constitution lays out its "Founding Principles." Its first section reads: "The Constitution of the Federal Republic of Somalia is based on the foundations of the Holy Quran and the Sunna of our prophet Mohamed (PBUH) [Peace Be Upon Him] and protects the higher objectives of **Shari'ah and social justice**."[279] [Emphasis added]

Rep. Omar's ties to Somalia go far beyond her upbringing. She clearly feels a sense of national pride with respect to her place of birth. Throughout the years, on social media, she has referred to Somalia as if she were still a citizen, including commemorating its independence. She has attended events in celebration of Somalia. Beyond such shows of affection, Rep. Omar has frequently expressed her political opinions on the country's internal workings. During Somalia's 2012 presidential election, in a series of tweets, Omar demonstrated her keen interest in Somalia's government, writing:

> "Right leader for the job!"[280] [Linking to a YouTube video featuring Somali Prime Minister and presidential candidate Abdiweli Mohamed Ali]

> "I have my favorite candidate, but anyone except Sheikh Sharif would make me happy. #SomaliaVotes2012."[281]

> "I thank Farmaajo, Abdiwali Gaas and Mahiga for the Roadmap [go-forward government plan], the difficult decisions and for bringing our dignity back.#Somalia2012"[282]

Following that election, she wrote, in response to speculation about who the president would appoint as prime minister: "…All new admin might be what we need," and later "I hope he [winner Hassan Sheikh Mohamud] takes the full 30 days to appoint the PM. There is no rush, we rather get a quality leader. Patience is a virtue. #Somalia2012."[283,284]

In 2013, Omar was arrested for trespassing at a Minneapolis hotel where a large group of Somali-Americans had migrated to receive the arriving Somali President Hassan Sheikh Mohamud, following an event held for him at the Minneapolis Convention Center.[285] Mohamud is described in Western media as a "moderate Islamist" with "links to al-Islah, Somalia's branch of the Muslim Brotherhood…"[286]

Later that year, Omar attended and wrote up a summary of her observations from a 2013 Minneapolis event celebrating the formation of a new regional state within Somalia, Jubaland.[287] Rep. Omar further demonstrated her keen interest in Somali politics when in March 2016, she shared a video from an event welcoming to Minnesota Puntland President Abdiwali Gaas—one of the runners-up in the 2012 race on which she had tweeted.[288]

The problem for Rep. Omar regarding Somalia is not her past apparent devotion to the Somali cause and its politics, but her associations with the Somali government as an elected official.

In December 2016, Minnesota state representative-elect Ilhan Omar took a trip to Somalia with her then-husband during its election season. While there, she met with the country's then-president—the aforementioned MB-tied Hassan Sheikh Mohamud.[289] Reports indicate that essentially, Mohamud wanted a photo op with Omar. She complied. Omar and her then-husband were welcomed at the presidential palace and pictured talking with him in his office.[290] Granting her significance as the first Somali lawmaker-elect in America at that time, as with President Erdoğan, one wonders what President Mohamud felt was so significant about Omar to merit such a visit.

The same question can be asked of another companion with whom Omar had arrived in Somalia. She had reportedly flown into Mogadishu, the capital, by way of Nairobi, on a plane with former Somali Prime Minister Mohamed Abdullahi Mohamed, aka "Farmaajo." Farmaajo shortly thereafter became president, selected, according to the American Enterprise Institute's (AEI) Michael Rubin, "by a parliament chosen by hand-picked Somali elders in a process marked by fraud and vote-buying."[291] *The New York Times'* headline on the election told the story: "Fueled by Bribes, Somalia's Election Seen as Milestone of Corruption."[292] Based on subsequent events, one might ask whether Rep. Omar was tied to that corruption.

In February 2017, Farmaajo nominated Hassan Ali Khayre as Somalia's prime minister. Upon the announcement of his selection, Rep. Omar's then-husband shared a Facebook post reading: "Congrats to our new PM Mudane Hassan Ali Khayre. New beginning! *Inshallah* Khayre [*Inshallah* means "Allah willing" in Arabic, and can be read as Hirsi sending his best wishes here]."[293] Shortly thereafter, at a celebration in Minneapolis for Farmaajo's election, then-State Rep. Omar and her then-husband delivered public remarks. As David Steinberg described it in *PJ Media*,

"Standing behind a podium bearing Farmaajo's image, and wearing a lapel button of the same, Ilhan exuberantly praised him and the newly formed Somali government in a brief speech marked by religious anecdotes and imagery.[xi] Hirsi similarly praised Farmaajo, adding a specific mention of Hassan Ali Khayre."[294]

Who was Khayre? Khayre worked for over a decade at an NGO before being named executive director of Soma Oil & Gas, a company controlled by Russian oil oligarch Alexander Dzhaparidze.[295] Khayre would end up under investigation for potential links to jihadist groups, including Al-Shabaab, while the company he was leading was also put under investigation for perhaps making bribery payments to Somalia's oil industry. Khayre was ultimately cleared by the UN monitoring group investigating him and remained at Soma until the day he became prime minister—which was just days after the celebratory speeches delivered by Omar and her then-husband.[296]

Khayre is an important figure because almost immediately after his ascension to office, he tabbed as his permanent secretary a man named Mohamed Keynan. Keynan is the husband of Rep. Omar's sister, Sahra Noor. Steinberg notes that per old address records, at one time Ilhan, Sahra, father Nur Said, and Keynan all resided at the same St. Paul address. Keynan, unsurprisingly, contributed $1,000 to Omar's successful 2016 campaign for the Minnesota House.[297]

Farmaajo's administration seems to be plagued by the same ills as those of his predecessors, as he has purportedly substantially enriched himself since taking office, while Somalia remains broken—a haven for corruption, jihadism, and, political persecution.[298] One story indicative of the tragedy that is Somalia is that of Canadian-Somali journalist Hodan Nalayeh. After moving to Somalia to showcase its beauty with positive stories, Nalayeh was murdered, along with her unborn child and husband, in an Al-Shabaab attack in July 2019.[299]

In spite of the nature of the Somali regime under Farmaajo, the Omar family appeared unconcerned about interacting with it. In a picture posted in November 2018, Rep. Omar was photographed flanked by Somali

---

xi   The author has written for *PJ Media* in the past.

Foreign Minister Ambassador Ahmed Isse Awad, and his predecessor Ambassador Yusuf Garaad Omar.[300,301] A Facebook photo dated August 2017 shows then-State Rep. Omar's then-husband Ahmed Hirsi pictured with Amb. Awad at an event in Minneapolis.[302] In July 2017, Hirsi had posted a picture on Facebook following what may have been the same event, including a note from Hirsi "express[ing] my profound gratitude for the continuous support rendered to us" by "our amazing ambassador [Amb. Awad]."[303] The Omar family had in fact interacted with the ambassador before the Farmaajo era. In a video posted in October 2016, after Omar won the DFL nomination for the Minnesota House, she spoke on stage alongside Amb. Awad at a celebration hosted by The Somali Museum of Minnesota.[304]

In October 2017, then-State Rep. Omar appeared at an event in Minneapolis in which she welcomed several members of the Somali Federal Parliament.[305] That same month, her then-husband posted images on social media indicating he was in Mogadishu at the Constitutional Review of the Federal Government of Somalia.[306] During his time there, Hirsi apparently met with Farmaajo, posting a picture seated next to him on Facebook indicating the two had "discussed various aspects of the ongoing process of political and security stabilization in Somalia..."[307] Hirsi also posted a picture alongside the Somali Minister of Constitutional Affairs, Abdi Hosh.[308] Too, he met with Abdi Gutale, a then-Senior Strategic Policy Advisor at the Somali Ministry of Justice. Gutale wrote in response to Hirsi's praise, in part, "We will revolutionise governance together."[309]

During her 2018 U.S. House primary race, Omar tweeted of her excitement about the prospect of "fighting for political representation like the creation of the Congressional Somalia Caucus."[310]

Because of the nature of the relationship between Rep. Omar, her family, and the Somali government—even fully setting aside her family history under the Barre regime—one must look at her positions on foreign policy with added scrutiny. Sometimes this concerns issues directly affecting Somalia, like when, as noted earlier, Rep. Omar slipped an amendment into the 2019 National Defense Authorization Act (NDAA) stipulating that the U.S. establish no permanent bases or installations in Somalia;[311] or when she claimed to secure substantial debt relief for Somalia from the United States in an appropriations bill passed in December 2019—albeit a bill she curiously voted against.[312] Other times, one must consider the broader international context.

Perhaps most notably, Omar's ties to Somalia may color her views in the ongoing clash between the Iran-Turkey-Qatar axis, and that of Saudi Arabia-Egypt-UAE-Bahrain. Somalia has become another battlefield in this competition, pitting the Saudi-aligned UAE against Turkey ally Qatar.[313,314] A *New York Times* article from July 2019 shared on Facebook by Omar's aforementioned husband-in-law, Mohamed Keynan, demonstrates this, reading in part:[315]

> When a small car bomb exploded outside a courthouse in the bustling port city of Bosaso in northern Somalia, local news reports chalked it up to Islamist militants retaliating for American airstrikes. At least eight people were wounded, and a local affiliate of the Islamic State claimed responsibility.
>
> The attack, however, may have also been part of a very different conflict: one among wealthy Persian Gulf monarchies competing for power and profits across the Horn of Africa.
>
> Over the last two years, war-torn Somalia has emerged as a central battleground, with the United Arab Emirates and Qatar each providing weapons or military training to favored factions, exchanging allegations about bribing local officials, and competing for contracts to manage ports or exploit natural resources.
>
> In an audio recording obtained by The New York Times of a cellphone call with the Qatari ambassador to Somalia, a businessman close to the emir of Qatar said that the militants had carried out the bombing in Bosaso to advance

Qatar's interests by driving out its rival, the United Arab Emirates.[316]

The UAE and Qatar have for several years been vying for influence by lavishing on Somalia hundreds of millions of dollars, in the case of the UAE to fund the development of and operate ports, and Qatar to subsidize infrastructure, education, humanitarian, and security assistance.[317] Qatar's "security assistance" may be a euphemism for something more dastardly. Reports from July 2019 indicate that a Qatari military team landed several hundred miles north of Mogadishu with a sizable Iranian weapons cache. There to greet the plane was Prime Minister Khayre.[318]

Beyond the efforts of partner UAE, the Saudis too have sought to directly expand their influence in Somalia by, for example, recognizing Somalia's secessionist federal states, as part of a broader regional strategy.[319,320]

Meanwhile, in 2017, Qatar's ally Turkey opened its largest overseas military base and training program in none other than Mogadishu.[321] Since, the Somali government has partnered with Turkey in a military training program involving SADAT, an Islamist paramilitary force that has aided and abetted Hamas.[322] The military dimension of the bilateral relationship has followed what Turkey has touted as a robust effort to provide humanitarian assistance to the struggling nation.[323,324] At present, Turkey is Somalia's largest foreign investor.[325] Its role in Somalia can be seen as just one part of its effort to expand Ankara's influence throughout the continent.[326] In fact, Turkish publications have referred to Turkey's military bases in Somalia and Qatar—where it opened its second base in November 2019—as two of the three points on the "Turkish Triangle," the third point being its base in Sudan.[327] Perhaps a figure we introduced before—and with which Rep. Omar is familiar—Somali Foreign Minister Ambassador Ahmed Isse Awad put it best, when, during a November 2019 visit to Turkey with counterpart Mevlut Cavusoglu, he reportedly told Turkey's state-run *Anadolu Agency* publication: "We don't have a better friend than Turkey in Somalia…The Somali people's hearts and minds are with the Turkish people."[328]

Returning to the UAE-Qatar competition, one of the troubling signs that Turkey's partner may be gaining an upper hand is that reportedly, in August 2019, Fahad Yasin was named Deputy Director of Somalia's National Intelligence Security Agency (NISA) during a shakeup of Somalia's security apparatus.[329,330,331] Who is Fahad Yasin? According to a report from Saudi Arabia's *Al-Arabiya* in July 2019, translated by *MEMRI*, in Qatar's bid for spreading its influence in the Horn of Africa, Yasin is:

> Its most prominent means in Mogadishu...Fahad Yasin... [is] one of the most important centers of power today in the Somali presidency, who is a former correspondent for the Qatari Al-Jazeera channel. **Yasin is known to have been a member of extremist organizations before joining Al-Jazeera TV as a reporter. This apparently enabled him to strengthen his ties with Qatari security and intelligence agencies.** Six years ago, he was the head of the Al-Jazeera Center for Studies in East Africa. Two years ago, he was appointed to an important position in the presidential palace. **Sources accuse him of spearheading Qatari schemes – not only in Somalia, but in neighboring countries, as well.** In Mogadishu, he strengthens his position and sidelines his rivals, like General Abdallah, the deputy director of the National Intelligence and Security Agency. Last August, the Kenyan government revealed that Yasin had obtained a Kenyan passport in an illegal and fraudulent manner.[332] [Emphasis added]

A subsequent report from London-based *7D News*, a UAE-tied English language source focused on the Arab world, citing several other news reports, added more color. It alleged that Yasin received training on intelligence in Qatar, and is a member of the Muslim Brotherhood with extensive ties to Qatar's ruling family, the leading scholar of the MB Sheikh Yusuf al-Qaradawi, and a prominent Al-Qaeda official. The report claims that Yasin has served as an intermediary between Qatar and Somali-based jihadist groups. It also claims Yasin helped facilitate money transfers between Qatar and Al-Shabaab, as well as between Qatar and Farmaajo, helping him win the presidency.[333,334]

Now, claims such as these from foreign sources, some of which may be backed by those adversarial to Qatar, need to be taken with a large grain of salt. But Yasin's senior position in the Farmaajo regime is well-established, as is the fact that he worked for Qatar's *Al-Jazeera*, which may be legitimately thought of as a propaganda arm—part of its information warfare machinery. The Qatar tie-in takes on new meaning when one considers that not just *Al-Jazeera*, but other Qatar-linked publications including *Middle East Eye*, and *The New Arab*, have also been vociferous defenders of Rep. Omar.[335] Meanwhile, in the greater battle between the Iran-Turkey-Qatar axis, and that of Saudi Arabia-Egypt-UAE-Bahrain, Omar clearly supports the former camp over the latter.

We must consider the links between Rep. Omar and her family, the Turkish and Somali regimes and their partners, and MB entities and those states that harbor them—collectively—alongside the hostile positions she has taken towards the anti-Islamist partnership led by the U.S. and its allies. When seen in this context, the potential danger of Rep. Omar sitting on the U.S. HFAC becomes all too clear.

It becomes all the more so when Rep. Omar goes out of her way to defend terror-supporting companies based in Somalia, as she did in August 2019, when she called for "Somali government and peacekeeping forces… to protect @Hormuud." Hormuud is a Somali telecommunications company that has been identified by the UN as an Al-Shabaab financier and backer.[336]

Further, Rep. Omar does not simply serve on the HFAC, but on its Subcommittee on Africa, Global Health, Global Human Rights and International Organizations, as well as the Subcommittee on Oversight and Investigations. The mere appearance of conflict and impropriety stemming from any one of the mass of individual threads parsed here should terrify the American people. Viewed in the aggregate, they ought to merit her never setting foot in Washington, D.C. again.

Collusion Conclusion

Rep. Omar's defenders will likely claim that the foregoing analysis of her extensive associations with Islamists and their partners—domestic and foreign—represents guilt by association. They might point to President George W. Bush as having stood onstage in solidarity with the likes of CAIR's Nihad Awad following the September 11th attacks; or the numerous congressmen of both parties who have accepted campaign contributions from prominent individuals in these MB-linked organizations;[337] or officials across the political establishment who have advocated for fostering closer relations with Turkish President Erdoğan as a necessary evil. Leaving aside that this would be an exercise in "whataboutism," such ties are a testament to the fact that America has a bipartisan problem with willful blindness with respect to Islamic supremacism—one key indicator that the Islamist's *dawa* strategy has paid off.[338]

Still, there is a difference between witting and unwitting ties. And there is also a difference between individual lapses in judgment resulting in questionable associations and actions, and an overwhelming trove of data gleaned by a single author purely relying on publicly available records showing consistently questionable views and behaviors.

Most Americans would be hard-pressed to come up with one person they know who has espoused anything resembling the views of the dozens of organizations and individuals with which Rep. Omar has associated. And what makes the myriad data points, or in Mueller mandate terms, "links," detailed herein, so alarming, are the words and actions from Omar that seem to flow so seamlessly from them. Of course, it would be no more reassuring if she spoke and acted as she does independent of these relationships, and was herself the influencer rather than the influenced.

At a minimum, Rep. Omar's sentiments echo those of the organizations, individuals, and governments with which she has consorted. These include her savaging of Israel and embracing BDS; running interference for Islamists by crying "Islamophobia," and alleging white supremacism and 2nd Amendment rights are the real problems;[339,340] dissembling by claiming jihadism has nothing to do with religion; opposing counterjihadist policies while attacking counterjihadists;[341,342] and expressing righteous indignation when asked to denounce Al-Qaeda, and outrage when questioned—even by progressive Muslim women—about her views on the female genital mutilation to which young Somali girls are disproportionately subjected.[343,344] They imply "coordination." The implication alone is proof enough of the threat Rep. Omar poses to America.

But perhaps the saddest element of all is that the Islamist positions on such matters have been accepted almost wholesale by the American Left, including its progressives. Indeed, it is hard to know in the progressive-Islamist axis where the progressivism ends, and the Islamism begins. What makes Rep. Omar even more of a ticking timebomb for America is her corruption, some allegedly criminal, and the rest definitively unethical.

CHAPTER 11

CORRUPTION: CRIMINAL & ETHICAL CONCERNS

Alleged Fraud on Capitol Hill

In the fall of 2019, it appeared a couple of dogged conservative journalists might be on the cusp of cracking one of the great scandals in U.S. history. The mainstream media, taking its cues from the person at its center, either ignored or maligned them. Yet the evidence raised by the likes of Scott Johnson of *Power Line,* and David Steinberg of *PJ Media*, was compelling. The evidence they accumulated continued to mount, even as their subject sought to disappear it from social media. As the story gradually built, so did the evasiveness of the person at its center, Rep. Ilhan Omar. She made quite clear she wanted the story to go away, and when backed into a corner played the victim while casting aspersions on those trying to get to the truth. She could have put the lingering issues to rest quite simply through any number of means, but instead refused to answer basic questions forthrightly, while she and her associates acted suspiciously. Along the way, two fundamental questions went from surreal to very real: Is Congresswoman Ilhan Omar a fraud? If so, how many crimes has she committed in perpetuating it?

There was a long and storied history of fraud in the Somali refugee population in the United States. The P-3 refugee "family reunification" program for example, which was used mainly by Somalis, Ethiopians, and Liberians, had to be suspended in 2008, twenty years after it had commenced, on account of rampant fraud. Fraud rates in the program, which resulted in the admission of tens of thousands of people to our shores, were estimated at well over 80 percent.[1] But would a U.S. congresswoman implicate herself in immigration fraud, not to mention other frauds arising therefrom, *after* having already become a U.S. citizen? And did a more fundamental fraud underlie it?

A Marriage Chronology & Family Relations That Raise Serious Concerns

The controversy started in the wake of Ilhan Omar's triumph in the 2016 DFL primary for Minnesota House District 60B, when a post since deleted popped up on a popular Somali internet forum called *Somali Spot*. It claimed, among other things, that Omar married a British citizen named Ahmed Nur Said Elmi, who had arrived in the U.S. in 2008. The post also contained a number of other assertions. It detailed that after Elmi married Omar, and attended college at NDSU, he returned to the United Kingdom in 2012. It claimed that the "Nur Said" in her alleged brother's name derived from Omar's confirmed father, who went by "Nur Said" on social media. It claimed Elmi's social media accounts had posts corroborating these points, including referring to Omar's children as his nieces and nephew. Further, it added that Omar's own social media accounts revealed that in spite of this legal marriage, she and her original husband Ahmed Hirsi never lived apart, nor did Omar enter into any other relationship. The post included photographic evidence in the way of social media screenshots.[2] The rest, as they say, is history—history that appears to validate most if not all of these assertions.

Here is a timeline of the critical events involving Rep. Omar's family history, based in part on what she said when the controversy first broke:[3]

- 2002: Ilhan Omar and Ahmed Abdisalan Aden (who would change his name to Ahmed Hirsi) apply for a marriage license, but for some unstated reason, never finalize it. Over the next six years, they have two children.

- 2008: Omar and Hirsi dissolve their marriage Islamically.

- 2009: Omar enters a relationship with British citizen Ahmed Nur Said Elmi, who she marries according to U.S. law.

- 2011-2012: Omar and Elmi dissolve their marriage Islamically, but not according to U.S. law. Before 2011 is over, Omar reunites with Ahmed Hirsi, based on the fact she delivers their third child in June 2012. At some point, Omar and Hirsi remarry Islamically.

- 2017: Omar divorces Elmi under U.S. law.

- 2018: Omar and Hirsi legally marry under U.S. law.[4]

- 2019: Omar and Hirsi legally divorce under U.S. law.[5]

The problem for Rep. Omar is what happened between these bullet points. What happened undermines the narrative she has sought to create, namely that conservative bogeyman are out to get her with absurd allegations. The evidence that has been compiled regarding Rep. Omar's factual claims, and her responses to them, make clear the potential scandal at play.

The scandal centers on the question of whether Ahmed Nur Said Elmi is Ilhan Omar's brother. This would seem to be the primary explanation for her other prevarications, contradictory accounts, and evasive actions relating thereto—although there is evidence of fraud and other crimes even if Elmi is not related to Omar. Below are some of the major elements of the case that call into question the story the congresswoman has constructed. Readers may judge for themselves the merits of the allegations raised:

- Ilhan Omar and Ahmed Nur Said Elmi both attended NDSU—Omar from 2009-2011 and Elmi from 2010-2012—overlapping in part with the timeframe in which they were married.[6] Address records between 2009 and 2011 indicate that over two periods, Omar, Elmi, and Hirsi resided at the same address. For a number of months in 2010, Omar and Hirsi are recorded as living at one address, at which Elmi did not arrive until nine months later.[7] In a 2013 article, Omar confirmed that Hirsi had moved with her to North Dakota so Omar could finish her undergraduate education.[8]

The questions are: Why was she living with two men simultaneously for any period of time? Why when she was living solely with one man was it the person she divorced Islamically, rather than the new husband she married legally? Additionally, is it purely coincidental that her relationship with Elmi seemed to track with Omar's time in school? Omar seemed to marry Elmi quickly after a long-term relationship with Hirsi that yielded two children. Are we to believe that just as quickly, Omar and Elmi split, and she was reunited with Hirsi, almost instantly becoming pregnant with their third child?[9] Is there any evidence indicating Omar's marriage to Elmi was not a sham?

- A woman named Wilecia Harris officiated the wedding between Omar and Elmi in 2009. She identified herself on the marriage certificate as a Minister.[10] Today Harris is associated with the "Great and Mighty Works Ministries," which describes itself as a "nondenominational, Bible believing, Bible teaching, and Bible living ministry that believes in being a living example of Jesus the anointed one!"[11] One can only wonder why someone who has gotten married and divorced multiple times in her "faith tradition," that faith being Islam, would just this one time, with Elmi, be married by a Christian Minister. That today Pastor Harris refuses to respond to questions regarding this matter only makes it more suspicious.[i,12]

- In August 2017, then-State Representative Omar filed a document in connection with her divorce proceedings that raised still more questions. Omar swore under penalty of perjury that, among other things: (i) she last knew of Elmi's location in the summer of 2011, (ii) her most recent contact with him was in June 2011, (iii) she did not know where he was last employed, (iv) she did not know

---

i   When the *Daily Mail* sought to question Harris at her home in August of 2019, she refused to open the door. Harris's husband has said: "My wife doesn't want to be involved or interviewed about Congresswoman Omar…Why do[n't] you all just leave Congresswoman Omar alone and stop trying to find dirt on her to discredit her?" See: https://www.dailymail.co.uk/news/article-7353277/Christian-minister-married-Ilhan-Omar-brother-refuses-shed-light-marriage.html.

the names and locations of his parents, siblings, children, and other close relatives, (v) she did not know the names and locations of others likely to know his whereabouts, and (vi) she had looked for him on social media (presumably to no avail). However, Omar would appear to have repeatedly perjured herself based on social media evidence. Beyond the apparent ample evidence of his location and work on social media, the only Ahmed Nur Said Elmi matching the man described in the original rumors about Omar's past, himself admitted to having appeared with Rep. Omar subsequent to June 2011 in photos that were then deleted from social media. The two communicated on social media via an Instagram post dated October 2013—in which Omar claimed she had "been calling and no one will answer. I hope you are ok and feeling better. Pls call me, I need to hear your voice." Elmi had posted that he was in the hospital.[13] Such examples abound. But perhaps most telling of all is a picture Elmi posted in June 2012, a selfie of Elmi holding a baby with the caption, "Nieces, fresh out (sic) the vagina!" Omar's third child was born in June 2012.[14] According to public records, Elmi was evicted from a Minneapolis apartment in July of that year, not in the summer of 2011 when Omar claimed she last knew of his location, and last had contact with him.[15] In a May 2013 Instagram post picturing two other children, Elmi writes, "These girls rock my world… #nieces…" pictured at what appears to be a school in Camden, a borough of London in the UK. Ilhan Omar liked the post. Two years later, Omar was pictured in Camden with two slightly older girls, to whom she referred as "my nieces."[16] As we will discuss shortly, it would appear one of Omar's sisters, with whom she has been pictured, lives in Camden. Were these her daughters? Lastly, regarding potential dishonesty around her divorce, Omar claimed that she had not gotten divorced as of October 2016 because "There are particular challenges to getting a legal divorce…One of those is getting the cooperation and presence of the other person who you are divorcing." However, this appears to be a falsehood because Minnesota is a "no fault" state.[17]

- Practically all of the social media evidence indicating interaction between Ilhan Omar and Ahmed Nur Said Elmi has been scrubbed, and Elmi deleted several of his social media accounts or at a minimum created new ones, claiming he was being inundated with messages, beginning in August 2016, when stories about his relationship with Rep. Omar started breaking.[18,19,20]

- Evidence collected by then-*Alpha News* writer Preya Samsundar in 2016 indicated that as individuals in the Minneapolis Somali community started to leak out information about Omar's family, a man going by "Guhaad Hashi," or "Gulaad Hashi," had been physically threatening people in the district into remaining silent. Rumors suggested that he was Omar's "campaign muscle," corroborated by social media evidence. This was seemingly not without merit, as Hashi had been convicted of stabbing a person shortly before becoming a member of Omar's campaign in 2016.[21] Samsundar reported that individuals felt their families back in Somalia could be threatened given the ties of Omar's associates more broadly to forces in the country, something also worth considering in the context of the last chapter.[22] A running theme throughout the investigations of the few journalists looking into this story has been their reporting that confidential sources—whose information has proven credible—have demanded confidentiality for fear of the dangerous consequences they might face were they to be outed.

- In October 2018, the *Star Tribune*, Minnesota's largest newspaper, reported that during an interview, Omar "showed a reporter cellphone photos of documents from her family's U.S. entry in 1995 after fleeing Somalia's civil war. She declined to provide copies of the papers, which included refugee resettlement approval forms and identification cards, but they appeared to list her father, siblings and Omar by order of birth, with Omar as the youngest of seven children. No one named Ahmed Nur Said Elmi, who is three years younger than Omar, could be seen listed in the documents."[23] Rep. Omar is not known to have shown digital versions of those documents, let alone hard copies, to anyone else. Kevin Diaz, the politics editor of the paper, noted in a July 2019 interview with *Politifact* that: "We've asked her these questions [about suspicious pieces of evidence regarding Omar's marriage to Elmi], and also asked her to make her father available. We've tried to reach Elmi. We've tried to reach her sisters. Her family could put this (the question of Elmi's relationship to Omar) to rest easily. No one will talk to us."[24] Bear in mind that the *Star Tribune* has historically been sympathetic to Congresswoman Omar, and generally reflects the progressive politics of the city it serves.

- In June 2019, the Minnesota Campaign Finance Board (CFB) revealed that as a state representative, Rep. Omar had unlawfully used campaign funds to cover personal expenses, including $2,250 to tax and immigration attorneys. The discovery related to that case indicated that these payments were related to a "crisis" that arose in August 2016—namely, the allegations regarding Omar's marriages. Emails show that Omar assembled a team that sought to coordinate efforts to combat the rumors, including characteristically painting those raising the allegations as bigots, and trying to "shut…down" the story by approaching local media figures directly. One of the emails circulated as the team sought to get its message straight and kill headlines it perceived as wrong and damaging, noted that "Ilhan is the ultimate decider on messaging and strategy…."

Those emails revealed why she retained immigration attorneys. According to one of the attorneys, Omar had claimed someone had reached out to her regarding an allegation that U.S. immigration authorities had issued a summons or were investigating her. The attorney said such an investigation would be unlikely "unless someone submitted very concrete evidence of fraud…proving her legal husband was a biological brother or something like that."[25] The emails indicated Omar's attorneys had filed a FOIA request with United States Citizenship and Immigration Services (USCIS) to obtain documents, and that they received them.

We do not know what those documents contained, but we do have an indication as to what the attorneys were looking for. According to a timesheet from the law firm representing Omar dated September 14, 2016, one of her attorneys prepared documents G-28 and G-639 for FOIA purposes, and forwarded along sample I-130 and I-751 forms to a representative from Omar's team.[26] In July 2019, the author corresponded with Jessica Vaughan, the Director of Policy Studies at the Center for Immigration Studies, and a former State Department Foreign Service Officer, to see what these forms might entail. She wrote:

> The I-130 is the petition to sponsor a qualifying family member for a green card or immigrant visa. The I-751 is the application to remove conditional residency and receive full permanent residency. The latter form was adopted relatively recently to address rampant marriage fraud. The law now imposes a 2 year period of conditional residency for marriage-based applications, and the couple has to go back at the conclusion of the time and essentially establish to USCIS that they are still married and it was not a sham marriage.

> What I find strange is that they sent Omar's representative a "sample" of these forms. For one thing they are easily available on the internet, most obviously on the USCIS web site... Secondly, these are forms that one would expect she would be familiar with since she would have had to sign them as the sponsor of a spouse. Sometimes people rely on their immigration attorney to prepare the forms, but they still have to sign them (and swear that the answers are truthful, under penalty of perjury).[ii]

---

ii   In a sworn deposition, Rep. Omar indicated that she had an archive of her immigration-related forms, that would have included the ones received via the FOIA request, but that these forms were likely collected so others could independently check them for any potential issues. When asked where the FOIA'd forms ultimately ended up, neither Rep. Omar nor her legal counsel could provide an answer as to their location. See: Minnesota Campaign Finance and Public Disclosure Board case docket pertaining to the "Complaint of Steve Drazkowski regarding Neighbors for Ilhan (Omar)," Document #72, pages 33-37.

These are the forms she would have had to fill out in order to sponsor the man who allegedly is her brother (Elmi).[27] [Emphasis added]

The request for the I-130 form alone would seem to be a critical clue in trying to understand what Rep. Omar's team was investigating in her background. To reiterate, her lawyers were seeking a form Omar would have filled out to establish her relationship with a relative who wished to immigrate here—in the midst of a crisis stemming from allegations Omar married her brother soon after he immigrated here. Needless to say, Omar never made the documents public.

Strangely, as the "crisis" unfolded in August 2016, the then-United States Attorney (USA) for Minnesota, Andy Luger, issued a statement seemingly intended to exonerate Rep. Omar, at the urging of her lawyer. USA Luger, a Democrat and Obama appointee, denied a news report indicating his office had opened an investigation into Omar's immigration status. He wrote, "There is no truth to this report and my office is not investigating, nor have we requested an investigation into Ms. Omar."[28] What made this statement particularly curious is that generally, U.S. Attorneys are not in the business of confirming or denying investigations. When *Power Line*'s Scott Johnson asked Luger directly via email in June 2019 whether he had reviewed any relevant documents before sending out his letter, or ever put out any other such letter while U.S. Attorney, Luger replied "Thanks. I will pass on this."[29]

As for the tax attorney fees, they concerned the September 2016 review and correction of one or several issues in Rep. Omar and Ahmed Hirsi's joint tax returns for 2014 and 2015. One known issue is that the couple filed jointly when they were not legally married. In fact, at the time, Rep. Omar was still legally married to Ahmed Nur Said Elmi. When asked by the *AP* in June 2019 if she would release her tax returns, Omar's campaign "did not acknowledge" the request. Yet Rep. Omar—clearly not seeing the inherent irony—has adamantly demanded President Trump release *his* tax returns. Her office has also not provided a response to the question of whether there might be issues with other tax returns she filed prior to her marriage to Hirsi in 2018.[30]

- Further indicating Rep. Omar's likely dishonesty with respect to the aforementioned document she filed in her divorce proceedings, Ahmed Nur Said Elmi was, in the summer of 2019, linked to Omar's sister Sahra Noor. As David Steinberg reported, the source code of the website for the Nairobi, Kenya-based company Sahra Noor had started, Grit Partners Consulting, contained Elmi's personal Instagram account handle, indicating he was running the site's Instagram account. Elmi's social media records revealed that he had been living in Nairobi since at least December 2018.[31,32]

- In September 2019, Rep. Omar deleted a 2013 post wishing "Nur Said" a happy Father's Day. A spokesman claimed it was merely a nickname, and Omar "isn't deleting it for the disturbing and hateful reasons that are being implied by conspiracy theorists and legitimate media outlets shouldn't be spreading conspiracy theories."[33] But her action and response contradicted substantial evidence that Rep. Omar's father is not named "Nur Omar Mohamed," but rather, "Nur Said Elmi Mohamed," or "Nur Said Elmi." If that is the case, it would greatly increase the odds he is Ahmed Nur Said Elmi's father, and therefore that Elmi is Omar's brother. Why? Because in Somali naming convention, children are given a first name followed by their father's first and middle names. If Omar's father is indeed "Nur Said Elmi Mohamed," it would follow that his children's names would end in "Nur Said Elmi."[34] Bear this in mind as we review some of the evidence pertaining to Rep. Omar's family tree, from her father down through her siblings:

- A 2013 document from the St. Anthony, Minnesota-based Jubaland Foundation published an open letter on the formation of Jubaland, listing among its signers Omar's brother-in-law Mohamed Keynan, as well as a "Nur Said Elmi Mohamed."

Recall that during that year, again, Omar published a write-up about an event held in Minneapolis celebrating the formation of Jubaland.[35] Campaign literature also referred to Omar's father as "Nur Mohamed."[36] A fall 2016 profile of Ilhan Omar from a local publication called *City Pages* originally referred to Rep. Omar's father as "Nur Said Elmi Mohamed." Shortly thereafter, it changed his name to "Nur Omar Mohamed." What was the author's explanation for the modification? "I screwed up on the reporting end, hence the corrections," he said.[37]

- David Steinberg reports that classmates of an "Ahmed N. Elmi"—who graduated from high school in St. Paul, MN in 2003, and based on a variety of evidence on social media and elsewhere is indeed the formerly UK-based Ahmed Nur Said Elmi—claimed that he lived with the man identified as Ilhan Omar's father.[38,39]

- Leila Nur Said Elmi, the only such Elmi in the United Kingdom according to David Steinberg's research, listed her father as "Nur Said Elmi" on her marriage certificate. Unsurprisingly, "Nur Said" on Facebook, Omar's father, was friends with Leila Elmi. After these revelations started to emerge, she changed her name on the social network to "Leyla Cilmi." As of September 2019, she had apparently shuttered that account altogether. Pictures from Ilhan Omar's Instagram account indicate that she was with what appears to be Leila Elmi, and definitively Omar's father, in 2011 in Kenya. In 2015, Elmi appears to have been pictured next to Omar again, this time in London, in a photograph with text superimposed over it reading, "I heart my sisters," with "#sisterhood" and "#londontrip" in the caption. Leila is the alleged Omar sister who historically resided in Camden, a borough of London, and whose daughters both Ahmed Nur Said Elmi and Omar may have referred to as "nieces." Records indicate that Ahmed Nur Said Elmi was living in the same neighborhood of the UK as Leila when she executed the aforementioned marriage certificate. Steinberg argues in his reporting that Leila was Ahmed's caretaker, given she was twelve years his senior. Social media postings indicate that a "Leila Elmi" accompanied Ilhan Omar on a trip to Washington, D.C. in December 2016, a visit in which Omar claimed she was harassed by a cab driver while traveling with what she described as her "sister."[40]

- Sources indicated to Samsundar back in August 2016 that indeed Nur Said, Ilhan, and sister Sahra emigrated to the U.S., while Leila, Ahmed, and a Mohamed Nur Said Elmi emigrated to the United Kingdom.[41]

- Scott Johnson shared a screenshot from a source showing a Facebook post from a "Mohamed Nur Said Dhaylule," tagging, among others, Ahmed Hirsi, with a message in Somali translating to, per *Alpha News*: "My sister Ilhan Omar made concise (sic) and very important speech in London, in that speech she announced she will run for Minnesota state Representative seat the year of 2016, (sic) I wish her victory, support her." That post was dated August 2015. August 2015 appears to have been the same period in which Omar posted about her London trip with her sisters, and during which she posted pictures with Ahmed Nur Said Elmi.[42]

- A supporter seemed to refer to Ilhan Omar as "Ilhan Nur Said," in a Facebook post in August 2016 celebrating Omar's DFL primary win. The poster tagged Omar's then-husband, Ahmed Hirsi, along with "Nuur Siciid," "Sahro Nuur," "Leila Elmi," and "Mohamed Nur Said," that is, presumably three of her four siblings, and her father.[43]

- That Omar appears to be one of five siblings, along with Mohamed, Ahmed, Leila and Sahra is significant. Three separate articles, two profiling Ilhan Omar, and another profiling sister Sahra Noor indicated Omar was one of *five*.

The aforementioned *City Pages* profile modified the number of siblings to seven, just as it had changed the name of Omar's father from "Nur Said Elmi Mohamed" to "Nur Omar Mohamed." *Seven* is the number of siblings today cited in, among other places, the *Star Tribune*. But the two articles regarding confirmed sister Sahra Noor still reference five siblings in total.[44]

- Perhaps lending credence to the foregoing, in a 2016 campaign finance filing, Ilhan Omar referred to herself as "Ilhan S Omar."[45] What that "S" stands for, we do not know. When asked for comment, neither Rep. Omar nor her office provided a response.

Tying a bow on much of the foregoing is David Steinberg's assertion, based on his sources, and as revealed in a July 2019 exposé, that the concept of an "Omar" family itself is a fraud. Steinberg asserts that Ilhan "Omar" is an "Elmi," and that her father had used another family currently living in the U.S., the Omars, to help him, Ilhan and Sahra receive asylum and ultimately citizenship.[46] Readers can judge Steinberg's work for themselves.

Regardless, the evidence discussed prior to his exposé is indicative of potential crimes—crimes involving fraud and perjury pertaining to immigration, marriage, taxes, and even potential student loans.[47] Those potential crimes exist irrespective of whether the man Ilhan Omar married in 2009 and divorced in 2017 was her brother.

Denials of Impropriety

Through it all, Rep. Omar has continually tried to quash any story pertaining to her personal life by attacking those raising these points—unsheathing the weapon of identity politics. This was clear from her very first denial in 2016, when she delivered this statement:

A number of baseless, absurd rumors that don't bear repeating have been made recently about my personal life and family. Let me be clear: they are categorically false.

Now, the question that needs to be asked is, "Why are these absurd and hateful rumors being circulated?"

It matters that I am a woman. It matters that I am a Somali-American woman. It matters that I am a Muslim and immigrant woman. It matters that our campaign won the primary by creating a multi-cultural coalition between longtime residents, East Africans immigrants and students. This campaign has always been about bringing people together across lines of difference and that's not going to change.

I know deeply that the people of District 60B oppose Donald Trump-style misogyny, racism, anti-immigration rhetoric and Islamophobic division. We stand together to build a more prosperous and equitable district and state.

Despite the best efforts of those who wish to divide us and stand in the way of progress, rest assured that petty rumors like these will not distract me from the important work that lies ahead for our communities.[iii,48]

This same narrative continued right through June 2019, when, after it was revealed that Omar had filed tax returns jointly with her non-legal then-husband Ahmed Hirsi in 2014 and 2015, her office told the *Star Tribune*:

---

iii   The response from Rep. Omar's Republican general election opponent at the time—a fellow Somali-American—remains relevant. It read in part: "The truly odd thing about the story is how Omar's campaign has chosen to respond. Instead of having her brother explain who he married or producing any sort of documentation, Omar released a statement calling the accusations a racist witch-hunt.

I'm obviously very much in favor of a Somali being elected in 60B, and my questions about this situation are like everyone's. The constituents that Omar wishes to represent, myself included, would simply like a clear non-political answer about the allegations. If she can't provide that, what kind of representative is she going to be?" [Emphasis added] See: https://www.fox9.com/news/ilhan-omars-marriage-certificate-questions-and-her-response.

Since before she was elected to office, Ilhan has been the subject of conspiracy theories and false accusations about her personal life. Emboldened by a president who openly treats immigrants, refugees and Muslims as invaders, these attacks often stem from the presumption that Ilhan—like others who share those identities—is somehow illegitimate or not fully American…

Ilhan has shared more than most public officials ever do about the details of her personal life—even when it is personally painful…Whether by colluding with right-wing outlets to go after Muslim elected officials or hounding family members, legitimate media outlets have a responsibility not to fan the flames of hate. Continuing to do so is not only demeaning to Ilhan, but to her entire family."[49]

Omar is forever the victim. And she is outspoken on everything but the personal behavior that has implicated her in all manner of potential crimes.

Other Ethical Concerns

Heretofore we have focused on Rep. Omar's allegedly criminal actions. However, there are other elements of her conduct that raise serious ethics concerns, some of which have violated Minnesota State law. These include:

- **Allegedly carrying on an affair with a married man whom Rep. Omar's staff has paid—through his consulting firm and as an individual—almost $380,000.**[50,51,52] This allegation stems in part from a divorce filing sworn to under penalty of perjury by Dr. Beth Mynett who claimed her now ex-husband Tim—who has worked as a paid political consultant for Omar since July 2018—was having an affair with Omar.[53] Both Rep. Omar and Mr. Mynett deny this claim, though it bears noting it came amid rumors of a fallout between Omar and then-husband Ahmed Hirsi, who again she divorced in November 2019.[54,55] Judicial Watch has incorporated these allegations into a pending complaint filed with the Office of Congressional Ethics.[56]

- **Potentially violating House ethics rules in receiving a book advance.** In January 2019, it was reported that Rep. Omar had inked a book deal containing a substantial advance. The *Washington Free Beacon* alleges that in so doing, Omar may have violated House ethics rules. This is because members of Congress are prohibited from receiving a book advance of any size, and Omar never disclosed any such payment in her 2018 financial report, implying it was paid in 2019. To avoid skirting House rules, Omar would have had to sign the contract between January 1, 2019, and her swearing-in on January 3, 2019. Since neither the congresswoman nor her publisher have confirmed the date whereby the two parties inked the book deal, this has fueled speculation she broke the rules.[57]

- **Receiving $2,500 in honoraria from two local community colleges as personal income.** Rep. Omar ultimately had to return these funds given Minnesota House rules barred the acceptance of payment from individuals or organizations with a direct interest in House business.[58]

- **Unlawfully using campaign funds for personal travel.** These charges were layered on top of the tax and immigration law fees Rep. Omar had to pay in connection with the Minnesota Campaign Finance Board case that exposed the issues with her tax records.[59]

- **Supposedly badgered one or several voters.** During the 2014 DFL primary election, Rep. Omar allegedly coordinated with an election judge, who interceded with one or several people, asking whether they were voting for "our Somali Brother" [candidate Mohamud Noor] or "the old Jewish lady" [incumbent State Representative Phyllis Kahn]."[60]

Rep. Omar Would Never Pass a Background Check

Based on publicly available information alone, it would appear that Rep. Ilhan Omar, a sitting member of the House Foreign Affairs Committee (HFAC), would not pass a standard background check administered for national security positions. This is no small assertion. The HFAC has a very broad mandate. Its members are responsible for oversight and legislation pertaining to:

> foreign assistance (including development assistance, Millennium Challenge Corporation, the Millennium Challenge Account, HIV/AIDS in foreign countries, security assistance, and Public Law 480 programs abroad); national security developments affecting foreign policy; strategic planning and agreements; war powers, treaties, executive agreements, and the deployment and use of United States Armed Forces; peacekeeping, peace enforcement, and enforcement of United Nations or other international sanctions; arms control and disarmament issues; the International Development Finance Corporation, the United States Agency for International Development; activities and policies of the State, Commerce, and Defense Departments and other agencies related to the Arms Export Control Act and the Foreign assistance Act, including export and licensing policy for munitions items and technology and dual-use equipment and technology; international law; promotion of democracy; international law enforcement issues, including narcotics control programs and activities; international cyber issues; U.S. Agency for Global Media; embassy security; international broadcasting; public diplomacy, including international communication and information policy, and international education and exchange programs; and all other matters not specifically assigned to a subcommittee.[61]

Her seat on the HFAC, in short, touches on nearly every issue vital to U.S. national security and foreign policy—the most sensitive matters of war and peace.

Juxtapose these responsibilities with the language and dictates of the "Questionnaire for National Security Positions," or "SF-86," which is a standard document required of those seeking government security clearances. The introduction to the form notes that:

> Background investigations for national security positions are conducted to gather information to determine whether you are reliable, trustworthy, of good conduct and character, and loyal to the U.S...

> In addition to the questions on this form, inquiry also is made about your adherence to security requirements, honesty and integrity, vulnerability to exploitation or coercion, falsification, misrepresentation, and any other behavior, activities, or associations that tend to demonstrate a person is not reliable, trustworthy, or loyal.[62]

In connection therewith, respondents must answer highly detailed and personal questions about their family members, friends, finances, foreign ties, and a whole host of other sensitive information. The purpose is to find out whether one is a threat to national security or could be vulnerable to compromise, thereby making one a potential threat to national security. Based on what we know about Rep. Omar from what is public, it would be unimaginable to think she could pass a background check. But as a sitting congresswoman, she need not obtain a security clearance—she is exempt from any vetting process. Assuming the authorities refuse to investigate Rep. Omar, only the voters in her district will have an opportunity to effectively deny Rep. Omar a security clearance, by voting her out of office. If they do not, we will all pay the price.

CONCLUSION

In September of 2019, we visited Rep. Omar's 5th Congressional District. We walked the streets of the Cedar-Riverside neighborhood where the congresswoman's journey to stardom began. The enclave at the heart of the Minnesota legislative district that helped sweep her into office is an apt metaphor for progressivism and its dystopic contradictions.

On one side of a highway stood a Minneapolis business district filled with trendy restaurants and posh new high-rises. On the other side of the highway, in the shadow of a glitzy new football stadium, stood an area that personified the ubiquitous "Coexist" bumper stickers.

Half of Cedar-Riverside is a self-described "Little Mogadishu." The other half is a college town. Literally adjacent to the looming low-income and subsidized housing towers where many Somalis first settle upon arriving in America are swanky modern condos. On street corners, one finds some women covered head to toe in burqas, and other women wearing barely anything at all. Dive bars sit next to Arab markets. The only thing that would seem to unite the inhabitants of the neighborhood is political sentiment, symbolized by spray-painted glass at a pickup area near the Somali-dominated housing towers reading "Fu*k Trump." This is "coexistence," but it is not assimilation into anything but Minneapolis's progressive milieu.

Lost on the area's college students is that while they cheer for social and economic justice, the congressional district in which Cedar-Riverside sits—Rep. Omar's—is rated as the worst for black people in the entire country. The students are cloistered away from those impacted by their beliefs, including the Somali underclass that embraces a culture anathema to them. Furthermore, for all of Minneapolis's focus on assuaging the concerns of its Somalis, supposedly scarred by the scourge of Islamophobia, it remains the terror capital of the United States. How can that be in such a welcoming progressive bastion?

Some members of the Islamic community are unabashed in their support for the jihadis. Describing one local trial in which several men were convicted on terror charges, *Power Line*'s Scott Johnson, a Minneapolis native, seemed to capture the issue of Twin Cities jihadism—and the folly of the progressive Left's view on it—when he wrote:

> Despite the gravity of the offenses committed by the defendants, all well-spoken males in their early 20s with access to education and employment, they enjoyed substantial support within the Somali community and among the Twin Cities crowd of social justice warriors, such as those gathered under the umbrella of Minnesotans Against Islamophobia. These supporters charged the FBI with entrapping the defendants and demanded their freedom. The incredibly incriminating evidence produced by the government—including 40 hours of recorded conversations with an informant—proved that accusation ludicrous. Even the defendants themselves rejected it. "I'm certainly not being persecuted for my faith. I was certainly not entrapped," Daud [one of the convicted terrorists] declared at his sentencing hearing. "I was not going there to pass out medical kits or food. I was going strictly to fight and kill on behalf of the Islamic State."[1]

In fact, prosecutors noted for the record that as one of the defendants was hauled off after sentencing, he flashed an Islamic State sign that was met with an "exuberant" reply from the gallery. Another defendant had done the same thing, albeit less emphatically.[2] Of the trial as a whole, the government's lawyers remarked that none:

> in the aggregate memory of the U.S. Attorney's Office has been conducted in more of an atmosphere of intimidation, harassment, and incipient violence than the trial of this

case. The families of cooperating defendants were harassed in the courtroom, in full view of the testifying witness; there was a fistfight in the corridor outside the courtroom; multiple individuals had to be ejected from the courtroom for not following the Court's rules of behavior.[3]

The trial in question was the very one in which Rep. Omar had written the presiding judge calling for leniency.[4]

On top of the terrorism issues, for all the talk of the unalloyed good of refugee resettlement, Rep. Omar's Cedar-Riverside has seen a dramatic rise in violent crime, driven by Somali gang warfare.[5] If one did not know any better, one might think the state's commitment to taking in refugees was really about importing a population of Democrats, rather than taking in people from a world away out of the goodness of its politicians' hearts, let alone improving the lives of the native population.

The Minnesota House district from which Omar was first elected is surely non-representative of America. But it is a reflection of what happens when a progressive-Islamist axis takes hold. It leads to crime, poverty, and misery—but always with the best of intentions. That that axis is represented at the national level by way of Rep. Omar, her Squad, and a Democratic Party that has cowered to them must give every American pause.

Perhaps most sobering is the fact that Rep. Omar is a symptom of our failings as a country—of our immigration policies, our education system, and more broadly our predominant progressive values and principles, that have conspired to make a person like the congresswoman viable. And let us be clear: She was elected to the Minnesota House in large part due to support from college students, and to the U.S. House with the helping hand of Leftist elites—not solely by dint of support from her fellow Somali-Americans. What does it say when our elites of the present and future bless such candidates?

We wrote this book in the hope that we can one day look back and view Rep. Omar as the zenith of a radical progressive-Islamist movement in our national politics, rather than just another step on the road to serfdom, if not suicide.

Acknowledging the size, scope, and nature of the problem is the first step to combating it. We have illustrated in this book that a single seditious representative can have an outsized negative influence on our nation. More importantly, she can foreshadow existential challenges to our very system of government.

These points underscore the importance of awakening our citizens to the threat we face. If we who love this country are not actively engaged in this War of Ideas, by definition we will lose it.

What can we do? First, we must re-embrace our timeless founding values and principles, forged as they were from the study of theology, philosophy, and the history of thousands of years of trial and error reflecting an unchanging human nature that validated their righteousness. We must re-inculcate in our progeny a knowledge of, and love for, these values and principles. This is no small task, of course, requiring a full mobilization of efforts from the academy to the arts—battlefields on which the Left has gone unopposed for decades. But it is imperative because we cannot expect to win political elections one day every two years if we are losing elections for the American Mind every other day of every year. All else flows from the right ideas: immigration policy, the education system, cultural dynamism, the conduct of our citizens, our peace, and prosperity.

In the short term and beyond we must vigilantly marshal all of our resources to defend free speech—for that is the first pillar the progressive elites and Islamists alike seek to abolish. Absent free speech, there can be no competition in the War of Ideas, and absent competition in the War of Ideas, the Leftists who predominate in the areas in which they are disseminated—namely academia, the media, and Silicon Valley—are guaranteed victory. Those in the progressive-Islamist axis, like those in the totalitarian movements that preceded it, seek to intimidate into silence those who stand in their way of achieving dominance. Rep. Omar is counting on us to shut up by questioning our motives and calling us Islamophobes, racists, and bad Americans. She put every American who cherishes the First Amendment on notice when she declared in December 2019 that "Hate, sinful, bigot [sic] rhetoric is very dangerous, and it's becoming synonymous with the Republican party"—since many progressives believe in censoring speech that is "hateful" as they define it.[6] Do not give her the satisfaction of letting these falsehoods, calumnies, and attacks on free expression stand unchallenged. Demand that Rep. Omar be held to the same standard of scrutiny as every other politician. Call things by their name rather than twisting language to appease the unappeasable. By standing up for what is right in the face of the crybullies' might, you will encourage others to do the same.

Next, demand of our elected leaders that they too stand up to progressive crybullies, as well as the initiatives of progressive colleagues that threaten American liberties. It is impossible to compete against a political adversary that genuinely wishes to destroy us by hamstringing ourselves with suicidal rules of engagement or naively dismissing the threat. President Trump's refusal to do so is perhaps the chief reason why he is so reviled by the progressives.

Finally, educate your friends and family members—and especially children—as to the history of totalitarianism, and the common theme of its rising under the banner of pleasant platitudes that mask a deadly core of censorship and tyranny.

Together, these actions can help expand our numbers, strengthen the resolve of our people, and serve as a bulwark against the erosion of our rights.

This book illustrates the danger posed if those who love this country do not engage with those who wish to see it consigned to the dustbin of a fallacious history. America is man's last, best hope on Earth. We must honor those who bequeathed it to us by protecting and preserving it for generations to come.

ENDNOTES

Chapter 1: Roots of Ilhan Omar's Rage and Rise

1.   https://www.theguardian.com/us-news/2018/nov/12/
      lesson-hopeful-ilhan-omar-journey-somali-refugee-us-congress

2   https://time.com/collection/firsts/4898550/ilhan-omar-firsts/?f-
      bclid=IwAR3PFu9SVWD8BN5E7PXn-YHZHMF-
      p462DVLbi7GgbRCxsKSYZ4Yyj53YRJw0

3   https://www.youtube.com/watch?v=Zi_Ex_MpzT4

4   http://mspmag.com/arts-and-culture/
      coffee-and-conversation-with-ilhan-omar/

5   https://www.washingtonexaminer.com/news/ilhan-omar-i-proba-
      bly-love-this-country-more-than-anyone-that-is-naturally-born

6   https://medium.com/airbel/refugee-resettlement-a-conversa-
      tion-with-congresswoman-ilhan-omar-e48602387f4

7   https://www.southwestjournal.com/news/2018/11/
      ilhan-omars-road-to-washington/

8   https://www.blackpast.org/african-american-history/
      omar-ilhan-1982/

9   https://web.archive.org/web/20190307192434/http://www.
      citypages.com/news/ilhan-omars-improbable-journey-from-refu-
      gee-camp-to-minnesota-legislature/398441901

10   https://psmag.com/magazine/countrys-first-somali-american-leg-
      islator-and-her-politics-of-inclusivity

11   https://www.youtube.com/watch?v=r2y-oRR2WKM&t=718s

12   https://www.thefader.com/2017/03/14/
      ilhan-omar-first-somali-muslim-politician-interview

13   https://www.chicagotribune.com/news/ct-xpm-1992-12-13-
      9204230505-story.html

14   https://www.nytimes.com/1977/10/11/archives/somalia-trys-to-
      live-by-both-the-koran-and-das-kapital.html
15   https://www.un.int/somalia/somalia/country-facts
16   https://www.un.int/somalia/somalia/country-facts
17   https://www.cia.gov/library/publications/the-world-factbook/
      geos/so.html
18   https://www.cia.gov/library/readingroom/docs/CIA-RDP90-
      00552R000100260010-3.pdf
19   https://www.un.int/somalia/somalia/country-facts
20   https://www.mprnews.org/story/2019/04/18/
      rep-ilhan-omar-politics-profile-timeline-history
21   https://freebeacon.com/politics/ilhan-omar-on-trump-voters-ig-
      norance-really-is-pervasive-in-many-parts-of-this-country/
22   http://web.archive.org/web/20180719142939/https://www.
      aaiusa.org/from_refugee_to_st_house_race_ilhan_omar_looks_
      to_break_new_ground
23   https://mshale.com/2015/11/10/
      ilhan-omars-legislative-race-shape/
24   https://www.youtube.com/watch?v=gWEQ9hhXQFM
25   https://www.thenation.com/podcast/ilhan-omar-next-left-politics/
26   https://www.thefader.com/2017/03/14/
      ilhan-omar-first-somali-muslim-politician-interview
27   http://archive.is/8EJTH
28   media.mnhs.org/things/cms/10395/527/10395527.pdf, pgs. 7-8
29   https://alphanewsmn.com/a-community-forced-into-silence/
30   https://www.thenation.com/podcast/ilhan-omar-next-left-politics/
31   http://web.archive.org/web/20161103134253/https://www.
      aaiusa.org/from_refugee_to_st_house_race_ilhan_omar_looks_
      to_break_new_ground
32   https://www.youtube.com/watch?v=7INpvY0J0RI at 18:57
33   https://www.ifes.org/sites/default/files/con00170.pdf#page=10
34   http://hrlibrary.umn.edu/research/Somalia-Constitution2012.pdf
35   https://nbcpalmsprings.com/2018/07/04/
      how-we-became-americans-the-story-of-immigrants/
36   https://www.youtube.com/watch?v=r2y-oRR2WKM

37 http://web.archive.org/web/20161103134253/https://www.
aaiusa.org/from_refugee_to_st_house_race_ilhan_omar_looks_
to_break_new_ground

38 http://web.archive.org/web/20160506180716/http://www.ilhan-
omar.com/bio/

39 https://www.westfargopioneer.com/news/government-and-pol-
itics/995826-Quiet-while-at-NDSU-U.S.-Rep.-Omar-now-
makes-national-headlines

40 https://www.nationalreview.com/2014/04/
roots-cairs-intimidation-campaign-andrew-c-mccarthy/

41 https://www.centerforsecuritypolicy.org/wp-content/
uploads/2018/01/HAMAS_CAIR_MB.pdf

42 https://www.cairmn.com/about-us/cair-mn-staff.html

43 https://kstp.com/kstpImages/repository/cs/files/Ilhan%20
Omar%20Statement.pdf

44 http://www.startribune.com/new-documents-revisit-questions-
about-rep-ilhan-omar-s-marriage/511681362/

45 https://apnews.com/05839987bd644e1385bc4b8d3ccd995d

46 http://bioguide.congress.gov/scripts/biodisplay.
pl?index=O000173

47 https://www.ilhanomar.com/about

48 https://bsmknighterrant.org/2014/05/31/
inside-the-somali-political-movement/

49 http://www.citypages.com/news/phyllis-kahn-alleges-elec-
tion-judge-called-her-old-jewish-lady-opponent-muslim-
brother-6569512

50 https://www.minnpost.com/politics-policy/2014/02/
allegations-threats-bullying-follow-cedar-riverside-caucus-brawl/

51 http://www.startribune.com/rival-s-analysis-shows-omar-domi-
nated-among-students/390088981/

52 https://twitter.com/startribune/status/905901491206094848

53 https://blog.thecurrent.org/2018/06/
minnesota-rep-ilhan-omar-featured-in-maroon-5-video/

54 https://www.timeforilhanfilm.com/

55 https://www.house.leg.state.mn.us/members/profile/
news/15286/37826

56   https://www.twincities.com/2019/06/06/ilhan-omar-violated-minnesota-state-campaign-finance-rules-board-says/

57   https://nypost.com/2019/09/03/rep-ilhan-omars-husband-wants-divorce-after-affair-bombshell-source/

58   https://www.washingtonexaminer.com/news/rashida-tlaib-says-minority-members-in-congress-are-token-diversity

Chapter 2: Omar Blames America First

1   https://spectator.org/is-ilhan-omar-a-communist/

2   https://www.nytimes.com/2018/02/13/arts/angela-davis-archive-harvard.html

3   https://www.wsj.com/articles/angela-davis-and-radical-chic-2016-1465254392

4   https://books.google.com/books?id=3jjNW-_Tnus-C&q=angela+davis#v=snippet&q=angela%20davis&f=false

5   https://spectator.org/is-ilhan-omar-a-communist/

6   https://books.google.com/books?id=3jjNW-_Tnus-C&q=angela+davis#v=snippet&q=angela%20davis&f=false

7   https://www.nytimes.com/1985/04/04/us/kirkpatrick-joins-republican-party.html

8   http://www.cnn.com/ALLPOLITICS/1996/conventions/san.diego/facts/GOP.speeches.past/84.kirkpatrick.shtml

9   https://www.nationalreview.com/2010/02/professor-contempt-roger-kimball/

10   https://www.city-journal.org/html/fbi-history-howard-zinn-10752.html

11   http://archive.is/Wfax3

12   http://archive.is/HMobY

13   https://www.washingtonexaminer.com/news/ilhan-omar-united-states-was-founded-by-genocide

14   http://archive.is/fK0GS

15   https://dailycaller.com/2019/07/05/ilhan-omar-independence-day-somali/

16   http://archive.is/F8g2z
17   https://www.newyorker.com/news/the-political-scene/
      ilhan-omars-embattled-first-months-in-office
18   https://grabien.com/story.php?id=236621
19   https://www.c-span.org/video/?460903-1/
      lawmakers-speak-iftar-dinner-capitol-hill
20   https://www.newsweek.com/2019/04/19/ilhan-omar-demo-
      crats-israel-trump-1389677.html
21   http://archive.is/nV3vH
22   https://www.jihadwatch.org/2019/03/ilhan-omar-thanks-fox-for-re-
      buking-jeanine-pirro-but-pirro-is-right-hijab-is-a-sharia-imperative
23   https://en.radiofarda.com/a/iran-activists-say-they-will-continue-
      anti-hijab-protests/29729246.html
24   https://www.militarytimes.com/news/
      pentagon-congress/2019/07/22/survey-public-confi-
      dence-in-the-military-is-high-especially-among-older-generations/
25   https://thefederalist.com/2019/04/23/fought-battle-mogadishu-
      heres-ilhan-omar-gets-wrong-black-hawk/
26   http://archive.is/OqEgy
27   https://www.investigativeproject.org/7894/
      ilhan-omar-slammed-us-soldiers-involved-in-black
28   https://www.nationalreview.com/2019/07/
      ilhan-omar-is-completely-assimilated/
29   https://www.foxnews.com/politics/
      ilhan-omar-unamerican-ice-detain-immigrants
30   https://www.washingtonexaminer.com/news/
      ilhan-omar-we-treat-dogs-better-than-migrant-children
31   https://omar.house.gov/media/press-releases/progressive-congress-
      women-joint-statement-ice-and-cbp-not-one-more-dollar
32   https://www.newyorker.com/news/dispatch/
      how-ilhan-omar-won-over-hearts-in-minnesotas-fifth
33   https://en.wikipedia.org/wiki/
      Application_of_Islamic_law_by_country
34   https://twitter.com/RealSaavedra/status/1146514097661284352
35   https://www.dailysignal.com/2018/06/26/
      fact-check-are-half-of-all-border-patrol-agents-hispanic/
36   http://archive.is/zTAm1

37 http://archive.is/ewkWm

38 https://omar.house.gov/media/press-releases/rep-ilhan-omar-state-ment-federal-court-blocking-president-trump-s-asylum

39 https://www.realclearpolitics.com/video/2019/06/22/rep_ilhan_omar_defends_aoc_there_are_camps_and_people_are_being_concentrated.html

40 https://twitter.com/IlhanMN/status/1131701844324102144

41 https://www.conservativereview.com/news/ilhan-omar-accuses-america-committing-atrocities-southern-border/

42 https://grabien.com/file.php?id=595261

43 https://grabien.com/file.php?id=620919

44 https://www.c-span.org/video/?460903-1/lawmakers-speak-iftar-dinner-capitol-hill

45 https://grabien.com/file.php?id=595763

46 http://archive.is/8oQFP

47 Mac Donald, Heather *The War on Cops*

48 https://benweingarten.com/2018/06/heather-mac-donald-identity-politics-criminal-justice/

49 http://archive.is/BBmZf

50 https://thefederalist.com/2019/07/10/left-managed-mainstream-anti-americanism/

51 http://americanradioworks.publicradio.org/features/blackspeech/adavis.html

52 https://www.congress.gov/congressional-record/2019/5/1/house-section/article/h3363-3?s=1&r=11

53 https://www.theamericanconservative.com/articles/want-to-fix-immigration-start-with-the-abused-asylum-system/

54 https://www.nationalreview.com/news/dhs-secretary-90-percent-of-recent-asylum-seekers-skipped-their-hearings/

55 https://www.foxnews.com/politics/ilhan-omar-bernie-sanders-minnesota-minneapolis

56 https://twitter.com/SaraCarterDC/status/1191354409671909376

57 https://spectator.org/is-ilhan-omar-a-communist/

58 https://witnessforpeace.org/about-us/mission-history/

59 https://www.centerforsecuritypolicy.org/2019/02/14/rep-ilhan-omar-cribbed-from-al-jazeera-while-grilling-elliott-abrams/

60   https://www.breitbart.com/national-security/2019/02/13/
     ilhan-omar-accuses-trump-official-elliot-abrams-of-glorif-
     ying-1980s-massacre-in-venezuela-hearing/
61   Ibid
62   https://www.dailywire.com/news/46657/
     watch-ilhan-omar-blames-us-venezuela-crisis-claims-ryan-saavedra
63   https://www.wsj.com/articles/
     no-dialogue-for-maduro-11549229078?mod=article_inline
64   https://twitchy.com/brettt-3136/2019/01/26/
     rep-ilhan-omars-tweet-backing-russia-on-venezuela-and-oppo-
     sing-trumps-coup-gets-even-worse/
65   https://www.powerlineblog.com/archives/2019/02/explicating-il-
     han-omar.php
66   https://www.washingtonpost.com/opinions/2019/02/14/
     venezuelas-regime-is-using-death-squads-today-where-is-ilhan-
     omars-outrage/?utm_term=.3a7e5d44c451
67   https://www.washingtonpost.com/
     opinions/ilhan-omar-sanctions-are-part-of-a-failed-for-
     eign-policy-playbook-stop-relying-on-them/2019/10/23/
     b7cbb1ca-f510-11e9-a285-882a8e386a96_story.html
68   https://www.reuters.com/article/us-iran-protests-usa/u-s-says-iran-
     may-have-killed-more-than-1000-in-recent-protests-idUSKB-
     N1Y926W
69   http://archive.is/ERPOX
70   https://twitter.com/IlhanMN/status/1212942887048101888
71   https://www.newyorker.com/news/the-political-scene/
     ilhan-omars-embattled-first-months-in-office
72   https://www.motherjones.com/politics/2017/07/
     minnesota-ilhan-omar-muslim/
73   https://www.youtube.com/watch?v=oL3atWiLRnc
74   Ibid
75   https://www.foxnews.com/politics/ilhan-omar-once-blamed-our-
     involvement-in-other-peoples-affairs-al-shabab-attack-on-kenyan-
     mall
76   https://dailycaller.com/2019/02/05/ilhan-omar-israel-hamas/

77   https://www.youtube.com/watch?v=qj_nkzcvJ1w

78   https://www.snopes.com/uploads/2019/01/Yasin-Daud-USA-Sentencing-Memo.pdf

79   http://www.startribune.com/isil-hearings-exposed-depth-of-terror-recruiting-in-minnesota/401984905/

80   https://www.foxnews.com/us/how-rep-ilhan-omars-minnesota-district-became-the-terrorist-recruitment-capital-of-the-us-officials-highly-concerned

81   https://www.justice.gov/usao-mn/pr/jury-trial-results-conviction-three-minnesotans-conspiring-join-isil-and-commit-murder-0

82   https://www.powerlineblog.com/archives/2016/11/sentencing-the-minnesota-men-4.php

83   http://www.fox9.com/news/minnesota-isis-sentencing-ilhan-omar-letter

84   https://www.pbs.org/wgbh/pages/frontline/shows/binladen/who/interview.html

85   https://www.meforum.org/2095/islams-doctrines-of-deception.

86   Coughlin, Stephen *Catastrophic Failure,* pgs. 177-182

87   https://www.nationalreview.com/2011/10/fears-and-smears-andrew-c-mccarthy/

88   http://deanbibleministries.org/dbmfiles/notes/2018-Chafer-Conf-Hadian-01-Document.pdf#page=620

89   https://www.wsj.com/articles/SB10001424052748704132204576136590964621006

90   Coughlin, Stephen *Catastrophic Failure,* pg. 538

91   http://web.archive.org/web/20150323064950/http://www.theblaze.com/contributions/obama-peddles-osamas-propaganda/

92   https://pjmedia.com/homeland-security/ilhan-omar-falsely-claims-that-white-men-are-greater-threat-than-jihadis/

Chapter 3: Omar, Intersectionality, and Identity Politics

1   https://chicagounbound.uchicago.edu/cgi/viewcontent.cgi?referer=&httpsredir=1&article=1052&context=uclf

2   http://shain003.grads.digitalodu.com/blog/wp-content/uploads/2014/09/Twenty-Years-of-Critical-Race-Theory-Looking-Back-to-Move-Forward.pdf#page=8

3   https://cyber.harvard.edu/bridge/CriticalTheory/critical4.htm

4   https://www.lifezette.com/2019/05/democrat-ilhan-omar-america-not-going-be-country-of-white-people/

5   https://dailycaller.com/2019/09/15/ilhan-omar-wants-kavanaugh-trump-impeached/

6   https://amgreatness.com/2019/08/11/the-strange-case-of-white-supremacy/

7   https://www.dissentmagazine.org/article/alinsky-for-the-left-the-politics-of-community-organizing

8   http://archive.is/I9ccg

9   https://www.minnpost.com/community-voices/2018/11/one-of-us-is-going-to-washington/

10   http://www.aei.org/publication/the-great-society-at-50/

11   http://spokesman-recorder.com/2019/06/12/the-omar-effect-on-the-pulse-of-controversy-and-change/

12   https://www.merriam-webster.com/dictionary/intersectionality

13   https://americanmind.org/essays/the-promises-and-perils-of-identity-politics/

14   https://twitter.com/evanmlips/status/1150576367676903425

15   https://en.vogue.me/culture/ilhan-omar-first-somali-american-hijabi-congresswoman/

16   https://www.pri.org/stories/2018-11-01/love-democracy-ilhan-omar-draws-diverse-supporters-bid-congress

17   https://www.youtube.com/watch?v=gWEQ9hhXQFM

18   https://quillette.com/2018/05/08/illiberal-logic-intersectionality/

19   https://twitter.com/ByRyanBrooks/status/1150059816238407681

20   https://minnesota.cbslocal.com/2019/08/15/minnesotas-5th-congressional-district-listed-as-worst-di-struct-for-black-americans-to-live/

21   https://www.blackpast.org/african-american-history/1998-clarence-thomas-speech-national-bar-association/

Chapter 4: Omar's Progressive Agenda

1   https://online.hillsdale.edu/document.doc?id=325

2   https://www.refinery29.com/en-us/2018/09/207297/democratic-socialists-midwest-young-women-2018-elections

3   https://keywiki.org/Ilhan_Omar#DSA_connections
4   https://www.dsausa.org/statements/
    dsa-statement-in-solidarity-with-representative-ilhan-omar/
5   https://www.foxnews.com/politics/
    ilhan-omar-bernie-sanders-minnesota-minneapolis
6   http://archive.is/I9ccg
7   https://www.ilhanomar.com/economic-justice
8   http://archive.is/Y4XNF
9   https://grabien.com/file.php?id=550497
10 http://archive.is/jt6jO
11 https://omar.house.gov/media/press-releases/rep-ilhan-omar-in-
    troduces-homes-all-act-new-21st-century-public-housing-vision
12 http://archive.is/prljC
13 http://archive.is/LDXCx
14 https://www.minnpost.com/national/2019/06/rep-omar-along-
    side-sen-bernie-sanders-releases-student-debt-cancellation-bill/
15 https://www.congress.gov/congressional-record/2019/5/1/
    house-section/article/h3397-7?s=1&r=10
16 https://www.tcdailyplanet.net/
    sentencing-reforms-offer-path-towards-justice/
17 https://www.thefader.com/2017/03/14/
    ilhan-omar-first-somali-muslim-politician-interview
18 https://psmag.com/magazine/countrys-first-somali-american-leg-
    islator-and-her-politics-of-inclusivity
19 https://www.thefader.com/2017/03/14/
    ilhan-omar-first-somali-muslim-politician-interview
20 https://nasro.org/frequently-asked-questions/
21 https://spokesman-recorder.com/2019/06/21/the-omar-agenda/
22 https://twitter.com/marclamonthill/
    status/1146908766992031744
23 https://alphanewsmn.com/ilhan-omar-calls-to-abolish-ice-in-re-
    sponse-to-trumps-immigration-proposal/
24 https://omar.house.gov/media/press-releases/rep-ilhan-omar-state-
    ment-federal-court-blocking-president-trump-s-asylum
25 http://archive.is/gLPwu

26 https://www.washingtonexaminer.com/news/
    aoc-and-ilhan-omar-warn-immigrants-of-impending-ice-raids
27 http://archive.is/QmwRP
28 https://psmag.com/magazine/countrys-first-somali-american-leg-
    islator-and-her-politics-of-inclusivity
29 https://www.nationalreview.com/2015/10/
    sanctuary-cities-illegal-immigration-confederates-nullification/
30 http://archive.is/1w4U6
31 http://archive.is/Biim2
32 https://www.foxnews.com/media/
    ilhan-omar-interview-2018-fearful-white-men-islam
33 https://alphanewsmn.com/
    omar-lesch-no-votes-ending-terrorist-life-insurance-payouts/
34 https://www.rescue.org/displaced-season-2/
    refugee-resettlement-conversation-congresswoman-ilhan-omar
35 http://archive.is/1kLll
36 https://www.congress.gov/congressional-record/2019/7/10/
    house-section/article/h5337-3?s=1&r=2
37 https://www.congress.gov/congressional-record/2019/7/16/
    house-section/article/h5858-1?s=1&r=1
38 https://www.congress.gov/congressional-record/2019/5/1/
    house-section/article/h3363-3?s=1&r=11
39 https://www.congress.gov/congressional-record/2019/5/22/
    house-section/article/h4115-1?s=1&r=7
40 https://www.dailysignal.com/2019/06/04/here-are-3-gaping-er-
    rors-ilhan-omar-made-in-attacking-pro-life-advocates-and-reli-
    gious-liberty/
41 https://www.congress.gov/congressional-record/2019/6/20/
    house-section/article/h4929-2?s=1&r=3
42 https://thefederalist.com/2019/11/19/
    americans-need-to-stop-funding-the-chinese-gulag/
43 https://www.congress.gov/congressional-record/2019/5/23/
    house-section/article/h4151-5?s=1&r=6
44 http://www.startribune.com/rep-ilhan-omar-with-perspective-of-
    a-foreigner-sets-ambitious-global-agenda/510489882/

45 https://www.foxnews.com/politics/
    ilhan-omar-bernie-sanders-minnesota-minneapolis
46 https://omar.house.gov/media/press-releases/
    rep-ilhan-omar-statement-bipartisan-budget-act-2019-hr-3877
47 http://spokesman-recorder.com/2019/06/12/
    the-omar-effect-on-the-pulse-of-controversy-and-change/
48 https://www.newyorker.com/news/dispatch/
    how-ilhan-omar-won-over-hearts-in-minnesotas-fifth
49 https://www.washingtonpost.com/opinions/
    ilhan-omar-we-must-apply-our-universal-values-to-all-nations-on-
    ly-then-will-we-achieve-peace/2019/03/17/0e2d66fc-4757-11e9-
    aaf8-4512a6fe3439_story.html
50 http://archive.is/VOb11
51 Ibid
52 https://www.wsj.com/articles/
    no-dialogue-for-maduro-11549229078?mod=article_inline
53 http://archive.is/ERPOX
54 https://www.congress.gov/bill/116th-congress/house-bill/2354/
55 https://jewishjournal.com/news/nation/293059/
    rep-omar-compares-israels-nation-state-law-to-iran/
56 http://archive.is/fDBgD
57 https://www.wsj.com/articles/rocket-attack-in-iraq-kills-u-s-con-
    tractor-wounds-four-u-s-troops-11577492632
58 https://www.politico.com/news/2019/12/29/
    strike-iraq-death-militia-090555
59 https://www.wsj.com/articles/protesters-attempt-to-storm-u-s-em-
    bassy-in-baghdad-11577787978
60 https://grijalva.house.gov/uploads/Rep%20Grijalva%20Iran%20
    Letter.pdf
61 https://home.treasury.gov/news/press-releases/sm780
62 https://www.jpost.com/American-Politics/Ilhan-Omar-calls-for-
    release-of-Egyptian-prisoner-with-terrorist-ties-586456
63 https://www.investigativeproject.org/7954/
    muslim-brotherhood-supporters-jihadists-label
64 http://archive.is/lTzkN

65   http://archive.is/JBQ91
66   https://twitter.com/byrdinator/status/1189303734163124227
67   http://clerk.house.gov/evs/2019/roll592.xml
68   http://archive.is/isRem
69   http://archive.is/mDvg8
70   https://www.washingtonpost.com/opinions/
      ilhan-omar-we-must-apply-our-universal-values-to-all-nations-on-
      ly-then-will-we-achieve-peace/2019/03/17/0e2d66fc-4757-11e9-
      aaf8-4512a6fe3439_story.html
71   https://thefederalist.com/2018/11/05/irans-hits-western-soil-re-
      veal-foreign-policy-establishments-hypocrisy/
72   https://www.rollingstone.com/politics/politics-features/
      ilhan-omar-congress-interview-797220/
73   https://omar.house.gov/media/press-releases/rep-ilhan-omar-ap-
      pointed-foreign-affairs-education-labor-committees-0
74   https://www.congress.gov/bill/116th-congress/
      house-joint-resolution/37/cosponsors
75   https://omar.house.gov/media/press-releases/rep-ilhan-omar-pass-
      es-amendments-national-defense-authorization-act
76   https://www.washingtonexaminer.com/opinion/
      the-us-may-be-funding-iran-backed-extremism-in-africa
77   http://archive.is/IeFrl
78   https://www.state.
      gov/u-s-ends-participation-in-the-global-compact-on-migration/
79   https://omar.house.gov/media/press-releases/reps-ilhan-omar-and-
      jim-mcgovern-lead-letter-trump-administration-efforts
80   https://www.theguardian.com/law/2019/apr/05/
      us-revokes-visa-of-international-criminal-courts-top-prosecutor
81   https://www.lawfareblog.com/
      national-security-adviser-john-bolton-remarks-federalist-society
82   https://progressive.org/dispatches/
      the-real-trouble-with-ilhan-omar-jaffe-190719/

Chapter 5: The Special Case of Israel and the Jews
1   http://archive.is/d1rHf
2   https://www.nytimes.com/2019/01/21/opinion/ilhan-omar-isra-
      el-jews.html

3   https://www.mercurynews.com/2019/02/13/
     mn-jewish-leaders-talked-with-ilhan-omar-about-anti-semitism-
     last-year-why-they-remain-frustrated/

4   https://www.twincities.com/2019/02/12/mn-jewish-leaders-talk-
     ed-with-ilhan-omar-about-anti-semitism-last-year-why-they-re-
     main-frustrated/

5   https://www.tcdailyplanet.net/house-60b-candidate-il-
     han-omar-challenges-outdated-notions-politicians-can/

6   https://tcjewfolk.com/
     huge-turnout-welcomes-cd-5-candidates-at-forum/

7   http://muslimgirl.com/50283/
     ilhan-omar-why-advocating-for-palestine-is-not-anti-semitic/

8   http://archive.is/4TrHj

9   https://bdsmovement.net/colonialism-and-apartheid/summary

10   https://www.jewishvirtuallibrary.org/
     myths-and-facts-human-rights-in-israel-and-the-territories#i

11   https://www.frontpagemag.com/fpm/2019/08/omar-turns-her-
     back-somalilands-aspiration-freedom-joseph-klein/

12   https://www.palestinianbasiclaw.org/
     basic-law/2003-amended-basic-law

13   https://thefederalist.com/2019/01/07/media-completely-ignores-
     isaam-akel-american-brutalized-like-khashoggi/

14   https://blogs.timesofisrael.com/
     which-countries-are-apartheid-states/

15   https://www.weeklyblitz.net/news/
     the-myth-of-hebrons-shuhada-street/

16   https://www.state.gov/defining-anti-semitism/

17   https://mailchi.mp/4d1ad2488cf3/zoa-congresss-anti-bds-resolu-
     tions-some-good-points-but-toothless-and-poisoned-by-promo-
     ting-dangerous-palestinian-state?e=19cf2d4779

18   https://www.congress.gov/bill/116th-congress/
     house-resolution/496/text

19   https://www.al-monitor.com/pulse/originals/2019/07/ilham-
     omar-pro-bds-legislation-trump-israel.html

20   https://www.bis.doc.gov/index.php/enforcement/
     oac#whatsprohibited

21 https://www.dailywire.com/news/49651/hammer-ilhan-omar-wrong-here-why-anti-bds-laws-are-josh-hammer

22 https://papers.ssrn.com/sol3/papers.cfm?abstract_id=2531130

23 https://il.usembassy.gov/ambassador-friedman-statement-on-israeli-government-decision-to-deny-entry-to-tlaib-omar-congressional-delegation/

24 https://www.speaker.gov/newsroom/32619/

25 https://www.schumer.senate.gov/newsroom/press-releases/on-senate-floor-schumer-condemns-anti-zionism-as-anti-semitism

26 https://www.wsj.com/articles/german-lawmakers-move-to-outlaw-hezbollah-in-new-effort-to-isolate-the-iran-backed-group-11576764299

27 https://www.jpost.com/Breaking-News/German-parliament-rejects-ban-of-Hezbollah-snubbing-US-and-German-Jews-591800

28 https://www.nytimes.com/2019/05/17/world/europe/germany-bds-anti-semitic.html

29 http://fathomjournal.org/holocaust-inversion-and-contemporary-antisemitism/

30 https://www.algemeiner.com/2018/12/05/what-palestinians-want-in-their-own-words-when-they-say-from-the-river-to-the-sea/

31 https://vimeo.com/75201955

32 https://www.meforum.org/campus-watch/25965/a-bds-lesson-in-dishonesty-incl-asad-abukhalil

33 https://www.middleeasteye.net/news/how-ilhan-omar-changing-way-americans-talk-about-israel

34 https://spectator.org/the-unmasking-of-bds/

35 https://twitter.com/bhweingarten/status/1156193930347786241

36 https://www.gov.il/en/Departments/General/terrorists_in_suits

37 https://dailycaller.com/2019/05/08/anti-israel-bds-palestinian-terrorist-pflp-hamas/

38 https://www.ngo-monitor.org/ngos/samidoun/#samidountiestopflp

39 http://www.thetower.org/7282-global-payment-giants-remove-account-of-bds-organization-over-purported-links-to-terrorists/

40 https://samidoun.net/2019/02/standwithilhan-samidoun-urges-broad-support-for-rep-ilhan-omar/

41 https://uscpr.org/about-us/

42   https://www.tabletmag.com/scroll/263409/bds-umbrella-group-linked-to-palestinian-terrorist-organizations

43   https://uscpr.org/about-us/

44   https://www.al-monitor.com/pulse/originals/2019/07/ilham-omar-pro-bds-legislation-trump-israel.html#ixzz5u3QsamNk

45   https://twitter.com/LizRNC/status/1151581659243909120

46   https://thefederalist.com/2019/08/26/squad-co-sponsors-bill-claiming-israel-tortures-children-terrorist-propaganda/

47   https://www.tabletmag.com/jewish-news-and-politics/271256/no-way-to-treat-children

48   http://archive.is/nJVwr

49   https://www.jpost.com/Opinion/Ilhan-Omars-ignorance-and-bigotry-on-Gaza-rockets-589307

50   https://www.algemeiner.com/2019/05/10/report-34-of-palestinians-killed-in-latest-gaza-flare-up-were-terrorists/

51   http://www.thetower.org/2129-how-the-idf-works-to-prevent-civilian-casualties/

52   Katz, Yaakov and Bohbot, Amir *The Weapon Wizards*

53   http://archive.is/1z9ij

54   http://archive.is/m2PET

55   https://alphanewsmn.com/ilhan-omar-to-speak-at-anti-israel-fundraiser/

56   https://www.jewishvirtuallibrary.org/history-of-jewish-settlements-in-gaza

57   https://www.jewishvirtuallibrary.org/israel-transfers-gush-katif-hothouses-to-palestinians-september-2005

58   https://www.jewishvirtuallibrary.org/the-original-palestine-national-charter-1964

59   https://www.mfa.gov.il/MFA/MFA-Archive/2003/Pages/DISPUTED%20TERRITORIES-%20Forgotten%20Facts%20About%20the%20We.aspx

60   https://twitter.com/IsraeliPM/status/1162039728725811202

61   https://twitter.com/gilicohen10/status/1162028501437992960

62   http://archive.is/YDWtk

63   https://tinyurl.com/whos953

64 http://archive.is/4isoM

65 http://archive.is/7qrqR

66 https://www.algemeiner.com/2019/08/20/end-which-occupation/

67 https://www.algemeiner.com/2019/08/22/palestinian-leader-abbas-declares-we-shall-enter-jerusalem-millions-of-fighters/

68 https://www.washingtoninstitute.org/fikraforum/view/half-of-palestinians-still-want-all-of-palestine-but-most-would-compromise

69 https://www.algemeiner.com/2019/08/20/end-which-occupation/

70 https://www.claremont.org/crb/article/the-chosen-and-the-woke/

71 https://www.tandfonline.com/doi/pdf/10.1080/23739770.2015.1037579#page=7

72 https://www.jewishvirtuallibrary.org/haj-amin-al-husseini

73 https://freebeacon.com/politics/omar-criticism-of-tlaib-part-of-efforts-to-eliminate-the-public-voice-of-muslims/

74 https://www.algemeiner.com/2019/08/16/rashida-tlaib-met-with-another-terror-supporter/

75 https://freebeacon.com/politics/omar-criticism-of-tlaib-part-of-efforts-to-eliminate-the-public-voice-of-muslims/

76 https://www.dailywire.com/news/42864/watch-ilhan-omar-suggests-israel-should-not-be-ryan-saavedra

77 https://mfa.gov.il/mfa/mfa-archive/1999/pages/human%20rights%20and%20the%20rule%20of%20law.aspx

78 https://www.jns.org/arab-mk-urges-boycott-of-israel-at-london-pro-bds-conference/

79 https://www.jpost.com/Arab-Israeli-Conflict/Interior-Ministry-keeping-BDS-leader-Barghouti-from-leaving-country-453634

80 http://archive.is/DKWMm

81 http://web.archive.org/web/20190201185403/https://twitter.com/maxberger/status/1091174801291571200

82 https://www.timesofisrael.com/final-text-of-jewish-nation-state-bill-set-to-become-law/

83 https://mfa.gov.il/mfa/foreignpolicy/peace/guide/pages/declaration%20of%20establishment%20of%20state%20of%20israel.aspx

84 https://en.wikipedia.org/wiki/List_of_Israeli_inventions_and_discoveries

85   https://www.tandfonline.com/doi/pdf/10.1080/23739770.2015.1037579#page=8

86   https://www.realclearpolitics.com/video/2019/08/19/ilhan_omar_israels_actions_not_consistent_with_being_an_ally_or_a_democracy.html

87   https://www.jpost.com/Middle-East/PA-bans-LGBT-activities-in-West-Bank-598980

88   https://www.newsweek.com/palestinian-lgbt-group-banned-ilhan-omar-1455333

89   http://archive.is/8J32O

90   http://archive.is/6aauD

91   http://archive.is/GIGxI

92   https://www.jewishvirtuallibrary.org/the-bible-on-jewish-links-to-the-holy-land

93   https://www.jpost.com/Opinion/Zachor-The-sanctity-of-Eretz-Yisrael-383716

94   https://www.jewishpress.com/indepth/opinions/the-dangerous-drive-to-correlate-islamophobia-with-anti-semitism/2019/07/02/

95   https://avalon.law.yale.edu/20th_century/hamas.asp

96   https://www.middleeasteye.net/news/hamas-2017-document-full

97   https://www.memri.org/reports/hamas-policy-document

98   https://www.fdd.org/analysis/2017/05/02/hamass-new-document-more-of-the-same/

99   https://www.jpost.com/Arab-Israeli-Conflict/UN-asks-Palestinians-to-explain-hate-speech-antisemitism-598536

100 https://jewishjournal.com/news/israel/302940/palestinian-authority-representative-dodges-un-questioning-of-anti-semitism/

101 https://unwatch.org/un-racism-committee-presses-palestinians-on-antisemitism-based-on-un-watchs-report/

102 https://www.ngo-monitor.org/reports/miftah_s_funders_share_responsibility_for_antisemitism_and_incitement/

103 https://www.ngo-monitor.org/reports/ngo-sponsorship-and-involvement-in-reps-tlaib-and-omar-trip-to-israel-west-bank/

104 https://twitter.com/IsraeliPM/status/1162039738162921475

105   http://archive.is/crJKv

106   https://www.meforum.org/campus-watch/58740/
mesa-demands-us-welcome-palestinian-terrorist

107   https://www.cnn.com/2019/05/13/politics/hanan-ashrawi-visa-re-jected/index.html

108   https://www.jta.org/2019/08/16/politics/heres-what-ilhan-omar-and-rashida-tlaib-were-going-to-do-on-their-trip-to-israel-and-the-west-bank

109   https://www.ngo-monitor.org/pdf/DCIP_Ties_to_PFLP.pdf

110   http://archive.is/OC4lV

111   https://twitter.com/bungarsargon/status/1162898365769748480

112   https://blogs.timesofisrael.com/at-conference-tlaib-and-omar-chose-speaker-who-promotes-violence-anti-semitism/

113   https://www.jns.org/opinion/
jesus-was-palestinian-an-old-big-lie-gets-new-legs/

114   https://www.newyorker.com/news/the-political-scene/
ilhan-omars-embattled-first-months-in-office

115   https://www.realclearpolitics.com/video/2019/01/17/
rep_ilhan_omar_defends_her_comment_accusing_israel_of_evil_
doings_and_hypnotising_the_world.html

116   https://thehill.com/blogs/blog-briefing-room/news/425842-ilhan-omar-addresses-2012-tweet-i-dont-know-how-my-comments

117   https://www.newyorker.com/news/the-political-scene/
ilhan-omars-embattled-first-months-in-office

118   http://archive.is/zRlA9

119   http://web.archive.org/web/20190211005046/https://twitter.
com/IlhanMN/status/1094747501578633216

120   http://archive.is/nyCMC

121   https://www.usatoday.com/story/news/politics/
onpolitics/2019/02/26/ilhan-omar-deletes-israel-tweets-that-drew-charges-of-anti-semitism/2989404002/

122   https://www.tabletmag.com/jewish-news-and-politics/281477/
how-influential-is-aipac

123   http://www.thetower.org/article/anti-zionism-of-j-street/

124   https://zoa.org/zoa-expose-j-street-sides-with-israels-enemies-works-to-destroy-support-for-israel/#noopener

125   http://archive.is/yK4nX

126 https://www.opensecrets.org/news/2019/02/aipac-dont-contribute-which-pro-israel-groups-do/

127 http://archive.is/PkUqR

128 https://www.washingtontimes.com/news/2019/feb/11/ilhan-omar-retweets-ady-barkan-thread-denouncing-n/

129 https://www.washingtonexaminer.com/opinion/reminder-ilhan-omar-and-rashida-tlaib-questioned-the-loyalty-of-americans-who-support-israel

130 https://besacenter.org/perspectives-papers/jews-dual-loyalty/

131 http://archive.is/R10Ar

132 https://www.dailywire.com/news/44170/omar-doubles-down-anti-semitism-accuses-jewish-ryan-saavedra

133 https://twitter.com/LizRNC/status/1151503467179053056

134 https://www.washingtonexaminer.com/news/al-jazeera-pushes-back-on-gop-effort-to-force-it-to-register-as-a-foreign-agent

135 https://jewishjournal.com/cover_story/298975/qatar-shows-two-faces-to-the-world/

136 http://blog.camera.org/2019/05/after_broadcasting_holocaust_d.html

137 https://www.jns.org/watchdog-group-uncovers-longstanding-disdain-for-jews-and-israel-among-al-jazeera-staff/

138 https://dailycaller.com/2019/05/21/ilhan-omar-aj-plus-holocaust/

139 https://www.bbc.com/news/world-asia-48171165

140 https://theintercept.com/2019/02/28/exclusive-ilhan-omar-speaks-out-on-her-twitter-scandal-anti-semitism-and-a-progressive-foreign-policy/

141 https://www.washingtonexaminer.com/news/ilhan-omar-equivocates-on-her-anti-semitism-statement-i-apologized-for-the-way-that-my-words-made-people-feel

142 https://www.nbcnews.com/news/amp/ncna1000296

143 https://www.jihadwatch.org/2012/08/did-the-muslim-brotherhood-invent-the-term-islamophobia

144 https://capitalresearch.org/article/islamophobia-hoax/

145 https://www.jpost.com/Middle-East/Three-far-right-leaders-promise-to-create-channel-to-fight-Islamophobia-603284

146 https://www.fbi.gov/news/stories/2018-hate-crime-statistics-released-111219

147   https://ucr.fbi.gov/hate-crime/2018/topic-pages/
      incidents-and-offenses
148   https://www.jewishvirtuallibrary.org/
      statistics-on-religious-hate-crimes
149   https://www.wsj.com/articles/anti-semitic-incidents-fuel-17-rise-
      in-hate-crimes-fbi-says-1542129814
150   https://www.voanews.com/usa/
      report-anti-muslim-hate-crimes-drop-second-year-row
151   https://web.archive.org/web/20170224235035/
      http://www.investors.com/politics/editorials/
      muslims-fake-hate-crimes-to-serve-political-agenda/
152   https://www.nationalreview.com/2015/12/
      anti-muslim-hate-crime/
153   https://www.pewforum.org/2017/04/05/the-changing-global-reli-
      gious-landscape/#global-population-projections-2015-to-2060
154   https://www.jewishpress.com/indepth/opinions/
      the-dangerous-drive-to-correlate-islamophobia-with-anti-semi-
      tism/2019/07/02/
155   https://twitter.com/RealSaavedra/status/1101205531069435906
156   https://isgap.org/wp-content/uploads/2015/05/Landes_Proud_
      to_be_Ashamed_Working_Paper.pdf
157   https://twitter.com/AdamMilstein/status/1158831109687238658
158   https://www.jcpa.org/phas/phas-sharansky-f04.htm
159   https://news.yahoo.com/ilhan-omar-trump-obsession-radical-sup-
      port-bernie-sanders-204041095.html?guccounter=1
160   https://scholar.harvard.edu/files/martinkramer/files/words_of_
      martin_luther_king.pdf

Chapter 6: Embodiment of the Progressive-Islamist Axis

1   https://www.andrewbostom.org/2019/08/from-hebron-1929-to-
      tlaib-omar-2019-the-jew-hating-jihadist-marxist-alliance/
2   https://www.realclearinvestigations.com/articles/2019/08/12/
      in_france_even_muslims_have_had_it_with_radical_
      muslims_119853.html
3   https://www.commentarymagazine.com/articles/
      is-corbynization-the-democratic-partys-future/

4 http://fathomjournal.org/wp-content/uploads/2019/03/Institutionally-Antisemitic-Report-FINAL-6.pdf, pgs. 20-21

5 http://fathomjournal.org/wp-content/uploads/2019/03/Institutionally-Antisemitic-Report-FINAL-6.pdf#page=21

6 https://mosaicmagazine.com/observation/history-ideas/2019/04/socialism-and-the-jews-a-brief-history/

7 https://www.commentarymagazine.com/articles/marxism-vs-the-jews/

8 https://www.lawliberty.org/2019/01/18/the-lefts-anti-semitism-problem-a-history/

9 Wistrich, Robert S. *From Ambivalence to Tragedy,* pg. 5

10 Johnson, Paul *A History of the Jews,* pg. 569

11 Ibid

12 Ibid

13 Wistrich, Robert S. From Ambivalence to Betrayal, pgs. 563-566

14 https://cairh.org/index.php/2019/09/30/koranic-antisemitism-striking-agreement-between-authoritative-modern-western-and-islamic-scholars/

15 http://www.jewishmag.com/57mag/dhimmi/dhimmi.htm

16 https://www.meforum.org/5275/jizya-fact-fiction

17 https://www.jihadwatch.org/2019/08/muslims-against-antisemitism-desinformatzia-deconstructed

18 http://www.israelnationalnews.com/Articles/Article.aspx/23721

19 https://www.andrewbostom.org/2019/09/prompted-elan-carr-becomes-1st-us-special-envoy-on-antisemitism-to-acknowledge-the-disproportionate-global-pandemic-of-muslim-antisemitism-video-transcript/

20 http://web.archive.org/web/20191105042900/https://global100.adl.org/public/ADL-Global-100-Executive-Summary.pdf, pg. 25

21 https://www.nytimes.com/2018/07/27/world/europe/france-new-anti-semitism.html

22 https://www.timesofisrael.com/anti-semitism-rampant-among-muslim-refugees-in-germany-study/

23 https://www.andrewbostom.org/2019/03/ilhan-omar-islam-and-the-global-pandemic-of-muslim-jew-hatred/

24 http://www.startribune.com/
    somali-americans-say-no-to-hatred/269464141/

25 https://docs.house.gov/meetings/JU/JU00/20190409/109266/
    HHRG-116-JU00-Wstate-KleinM-20190409.pdf

26 http://ajcarchives.org/ajcarchive/FileViewer.aspx?id=13663

27 https://www.jpost.com/Arab-Israeli-Conflict/
    Despite-alignment-with-Israel-Arab-powers-still-spreading-an-
    tisemitism-558806

28 https://www.fdd.org/analysis/2012/02/24/
    spotlight-on-modern-loathing/

29 https://www.worldjewishcongress.org/en/news/
    robert-wistrich-post-mubarak-egypt-the-dark-side-of-islamic-uto-
    pia-israel-journal-of-foreign-affairs

30 https://www.jpost.com/Middle-East/Ex-Muslim-to-Post-Trying-
    to-teach-naive-West-about-true-nature-of-Islam-598946

31 https://www.andrewbostom.org/2019/03/audio-the-contrite-mea-
    culpa-based-honesty-of-ayaan-hirsi-ali-on-the-islam-animating-
    muslim-jew-hatred-holy-koranic-verses-support-hatred-of-jews/

32 Johnson, Paul *A History of the Jews,* pgs. 572-575

33 https://web.archive.org/web/20140310064725/http://www.
    theblaze.com/blog/2014/02/10/an-interview-with-lt-gen-ion-pace-
    pa-the-highest-ranking-soviet-bloc-intel-officer-to-ever-defect/

34 Johnson, Paul *A History of the Jews,* pg. 578

35 https://www.wsj.com/articles/SB106419296113226300

36 http://fathomjournal.org/
    soviet-anti-zionism-and-contemporary-left-antisemitism/

37 https://www.tabletmag.com/jewish-arts-and-culture/285781/
    soviet-anti-semitic-cartoons

38 https://spectator.us/anti-semitic-cartoon-nyt/

39 Johnson, Paul *A History of the Jews,* pg. 575

40 http://fathomjournal.org/1967-and-the-global-left-the-case-of-
    the-east-german-regime-and-the-west-german-radicals/

41 Muravchik, Joshua *Making David Into Goliath,* Chapter 2 "The
    Arab Cause Becomes Palestinian (and "Progressive")

42 https://www.jewishvirtuallibrary.org/
    the-seven-points-of-fatah-january-1969

43 Ibid

43 https://tinyurl.com/w4thv6v

45 Wistrich, Robert S. *From Ambivalence to Betrayal,* pg. 564

46 https://www.tandfonline.com/doi/pdf/10.1080/23739770.2015.
    1037579#page=6

47 Muravchik, Joshua *Making David Into Goliath,* pgs. 99-102

48 https://jewishjournal.com/news/los_angeles/298850/
    ucla-guest-lecturer-calls-zionists-white-supremacists/

49 https://thefederalist.com/2019/12/04/israel-equals-jewish-su-
    premacy-linda-sarsour-again-stoops-to-antisemitism/

50 https://www.jta.org/quick-reads/linda-sarsour-clarifies-her-com-
    ment-that-israel-is-built-on-the-idea-that-jews-are-supreme-to-ev-
    eryone-else

51 https://tinyurl.com/vnn4qml

52 https://www.newcriterion.com/issues/2019/6/the-left-against-zion

53 https://www.claremont.org/crb/article/the-chosen-and-the-woke/

54 https://www.nytimes.com/2019/02/08/opinion/sunday/isra-
    el-progressive-anti-semitism.html

55 https://www.tabletmag.com/jewish-news-and-politics/276694/
    is-the-womens-march-melting-down

56 https://alphanewsmn.com/ilhan-omar-meets-with-anti-semite-
    linda-sarsour-first-day-of-congress/

57 https://www.cnsnews.com/news/article/patrick-goodenough/
    linda-sarsour-urges-muslims-support-rep-ilhan-omar-best-our

58 https://legalinsurrection.com/2017/05/linda-sarsours-little-lie-
    about-her-vile-attack-on-ayaan-hirsi-ali-is-a-big-deal/

59 https://jewishjournal.com/cover_story/299926/how-jewish-wom-
    en-are-being-harassed-online-for-fighting-anti-semitism/

60 https://www.foxnews.com/tech/
    ben-shapiro-slams-google-over-email-describing-him-as-a-nazi

61 https://www.wsj.com/articles/twitter-suspends-accounts-linked-
    to-hamas-hezbollah-11572888026

62 https://www.thenational.ae/world/dangerous-muslim-brother-
    hood-fatwa-app-in-apple-store-s-top-100-downloads-1.877092

63   https://www.huffpost.com/entry/ilhan-omar-profile_n_5c-cc987ae4b0548b7359ee0f?guccounter=1&guce_referrer=aHR0cHM6Ly93d3cuZ29vZ2xlLmNvbS88&guce_referrer_sig=AQAAAKP9Y0Hk8xntZQK_xWD13EnS9aTcKpBffke20w-g8qql5qEXwE2_aeGNfn6NZV-6jDID02871ISrBM-pKAf-4ScVFQre74u48AlafEFQw8hI2nRCSfspIRZMn7BqamDv69Rs-PiAkw2BD18KRl_DSc4pOgdjEiiKnAe9cg2Cjc45IOd

64   https://www.newcriterion.com/issues/2019/6/the-left-against-zion

65   https://www.lawliberty.org/2019/01/18/the-lefts-anti-semitism-problem-a-history/

66   https://thefederalist.com/2019/12/29/identity-politics-enables-anti-semitic-violence-enough/

67   https://twitter.com/davereaboi/status/1211287310114930689

68   https://twitchy.com/samj-3930/2019/12/29/is-this-a-joke-andrew-cuomos-statement-on-stabbing-in-rabbis-monsey-home-during-hanukkah-celebration-goes-so-wrong/

69   https://twitter.com/Cameron_Gray/status/1210663824573050881

70   https://twitter.com/AGHamilton29/status/1210704604180156416

Chapter 7: The Democrats' Cave on Israel and the Jews

1   https://thefederalist.com/2019/05/22/democratic-establishment-wont-stand-partys-anti-semites/

2   https://www.gingrich360.com/2019/05/no-mayor-pete-erasing-thomas-jefferson-is-not-the-right-thing-to-do/

3   Johnson, Paul *A History of the Jews*, pg. 569

4   https://www.jewishvirtuallibrary.org/jewish-voting-record-in-u-s-presidential-elections

5   https://news.gallup.com/opinion/polling-matters/265898/american-jews-politics-israel.aspx

6   https://www.washingtontimes.com/news/2019/jan/18/nancy-pelosi-faces-backlash-for-placing-ilhan-omar/

7   https://www.thenation.com/article/nancy-pelosi-speaker-progressives/

8   https://dailycaller.com/2019/01/16/
     omar-defends-anti-israel-tweet/

9   https://www.speaker.gov/newsroom/21119/

10   https://www.politico.com/story/2019/02/11/
     house-democrats-ilhan-omar-antisemitism-1163728

11   https://www.newsbusters.org/blogs/nb/
     kristine-marsh/2018/08/20/nyts-goldberg-course-trump-would-
     round-people-and-murder-them

12   https://www.nytimes.com/2019/02/11/opinion/ilhan-omar-an-
     tisemitism.html

13   https://docs.house.gov/billsthisweek/20190304/BILLS-
     116hres183-SUS.pdf

14   https://www.nytimes.com/2019/03/05/us/politics/ilhan-omar-is-
     rael.html

15   http://archive.is/WHtxf

16   https://www.politico.com/story/2019/02/11/
     house-democrats-ilhan-omar-antisemitism-1163728

17   https://www.apnews.com/890c970cbbe3b0e631504f47e2e5a5cc

18   https://www.investigativeproject.org/7855/
     pelosi-caves-to-anti-semites-and-supporters

19   https://www.cnn.com/politics/live-news/anti-semi-
     tism-house-democrats/h_2b22ff9a855ff5bfa7935796b04a646e

20   https://www.speaker.gov/newsroom/3719-2

21   https://thehill.com/homenews/house/433263-pelosi-omar-not-
     anti-semitic-has-different-use-of-words

22   https://foreignaffairs.house.gov/2019/3/
     engel-statement-on-representative-omar-s-comments

23   https://thehill.com/homenews/house/432805-chairman-says-he-
     wont-remove-omar-from-house-foreign-affairs-committee

24   https://www.axios.com/bernie-sanders-kamala-harris-elizabeth-
     warren-defend-ilhan-omar-6e45b0a8-b28d-4db4-ae21-bd-
     1307cca672.html

25   https://thehill.com/homenews/
     house/432968-new-cracks-emerge-in-dem-unity

26   https://www.speaker.gov/newsroom/32619/

27 https://thehill.com/homenews/house/435841-omar-hits-back-at-pelosi-over-bds-remarks

28 https://jewishinsider.com/2019/05/how-canadian-barry-zekelman-ended-up-in-a-private-dining-room-with-potus-pompeo-to-meet-jewish-leaders-steve-cohens-91m-rabbit/

29 https://twitter.com/realdonaldtrump/status/1150381395078000643

30 https://www.usatoday.com/story/news/politics/2019/07/14/trump-tells-congresswomen-go-back-counties-they-came/1728253001/

31 https://www.nbcnews.com/news/amp/ncna1042756

32 https://twitter.com/SpeakerPelosi/status/1128022871442382852

33 https://thefederalist.com/2019/05/13/bowing-to-the-socialists-hoyer-says-tlaib-deserves-an-apology/

34 https://www.washingtonexaminer.com/opinion/rashida-tlaib-says-thinking-of-the-holocaust-provides-her-a-calming-feeling-shockingly-claims-palestinians-created-safe-haven-for-jews

35 https://www.senate.gov/legislative/LIS/roll_call_lists/roll_call_vote_cfm.cfm?congress=116&session=1&vote=00016

36 https://www.nytimes.com/interactive/2019/us/politics/israel-human-rights-democratic-candidates.html

37 https://www.realclearpolitics.com/epolls/2020/president/us/2020_democratic_presidential_nomination-6730.html#polls

38 http://www.israelnationalnews.com/News/News.aspx/265917

39 https://www.nytimes.com/2019/06/16/us/politics/2020-democratic-donors-wall-street.html

40 https://theintercept.com/2019/07/13/pete-buttigieg-joe-biden-condemn-israeli-occupation-young-american-jews-urge-democrats-press-israel/

41 https://www.timesofisrael.com/how-ifnotnow-is-getting-2020-democrats-to-talk-occupation/

42 https://www.jta.org/quick-reads/bernie-sanders-absolutely-would-cut-us-aid-to-israel-to-pressure-government

43 https://www.timesofisrael.com/how-ifnotnow-is-getting-2020-democrats-to-talk-occupation/

44 https://www.jns.org/warren-supports-anti-israel-group-call-to-pressure-israel-to-end-the-occupation/

45 https://freebeacon.com/politics/warren-threatens-israel-everything-table/

46 https://thefederalist.com/2019/07/17/hiring-pro-hamas-aide-completes-elizabeth-warrens-anti-israel-pivot/

47 Ibid

48 https://www.jpost.com/Opinion/Cory-Bookers-Jewish-enablers-580363

49 https://graphics.axios.com/2019-07-14-dem-responses/index.html?subset=israe-li-embassy#_ga=2.180810727.1536161833.1575823563-1972021019.1537800491

50 https://www.axios.com/2020-democrats-embassy-israel-jerusa-lem-trump-d4dc1cf5-96d6-4801-8205-6f0ef0858303.html

51 https://www.jpost.com/American-Politics/Buttigieg-recogni-tion-of-Golan-interference-in-Israeli-politics-598557

52 https://www.jta.org/quick-reads/democratic-candidates-criti-cize-trump-administration-decision-on-settlements

53 https://observer.com/2019/06/pete-buttigieg-palestine-support-bernie-sanders/

54 https://www.frontpagemag.com/fpm/274003/how-buttigieg-entered-anti-israel-echo-chamber-daniel-greenfield

55 http://archive.is/bIa5Q

56 http://archive.is/DqPwA

57 http://english.wafa.ps/page.aspx?id=OEscdva110496619794aOEscdv

58 https://jewishinsider.com/2019/06/plos-hanan-ashrawi-re-verse-jerusalem-golan-heights-recognition-to-bring-palestin-ians-to-the-negotiating-table/

59 https://mailchi.mp/jewishinsider/daily-kickoff-august-775741?e=f4b3aa1480

60 https://www.cfr.org/article/democratic-candidates-iran-nuclear-deal

61 https://mailchi.mp/4d1ad2488cf3/zoa-congresss-anti-bds-resolu-tions-some-good-points-but-toothless-and-poisoned-by-promo-ting-dangerous-palestinian-state?e=19cf2d4779

62   https://thefederalist.com/2019/07/26/
     new-house-resolutions-democrats-finally-allow-israel-divide-open/

63   https://www.washingtonexaminer.com/news/
     democratic-house-member-suggests-ilhan-omar-rashida-tlaib-
     dont-understand-the-impact-of-the-bds-movement

64   https://www.cnsnews.com/article/
     international/patrick-goodenough/
     democrats-want-israeli-occupation-language-2020-party

65   https://www.foxnews.com/politics/
     pompeo-israel-settlements-democrats-palestinians

66   https://andylevin.house.gov/sites/andylevin.house.gov/
     files/191122_Pompeo%20Letter.pdf

67   https://twitter.com/andrewbostom/
     status/1127952118810386432

68   https://twitter.com/repleezeldin/status/1126831143158976512

69   https://twitter.com/IlhanMN/status/926191227279691783

70   https://theintercept.com/2019/06/18/
     eliot-engel-primary-challenge/

71   https://www.huffpost.com/entry/roots-action-bad-blues-re-
     port-progressive-primary-challenges-house-democrats-dccc_n_5d-
     0d4e93e4b07ae90d9d21e8?0pu

72   https://www.cbsnews.com/news/new-york-democrats-face-prima-
     ry-challenges-from-progressive-candidates-2019-07-13/

73   https://www.rollcall.com/news/congress/
     lowey-faces-primary-challenge-her-first-in-three-decades

74   https://www.nytimes.com/2019/10/10/nyregion/chelsea-clin-
     ton-nita-lowey.html

75   https://jewishinsider.com/2019/05/daily-kickoff-gottheimer-on-
     tlaibs-unprovoked-attack-pelosi-praises-israel-as-one-of-greatest-
     20th-century-accomplishments-sam-fox-turns-90/

76   https://theintercept.com/2019/05/08/
     josh-gottheimer-democrats-yemen/

77   https://theintercept.com/2019/05/22/josh-gottheimer-staff/

78   https://www.frontpagemag.com/point/274467/leftists-ob-
     sessed-wdestroying-jewish-dem-who-stood-daniel-greenfield

79   http://archive.is/Oz6lJ
80   https://jewishinsider.com/2019/03/at-town-hall-rep-max-rose-apologizes-to-jewish-constituents-for-omars-rhetoric/
81   https://www.washingtonexaminer.com/news/franken-after-me-too-scandal-people-that-know-me-know-im-not-that-guy
82   https://ballotpedia.org/Minnesota%27s_5th_Congressional_District_election,_2020
83   https://thehill.com/homenews/campaign/433970-democrats-upset-over-omar-seeking-primary-challenger
84   http://www.israelnationalnews.com/News/News.aspx/264041
85   https://freebeacon.com/blog/latest-progressive-assault-israel/
86   https://nypost.com/2016/07/27/democrats-have-an-ugly-anti-israel-obsession/
87   https://web.archive.org/web/20170222081026/https://www.conservativereview.com/commentary/2016/07/anti-semite-anti-american-protesters-burn-israeli-flag-at-dnc
88   https://thehill.com/blogs/ballot-box/presidential-races/280941-sanders-names-cornel-west-keith-ellison-to-platform
89   https://www.middleeasteye.net/news/how-ilhan-omar-changing-way-americans-talk-about-israel
90   https://www.nytimes.com/2012/09/06/us/politics/pushed-by-obama-democrats-alter-platform-over-jerusalem.html
91   https://freebeacon.com/politics/pro-israel-language-removed-from-democratic-party-platform/
92   https://www.presidency.ucsb.edu/documents/2012-democratic-party-platform
93   https://www.reuters.com/article/us-usa-israel/israels-netanyahu-draws-rebuke-from-obama-over-iran-speech-to-congress-idUSKBN0LZ0BS20150303
94   http://archive.is/A56wi
95   https://www.commentarymagazine.com/american-society/bob-menendez-corruption-charges-iran-nuclear-deal/
96   https://www.vice.com/en_us/article/a3bvyk/israel-is-becoming-a-wedge-issue-for-democrats
97   https://www.nytimes.com/2018/10/07/us/politics/democrats-israel-palestinians.html?module=inline

98   https://www.nytimes.com/2019/03/28/magazine/
     battle-over-bds-israel-palestinians-antisemitism.html

99   https://www.pewresearch.org/fact-tank/2017/09/07/demo-
     cratic-voters-are-increasingly-likely-to-call-their-views-liberal/
     ft_17-09-07_democratliberal_in2017/

100 https://www.people-press.org/2018/01/23/republicans-and-dem-
     ocrats-grow-even-further-apart-in-views-of-israel-palestinians/

101 https://news.gallup.com/poll/247376/americans-not-liberal-dem-
     ocrats-mostly-pro-israel.aspx

102 https://www.haaretz.com/israel-news/.premium-poll-shows-sup-
     port-for-israel-plummeting-among-u-s-liberals-millennials-and-
     women-1.6594182

103 https://news.gallup.com/poll/247376/americans-not-liberal-dem-
     ocrats-mostly-pro-israel.aspx

104 https://www.nytimes.com/2019/03/28/magazine/
     battle-over-bds-israel-palestinians-antisemitism.html

105 https://www.nationalreview.com/news/tamika-mallory-defends-
     decision-to-praise-farrakhan-as-the-greatest-of-all-time/

106 https://www.tabletmag.com/jewish-news-and-politics/276694/
     is-the-womens-march-melting-down

107 https://www.washingtontimes.com/news/2019/feb/12/
     womens-march-leaders-tamika-mallory-linda-sarsour-/

108 http://archive.is/wLdcN

109 https://www.haaretz.com/us-news/chicago-dyke-march-flies-pal-
     estinian-flags-after-banning-jewish-ones-1.6216718

110 https://forward.com/fast-forward/425533/
     dc-dyke-march-bans-jewish-pride-flag/

111 https://jewishinsider.com/2019/06/
     dyke-march-bans-jewish-flags-to-be-inclusive/

112 Ibid

113 https://www.city-journal.org/html/delusions-justice-15855.html

114 https://www.nytimes.com/2016/12/22/world/middleeast/
     donald-trump-united-nations-israel-settlements.html

115 https://www.axios.com/us-cuts-all-funding-to-unrwa-palestinian-
     refugees-05739016-176a-421f-bac2-73a5e7492531.html

116   https://www.meforum.org/articles/2011/unrwa-s-anti-israel-bias

117   https://www.foxnews.com/politics/us-hardens-pro-israel-stance-at-un-votes-down-resolution-on-golan-heights

118   https://www.state.gov/the-international-criminal-court-unfairly-targets-israel/

119   https://www.whitehouse.gov/presidential-actions/proclamation-recognizing-golan-heights-part-state-israel/

120   https://www.jpost.com/Israel-News/US-report-does-not-refer-to-Golan-West-Bank-Gaza-as-occupied-territories-583328

121   https://www.wsj.com/articles/trump-administration-to-close-palestine-liberation-organization-office-in-washington-1536546125

122   https://www.bloomberg.com/news/articles/2018-08-24/us-cuts-aid-to-palestinians-by-more-than-200-million

12   https://www.jpost.com/American-Politics/State-Department-redefines-antisemitism-Dont-compare-Israel-to-the-Nazis-597905

124   https://www.politico.com/story/2018/09/11/trump-anti-semitism-schools-781917

125   https://www.insidehighered.com/sites/default/server_files/media/Rutgers%20Appeal.pdf

126   https://www.whitehouse.gov/presidential-actions/executive-order-combating-anti-semitism/

127   https://www.timesofisrael.com/full-text-of-pompeos-statement-on-settlements/

128   https://www.whitehouse.gov/briefings-statements/president-donald-j-trump-keeps-promise-open-u-s-embassy-jerusalem-israel/

129   https://news.gallup.com/poll/247376/americans-not-liberal-democrats-mostly-pro-israel.aspx

130   https://www.jewishpress.com/indepth/analysis/caroline-glick-analysis/american-jewrys-days-of-reckoning/2019/10/07/

131   http://www.pewforum.org/2017/07/26/findings-from-pew-research-centers-2017-survey-of-us-muslims/

132   https://www.npr.org/2018/07/18/630132952/muslim-americans-running-for-office-in-highest-numbers-since-2001

133   http://www.pewresearch.org/fact-tank/2016/01/06/a-new-estimate-of-the-u-s-muslim-population/

134 https://newrepublic.com/article/154918/
democrats-need-decide-whether-care-muslim-voters

135 https://www.texastribune.org/2019/08/31/
julian-castro-bernie-sanders-court-muslim-vote-houston/

136 http://www.pewforum.
org/2015/08/26/a-portrait-of-american-orthodox-jews/

137 https://www.city-journal.org/html/democratic-par-
ty-prayer-14816.html

138 https://benweingarten.com/2018/08/how-leftism-supplanted-ju-
daism-and-subverted-israel-and-zionism-under-tikkun-olam-so-
cial-justice-with-a-perverse-and-baseless-religious-veneer/

139 https://news.gallup.com/opinion/polling-matters/265898/ameri-
can-jews-politics-israel.aspx

140 https://www.jewishelectorateinstitute.org/poll-domestic-is-
sues-dominate-the-priorities-of-the-jewish-electorate/

141 https://www.jta.org/2019/07/08/opinion/get-ready-for-the-new-
wave-young-passionately-jewish-and-anti-zionist

142 https://www.jns.org/new-report-highlights-ties-between-ifnot-
now-and-anti-semitic-pro-palestinian-group/

143 https://www.politico.com/story/2019/03/15/
trump-jexodus-jewish-republican-1222890

144 https://www.commentarymagazine.com/articles/
is-corbynization-the-democratic-partys-future/

125 https://amchainitiative.org/wp-content/uploads/2019/09/Elimina-
tionist-Anti-Zionism-and-Academic-BDS-on-Campus-Report.pdf

146 https://downloads.frc.org/EF/EF18C11.pdf

147 https://www.algemeiner.com/2019/07/22/opposi-
tion-grows-to-pro-bds-resolution-set-to-be-voted-on-by-major-ac-
ademic-association/?utm_content=news1&utm_medium=daily_
email&utm_campaign=email&utm_source=internal/

148 https://www.the-american-interest.com/2015/09/18/
the-politicization-of-middle-east-studies/

149 https://www.algemeiner.com/2019/07/17/enshrined-anti-zi-
onism-at-san-francisco-state-university-and-many-us-campus-

es/?utm_content=blog1&utm_medium=daily_email&utm_campaign=email&utm_source=internal/

150 https://nas.org/blogs/dicta/how-anti-semitism-became-a-stable-of-woke-activism-on-campus?mc_cid=faf4f9e8f9&mc_eid=688658a0cc

151 https://www.nytimes.com/2019/03/28/magazine/battle-over-bds-israel-palestinians-antisemitism.html

152 https://www.algemeiner.com/2019/12/03/professors-continue-to-advocate-for-bds-on-campus/

153 https://anthroboycott.wordpress.com/signatories/

154 https://mondoweiss.net/2014/08/scholars-librarians-institutions/

155 https://amchainitiative.org/amcha-publishes-list-of-over-200-anti-israel-middle-east-studies-professors/

156 https://drive.google.com/file/d/0B5SS7zLUxlHqaDlqbmlYRlppMHc/view

157 https://www.insidehighered.com/news/2018/09/19/professor-cites-boycott-israeli-universities-declining-write-recommendation-letter

158 https://www.change.org/p/stand-with-john-cheney-lippold

159 American-Israeli Cooperative Enterprise email titled "Reminder: Did you know more than 2,000 professors advocate boycotting Israel?" December 6, 2019

160 http://apartheidweek.org/

161 https://www.nytimes.com/2019/03/28/magazine/battle-over-bds-israel-palestinians-antisemitism.html

162 https://docs.house.gov/meetings/JU/JU00/20190409/109266/HHRG-116-JU00-Wstate-KleinM-20190409.pdf#page=5

163 https://amchainitiative.org/search-by-incident#incident/search/display-by-date/search/

164 https://www.justice.gov/opa/speech/attorney-general-william-p-barr-delivers-keynote-speech-us-department-justices-summit

165 https://mosaicmagazine.com/picks/israel-zionism/2019/09/in-the-campus-anti-israel-campaign-zionists-must-be-driven-from-all-student-activist-groups/

166   https://www.washingtonexaminer.com/opinion/op-eds/
       the-left-is-mainstreaming-palestinian-marxist-terrorists

167   https://amgreatness.com/2019/08/13/california-readies-new-an-
       ti-semitic-curriculum-for-high-school-students/

168   https://www.theatlantic.com/international/archive/2014/11/
       how-the-media-makes-the-israel-story/383262/

169   https://www.tabletmag.com/jewish-news-and-politics/183033/
       israel-insider-guide

170   http://archive.is/jM8x7

171   https://www.conservativereview.com/news/
       legacy-media-celebrates-election-of-anti-israel-radicals/

172   https://pjmedia.com/davidsteinberg/
       ilhan-omar-happened-because-media-chose-to-lie-to-you/

173   https://www.dailysignal.com/2019/08/23/new-york-times-de-
       motes-editor-for-tweets-mocking-jews-native-americans/

174   https://jewishjournal.com/news/nation/302153/
       cnn-photo-editor-resigns-over-anti-semitic-tweets/

175   https://www.nationalreview.com/2019/01/
       new-anti-semitism-woke-progressives-old-stereotypes/

176   https://www.jns.org/opinion/
       ilhan-omars-anti-semitism-wins-the-pop-culture-primary/

Chapter 8: How Barack Obama Made Ilhan Omar Possible

1   http://archive.discoverthenetworks.org/viewSubCategory.
       asp?id=2374

2   https://www.realclearpolitics.com/articles/2018/02/01/
       had_news_media_done_its_job_obama_would_not_have_
       become_president_136153.html

3   https://www.jpost.com/Opinion/Why-UN-resolution-2334-
       leads-the-Simon-Wiesenthal-Centers-top-10-list-for-2016-477187

4   https://www.un.org/press/en/2016/sc12657.doc.htm

5   https://www.factsandlogic.org/ad_170-what-is-palestinian-territo-
       ry/?eType=EmailBlastContent&eId=4b55e006-fac7-404d-ac69-b
       9ecd03d1704

6   https://www.ynetnews.com/articles/0,7340,L-4897773,00.html

7   https://www.jpost.com/Opinion/Column-One-Obama-and-Israel-strike-and-counter-strike-476948

8   https://www.jpost.com/Opinion/Our-World-Obamas-war-against-America-476598

9   https://www.discoverthenetworks.org/individuals/rashid-khalidi/

10 https://www.nytimes.com/2016/12/29/opinion/john-kerry-and-israel-too-little-and-too-late.html

11 https://www.foxnews.com/opinion/the-united-nations-anti-israel-bias-is-undeniable-lets-stop-pretending-otherwise

12 https://thehill.com/policy/defense/311712-obama-faces-widespread-backlash-after-abstaining-from-un-israel-vote

13 https://blogs.timesofisrael.com/joining-the-jackals-an-open-letter-to-amb-samantha-power-the-case-against-u-n-resolution-2334/

14 https://www.nytimes.com/2019/03/28/magazine/battle-over-bds-israel-palestinians-antisemitism.html

15 https://freebeacon.com/politics/official-obama-white-house-pushed-delay-of-anti-israel-u-n-resolution-to-provide-cover-for-clinton/

16 https://www.nytimes.com/2019/03/28/magazine/battle-over-bds-israel-palestinians-antisemitism.html

17 http://www.cnsnews.com/news/article/patrick-goodenough/netanyahu-we-have-unequivocal-evidence-obama-administration-led-un

18 https://www.wsj.com/articles/SB10001424053111904353504576568710341742174

19 https://www.unwatch.org/un-israel-key-statistics/

20 https://www.theblaze.com/contributions/why-americas-foreign-policy-has-failed-from-bush-to-obama-and-the-antidote

21 https://www.heritage.org/europe/report/barack-obamas-top-10-apologies-how-the-president-has-humiliated-superpower

22 https://www.forbes.com/sites/mikegonzalez3/2016/03/25/obamas-apology-tour-and-latin-american-dictators/#58a64769261b

23 http://archive.discoverthenetworks.org/viewSubCategory.asp?id=2376

24 https://www.nationalreview.com/corner/obama-administra-tion-opens-formal-contacts-muslim-brotherhood-andrew-c-mcca-rthy/

25 https://www.nationalreview.com/2014/09/search-moderate-islamists-andrew-c-mccarthy/

26 https://www.jpost.com/Opinion/Why-did-the-Obama-adminis-tration-support-Morsis-Muslim-Brotherhood-563641

27 https://www.newyorker.com/news/daily-comment/obamas-bumpy-road

28 https://www.nationalreview.com/2014/09/its-not-misnomer-andrew-c-mccarthy/

29 https://www.jpost.com/Opinion/Column-One-Obama-and-the-moderate-Muslims-457032

30 https://www.frontpagemag.com/fpm/104728/are-president-obamas-actions-hostile-jews-and-morton-klein

31 https://www.usatoday.com/story/news/politics/2016/06/13/obama-orlando-terror-attack-homegrown/85824538/

32 https://www.memri.org/reports/they-are-neither-losers-nihilists-worshipers-death-nor-sick-cowards--rather-believers-and

33 https://www.timesofisrael.com/french-group-slams-obama-for-calling-market-attack-random/

34 https://pjmedia.com/blog/omitted-is-the-sine-qua-non-of-ameri-cas-see-no-islam-national-security-policy/

35 Coughlin, Stephen *Catastrophic Failure*

36 https://www.conservativereview.com/news/inside-muellers-pc-purge-of-counter-terror-material-at-the-fbi/

37 https://www.realclearpolitics.com/video/2015/03/16/obama_isis_unintended_consequence_of_invading_iraq_which_is_why_we_should_aim_before_we_shoot.html

38 https://www.city-journal.org/html/did-inequali-ty-cause-isis-14071.html

39 https://www.theatlantic.com/international/archive/2015/05/obama-interview-iran-isis-israel/393782/#Israel

40 https://www.wsj.com/articles/SB100014240531119043535045765687 10341742174

41 https://legalinsurrection.com/2016/11/
    did-obamas-daylight-with-israel-bring-peace/
42 http://www.jewishworldreview.com/0609/bayefsky060909.php3
43 https://obamawhitehouse.archives.
    gov/the-press-office/2016/01/27/
    remarks-president-righteous-among-nations-award-ceremony
44 https://www.nationalreview.com/2015/10/
    obama-palestinians-istaelis/
45 http://archive.discoverthenetworks.org/viewSubCategory.
    asp?id=1521
46 Ibid
47 https://www.cnn.com/2011/POLITICS/05/19/obama.israel.
    palestinians/index.html
48 https://www.jewishpress.com/blogs/the-lid-jeffdunetz/
    the-pre-1967-israeli-borders-never-existed/2016/12/26/
49 http://campus.zoa.org/wp-content/uploads/sites/2/2015/05/
    FACT-SHEET-The-1949-Armistice-Lines-_1967-Borders_-Inde-
    fensible-Borders-.pdf
50 https://www.washingtonpost.com/blogs/right-turn/
    wp/2016/01/20/why-its-correct-to-label-the-obama-administra-
    tion-anti-israel/?utm_term=.4cbc42bfa661
51 https://www.telegraph.co.uk/news/worldnews/middleeast/
    israel/10613055/John-Kerry-labelled-anti-Semite-for-warning-of-
    possible-boycott-of-Israel.html
52 https://www.timesofisrael.com/
    kerry-warns-of-3rd-intifada-isolation-of-israel-if-talks-fail/
53 https://www.commentarymagazine.com/foreign-policy/
    middle-east/israel/the-presidents-prophetic-threats-to-israel/
54 http://archive.discoverthenetworks.org/viewSubCategory.
    asp?id=1521
55 Ibid
56 http://www.frontpagemag.com/2014/caroline-glick/
    obama-the-virtuoso-manager/
57 http://www.worldtribune.com/2014/08/15/furious-obama-
    blocked-arms-deliveries-israel-state-dept-approved-july-request/

58   https://www.nytimes.com/2016/05/08/magazine/the-aspir-ing-novelist-who-became-obamas-foreign-policy-guru.html

59   https://www.tabletmag.com/scroll/192794/the-white-houses-iran-sell-and-the-jews-a-debate-2

60   https://www.tabletmag.com/scroll/192751/crossing-a-line-to-sell-a-deal

61   https://www.wsj.com/articles/u-s-spy-net-on-israel-snares-congress-1451425210

62   http://archive.is/LJNKr

63   http://archive.discoverthenetworks.org/viewSubCategory.asp?id=1521

64   http://www.israelnationalnews.com/News/News.aspx/193175#.VRVsDmaqBWM

65   https://www.timesofisrael.com/israel-furious-with-white-house-for-leak-on-syria-strike/

66   https://abcnews.go.com/blogs/headlines/2012/03/obama-admin-istration-media-campaign-to-stop-israeli-strike-on-iran/

67   https://www.wsj.com/articles/how-obama-abandoned-israel-1434409772

68   http:/www.washingtontimes.com/news/2016/jul/12/obama-admin-sent-taxpayer-money-oust-netanyahu/

69   https://freebeacon.com/issues/state-department-purged-emails-secret-anti-netanyahu-campaign/

70   http://archive.discoverthenetworks.org/viewSubCategory.asp?id=1521

71   https://web.archive.org/web/20170222143252/https://www.conservativereview.com/commentary/2016/12/why-john-ker-ry-thinks-israel-is-the-real-oppressive-middle-eastern-theocracy

72   http://startribune.com//omar-tlaib-host-news-conference-on-trav-el-restrictions/553720092/

73   http://archive.discoverthenetworks.org/viewSubCategory.asp?id=1521

74   http://www.dailymail.co.uk/news/article-4149484/US-sent-221-million-Palestinians-Obamas-hours.html

75   https://www.washingtonexaminer.com/weekly-standard/
      obama-campaign-flattered-by-hamas-endorsement

76   https://www.politico.com/interactives/2017/
      obama-hezbollah-drug-trafficking-investigation/

77   http://thefederalist.com/2018/01/15/will-obama-administration-
      ever-brought-justice-iran-deal-scandals/

78   https://www.reuters.com/article/us-usa-security-iran/
      iranians-charged-in-u-s-over-assassination-plot-idUS-
      TRE79A5E020111011

79   https://www.tabletmag.com/jewish-news-and-politics/255801/
      iran-deal-disaster

80   https://www.tabletmag.com/jewish-news-and-politics/212698/
      obamas-syria-policy

81   https://www.hudson.org/
      research/10989-obama-s-secret-iran-strategy

82   http://web.archive.org/web/20170216225800/
      https://now.mmedia.me/lb/en/
      commentaryanalysis/564899-extraordinary-concessions

83   https://www.hudson.org/research/9885-the-paradoxes-of-shiism

84   https://www.whitehouse.gov/briefings-statements/
      remarks-president-trump-commemorating-35th-anniversary-at-
      tack-beirut-barracks/

85   https://www.militarytimes.com/news/your-military/2019/04/04/
      iran-killed-more-us-troops-in-iraq-than-previously-known-penta-
      gon-says/

86   https://www.counterextremism.com/content/
      muslim-brotherhood%E2%80%99s-ties-isis-and-al-qaeda

87   https://www.centerforsecuritypolicy.org/2018/11/26/
      decision-brief-president-trump-must-declassify-obamas-secret-
      psd-11-strategy-to-support-the-muslim-brotherhood/

88   https://www.washingtonexaminer.com/policy/
      defense-national-security/act-of-war-mattis-says-obamas-inept-re-
      sponse-to-cafe-milano-bomb-plot-emboldened-iran

89   https://www.investigativeproject.org/3827/
      obama-administration-oversells-morsi

90   http://www.nationalreview.com/article/425787/
     moral-equivalence-middle-east-victor-davis-hanson

91   https://www.washingtontimes.com/news/2009/may/29/
     obamas-open-hand-slapped-by-adversaries/

92   https://www.latimes.com/world/middleeast/la-fg-cia-pentagon-
     isis-20160327-story.html

93   https://obamawhitehouse.archives.gov/
     the-press-office/2015/02/16/background-conference-call-se-
     nior-administration-officials-previewing-wh

94   http://www.judicialwatch.org/press-room/press-releases/
     documents-obtained-by-judicial-watch-reveal-fbi-training-curric-
     ula-purged-of-material-deemed-offensive-to-muslims/

95   https://www.jihadwatch.org/2008/01/the-implications-of-the-dis-
     missal-of-stephen-coughlin-joint-staff-pentagon

96   https://www.city-journal.org/html/see-no-islam-hear-no-is-
     lam-14091.html

97   https://www.theblaze.com/contributions/10-troubling-as-
     pects-of-president-obamas-countering-violent-extremism-summit

98   https://www.judiciary.senate.gov/imo/media/doc/06-28-16%20
     McCarthy%20Testimony.pdf#page=17

99   https://www.city-journal.org/html/anti-free-speech-mayor-14774.
     html

100 https://www.theblaze.com/contributions/
     hillary-clintons-hypocritical-and-totalitarian-war-on-free-speech

101 https://www.gatestoneinstitute.org/7176/
     criminalizing-free-speech

102 https://www.politico.com/blogs/under-the-radar/2015/12/
     lynch-recalibrates-message-on-hateful-speech-216488

103 https://www.cruz.senate.gov/?p=news&id=2987

104 https://thehill.com/blogs/congress-blog/homeland-security/268282-
     dhs-ordered-me-to-scrub-records-of-muslims-with-terror

105 https://www.washingtonexaminer.com/examiner-editori-
     al-how-the-fbi-was-blinded-by-political-correctness

106 https://dailycaller.com/2016/06/13/fbi-called-off-investigation-of-
     orlando-shooter-because-they-thought-his-coworkers-were-racist/

107 http://archive.is/OKIT8

108 http://archive.is/G9mKV

109 https://www.washingtonexaminer.com/weekly-standard/
obama-on-occupy-wall-street-we-are-on-their-side

110 http://web.archive.org/web/20111102163616/
https://www.theroot.com/blogs/predatory-lending/
obama-weighs-occupy-wall-street

111 http://archive.discoverthenetworks.org/viewSubCategory.
asp?id=2378

112 https://www.dailysignal.com/2016/11/16/
obamas-contribution-to-our-identity-politics-climate/

113 https://fivethirtyeight.com/features/barack-obama-won-the-
white-house-but-democrats-lost-the-country/

114 https://www.vox.com/policy-and-politics/2017/1/10/14211994/
obama-democrats-downballot

115 https://www.apnews.com/21dbd1254fea4738b662a12612c5fbf1

116 https://spectator.org/
al-charlatan-the-race-baiters-race-ta-wanna-a-brawley/

117 https://www.jewishpress.com/blogs/the-lid-jeffdunetz/
how-al-sharpton-inflamed-the-crown-heights-riot-and-how-the-
media-lied/2018/08/15/

118 https://www.mrctv.org/blog/happy-anniversa-
ry-rev-al-20-years-shapton-incited-firebombing-freddys-fash-
ion-mart

119 https://www.latimes.com/politics/la-na-pol-sharpton-demo-
crats-presidential-20190404-story.html

120 http://www.israelnationalnews.com/Articles/Article.aspx/19883

121 https://www.wsj.com/articles/SB122212856075765367

122 https://www.discoverthenetworks.org/individuals/
barack-hussein-obama/

123 https://www.latimes.com/archives/la-xpm-2008-apr-10-na-
obamamideast10-story.html

124 Ibid

125 https://www.thenation.com/article/
amy-kaplan-our-american-israel-book-review/

126 https://www.investigativeproject.
org/3777/a-red-carpet-for-radicals-at-the-white-house

127 https://www.cnn.com/2016/09/15/politics/john-brennan-cia-communist-vote/index.html

128 https://www.nationalreview.com/corner/obamas-moderate-hezbo-guy-city-i-have-come-love-most-al-quds-andrew-c-mccarthy/

129 https://www.meforum.org/2949/
john-brennan-jihad-holy-struggle

130 https://www.discoverthenetworks.org/individuals/john-brennan/

131 https://www.timesofisrael.com/can-one-time-proponent-of-out-reach-to-islamists-get-obamas-is-strategy-in-sync/

132 https://thefederalist.com/2019/03/12/ilhan-omar-barack-obama-mainstreamed-anti-semitism-democratic-party/

133 https://www.cruz.senate.gov/?p=press_release&id=1875

134 https://www.nationalreview.com/2014/09/
search-moderate-islamists-andrew-c-mccarthy/

135 http://archive.discoverthenetworks.org/individualProfile.
asp?indid=2562

136 https://www.nationalreview.com/2014/09/
obamas-go-moderate-islamist-andrew-c-mccarthy/

137 https://www.centerforsecuritypolicy.org/2014/09/05/
mohamed-elibiary-has-left-the-building/

138 https://www.investigativeproject.org/1904/
dalia-mogahed-a-muslim-george-gallup-or-islamist

139 http://archive.discoverthenetworks.org/individualProfile.
asp?indid=2428

140 http://www.jewishworldreview.com/cols/sowell070808.php3

141 https://youtu.be/zA_YcObRqqM?t=9075

142 https://www.politico.com/magazine/story/2019/03/08/
ilhan-omar-dean-phillips-minnesota-democratic-party-225696

Chapter 9: The Progressive Takeover of the Democratic Party

1 https://www.newyorker.com/news/dispatch/
how-ilhan-omar-won-over-hearts-in-minnesotas-fifth

2 https://www.politico.com/story/2018/11/16/
pelosi-speaker-progressives-congress-998595

3   https://www.pewresearch.org/fact-tank/2017/09/07/demo-
    cratic-voters-are-increasingly-likely-to-call-their-views-liberal/
    ft_17-09-07_democratliberal_in2017/

4   https://news.gallup.com/poll/225074/conservative-lead-ideolo-
    gy-down-single-digits.aspx

5   https://www.axios.com/axios-hbo-poll-55-percent-women-prefer-
    socialism-f70bf87e-34fd-4b63-b1f6-2f2b6900f634.html

6   https://news.gallup.com/poll/257639/four-americans-em-
    brace-form-socialism.aspx

7   https://www.theamericanconservative.com/dreher/
    america-future-childless-godless-unpatriotic/

8   https://assets.documentcloud.org/documents/6336787/19305-
    NBCWSJ-August-Social-Trends-Poll.pdf

9   https://www.flagusa.org/patriotismreport/

10 https://www.theatlantic.com/ideas/archive/2019/06/
    aoc-isnt-interested-american-exceptionalism/592213/

11 https://www.vox.com/2019/3/22/18259865/
    great-awokening-white-liberals-race-polling-trump-2020

12 https://www.claremont.org/crb/article/the-chosen-and-the-woke/

13 https://www.tabletmag.com/jewish-news-and-politics/284875/
    americas-white-saviors

14 Ibid

15 Ibid

16 https://www.nbcnews.com/politics/politics-news/
    far-washington-rep-omar-s-constituents-see-israel-controversy-dif-
    ferent-n981441

17 https://censusreporter.org/
    profiles/50000US2705-congressional-district-5-mn/

18 https://slate.com/news-and-politics/2019/08/new-york-times-
    meeting-transcript.html

19 https://pulitzercenter.org/sites/default/files/full_issue_of_
    the_1619_project.pdf

20 https://slate.com/news-and-politics/2019/08/new-york-times-
    meeting-transcript.html

21 Ibid

22 https://ballotpedia.org/Congressional_Progressive_Caucus

23 https://www.huffingtonpost.com/entry/congressional-progressive-caucus-more-influential-pramila-jayapal_us_5bfd8d84e4b-0771fb6bee520

24 https://www.thenation.com/article/progressive-caucus-and-obama/

25 https://cpc-grijalva.house.gov/caucus-members/

26 https://thefederalist.com/2019/05/21/democratic-frontrunners-voted-religious-freedom-restoration-act/

27 https://en.wikipedia.org/wiki/Results_of_the_2016_Democratic_Party_presidential_primaries

28 https://www.realclearpolitics.com/video/2019/08/04/bill_maher_democrats_are_blowing_their_chance_to_beat_trump.html

29 https://www.axios.com/2020-democrats-centrists-progressives-attacks-77242ddb-bb37-4b15-98c6-7d107ef55d51.html

30 http://nymag.com/intelligencer/2019/09/democrats-presidential-candidates-old-radical-biden-warren-bernie.html

31 https://www.politico.com/2020-election/candidates-views-on-the-issues/health-care/medicare-for-all/

32 https://thefederalist.com/2019/06/28/democrats-agree-taxpayers-cover-medical-bills-everyone-breaks-united-states/

33 https://www.huffpost.com/entry/decriminalizing-border-crossing-democrats-2020_n_5d15884ee4b03d6116392906

34 https://www.axios.com/2020-presidential-candidates-green-new-deal-22faff60-3fee-45f3-8636-09e437c82431.html

35 https://thefederalist.com/2019/09/05/climate-change-hysteria-dangerous/#.XXFRRIN-PFQ.twitter

36 https://thefederalist.com/2019/08/26/every-top-2020-democrat-wants-taxpayers-shoulder-college-tuition/

37 https://townhall.com/tipsheet/guybenson/2019/07/23/ilhan-omar-american-taxpayers-have-a-responsibility-to-provide-abortions-to-illegal-immigrants-n2550456

38 http://archive.is/qVuAw

39   https://www.businessinsider.com/who-supports-impeachment-major-democrats-2020-candidates-want-impeach-trump-2019-5#in-a-may-31-statement-rep-alma-adams-of-north-carolina-said-she-supports-opening-an-impeachment-inquiry-because-congress-has-a-sacred-responsibility-to-obtain-the-information-necessary-to-determine-the-next-steps-53

40   https://www.nationalreview.com/2019/08/progressive-democratic-candidates-renounce-former-centrist-views/

41   https://www.nytimes.com/2019/06/06/us/politics/joe-biden-hyde-amendment.html

42   https://www.cnn.com/2019/03/01/politics/joe-biden-mike-pence-2020/index.html

43   https://www.politico.com/magazine/story/2019/04/12/elizabeth-warren-profile-young-republican-2020-president-226613

44   https://www.huffpost.com/entry/kamala-harris-criminal-justice-reform-presidential-debate_n_5d7af28be4b00d690595c769

45   https://www.vanityfair.com/news/2019/08/kamala-harris-medicare-for-all

46   https://nypost.com/2019/07/10/ocasio-cortez-harris-team-up-for-bill-aimed-at-helping-criminals-get-housing/

47   http://archive.is/wz0vY

48   https://thefederalist.com/2019/06/28/moderate-democrat-candidates-arent-socialists-like-bernie-still-wildly-extreme/

49   https://www.wsj.com/articles/trump-isnt-the-one-dividing-us-by-race-11566158729?shareToken=stc50b630f49c645a49aa3cf6cfada956e

50   https://www.axios.com/joe-biden-white-supremacy-speech-a3e64c52-0753-4704-b841-5ee663f2f6e9.html

51   https://www.axios.com/reparations-2020-presidential-candidates-02cce9ac-082e-4777-955b-33c8196e64c0.html

52   https://www.vox.com/2019/3/22/18259865/great-awakening-white-liberals-race-polling-trump-2020

53   http://archive.is/FXXCd

54   http://archive.is/I5WEi

55 https://thehill.com/homenews/campaign/453526-buttigieg-the-squad-is-very-healthy-for-our-party

56 http://archive.is/dWz67

57 https://thehill.com/policy/energy-environ-ment/416411-youth-protestors-fill-nancy-pelosis-office-demand-ing-climate-change

58 https://www.theatlantic.com/science/archive/2019/03/climate-change-which-democrats-oppose-green-new-deal/585802/

59 https://www.usatoday.com/story/news/politics/2019/03/27/green-new-deal-democrats-push-to-stay-in-paris-agree-ment/3284225002/

60 https://www.washingtonpost.com/news/magazine/wp/2019/07/10/feature/how-saikat-chakrabarti-became-aocs-chief-of-change/

61 https://www.cnn.com/2019/04/14/politics/pelosi-aoc-60-min-utes/index.html

62 https://nypost.com/2019/04/08/pelosi-takes-jab-at-aoc-over-attention-to-twitter-followers/

63 https://thehill.com/homenews/house/450363-the-4-house-demo-crats-who-voted-against-the-border-funding-bill

64 https://www.nytimes.com/2019/06/25/us/politics/border-fund-ing-vote.html

65 https://www.nytimes.com/2019/06/27/us/politics/border-fund-ing-immigration.html

66 https://www.theguardian.com/us-news/2019/jul/07/house-border-bill-funding-democratic-progressive-moderate-split

67 https://thefederalist.com/2019/07/16/house-democrats-uncivil-war-fueled-identity-politics/

68 https://www.businessinsider.com/ocasio-cortez-says-pelosi-sin-gling-out-newly-elected-women-color-2019-7

69 https://www.nytimes.com/2019/07/13/us/politics/alexandria-oca-sio-cortez-democrats.html

70 http://archive.is/3HAaa

71 http://archive.is/zOHSA

72 https://www.mediaite.com/tv/watch-alexandria-ocasio-cortez-and-rashida-tlaib-blame-speaker-pelosi-for-attacks-and-death-threats/

73 https://www.axios.com/newsletters/axios-am-3fad5f0e-20ee-49fa-ac59-b557841834c5.html?chunk=0&utm_term=emshare#story0

74 https://www.businessinsider.com/democrat-ic-group-leaked-poll-unfavorable-alexandria-ocasio-cortez-2019-7

75 https://www.politico.com/story/2019/07/10/pelosi-progressives-twitter-1405763

76 https://www.apnews.com/ee40bb3f2bfc42c481bbe23ed9bf9d04

77 https://www.newsweek.com/ilhan-omar-instagram-picture-nancy-pelosi-africa-send-her-back-1452249

78 https://www.c-span.org/video/?462678-1/representatives-omar-pressley-ocasio-cortez-tlaib-respond-president-trump

79 https://www.c-span.org/video/?463543-1/representatives-omar-tlaib-hold-news-conference-travel-restrictions

80 https://thehill.com/homenews/campaign/452701-cbc-members-accuse-aoc-linked-justice-democrats-of-targeting-black

81 https://www.congress.gov/bill/116th-congress/house-bill/40

82 https://www.politico.com/story/2019/07/29/top-dccc-staffer-out-amid-diversity-uproar-1439525

83 https://www.politico.com/story/2019/07/29/cheri-bustos-democrats-diversity-1438867

84 https://www.politico.com/story/2019/09/11/hoyer-nadler-impeachment-1489506

85 https://spectator.org/nadlers-fake-impeachment-inquiry/

86 https://engel.house.gov/latest-news/engel-calls-for-formal-impeachment-inquiry/

87 https://assets.documentcloud.org/documents/6146001/Document.pdf, pgs. 47-48.

88 https://www.usatoday.com/story/news/politics/2019/09/29/nancy-pelosi-impeachment-inquiry-trump-ramps-up-plan/3791214002/

89 https://www.nationalreview.com/2019/12/the-articles-of-impeachment-are-very-weak/

90	https://www.nytimes.com/interactive/2019/12/18/us/politics/trump-impeachment-vote.html

91	https://www.politico.com/news/2019/12/30/van-drews-party-switch-upends-gop-primary-race-090998

92	https://www.wsj.com/articles/pelosis-rolling-impeachment-11577400108

93	https://thefederalist.com/2019/12/05/impeachment-is-slowly-destroying-democrats-2020-political-hopes/

94	https://www.republicanleader.senate.gov/newsroom/remarks/mcconnell-remarks-on-house-democrats-impeachment-of-president-trump-

95	http://archive.is/xpTAm

96	http://archive.is/vY5bz

97	http://archive.is/QtwAA

98	http://archive.is/v3veH

99	http://archive.is/zbugM

100	http://archive.is/CKqW9

101	http://archive.is/k1qY3

102	https://theunitedstateofwomen2018.sched.com/

103	http://archive.is/udnlt

104	https://www.reuters.com/article/us-usa-trump-democrats/apologize-to-america-trump-tells-democratic-congresswomen-idUSKCN1UG0J2

105	https://thinkprogress.org/rep-ilhan-omar-we-were-sent-to-washington-to-lead-with-our-values-5eba273ff041/

106	https://www.cnn.com/2019/04/09/politics/democratic-party-voters-analysis/index.html

Chapter 10: Collusion: Omar's Troubling Ties to America's Enemies

1	https://www.tampabay.com/opinion/columns/read-the-transcript-of-rep-ilhan-omars-speech-20190415/

2	https://www.foxnews.com/us/9-11-anniversary-mourner-who-lost-mother-in-attacks-criticizes-ilhan-omars-some-people-did-something-comment

3   https://slate.com/news-and-politics/2019/09/ilhan-omar-responds-criticism-son-september-11-victim.html
4   https://www.cair.com/about_us
5   https://www.justice.gov/opa/pr/individual-charged-connection-2001-terrorist-attack-jerusalem-resulted-death-americans
6   https://www.investigativeproject.org/documents/misc/110.pdf#page=4
7   Ibid
8   https://www.youtube.com/watch?v=1mVxkQUus38
9   http://archive.is/cBQKP
10 http://archive.is/iTAh5
11 http://archive.is/ASrgF
12 https://www.investigativeproject.org/documents/misc/1059.pdf
13 https://www.justice.gov/opa/pr/federal-judge-hands-downs-sentences-holy-land-foundation-case
14 https://www.investigativeproject.org/documents/case_docs/717.pdf#page=6
15 https://www.investigativeproject.org/documents/case_docs/441.pdf
16 https://www.investigativeproject.org/documents/case_docs/439.pdf#page=5
17 https://www.dallasnews.com/news/crime/2008/10/07/fbi-cair-is-a-front-group-and-holy-land-foundation-tapped-hamas-clerics-for-fundraisers/
18 https://www.investigativeproject.org/documents/misc/122.pdf#page=12
19 https://www.investigativeproject.org/781/holy-land-evidence-establishes-hamas-link
20 http://www.investigativeproject.org/documents/case_docs/1425.pdf#page=19
21 http://www.investigativeproject.org/documents/misc/185.pdf#page=14
22 https://www.nationalreview.com/2014/04/roots-cairs-intimidation-campaign-andrew-c-mccarthy/

23   https://www.investigativeproject.org/documents/misc/122.pdf#page=7

24   http://web.archive.org/web/20070816165050/http://counterterrorismblog.org/2007/08/cair_identified_by_the_fbi_as.php

25   https://www.investigativeproject.org/documents/case_docs/717.pdf#page=6

26   http://archive.is/ig7SL

27   https://www.cair.com/cair_calls_on_leaders_to_say_istandwithilhan_after_trump_tweet_endangers_rep_ilhan_omar

28   http://archive.is/WOrwb

29   https://www.newsweek.com/2019/04/19/ilhan-omar-democrats-israel-trump-1389677.html

30   Ibid

31   https://www.investigativeproject.org/documents/misc/110.pdf, pgs. 1-2

32   https://www.investigativeproject.org/documents/case_docs/1425.pdf#page=15

33   https://www.investigativeproject.org/2340/federal-judge-agrees-cair-tied-to-hamas

34   https://www.investigativeproject.org/documents/misc/265.pdf

35   https://www.investigativeproject.org/2845/cair-great-fbi-scare-lecture

36   https://www.investigativeproject.org/2492/cair-imagery-makes-obstructionist-goal-clear

37   https://www.investigativeproject.org/documents/case_docs/225.pdf#page=33

38   https://www.govinfo.gov/content/pkg/CHRG-112hhrg72541/pdf/CHRG-112hhrg72541.pdf

39   https://www.foxnews.com/us/how-rep-ilhan-omars-minnesota-district-became-the-terrorist-recruitment-capital-of-the-us-officials-highly-concerned

40   https://www.investigativeproject.org/6126/trump-continues-obama-dhs-policy-of-engaging-cair

41   https://www.cairchicago.org/blog/2019/10/cair-chicago-trains-us-customs-amp-border-patrol-officers?fb-

clid=IwAR2T8ydIPy6wYzAOJ4pnjkxvsae_08Is0YVccI9Og-
ka0qRSst9MNRHAB0xU

42   https://www.investigativeproject.org/7682/
ipt-obtains-letters-of-support-to-hamas-front-group

43   https://www.justice.gov/opa/press-release/file/967231/download

44   https://thefederalist.com/2018/02/21/russia-collusion-mon-
gers-hurt-america-far-worse-indicted-russians/

46   https://thefederalist.com/2018/03/15/
okay-adam-schiff-show-us-the-russia-collusion/

46   https://thefederalist.com/2018/05/17/
far-russia-investigations-keep-leading-back-investigators/

47   https://thefederalist.com/2019/04/02/
media-failed-collusion-wanted-trump-traitor/

48   https://www.nationalreview.com/2019/12/
the-articles-of-impeachment-are-very-weak/

49   https://www.wsj.com/articles/SB1000142405274870413220457
6136590964621006

50   https://pjmedia.com/homeland-security/2016/08/14/revisiting-
the-muslim-brotherhoods-august-2013-reign-of-terror-targeting-
egypts-christians/?utm_source=twitterfeed&utm_medium=twitter

51   https://pjmedia.com/homeland-security/2017/05/29/
muslim-brotherhood-incites-more-terror-attacks-target-
ing-egypts-coptic-christians/

52   https://www.nationalreview.com/2010/07/
raufs-dawa-world-trade-center-rubble-andrew-c-mccarthy/

53   https://pjmedia.com/blog/pulitzer-prize-winners-journalistic-mal-
practice-over-the-u-s-muslim-brotherhood/3/

54   https://www.investigativeproject.org/documents/20-an-explanato-
ry-memorandum-on-the-general.pdf#page=18

55   https://www.investigativeproject.org/documents/20-an-explanato-
ry-memorandum-on-the-general.pdf#page=19

56   https://www.investigativeproject.org/documents/20-an-explanato-
ry-memorandum-on-the-general.pdf#page=21

57   https://www.investigativeproject.org/documents/20-an-explanato-
ry-memorandum-on-the-general.pdf, PDF pgs. 24-26

58   https://www.investigativeproject.org/documents/20-an-explanatory-memorandum-on-the-general.pdf#page=32

59   https://www.investigativeproject.org/documents/misc/1059.pdf

60   https://www.newenglishreview.org/Jerry_Gordon/CAIR_and_Lawfare:_an_Interview_with_Brooke_Goldstein/

61   https://www.city-journal.org/html/see-no-islam-hear-no-islam-14091.html

62   https://www.cair.com/cair_to_announce_complete_victory_in_constitutional_challenge_to_federal_terror_watchlist

63   https://www.nationalreview.com/2014/04/roots-cairs-intimidation-campaign-andrew-c-mccarthy/

64   https://www.nationalreview.com/2014/11/cair-terror-group-daniel-pipes/

65   https://www.gatestoneinstitute.org/9908/jihadist-groups-cair

66   https://www.danielpipes.org/2627/cairs-hate-crimes-nonsense

67   http://web.archive.org/web/20180921111747/https://www.ilhan-omar.com/about/

68   http://archive.is/kX0Ci

69   https://www.seattleglobalist.com/2019/05/21/rep-ilhan-omar-to-headline-cair-wa-ramadan-fundraiser/85231

70   https://freebeacon.com/issues/omar-holding-secret-fundraisers-with-islamic-groups-tied-to-terror/

71   http://archive.is/Xynsw

72   https://www.cair.com/1_200_expected_to_attend_cair_sfba_23rd_annual_banquet

73   https://cair-az.org/2017/06/18/cair-az-first-somali-american-lawmaker-ilhan-omar-muslims-no-longer-alone/

74   https://www.facebook.com/CAIR.Minnesota/videos/1278447728929628/

75   https://www.cairchicago.org/speaker-bios-2017

76   http://clerk.house.gov/public_disc/financial-pdfs/2018/10024006.pdf

77   https://www.fec.gov/data/receipts/?data_type=processed&committee_id=C00680934&contributor_name=C00396556&two_year_transaction_period=2018&line_number=F3-11C

78   https://www.investigativeproject.org/profile/113/nihad-awad

79   https://www.investigativeproject.org/documents/misc/1059.pdf, pgs. 13-14

80   https://www.investigativeproject.org/profile/113/nihad-awad

81   https://www.investigativeproject.org/2749/nihad-awad-cair-anti-semite

82   https://www.cair.com/cair_to_announce_complete_victory_in_constitutional_challenge_to_federal_terror_watchlist

83   https://www.jpost.com/American-Politics/Omar-Tlaib-welcome-decision-ruling-US-terror-watchlist-unconstitutional-600829

84   https://www.cair.com/action_alert_cair_cair_minnesota_call_on_twitter_to_suspend_trump_s_account_over_false_9_11_smear_of_rep_ilhan_omar

85   https://omar.house.gov/media/press-releases/rep-ilhan-omar-members-congress-send-letter-secretary-mike-pompeo-protect

86   http://archive.is/FOA9i

87   http://archive.is/XjyB2

88   http://archive.is/9y638

89   https://www.investigativeproject.org/documents/misc/120.pdf

90   http://www.danielpipes.org/blog/2016/11/cair-leader-overthrow-the-us-government

91   https://www.investigativeproject.org/4214/cair-ayloush-gives-dishonest-bullying-answer-to

92   http://archive.is/ciEXY

93   http://archive.is/enYZm

94   https://www.investigativeproject.org/3837/cair-targets-morsi-brotherhood-critics

95   http://archive.is/CvfeK

96   https://tinyurl.com/sfnxpfc

97   https://www.meforum.org/islamist-watch/money-politics/recipient/682/

98   https://www.foxnews.com/us/womens-march-zahra-billoo-anti-semitism-board-member

99   https://twitter.com/JordanSchachtel/
      status/1150602302560116737
100   https://www.mpac.org/programs/hollywood-bureau-old/were-
      bringing-hollywood-to-you.php
101   https://www.nationalreview.com/2012/08/
      history-mpac-andrew-c-mccarthy/
102   http://archive.is/r4xCc
103   https://twitter.com/RealSarahIdan/status/1174020645442576384
104   https://www.investigativeproject.org/7799/twitter-gives-islamist-
      anti-semites-a-pass-but#.XX_WssPMB-o.twitter
105   https://twitter.com/RealSaavedra/status/1173660856111943680
106   https://capitalresearch.org/article/keeping-up-with-cair/
107   https://twitter.com/RealSaavedra/status/1173660892799455232
108   https://canarymission.org/individual/Zahra_Billoo
109   http://archive.is/UPad8
110   https://www.meforum.org/59007/zahra-biilloo
111   https://thehill.com/hilltv/rising/436933-muslim-rights-advocate-
      says-omar-as-broadened-the-conversation-on-how-to
112   https://www.wnd.com/2017/11/cair-leader-refuses-to-de-
      nounce-hamas-muslim-brotherhood/#PuZqZua22bp8FveT.99
113   https://pjmedia.com/homeland-security/2016/09/18/
      mass-stabbing-at-mall-in-st-cloud-minnesota-suspect-asked-vic-
      tims-in-they-were-muslim-per-local-police/2/
114   http://www.startribune.com/one-year-later-motive-of-st-cloud-
      mall-attacker-remains-unclear/444894453/
115   https://www.city-journal.org/html/alice-terrorland-14747.html
116   https://www.prairiebusinessmagazine.com/news/
      government-and-politics/4592624-quiet-while-ndsu-us-rep-omar-
      now-makes-national-headlines
117   https://www.theguardian.com/us-news/2015/sep/14/
      somali-muslims-minnesota-counter-extremism-program
118   https://www.cair.com/action_alert_cair_cair_minnesota_call_on_
      twitter_to_suspend_trump_s_account_over_false_9_11_smear_
      of_rep_ilhan_omar

119   https://www.powerlineblog.com/archives/2016/10/meet-ilhan-omar-daily-beast-style.php

120   https://www.investigativeproject.org/documents/misc/1059.pdf

121   http://archive.is/JsxQI

122   https://www.cairflorida.org/mediacenter/1455-cair-florida-exec-dir-hassan-shibly-addressed-president-trump-s-tweet-endangering-rep-ilhan-omar

123   http://www.investigativeproject.org/documents/case_docs/542.pdf#page=58

124   http://archive.is/KYUn0

125   http://www.investigativeproject.org/documents/misc/85.pdf#page=2

126   http://web.archive.org/web/20021206132514/www.masmn.org/Other/About_Us.htm

127   https://www.thenational.ae/uae/government/list-of-groups-designated-terrorist-organisations-by-the-uae-1.270037

128   https://www.memri.org/reports/children-philadelphia-muslim-society-we-will-sacrifice-ourselves-al-aqsa-will-chop-their

129   https://thefederalist.com/2019/05/07/rep-ilhan-omar-supports-group-that-produced-child-beheading-skit/

130   http://archive.is/hUsdA

131   https://www.jns.org/opinion/minnesota-lawmakers-nominate-anti-semites-to-fight-anti-semitism/

132   https://www.investigativeproject.org/6947/isna-president-addresses-jamaat-e-islami-crowd-in

133   https://www.cair.com/about_us

134   https://www.cair.com/search?q=social+justice

135   https://www.masmn.org/claiming-our-voices-2019/

136   http://archive.is/mDvg8

137   https://www.dailywire.com/news/48591/swindle-california-islamist-activists-protest-david-m-swindle

138   https://www.reuters.com/article/us-usa-trump-muslimbrotherhood-explainer/explainer-who-is-targeting-the-muslim-brotherhood-idUSKCN1S90YX

139 https://www.muslimamericansociety.org/a-call-for-international-investigation-into-death-of-mohamed-morsi-and-human-rights-violations-in-sudan-and-saudi-arabia/

140 https://uscmo.org/index.php/about-us/

141 https://www.meforum.org/7364/
islamists-with-ties-to-terror-lobby-congress

142 https://uscmo.org/index.php/our_board/

143 https://www.washingtontimes.com/news/2015/jan/12/
imam-linked-to-1993-wtc-bombing-to-speak-at-stand-/

144 https://www.meforum.org/islamist-watch/51649/
siraj-wahhaj-on-jihad

145 https://www.discoverthenetworks.org/individuals/siraj-wahhaj/

146 http://www.washingtonpost.com/wp-dyn/articles/A48936-
2004Aug7.html

147 https://www.centerforsecuritypolicy.org/wp-content/
uploads/2015/09/Star_Spangled_Shariah1.pdf#page=37

148 https://uscmo.org/index.php/portfolio-items/
uscmos-annual-national-muslim-advocacy-day-on-capitol-hill-2/

149 https://www.centerforsecuritypolicy.org/wp-content/
uploads/2015/09/Star_Spangled_Shariah1.pdf

150 https://uscmo.org/index.php/portfolio-items/
uscmos-annual-ramadan-iftar/

151 https://uscmo.org/index.php/2018/09/11/usmco-celebrates-rashida-tlaib-and-ilhan-omar-two-democrats-set-to-become-the-first-muslim-women-in-congress/

152 http://archive.is/YeMsF

153 http://archive.is/ERp7t

154 http://archive.is/HZo9y

155 http://archive.is/WTonC

156 https://www.meforum.org/7281/
mef-reveals-islamic-relief-under-investigation

157 https://www.meforum.org/7403/
islamic-relief-charity-extremism-terror

158 https://www.meforum.org/MiddleEastForum/media/MEFLibrary/pdf/Islamic-Relief-Dossier-v3.pdf

159 https://www.meforum.org/7281/
mef-reveals-islamic-relief-under-investigation

160 https://www.meforum.org/islamist-watch/57764/
ilhan-omar-to-speak-alongside-charity-official

161 https://www.investigativeproject.org/7871/
new-islamist-group-in-chicago-dominated-by

162 https://www.mlfa.org/ilhan17/#.XYU_i5NKijg

163 http://clerk.house.gov/public_disc/finan-
cial-pdfs/2018/10024006.pdf

164 https://www.meforum.org/islamist-watch/money-politics/
recipient/682/

165 https://ethnicstudies.berkeley.edu/people/hatem-bazian/

166 https://www.discoverthenetworks.org/individuals/hatem-bazian/

167 https://www.adl.org/resources/profiles/
american-muslims-for-palestine

168 https://www.investigativeproject.org/3346/
american-muslims-for-palestine-web-of-hamas

169 https://www.meforum.org/campus-watch/58975/
ilhan-omar-pro-bds-resolution-isnt-about-free

170 https://www.discoverthenetworks.org/individuals/hatem-bazian/

171 https://www.centerforsecuritypolicy.org/2019/02/13/
red-green-axis-chokes-on-omars-antisemitism/

172 http://www.hatembazian.com/content/
israel-bds-and-congresswomen-elect-ilhan-omar-and-rashida-tlaib/

173 https://www.dailysabah.com/columns/hatem-bazian/2019/04/19/
trumps-attacks-on-ilhan-omar-and-fascism

174 https://www.meforum.org/islamist-watch/money-politics/
donor/1300/

175 https://www.investigativeproject.org/8065/
sanders-doubles-down-on-anti-semite-sarsour

176 https://zoa.org/2017/07/10369225-zoa-jihadist-jew-hater-linda-
sarsours-speech-was-call-for-sedition-violence-against-pres-trump-
and-u-s/

177 https://www.jpost.com/American-Politics/Bernie-Sanders-chose-
Linda-Sarsour-Can-Jews-overlook-her-views-on-Israel-601691

178 https://www.cnsnews.com/news/article/patrick-goodenough/
linda-sarsour-urges-muslims-support-rep-ilhan-omar-best-our

179 http://archive.is/j8FHe

180 http://archive.is/CKHUF

181 https://spectator.org/misleading-while-muslim/

182 https://www.meforum.org/campus-watch/12867/
cair-vs-the-nypd-incl-dhabah-debbie-almontaser

183 https://www.meforum.org/islamist-watch/58714/
misleading-while-muslim

184 https://www.foxnews.com/politics/
new-york-post-ilhan-omar-911-attacks

185 http://archive.is/z5jVZ

186 https://www.fec.gov/data/receipts/?cycle=2018&data_type=pro-
cessed&committee_id=C00680934&contributor_name=almon-
taser&two_year_transaction_period=2018&line_number=F3-
11AI

187 Minnesota Campaign Finance and Public Disclosure Board
- Neighbors for Ilhan "Report of Receipts and Expenditures
for Principal Campaign Committees" for 1/1/2017 through
12/31/2017, pg. 3

188 https://www.meforum.org/campus-watch/17201/
dalia-mogahed-a-muslim-george-gallup-or-islamist

189 http://archive.is/z5jVZ

190 Minnesota Campaign Finance and Public Disclosure Board
- Neighbors for Ilhan "Report of Receipts and Expenditures
for Principal Campaign Committees" for 1/1/2018 through
12/31/2018, pg. 4

191 https://www.algemeiner.com/2019/02/17/
ilhan-omar-is-funded-by-israel-hating-bds-promoters-and-pacs/

192 https://www.fec.gov/data/receipts/?cycle=2020&data_type=pro-
cessed&committee_id=C00680934&contributor_name=zog-
by&line_number=F3-11AI

193 https://www.investigativeproject.org/691/
isna-nait-seek-to-edit-history

194 https://www.nationalreview.com/corner/international-institute-is-lamic-thought-and-muslim-brotherhood-andrew-c-mccarthy/

195 https://counterjihad.com/obama-appoints-zaki-barzinji-grand-son-muslim-brotherhood-leader-white-house-muslim-out-reach-position

196 https://www.fec.gov/data/receipts/individual-contributions/?data_type=processed&contributor_name=barzinji&two_year_transaction_period=2018&two_year_transaction_period=2020&min_date=01%2F01%2F2017&max_date=12%2F31%2F2020

197 http://archive.is/GFmSY

198 https://www.jns.org/opinion/minnesota-lawmakers-nominate-anti-semites-to-fight-anti-semitism/

199 https://www.investigativeproject.org/5288/islamic-university-of-minnesota-a-hotbed

200 https://www.brotherhoodunmasked.net/naif

201 https://ianaonline.org/ianas-director-sh-hassan-dhooye-met-our-future-scholars/

202 https://www.meforum.org/58043/minnesota-lawmakers-nominate-anti-semites

203 http://www.startribune.com/voices-for-palestine-3/270129611/

204 http://archive.is/L2wEi

205 http://archive.is/oqpmd

206 https://www.memri.org/tv/minneapolis-imam-shaaban-abou-badria-western-civilization-built-bloodshed-terrorism/transcript

207 https://www.mprnews.org/story/2015/04/29/fears-of-spying-intensify-after-twin-cities-terror-arrests

208 http://www.timberjay.com/stories/breaking-bread-breaking-barriers,13647

209 https://web.archive.org/web/20171003081153/http:/www.tusmotimes.com/xildhibaan-ilhaan-cumar-iyo-madaxweyne-recep-erdogan-oo-magaalada-new-york-ku-kulmay/

210 https://www.conservativereview.com/news/omar-met-erdogan/

211 http://www.timberjay.com/stories/breaking-bread-breaking-barriers,13647

212   https://www.city-journal.org/html/where-democracy-real-ly-does-die-darkness-15184.html
213   https://www.washingtonexaminer.com/opinion/yes-turkey-has-definitely-become-a-rogue-regime
214   https://www.politurco.com/erdogans-anti-semitism.html
215   https://www.city-journal.org/html/who-planned-turkeys-coup-14656.html
216   https://abcnews.go.com/International/3rd-straight-year-turkey-jailed-journalists-country-report/story?id=59791362
217   https://thefederalist.com/2019/04/30/ilhan-omars-collusion-islamists-acceptable/
218   http://archive.is/j0InS
219   http://archive.is/4Deks
220   http://archive.is/PHpww
221   https://www.memri.org/reports/call-campaign-funds-us-rep-il-han-omar-%E2%80%93-who-has-met-turkish-president-erdo-gan-%E2%80%93-turkish-pro
222   http://archive.is/pNbCG
223   http://archive.is/EHaQK
224   http://archive.is/HO9SP
225   https://www.memri.org/reports/call-campaign-funds-us-rep-il-han-omar-%E2%80%93-who-has-met-turkish-president-erdo-gan-%E2%80%93-turkish-pro
226   https://diyanetamerica.org/news/dca-board-members-met-congressman-and-congresswomen/
227   https://www.meforum.org/7436/turkey-is-building-islamist-beachheads-in-america
228   https://diyanetamerica.org/about-us/what-is-dca/
229   https://www.jns.org/turkish-media-calls-for-turks-to-fund-us-rep-ilhan-omars-campaign/
230   https://www.yenisafak.com/en/world/media-flak-directed-at-ilhan-omar-no-surprise-at-all-3477913
231   https://www.memri.org/reports/call-campaign-funds-us-rep-ilhan-omar---who-has-met-turkish-president-erdogan---turkish-pro

232 https://www.dailywire.com/news/top-ally-of-turkish-president-er-dogan-donated-to-omars-campaign-last-month

233 https://web.archive.org/web/20170222153513/https:/www.conservativereview.com/commentary/2016/08/why-nato-members-including-the-us-should-not-coddle-turkey/

234 https://www.sbs.com.au/news/deeply-offended-pm-demands-tur-key-s-erdogan-withdraws-gallipoli-coffins-comment

235 https://www.dailywire.com/news/rossomando-emerson-while-erdo-gan-slammed-israel-at-u-n-turkish-support-for-terror-was-revealed

236 https://nypost.com/2019/09/23/turkey-is-now-a-haven-for-terrorists-and-an-enabler-of-terrorism/

237 https://foreignpolicy.com/2019/12/10/us-lawmakers-move-pun-ish-turkey-buying-russian-missile-system-s400/

238 https://www.wsj.com/articles/turkey-has-legitimate-grievances-against-the-u-s-11570576128

239 https://www.nationalreview.com/2019/10/turkey-and-the-kurds-its-more-complicated-than-you-think/

240 https://www.nationalreview.com/2019/10/kurdish-syrian-turkish-ironies/

241 https://www.dailywire.com/news/bds-supporter-ilhan-omar-sanc-tions-unjustly-target-citizens-are-failed-foreign-policy

242 https://omar.house.gov/sites/omar.house.gov/files/documents/Turkey%20Letter.pdf

243 https://www.gatestoneinstitute.org/11484/erdogan-moderate-islam

244 https://www.gatestoneinstitute.org/13704/turkey-erdogan-muslim-brotherhood

245 https://www.haaretz.com/middle-east-news/.premium-is-turkey-s-erdogan-quietly-courting-indian-muslims-to-crown-him-caliph-1.6786101

246 https://www.miamiherald.com/latest-news/article1938672.html

247 https://www.vanguardngr.com/2019/06/turkeys-erdogan-pays-tribute-to-martyr-morsi-after-his-death/

248 https://www.gatestoneinstitute.org/11933/turkey-hamas-erdogan

249 https://www.timesofisrael.com/topic/hamas-turkey-relations/

250 https://www.israelhayom.com/2019/07/28/
erdogan-says-turkey-is-opposed-to-anyone-that-stands-by-israel/

251 https://www.israelhayom.com/2018/12/24/
netanyahu-calls-turkish-leader-erdogan-an-anti-semitic-dictator/

252 https://www.algemeiner.com/2019/09/25/
us-islamists-effusively-praise-erdogan-in-new-york-meeting/

253 https://www.investigativeproject.org/7365/
erdogan-allies-lobbied-congress-against-kurds

254 https://www.algemeiner.com/2019/09/25/
us-islamists-effusively-praise-erdogan-in-new-york-meeting/

255 http://archive.is/tUkiA

256 https://www.aa.com.tr/en/world/
us-muslim-leaders-hail-erdogan-for-islamic-leadership/1591054

257 https://www.yenisafak.com/en/news/erdogan-meets-with-repre-
sentatives-of-muslim-community-in-the-us-2535813

258 https://www.investigativeproject.org/5492/
will-turkey-new-diplomatic-push-reduce-its

259 https://www.investigativeproject.org/5631/
cair-awad-continue-aggressively-shilling-for

260 https://www.investigativeproject.org/5548/
erdogan-coup-survival-dont-call-it-democracy

261 https://www.algemeiner.com/2018/09/26/
cair-chief-meets-with-turkish-and-iranian-presidents/

262 https://www.investigativeproject.org/7365/
erdogan-allies-lobbied-congress-against-kurds

263 https://www.apnews.com/dbb5fa7d8f8c4d0d99f297601c83a164

264 https://www.investigativeproject.org/5548/
erdogan-coup-survival-dont-call-it-democracy

265 https://www.investigativeproject.org/5492/
will-turkey-new-diplomatic-push-reduce-its

266 http://www.hurriyetdailynews.com/turkey-calls-oic-for-an-ex-
traordinary-summit-on-jerusalem-in-istanbul-131817

267 https://www.apnews.com/1d46396a70834980a08a02bad9
70b017

268   https://www.centerforsecuritypolicy.org/2017/12/20/
      turkish-president-erdogan-declared-ummah-leader-at-washing-
      ton-dc-muslim-brotherhood-rally-condemning-trump-recogni-
      tion-of-jerusalem/

269   https://www.investigativeproject.org/7631/
      cair-chief-to-meet-with-turkish-and-iranian

270   http://www.cometoturkey.com/president-erdo-
      gan-meets-with-representatives-of-muslim-community-in-the-us.
      html

271   https://uscmo.org/index.php/2014/08/27/
      witnessing-turkish-democracy-in-action/

272   https://www.investigativeproject.org/5492/
      will-turkey-new-diplomatic-push-reduce-its

273   https://web.archive.org/web/20160211043643/
      http://www.yenisafak.com/en/columns/yasinaktay/
      greetings-and-a-message-from-western-muslims-2026629

274   https://www.investigativeproject.org/7365/
      erdogan-allies-lobbied-congress-against-kurds

275   https://www.centerforsecuritypolicy.org/wp-content/
      uploads/2018/04/Turkey_Final.pdf, Chapter 2

276   https://www.hrw.org/world-report/2019/country-chapters/
      somalia

277   https://www.radiodalsan.com/en/2018/12/31/
      somalia-most-corrupt-country-in-the-world-transparency-int/

278   http://hrlibrary.umn.edu/research/Somalia-Constitution2012.pdf

279   Ibid

280   http://archive.is/pg8dq

281   http://archive.is/onpX8

282   http://archive.is/XHqx5

283   http://archive.is/OKGjP

284   http://archive.is/6GMSK

285   https://alphanewsmn.com/ilhan-omar-arrested-in-2013-for-tres-
      passing-booked-at-hennepin-county-jail/

286   https://www.bbc.com/news/world-africa-19557884

287 https://www.tcdailyplanet.net/community-voices-somali-americans-minnesota-celebrate-new-state-jubbaland/

288 http://archive.is/lAL6O

289 https://www.hiiraan.com/news4/2016/Dec/139425/ilhan_omar_meets_with_president_mohamud_at_villa_somalia.aspx

290 Ibid

291 https://www.washingtonexaminer.com/red-alert-politics/10-questions-somalias-prime-minister-should-answer-in-washington

292 https://www.nytimes.com/2017/02/07/world/africa/somalia-election-corruption.html

293 http://archive.is/kfjUZ

294 https://pjmedia.com/davidsteinberg/ilhan-omar-endorsed-somalias-new-president-four-days-later-omars-brother-in-law-had-a-powerful-job-in-his-administration/

295 https://www.scribd.com/document/370313106/2018-01-29-Treasury-Caatsa-241-Final#from_embed

296 https://pjmedia.com/davidsteinberg/ilhan-omar-endorsed-somalias-new-president-four-days-later-omars-brother-in-law-had-a-powerful-job-in-his-administration/

297 Minnesota Campaign Finance and Public Disclosure Board - Neighbors for Ilhan "Report of Receipts and Expenditures for Principal Campaign Committees" for 1/1/2016 through 7/18/2016, pg. 4

298 https://www.washingtonexaminer.com/opinion/10-topics-somalian-president-mohamed-farmajo-should-address-when-he-visits-d-c

299 https://www.bbc.com/news/world-africa-48975875

300 http://archive.is/oS0pC

301 http://archive.is/7ie1s

302 http://archive.is/TVGl5

303 http://archive.is/eOtHN

304 https://www.youtube.com/watch?v=eC4yGngGBOQ

305 http://archive.is/nYPcy

306 http://archive.is/MeVWZ

307 http://archive.is/oPpmE

308   http://archive.is/RHGbO

309   http://archive.is/y4fMX

310   http://archive.is/kRKkh

311   https://omar.house.gov/media/press-releases/rep-ilhan-omar-pass-es-amendments-national-defense-authorization-act

312   https://www.powerlineblog.com/archives/2019/12/no-relief-from-ilhan-omar.php

313   https://thearabweekly.com/qatari-ties-iran-turkey-undermine-regional-security

314   https://www.haaretz.com/world-news/asia-and-australia/somalia-the-latest-saudi-arabia-qatar-battleground-1.6051936

315   http://archive.is/L5EWQ

316   https://www.nytimes.com/2019/07/22/world/africa/somalia-qatar-uae.html?fbclid=IwAR08qyhNnu-11ubRQwRADU4D-1yIfxiL7XHJjKb9D7pBvrilVfuAk5_kJtec

317   https://www.nytimes.com/2019/07/22/world/africa/somalia-qatar-uae.html?fbclid=IwAR08qyhNnu-11ubRQwRADU4D-1yIfxiL7XHJjKb9D7pBvrilVfuAk5_kJtec

318   https://www.washingtonexaminer.com/opinion/the-us-may-be-funding-iran-backed-extremism-in-africa

319   https://www.haaretz.com/world-news/asia-and-australia/somalia-the-latest-saudi-arabia-qatar-battleground-1.6051936

320   https://www.alaraby.co.uk/english/indepth/2019/9/20/the-saudi-arabia-qatar-rift-over-somalia

321   https://www.reuters.com/article/us-somalia-turkey-military/turkey-opens-military-base-in-mogadishu-to-train-somali-sol-diers-idUSKCN1C50JH

322   https://ahvalnews.com/israel-turkey/turkey-gives-hamas-military-assistance-israeli-intelligence

323   https://www.csis.org/neo-ottomanism-turkeys-foreign-policy-approach-africa

324   https://www.dailysabah.com/op-ed/2019/10/16/turkeys-humanitarian-diplomacy-in-somalia-from-past-to-present

325   https://www.fdd.org/analysis/2019/12/11/brothers-in-arms/

326   https://www.nationalreview.com/2019/06/
turkey-africa-strategy-threatens-to-breed-islamist-extremism/

327   https://www.memri.org/reports/turkey-qatar-relations-bilater-
al-ties-strategic-partnership-introduction

328   https://www.aa.com.tr/en/africa/
top-somali-diplomat-lauds-turkeys-continued-support-/1658412

329   http://archive.is/XJ2Eu

330   http://archive.is/Ab2gw

331   https://7dnews.com/news/
al-jazeera-journalist-promoted-to-intelligence-leader-in-somalia

332   https://www.memri.org/tv/saudi-airs-report-fa-
had-yasim-fmr-jazeera-reporter-somalia-senior-fraud-
ulent-kenyan-passport-extremist-organization/
transcript

333   https://7dnews.com/news/
al-jazeera-journalist-promoted-to-intelligence-leader-in-somalia

334   https://web.archive.org/web/20170604020458/
http://somaliupdate.com/articles/10246/
Somalia-Villa-Somalia-Gets-Qatar-Backed-Chief-of-Staff

335   https://blogs.timesofisrael.com/
qatari-medias-promotion-of-rep-ilhan-omar-is-alarming/

336   http://archive.is/rx06C

337   https://www.meforum.org/islamist-watch/money-politics/party/
Republican/

338   https://www.judiciary.senate.gov/imo/media/doc/06-28-16%20
McCarthy%20Testimony.pdf

339   https://pjmedia.com/homeland-security/ilhan-omar-falsely-
claims-that-white-men-are-greater-threat-than-jihadis/

340   https://www.justice.gov/opa/pr/doj-dhs-report-three-out-four-in-
dividuals-convicted-international-terrorism-and-terrorism

341   https://twitter.com/bhweingarten/
status/1156001698940252160?s=20

342   http://archive.is/54c3u

343   https://www.unicef.org/media/media_90033.html

344   https://mosaicmagazine.com/picks/
politics-current-affairs/2019/08/
how-ilhan-omars-politics-set-her-against-liberal-muslims/

Chapter 11: Corruption: Criminal & Ethical Concerns

1   http://ilw.com/articles/Policy-Paper-A-Decade-of-Policy-Failure
2   https://www.powerlineblog.com/archives/2016/08/ilhan-omar-
her-back-pages.php
3   https://kstp.com/kstpImages/repository/cs/files/Ilhan%20
Omar%20Statement.pdf
4   http://www.startribune.com/new-documents-revisit-questions-
about-rep-ilhan-omar-s-marriage/511681362/
5   https://apnews.com/05839987bd644e1385bc4b8d3ccd995d
6   https://www.apnews.com/cc2ccd70de56405098d2f259bf0e46c5
7   https://www.tcdailyplanet.net/refugee-par-
ent-finds-sense-home-minneapolis-neighborhood-school/
8   https://pjmedia.com/davidsteinberg/address-records-show-rep-
ilhan-omar-d-mn-still-lived-with-her-first-husband-throughout-
her-second-marriage/
9   https://www.apnews.com/cc2ccd70de56405098d2f259bf0e46c5
10   https://alphanewsmn.com/
evidence-confirms-rumors-candidates-marriages/
11   http://archive.is/dwrCw
12   https://alphanewsmn.com/
the-curious-case-of-ilhan-omar-revisited/
13   https://pjmedia.com/homeland-security/state-rep-ilhan-omar-d-
mn-swore-to-apparent-falsehoods-in-court-while-divorcing-her-
alleged-brother/
14   Ibid
15   https://alphanewsmn.com/
evidence-confirms-rumors-candidates-marriages/
16   https://alphanewsmn.com/
investigation-suggests-omar-married-brother/
17   https://alphanewsmn.com/city-pages-expose-omar-family-secrets/

18   https://alphanewsmn.com/investigation-suggests-omar-married-brother/

19   https://pjmedia.com/davidsteinberg/new-photos-corroborate-perjury-claims-against-rep-ilhan-omar-as-she-deletes-social-media-evidence/

20   https://alphanewsmn.com/brother-ilhan-omar-married-send-email/

21   http://archive.is/lofOU

22   https://alphanewsmn.com/a-community-forced-into-silence/

23   http://www.startribune.com/at-history-s-doorstep-yet-again-ilhan-omar-confronts-fresh-wave-of-scrutiny/498738831/

24   https://www.politifact.com/truth-o-meter/article/2019/jul/18/did-ilhan-omar-marry-her-brother-her-hometown-news/

25   Minnesota Campaign Finance and Public Disclosure Board case docket pertaining to the "Complaint of Steve Drazkowski regarding Neighbors for Ilhan (Omar)," Document #35, PDF pg. 42

26   Minnesota Campaign Finance and Public Disclosure Board case docket pertaining to the "Complaint of Steve Drazkowski regarding Neighbors for Ilhan (Omar)," Document #13, pg. 18, entry dated August 16, 2016

27   Email correspondence with Jessica Vaughan dated July 26, 2019

28   http://archive.is/6dOxF

29   https://www.powerlineblog.com/archives/2019/06/loose-threads-in-the-curious-case.php

30   https://www.apnews.com/b49ee5604ec2435a90945820b7c973eb

31   http://archive.is/sLv4N

32   https://dailycaller.com/2019/06/23/ilhan-omar-sister-website-husband/

33   http://archive.is/XSwr7

34   https://www.fbiic.gov/public/2008/nov/Naming_practice_guide_UK_2006.pdf

35   https://alphanewsmn.com/investigation-suggests-omar-married-brother/

36   Ibid

37   https://alphanewsmn.com/city-pages-expose-omar-family-secrets/

38   https://pjmedia.com/davidsteinberg/official-school-records-sup-port-claims-that-rep-ilhan-omar-d-mn-married-her-brother/

39   https://pjmedia.com/davidsteinberg/new-photos-corroborate-per-jury-claims-against-rep-ilhan-omar-as-she-deletes-social-media-ev-idence/

40   https://www.powerlineblog.com/archives/2019/07/david-stein-berg-tying-up-loose-threads-in-the-curious-case.php

41   https://alphanewsmn.com/investigation-suggests-omar-married-brother/

42   Ibid

43   Ibid

44   https://alphanewsmn.com/city-pages-expose-omar-family-secrets/

45   Minnesota Campaign Finance and Public Disclosure Board - Neighbors for Ilhan "Report of Receipts and Expenditures for Principal Campaign Committees" for 1/1/2016 through 7/18/2016, Schedule A1-IND, pg. 6

46   https://www.powerlineblog.com/archives/2019/07/david-stein-berg-tying-up-loose-threads-in-the-curious-case.php

47   https://www.judicialwatch.org/wp-content/uploads/2019/07/Omar-ethics-complaint-07-22-19-1.pdf

48   https://www.fox9.com/news/ilhan-omars-marriage-certificate-questions-and-her-response

49   http://www.startribune.com/new-documents-revisit-questions-about-rep-ilhan-omar-s-marriage/511681362/

50   https://www.fec.gov/data/disbursements/?data_type=pro-cessed&committee_id=C00680934&recipient_name=E+STREET+GROUP+LLC&recipient_name=my-nett&two_year_transaction_period=2020&two_year_transac-tion_period=2018

51   https://www.nationalreview.com/news/ilhan-omars-campaign-has-paid-over-200000-to-her-alleged-lover-for-fundraising-con-sulting/

52   https://freebeacon.com/politics/omar-campaign-payments-to-al-leged-boyfriends-firm-increased-in-third-quarter/

53 https://www.judicialwatch.org/wp-content/uploads/2019/09/Supplemental-Ethics-Complaint-Against-Rep.-Ilhan-Omar.pdf

54 http://www.startribune.com/dc-doctor-alleges-her-husband-left-her-for-rep-ilhan-omar/558480212/

55 https://nypost.com/2019/09/03/ilhan-omars-alleged-lover-tim-mynett-denies-having-affair/

56 https://www.judicialwatch.org/wp-content/uploads/2019/09/Supplemental-Ethics-Complaint-Against-Rep.-Ilhan-Omar.pdf

57 https://freebeacon.com/issues/publisher-stonewalls-ethics-questions-swirl-omar-book/

58 http://www.startribune.com/legislator-calls-on-rep-ilhan-omar-to-pay-back-2-500-in-college-speaking-fees-a-violation-of-house-rules/489557921/

59 https://cfb.mn.gov/pdf/bdactions/1464_Findings.pdf?t=1559852555

60 http://www.startribune.com/legal-disputes-escalate-in-kahn-noor-legislative-race/266123441/

61 https://foreignaffairs.house.gov/about

62 https://www.opm.gov/forms/pdf_fill/sf86.pdf

Conclusion

1 https://www.washingtonexaminer.com/weekly-standard/minnesota-men-go-to-prison

2 U.S. v. Farah, Crim. No. 15-49 (2) (MJD/FLN), United States District Court District of Minnesota, Sentencing Hearing Transcript dated November 16, 2016 (Document #877), pg. 57

3 https://www.powerlineblog.com/archives/2016/11/sentencing-the-minnesota-men-2.php

4 https://www.justice.gov/usao-mn/pr/nine-twin-cities-men-sentenced-providing-material-support-isil

5 https://alphanewsmn.com/large-violent-crime-increase-in-minneapolis-cedar-riverside-neighborhood/

6 https://freebeacon.com/politics/anti-semitic-dem-gop-synonymous-hate-speech/

ACKNOWLEDGMENTS

There are a great many people who deserve recognition for helping make this book become a reality. First and foremost, I would like to thank my loving, talented, and inspiring wife for her unfailing encouragement, patience, and support as I scrambled to write this book—and in all of my related endeavors. I love you so dearly, and cannot adequately express in words how appreciative I am for everything you do.

I would also like to thank my parents and in-laws for all manner of assistance—editorial, familial, and beyond—that they provided in the course of my writing this book, without which it would not have been possible. I love you all dearly as well.

A special thanks must go to David Bernstein of Bombardier Books for suggesting this project, supporting my pursuit of it, and then, alongside the fine folks at Post Hill Press including, among others, Heather King and Meredith Didier, helping to bring it to fruition.

Andrew C. McCarthy's generosity extends well beyond his penning the Foreword to this book. Andy, I cannot thank you enough for your tutelage, friendship, and service to country.

American Ingrate might have never come about had Ben Domenech not prodded me on the basis of a lone tweet to write a related op-ed at *The Federalist*. So thank you for that, Ben, and for the opportunity to contribute to such a vital publication.

This book combines a variety of threads that I had been pulling at for many years on political philosophy, religion, national security and foreign policy, and all manner of other subjects. It builds on the scholarship of an inordinate number of exceptional thinkers, as the endnotes to the book attest. That said, a few individuals whose work I found particularly invaluable in the drafting of this book include: Ayaan Hirsi Ali, Dr. Andrew

Bostom, and Stephen Coughlin—all of whom I greatly admire. A special thanks must also go to organizations including the Center for Security Policy and the Investigative Project on Terrorism.

In writing this book, several people were most helpful in providing insights about Rep. Omar and her district, including the likes of *Power Line*'s Scott Johnson, former *PJ Media* New York City Editor David Steinberg, Minnesota state representative Steve Drazkowski, and former Minnesota state representative Phyllis Kahn.

Many other people have helped me professionally and personally since I decided to devote my career to engaging in the War of Ideas on behalf of conservative principles. Some that I would like to personally recognize are: Tom Klingenstein, Ryan Williams, and the many other exceptional folks at the Claremont Institute; the late and great Herb London of the London Center for Policy Research and various and sundry other critical initiatives; Roger Kimball, Sam Schneider, and their colleagues at Encounter Books, and *The New Criterion*; Chris and Kevin Balfe, Glenn Beck, Gaston Mooney, Betsy Morgan, Eric Pearce, Buck Sexton, Andrew Wilkow, and the many other wonderful people who supported me at *The Blaze/Conservative Review*, and who have continued to do so in myriad ways; those who have seen fit to publish my writings at a number of other publications I so greatly respect; and many other confidantes, teachers, and friends whose names I shall omit. You know who you are, and I owe you an unpayable debt of gratitude.

ABOUT THE AUTHOR

Benjamin Weingarten is a Senior Fellow at the London Center for Policy Research, Fellow at the Claremont Institute and Senior Contributor at *The Federalist*. He was selected by The Fund for American Studies as a 2019 Robert Novak Journalism Fellow.

Blackhawk Down__ p. 35-36

Abortion irony - p. 36

Made in the USA
Middletown, DE
25 February 2020